The Mammoth Book of
World Sports

Every Sport Ever Played

ALSO AVAILABLE

The Mammoth Book of Vintage Science Fiction
The Mammoth Book of New Age Science Fiction
The Mammoth Book of Fantastic Science Fiction
The Mammoth Book of Modern Science Fiction
The Mammoth Book of Great Detective Stories
The Mammoth Book of True Murder
The Mammoth Book of Modern War Stories
The Mammoth Book of Ghost Stories
The Mammoth Book of Ghost Stories 2
The Mammoth Book of the Supernatural
The Mammoth Book of Astounding Puzzles
The Mammoth Book of Terror
The Mammoth Book of Vampires
The Mammoth Book of Killer Women
The Mammoth Book of Historical Whodunnits
The Mammoth Book of Werewolves
The Mammoth Book of Golden Age Detective Stories
The Mammoth Book of Erotica
The Mammoth Book of Frankenstein
The Mammoth Book of Battles
The Mammoth Book of Astounding Word Games
The Mammoth Book of Mindbending Puzzles
The Mammoth Book of Historical Detectives
The Mammoth Book of Victorian & Edwardian Ghost Stories
The Mammoth Book of Dreams
The Mammoth Book of Symbols
The Mammoth Book of Brainstorming Puzzles
The Mammoth Book of Great Lives
The Mammoth Book of International Erotica
The Mammoth Book of Pulp Fiction
The Mammoth Book of The West
The Mammoth Book of Love & Sensuality
The Mammoth Book of Chess
The Mammoth Book of Fortune Telling
The Mammoth Puzzle Carnival
The Mammoth Book of Dracula
The Mammoth Book of Gay Short Stories
The Mammoth Book of the Third Reich at War
The Mammoth Book of Best New Horror
The Mammoth Book of Tasteless Lists
The Mammoth Book of Comic Fantasy
The Mammoth Book of New Erotica
The Mammoth Book of Arthurian Legends
The Mammoth Book of True Crime (Second edition)

The Mammoth Book of
World Sports

Edited by Noam Friedlander

CARROLL & GRAF PUBLISHERS, INC.
New York

√RAP 430·2305

Carroll & Graf Publishers, Inc.
19 West 21st Street
New York, NY 10010-6805

First published in the UK by the Oxford University Press
in 1975.
Updated version published by Robinson Publishing in 1999.
First Carroll & Graf edition 1999.

This work is based on material originally published as
The Oxford Companion to Sports and Games © Oxford
University Press 1975 and is published by arrangement
with Oxford University Press. Additional material
© Robinson Publishing 1999.

Original selection of material for OUP edition © John Arlott
Line drawings by Carl James
Produced by Essential Books
Text designed by Neal Townsend for Essential Books
Edited by Emma Dickens for Essential Books

A copy of the Cataloguing in Publication Data for this title is
available from the Library of Congress.

ISBN 0 7867 0625 2

Printed and bound in the UK

CONTENTS

Aikido **8**
Aquabobbing **9**
Archery **11**
Archery, Crossbow **14**
Archery, Target **16**
Athletics **18**
Austball **31**
Autocross **31**
Badminton **32**
Ballooning **38**
Ballroom Dancing **39**
Bandy **40**
Baseball **42**
Baseball, Welsh **46**
Basketball **48**
Batinton **59**
Beach Volleyball **61**
Biathlon **63**
Biathlon, Skiing **64**
Bicycle Polo **66**
Biddy Basketball **70**
Billiards, Carom **71**
Billiards, English **73**
Bobsleigh **75**
Bowl-Playing **78**
Bowls **79**
Boxing **88**
Boxing, Chinese **92**
Boxing, Thai **94**
Broomball **95**
Bull **97**

Caber, Tossing The **99**
Camel Wrestling **100**
Camogie **100**
Canoe Polo **102**
Canoe Sailing **103**
Canoe Slalom **104**
Canoeing **107**
Club Ball **112**
Cricket **113**
Croquet **123**
Curling **129**
Cycle Ball **132**
Cycling **133**
Cyclo-Cross **138**
Dakyu **141**
Darts **141**
Deck Cricket **143**
Deck Games **144**
Deck Quoits **146**
Deck Tennis **147**
Diving **150**
Equestrian Events **155**
Eton Field Game **165**
Eton Fives **170**
Eton Wall Game **174**
Fell Running **178**
Fencing **179**
Fishing **186**
Fly Ball **189**
Flying, Sporting **189**
Football **193**

Futevolei	226	Lacrosse, Women's	348
Gliding	227	Lawn Tennis	352
Golf	232	Logrolling	357
Grass Skiing	241	Marathon	358
Gymnastics	243	Moto-Cross	359
Handball	250	Motor Racing	361
Handball, Court	255	Motorcycle Racing	367
Handball, Irish	259	Mountain Running	375
Hare and Hounds	260	Netball	375
Hockey, Field	261	Nine Men's Morris	382
Hockey, Indoor	267	Orienteering	383
Holani	269	Padder Tennis	387
Horse Racing	269	Paddleball	389
Horseshoe Pitching	272	Parachuting	391
Hurling	273	Pato	394
Ice Hockey	277	Pelota	396
Ice Skating	284	Pesäpallo	401
Ice Yachting	292	Pétanque	404
In-Line Roller Hockey	295	Pigeon Racing	407
Jeu Provencal	297	Ping Ball	410
Jousting	300	Polo	410
Joutes Lyonnaises	302	Polocrosse	416
Judo	303	Pool	418
Ju-jitsu	309	Powerboat Racing	419
Kabaddi	310	Punting	421
Karate	313	Quoits	423
Karting	322	Race Walking	425
Kendo	326	Rackets	427
Kick Boxing	332	Real Tennis	431
Kite Fighting	334	Rhythmic Gymnastics	438
Knur and Spell	335	Ring Tennis	440
Korfball	338	Rock Climbing	442
Kuningaspallo	342	Rodeo	443
Lacrosse, Men's	343	Roller Hockey	448

Roller Skating. **452**
Roque **454**
Rounders **455**
Rounders, Irish. **459**
Rowing **459**
Rugby Fives **465**
Rugby League Football. **469**
Rugby Union Football . . **473**
Sailing **479**
Sepak Takraw **479**
Shinty **481**
Shooting, Air Weapons **484**
Shooting, Clay Pigeon . **486**
Shooting, Pistol **490**
Shooting, Rifle **495**
Shuffleboard **498**
Skibobbing **500**
Skiing **502**
Skittles **509**
Sled Dog Racing **516**
Snooker **517**
Snowboarding **518**
Softball **520**
Spaceball **524**
Squash Rackets **527**
Stoolball **531**
Surfing **535**
Swimming **542**
Table Tennis **553**
Takraw **558**
Tejo. **560**
Tobogganing, Luge **560**
Touch Ball **562**
Trampolining **564**

Trapball **568**
Trotting **569**
Tug of War **572**
Underwater Hockey . . .**576**
Underwater Swimming **577**
Volleyball **581**
Waterpolo **586**
Waterskiing **589**
Weightlifting **596**
Winchester Fives **601**
Windsurfing **604**
Wrestling **607**
Yachting **615**
Yachting, Ice **620**
Yachting, Sand **621**
Index **622**

AIKIDO
Introduction
There are two types of Aikido, competitive and non-competitive. Aikido is not just a system of combat, but of self-cultivation and improvement. According to the founder, the goal of Aikido is not the defeat of others but the defeat of negative characteristics which occupy one's mind.

History
Aikido was founded by Morihei Ueshiba (1883-1969) who was born in Japan on 14 December, 1883. His father was often physically attacked for political reasons so Ueshiba devoted himself to martial arts and studied religion to find a deeper significance to life. By combining his martial training with his religious and political ideologies, he created the modern martial art of Aikido. Aikido has roots in JUJITSU, particularly Daitoryu-jujitsu, as well as sword and spear fighting, and also Omotokyo – part Neo-Shintoism and part neo-Shintoism.

Venue
At least 9m square, preferably with a surrounding safety area.

Rules
The competitive fighting version of Aikido is referred to as "Tomiki" Aikido. Here force is not met with counter-force but avoiding action, enabling the defender to take advantage of the attacker's temporary loss of balance to score with a successful technique.

Clothing
The costume is similar to that of JUDO costume. It is white or off-white. The jacket must be long enough to cover the thighs and have a minimum reach to the fists when the arms are fully extended downward. The trousers must be long enough to

cover the legs, while a belt fastens the jacket at the waist and is long enough to go twice around the body. For identification in a competition, one contestant wears a red belt, or string or tape at the belt, while the other wears a white belt.

AQUABOB

Introduction

This is a water sport which involves skiing on water and requires no special athletic abilities. A vehicle like a tricycle, but with three water skis in place of wheels, is towed over the water by a motor launch. Unlike WATER SKIING, but as on a tricycle, no skill in maintaining equilibrium is needed. The aquabobber sits comfortably in an upright position in the saddle, holding the handlebars firmly, with his/her feet resting on the side skis, and skims the water at 25mph (40km/h) or more without any danger of falling.

History

Aquabobbing first appeared in Switzerland in the spring of 1967 on the lake of Neuchâtel. In the previous winter Guggi, a 22-year-old medical student at the University of Lausanne, was given the job of repairing his father's skibob. He took it to a friend, Gaille, who worked in the family factory making metal furniture fittings. The discussion over the skibob soon turned to water-skiing, which they both practiced in the summer with considerable skill. The medical student wondered why the skibob could not go on the water. Guggi made a small model, Gaille manufactured a prototype, and the idea was born.

Rules

Aquabobbing requires a minimum of effort. Since motion is achieved solely by the vehicle being pulled, there is practically

Aquabob

no strain on the arms or legs. Only a twist of the handlebars, or a lean to right or left, is necessary to keep on course.

Runs are generally from 2 or 3 miles (3–5km). The start is made either touching the bottom or in deep water, the aquabobber lying on his stomach at full length on the saddle with his legs stretched out behind in an open scissors position to keep both machine and rider in balance. When the pulling rope is in tension, the go-ahead is given and the aquabobber waits until he is well out of the water and travelling at a good speed before sliding into the upright sitting position.

The ideal cruising speed of around 25mph (40 km/h) may be increased or diminished without danger. Slaloming across the waves at a speed approaching 40mph (64km/h) is easily mastered and acrobatic feats are possible.

If the rider falls off, the aquabob automatically slides free of the pulling rope. To bring the aquabob to a stop the rider waits until the boat slows almost to a halt and then jumps clear in the manner of a cyclist on a bicycle.

Equipment
The aquabob is built on a rustless steel frame. The three skis are of wood, the two side ones fixed rigidly to the frame, while the front ski, positioned slightly lower, is movable to allow steering. At the rear of each ski is a small fin. The rubber-cushioned saddle is made of wood to ensure that the aquabob floats. The overall length is 6ft (1.83m), width 2ft (0.61m), and the height of the saddle above water 1ft 6in (0.45m).

Clothing
No special dress is necessary, but for course at high speed and stunting a Mae West rubber suit like that used by water-skiers is worn.

ARCHERY

Introduction

In its modern form, archery is the art of shooting arrows from a bow at a target. Although it is essentially an individual pursuit it is possible to participate as a member of a team. In this case the individual is encouraged to record his performance with a view to improving his standard of shooting.

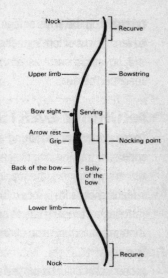

History

The traditional longbow, made of yew or other exotic woods, was used for target archery up to the 1940s but was replaced, firstly by tubular steel weapons and then by the composite bow made of wood, plastic, and fibreglass, whose construction derives from the ancient Asiatic bow used by the Saracens and the conquering hordes of Ghengis Khan. In the US, where the bow and arrow had long been the first choice weapon for Native Americans, the first archery group was formed in Philadelphia in 1879.

Clothing

Normal clothing is worn, but it must be closefitting above the waist to prevent catching the bowstring. Glasses may be worn and binoculars used to spot arrows between shots. For some forms of archery, archers should wear white attire, with some colour. All targets are numbered and archers should wear their target numbers.

Other variants

Rovers, clout-shooting, flight-shooting, popinjay-shooting, and novelties such as archery golf and archery darts. (All described below.)

• ARCHERY DARTS/GOLF

These forms of shooting are also valuable in providing additional training in aiming and accuracy. In matches between archers and golfers, the tee shot of the golfer is duplicated with a flight shot from a bow, the approach shot is matched by shooting a standard target arrow, and the archer holes out by shooting at a white disc of card.

Rules

Archery darts can be played against regular DARTS players. The archers use an enlarged target face patterned like a dart board and shoot at about 10 yds (9.244m) while the darts players use their normal dart board. Scoring is as for a regular darts match.

• CLOUT-SHOOTING

The principle object of clout-shooting is to shoot arrows high up into the air in order that they fall on a target marked out on the ground at much greater distances than those normally used in target archery.

Rules

The distance shot are measured by the scores of yards and are from 8 to 10 score (146.304-182.880m) for men to from 6 to 8 score (109.728-146.304m) for women.

The traditional "clout" was a small target with a black aiming-spot set up in the centre of the marked-out target. This has now been replaced by a flag. The target measured 24ft (7.315m) in diameter and has five scoring areas defined by rings at radii of 18in (0.457m), 3ft (0.914m), 6ft (1.829m), 9ft (2.743m), and 12ft (3.658m), respectively: by ancient custom these are designated "a foot", "half a bow", "a bow", "a bow and a half", and "two bows". Scoring from the central ring outwards, is 5, 4, 3, 2, and 1.

• FLIGHT-SHOOTING

Flight-shooting is a highly specialized pursuit with the sole object of reaching great distances – an exacting but extremely satisfying form of archery. Modern flight equipment is the result of advanced technological development and involves a short and powerful bow shooting slender lightweight arrows of special design.

Competition may take place in a "target-bow class", which is reserved for competitors using specially made equipment, or a "free-style class", in which any form of shooting is allowed.

• POPINJAY-SHOOTING

Popinjay-shooting is rarely seen outside the continent of Europe. The target consists of a series of wooden cylinders with feathers attached, variously called cocks, hens, and chicks, set on a frame, called a roost, on top of a mast 85ft (25.908m) high.

Rules

The object is to dislodge these "birds", each of which has a score value, by shooting bluntheaded arrows vertically from the base of the mast.

ARCHERY, CROSSBOW

Introduction

There are two major types of crossbow archery – match (traditional style) and field. Match shooting takes place on purpose-built ranges equipped with mechanized target transport systems. Field crossbow shooting shares many of the rules of Olympic style target archery and takes place on an open sports field.

Rules

The technique of shooting employed by field archers, where no aids to sighting are used is termed "instinctive". Here the archer adopts a stance quite unsuited to other forms of archery. These techniques are quite similar in many respects to those used in hunting wild game with a bow and arrow. American archers have excelled in field archery, although it is now becoming popular in Europe where special tournaments are now regularly recognized for this form of sport.

Equipment

Stocks for both match and field events are usually of hardwood and the bow or "prod" produced from glass or carbon fiber composites. Sights must be magnifying, correcting lenses may not be part of the crossbow. Most field archers use a bow of a heavier wright than they would normally use in target practise.

The bow strings of match crossbows are made from steel wire or synthetic fibers and are cocked (loaded) with the aid of a lever. Triggers may be mechanical or electronic action. A match "bolt" consists of a rounded steel head with a blunt cylindrical point. The tail of the bolt is flightless and may be made of compressed hardwood or high-tensile aluminum tube.

The field crossbow's strings must be non-metallic and may

be made from synthetic fibers. Triggers must be mechanical. Bolts may be made from any safe material and may be between 30.4 and 45.7cm in length. Bolts are usually made of high-tensile aluminum alloy or carbon fiber arrow tubing. They must carry vanes or "fletching" (usually 3). All bolts in a set must be identical and clearly marked for identification.

The match crossbow's target consists of a wooden holder with a cast lead centre. The target faces are made of paper, a black aiming mark being printed on a white background.

Field targets are portable buttresses made from woven straw, insulation board or polyethylene foam. They may be round or square in shape and are mounted on folding wooden stands. The standard 60cm diameter archery target face is made from laminated paper. These faces are divided into five concentric colour zones (yellow, red, blue, black and white).

Field archery consists of shooting animal figures, which may be coloured to add realism, upon which are superimposed the scoring rings. They are fastened to straw bales or other suitable backstops and set up in position as varied and as ingenious as the organizers can devise.

As the ground selected for field shooting is invariably rough, there is a danger of losing or breaking arrows. To prevent this, special arrows, with stouter shafts, heavier piles and longer fletchings are used for this form of shooting.

Shooting

A competition "round" lasts for a specified number of shots. Bolts are shot in sets or "ends" of 3 bolts – in competition, 3 minutes being allowed per end.

The match crossbow competitor has a mechanized target which returns to him/her after each shot.

Scoring

Scoring values are: inner "gold" 10 points; outer "gold" 9 points; and so on, down to 1 point for the outer white.

Clothing

Lightweight sports clothings.

ARCHERY, TARGET

This consists of shooting arrows from various distances at a target of standard size.

Venue

The ideal archery range consists of a level area of closely cropped grass in a reasonable sheltered position. In the most favoured arrangement, the ground is laid out on a north-and-south axis, and the targets set up at the northern end. There should be a safety zone of at least 25yds (22.860m) behind the targets.

Rules

Archers stand astride a clearly defined shooting line or mark to shoot, with a waiting line at least 5yds (4.572m) behind them. The various distances being shot are clearly defined on the ground by means of white lines, tapes or spots, and the targets, which are set up at least 12ft (3.658m) apart for communal shooting, are usually numbered from left to right for identification purposes.

Equipment

The target consists of a boss about 4in (10.16cm) thick and approximately 4ft (1.219m) in diameter, made of tightly coiled straw rope. On this is stretched a target face of canvas or similar material painted with coloured scoring rings.

Scoring

For the standard British five-zone target face, the arrangement is as follows: a circle in the centre measuring 9.6in (24.4cm) ringed by four concentric bands each 4.8in (12.2cm) wide. From the centre outwards the colours are yellow (called "the gold"), red, blue, black and white, their scoring values being 9, 7, 5, 3 and 1 respectively. The target is erected on a wooden stand of a height such that its exact centre, the pin-hole, is 52.25in (130cm) vertically above the ground. Two sizes of international rules, each at a different shooting distance. A 122cm (approx. 48in) target face is used for distances of 90, 70 and 60m, and an 80cm face for distances of 50 and 30m. Both these faces are divided into 10 zones, each colour of the standard five-zone target face being halved, the scoring values then ranging from 10 for the central gold down to 1 for the outermost ring of the white.

In target archery a "round", consisting of a specified number of arrows shot at predetermined distances, must be completed before a score is recorded. Rounds may vary according to the standard of proficiency, the age and the sex of the archer, and the particular form of archery chosen.

When a round is shot, each archer, after shooting six arrows as non-scoring sighters, shoots three arrows and then retires until all the other archers shooting at the same target have also shot three. A repetition of this process marks the completion of an "end" of six arrows. Scores are then taken, the arrows withdrawn from the target, and the next end shot. Further ends are shot in this fashion until the total number of arrows in the round has been discharged. Lunch and tea breaks are arranged at convenient intervals during the shooting of a round. The score from a round cannot be recorded unless it is completed in one day, but the only time limit imposed is a maximum of two and a half minutes per shot.

ATHLETICS, TRACK & FIELD

(Discus, Hammer, High Jump, Hurdling, Javelin, Long Jump, Pole Vault, Relay, Shot Put, Steeple Chase and Triple Jump)

Introduction

Known in Great Britain and the Commonwealth as athletics, or more fully in the USA as track and field athletics, this composite sport for amateurs embraces the group of activities concerned with running, jumping, and throwing contests: cross-country running; decathlon; discus; hammer; high jump; hurdling; javelin; long-distance running; long jump; marathon; middle-distance running; pentathlon; pole vault; race walking; relay running; road running; shot put; sprinting; steeplechase; triple jump. (Discus, hammer and javelin are all unsuitable for indoor events.) All of these events are contested by both men and women except the decathlon, hammer, marathon, pole vault and steeplechase, which are contested only by men.

Running distances for athletics vary according to the discipline: sprints: 100m, 200m, 400m; middle distance: 800m, 1,500m; long distance: 5,000m, 10,000m; steeplechase: 1,500m (rarely), 2,000m or 3,000m; hurdles: 110m (100m women), 400m (both men and women) indoors: 50m women/60m men; relays: 4x100m and 4x400m.

The sport is governed at international level by the International Amateur Athletic Federation (IAAF), which defines an amateur as "one who competes for the love of sport and as a means of recreation, without any motive of securing any material gain from such competition." The most important international competition in athletics is the Olympic Games which embraces many other sports and is organized by the International Olympic Committee (IOC).

History

Athletics has its origins in remote antiquity. Its history has been traced as far as the ancient Greek Olympic Games in the thirteenth century BC. Evidence exists of athletic contests in England in about 1154, but the first organized competitions were held at the Royal Military Academy, Woolwich, London, in 1849. The first competition held regularly was probably that first staged at Exeter College, Oxford, in 1850.

Clothing

Athletes should wear clothing which is decent and presentable – vest and shorts (or equivalent), which are clean and non-transparent (even if wet). Shoes should give traction and protection with minimum weight, although athletes may compete in bare feet, or with footwear on only one foot, if they wish. Shoes may not be constructed so as to give a competitor any additional assistance (for example extra spring).

Official Shoe Rules

Any number of spikes up to 11 may be used on the sole and heel of each shoe. In a competition taking place on a synthetic surface, the part of the spike projecting from the sole or heel must not exceed 9mm (approx. 0.5in) or 12mm in the high jump and javelin. The spikes should have a maximum diameter of 4mm. For non-synthetic surfaces the maximum spike length should be 25mm (1in), again with a maximum diameter of 4mm. For track and field events other than the high jump, a shoe's sole and/or heel may be of any thickness. It may have grooves, ridges, or other design features, provided these are constructed of the same or similar material as the basic sole itself. For the high jump, the soles must be more than 13mm and the heels over 19mm thickness.

• DISCUS

This event entails throwing a discus (no less than 2kg – men, 1kg – women) through the air for the maximum distance possible.

History

Throwing the discus is first mentioned in the writings of Homer, and was first contested in the ancient Greek Olympic Games in about 708 BC.

Rules

The discus is thrown with one hand from within the limits of a circle (2.5m in diameter). The thrower commences the throw from the back of the circle, holding the discus flat against their hand with their fingers curled round the rim. After a few preliminary swings of the throwing arm, the athlete drives across the circle, turning as s/he goes, and lands in the first half of the circle in a position to release the discus.

Disqualification may occur if:

You touch the ground outside the circle or the top of the circle rim with any part of the body having started to make a throw.

You leave the circle before the discus has touched the ground.

The discus lands outside the line markings in a sector of 40 degrees.

Measuring the throw: Throws are measured from the nearest mark in the ground at the landing point to the circumference to the circle along a line drawn to the centre of the circle. Measurements are made immediately after the throw and recorded in even centimeter units. The distance is rounded down to the nearest unit below if it goes over an even centimeter.

Competitors are allowed two practise trials before having six chances to hurl the discus the furthest distance.

• HAMMER

The hammer event entails throwing a "hammer" through the air for the maximum distance possible. For the throw, the implement thrown is not an actual hammer but a metal ball (no less than 16lb for men, 9lb for women) attached to a wire which has a handle at its other end.

History

Throwing the sledge-hammer was an amusement enjoyed by Englishmen in the sixteenth century and it was probably developed long before that time, as was shotputting, in the Scottish Highland Games.

Rules

The thrower stands at the rear of the circle with his/her back in the direction of throwing. S/he grips the handle with both hands, a glove can be worn on the hand closest to the grip. Two preliminary swings are made with the hammer rotating around the stationary thrower's body. The high point of each swing is behind the throwing and the low point is in front. They then describe three full turns while swinging the hammer and moving across the circle. The delivery is a sweeping movement starting from the very high point of the final turn, through the final low point, the hammer being released over the thrower's shoulder.

Measuring the throw: A throw is measured from the nearest indentation in the ground made by the head of the hammer to the inside of the circumference of the throwing circle, along a line drawn to the centre of the circle. Measurements are made immediately after the throw, recorded in even centimeter units to the nearest unit below, if that distance is not a whole even centimeter.

Before a competition, you may only have two practise trials after which the hammer is thrown, and the winner is the one with the best distance after six trials. For a throw to be valid, the hammer head must land completely within the inner edges of lines marking a sector of 40 degrees set out on the ground. If the hammer first strikes the cage before landing within the sector, the throw should not be considered invalid.

Disqualification may occur if:

You apply any substance to your shoes or to the surface of the throwing circle.

You touch the ground outside the circle or the top of the circle rim with any part of the body.

You interrupt the throw so as to begin a trial again, the head of the hammer may touch the ground during your preliminary swings and turns.

You leave the circle before the hammer has touched the ground.

When leaving the circle, the first contact with the top of the circle rim or the ground outside the circle is in front of the white line which is drawn outside the circle and runs theoretically through its centre.

• HIGH JUMP

Competitors try to propel themselves over a crossbar, without knocking it off its supporting uprights, at successively greater heights. The height at which the competitor starts, and to what height the bar is raised at the end of each round is decided by the judge.

Rules

There are four main styles: the scissors; the eastern cut-off; the western roll; and the straddle. The first three are virtually obsolete. In the straddle style of jumping, the athlete takes off from the foot nearest to the bar, and swings his/her other foot up and over the bar, crossing the bar stomach-downwards in a draped position. At the 1968 Olympics Fosbury won a gold medal with his head-first, face-upwards technique, known as the "Fosbury Flop", and this method superseded the straddle as the most popular high-jump technique for men and women.

Measuring the jumps: All height measurements should be made in whole centimetres perpendicularly from the ground to the lowest part of the upper side of the crossbar. Any measurement of a new height should be made before competitors attempt that height. Unless only one competitor remains, the bar should not be raised by less than 2cm in the high jump (5cm in the pole vault) after each round.

Disqualification may occur for:

Taking off from both feet.

Dislodging the crossbar so that it falls from the supports (or pegs) on the uprights.

Touching the ground, including the landing area, beyond the uprights (either between them or outside them) without first clearing the bar.

• HURDLES

Hurdling events combine sprinting with clearing a series of obstacles called hurdles.

A good hurdling style involves leaning forward and clearing each hurdle in a smooth action without breaking the rhythm of the running stride. In clearing a hurdle, the athlete may take off from either foot. The alternate leg is lifted with the knee bent and then extended across the bar of the hurdle and along the line of running. The trailing leg is lifted laterally and rotated about the hip, crossing the hurdle in a horizontal position. Forward lean contributes to the impetus which brings the hurdler down beyond the obstacle when their trailing leg lifts high into the getaway struggle.

Rules

All hurdle races are run in lanes and the hurdles themselves are designed such that a force at least equal to the weight of 3.6kg (7lb) applied to the centre of the crossbar's top is needed to overturn it. It may be adjustable in height for each event.

Disqualification may occur for:

Trailing a foot or leg below the horizontal plane of the top of any hurdle at the instance of clearance.

Jumping any hurdle not in your own lane.

Deliberately (in the referee's opinion) knocking down any hurdle by hand or foot.

• JAVELIN

The javelin event entails throwing a javelin through the air for maximum distance.

History

The spear has been a weapon from the earliest times.

Rules

The javelin must be held at the grip and be thrown with one hand only over the shoulder or upper part of the throwing arm. It can't be slung or hurled. You can't turn your back to the arc after preparing to throw and discharge the javelin.

Measuring the throw: The throw is measured from the nearest mark made by the head of the javelin to the inner edge of the circumference of the arc. It is measured along a line from the mark and through the centre of the radius of the arc. Measurements are made immediately after the throw, recorded in even centimetre units to the nearest unit below the distance measured if that distance is not a whole even centimetre.

Before a competition, you may only have two practise trials from near the circles or scratch line after which you throw the javelin and the winner is the one with the best distance after six trials.

• LONG JUMP

The athletes try to clear the longest distance following a sprint along a runway up to a take-off board.

The technique of long jumping consists of a high knee-lift of the alternate leg on take-off leading to a running stride in the air. The trailing leg is pulled forward to join its pair in forward extension in the downward trajectory. While still in the air the long jumper throws both feet forward of the body before landing in the sand.

Rules

Measuring the jumps: The rearmost imprint left by the jumper on landing is the mark to which the measurement is made.

Disqualification may occur if:

You touch the ground beyond the take-off line with any part of your body, whether in the act of jumping or running up without jumping.

You take off from outside either end of the take off board, whether beyond or before the take-off line.

In the course of landing, you touch the ground outside the landing area at a point nearer to the take-off than the nearest break in the sand made by the jump.

You walk back through the landing area after a completed jump.

You somersault in any fashion while in the run-up or in the act of jumping.

If an athlete takes-off before reaching the board, but within its width span, the jump should not be counted as a failure.

• POLE VAULT

Pole vaulting is a jumping contest for height, competitors using a pole to lever their bodies over a bar which is raised according to a fixed progression. Vaulters failing to clear each height within three attempts are eliminated and the winner is the athlete who clears the greatest height.

Rules

An approach run of not less than about 36m (120ft) is used, the vaulter holding the pole almost parallel with the ground. The pole is planted into a box, sunk below ground level, the athlete's impetus causing it both to flex and lift, levering his/her body from the ground. S/he hangs from the pole until it unflexes, then uses his/her arms to pull him/herself, feet first, upward, simultaneously turning about the pole so that s/he can cross the bar face downwards before dropping onto a thick, soft pad.

Measuring the jumps: See High Jump

Disqualification may occur if:

You dislodge the crossbar so that it falls from the supports (or pegs) on the uprights.

You touch the ground, including the area beyond the vertical plane of upper part of the box, without first clearing the bar.

You change the grip after leaving the ground (moving the lower hand above the upper one or the upper hand higher on the pole).

Equipment

The pole may be of any material or combination of materials and of any length or diameter, providing that the basic surface is smooth. It may have a binding of not more than two layers of adhesive tape to protect it when it strikes the back of the take-off box.

• RELAY RACES

Relay races are for teams of four runners, each carrying a baton for a given distance or stage before passing it to the next team member. The final team member races to the finish line with high knee-lift, free-swinging arm movements and a forward lean of some 25 degrees.

Rules

For the 4x100m relay, runners must run in their lanes and must not run more than 10m outside the take-over zone. In the 4x400m relays, the first runner must stay in his/her lane and the next runner must stay in their lane for part of the lap before moving over to the inside after the first bend. The baton pass starts when it is first touched by the receiving runner and is completed the instant it is solely in the recipient's hand. It is only the position of the baton within the take-over zone, rather than the position of the body or limbs of the runners, that is decisive. Having passed on the baton, competitors should remain in their lanes or zones until the course is clear of other athletes. Deliberate obstruction or jostling of members of another team warrants disqualification.

If a runner drops the baton (a rigid hollow tube, distinctly coloured to be visible during a race, 12–13cm in circumference, no more than 30cm long nor less than 50g), he or she can retrieve it, leaving the lane to do so if necessary. However, other athletes must not be impeded and the distance covered must not be lessened, otherwise disqualification may result.

• SHOT PUT

The shot put event entails pushing the shot, rather than throwing, a solid metal ball (no less than 16lb for men, 9lb for women) through the air for the maximum distance possible.

History

Shot-putting is a sport of martial origin, soldiers having used cannon balls for throwing contests for hundreds of years. Casting the stone was an exercise practiced by young Londoners in the twelfth century.

Rules

The shot putter stands at the rear of the circle with his/her back to the direction of the throw. The shot is cupped at the base of the fingers, not in the palm, and held in the hollow of the neck. The putter shifts backwards across the circle on one foot and delivers the shot following a full 180-degree rotation which blends with the extension of the throwing arm, thrusting the shot away, in front of his/her shoulder.

Measuring the shot: For a put to be valid, the shot has to land completely within the inner edges of lines marking a sector of 40 degrees set out on the ground. It is measured from the nearest indentation in the ground made by the shot, to the inside of the circumference of the throwing circle, along a line drawn to the centre of the circle.

Measurements should be made immediately after each put, and recorded to the nearest centimetre below the distance measured if that distance is not a whole centimetre.

When there are more than eight athletes in an event, each should be allowed three trials, and the eight competitors with the best valid throws should be allowed three additional trials. If there is a tie for the eighth place, those competitors should have three extra trials. If there are eight competitors or fewer, each should be allowed six throws.

Disqualification may occur if:

Having started the throw, you touch the ground outside the circle, or the top of the circle rim, or the top of the stopboard with any part of the body.

You leave the circle before the shot has touched the ground.

When leaving the circle, the first contact with the top of the circle rim or the ground outside the circle is in front of a white line which is drawn outside the circle and runs theoretically through its centre.

• THE STEEPLECHASE

The Steeplechase is a test of middle distance running, endurance and hurdling skill.

Rules

A typical 3,000m steeplechase must include 28 hurdle jumps and seven water jumps with five evenly spaced jumps per lap, the fourth being the water jump. For the 2,000m there should be 18 hurdle jumps and five water jumps.

Distance runners have to regulate their speed to avoid exhaustion. Knee action is less pronounced with steeplechase than with Hurdling, the strike is shorter and the forward lean less extreme.

• TRIPLE JUMP

The triple jump involves a complicated hop, step and jump sequence of actions before landing in sand. In the first phase of the triple jump the jumper lands on the take off foot; in the second phase he lands on the alternate foot and springs from the same foot for his/her final jump.

The technique of the first and third phases of the triple jump correspond to that for the long jump, the best distances being achieved only by effective dovetailing of the three jumps into a continuous sequence.

Rules

Measuring the jumps: See Long Jump

Disqualification: See Long Jump.

Also, in the hop manoeuvre of the sequence competitors should land upon the same foot with which they took off; in the step phase they should land on the other foot from which, subsequently, the jump is performed. If, in performing the step, a competitor's sleeping leg touches the ground, the jump is not considered a failure.

AUSTBALL

Introduction

Austball is a German bat-and-ball team game of the fives-tennis type and a forerunner to VOLLEYBALL.

Rules

It is played between two teams of five players each and the ball is hit with one fist. The object of the game is to hit and return the ball over a rope 2m (78in) high. No player may go nearer the rope than the line drawn 3m back from it on either side. A game consists of two 15-minute halves.

Scoring

Austball is decided on points, one of which is ceded to the other side when the ball:

Bounces more than three times without being returned.

Is hit out of court.

Is struck with two firsts or the open hand.

Is played more than three times on one side without crossing the net.

Equipment

The ball is 65–71cm (25–28in) in diameter, and 300-50g (about 12 1/2oz) in weight.

AUTOCROSS

Introduction

Autocross is a form of MOTOR RACING or speed event run against the clock on a grass or unsealed surface. Two or more cars are run simultaneously to add competition and spectator interest.

History

Autocross orginated in England after the Second World War. Its roots are embedded in the history of sporting motoring.

Rules

The circuits themselves are of a temporary nature, usually marked out with flags and straw bales in a field hired for the purpose by the organizing club. Strict regulations governing the precise character of the event and the nature of the courses have been laid down by the Royal Automobile Club (RAC) and these, in general, apply to other countries where the sport has found a footing.

Equipment

Pure racing cars are prohibited from autocross, and specials with a capacity of more than 3 litres are banned. Eligible cars comply with a number of regulations designed to make the sport as safe as possible. Each car must have not less than four road wheels, must be of sound construction and mechanical condition, and must have a sealed fireproof bulkhead, a complete floor, a flame-proof bonnet, and sprung suspensions.

AUTORACING

See MOTOR RACING

BADMINTON

Introduction

Badminton is an indoor game played by one or two players opposing an equivalent number across a net which is 5ft1in (1.55m) high at the posts and 5ft (1.524m) high in the centre, on a court whose overall dimensions are 44ft (13.41m) by 20ft (6.10m).

The court must be laid out on a level and smooth surface, wood or composition flooring being most common, and the floor must not be slippery.

History

Badminton derives its name from the seat of the Duke of Beaufort at Badminton in Gloucestershire where the game is supposed to have evolved in about 1870, from the ancient children's game of battledore and shuttlecock. From the outset it gained popularity with army officers who took it to India and played it out of doors.

The first rules were drawn up in Poona in the mid-1870s. These were used by several groups who first adopted the game at English seaside resorts and then, soon after, in the suburbs of London. Variations soon occurred and it was discovered that even the size of courts differed to an alarming extent. At this point, in 1893, a meeting was convened in Southsea, Hampshire, at which representatives from 14 clubs founded the Badminton Association. There and then they adopted a uniform set of rules.

Rules

In competitive play a match consists of the best of three games, each of 15 points. The rules actually allow for games going up to 21 points, but this method is used only in "American" or "Round Robin" handicap events. The toss of a coin at the beginning of a match decides which side is to serve first. That side will continue serving from alternate courts until it loses a rally, when the advantage of serving passes to the other side.

In doubles play, the first (right hand) player serves to the player diagonally opposite. The two partners serve consecutively, and after both have been downed, the right to service passes to the opposing side, which similarly commence from the right-hand service court. Thus, in doubles, the receiving side must win two rallies before it gains service.

A side loses a rally when it commits a fault:

(a) if the service is not underhand or if the receiver allows it to drop and it falls outside the correct service court;

(b) if either in service or play the shuttle hits the surface of the court, falls outside the boundaries, or does not pass the net;

(c) if the shuttle is caught on the racket or slung, or if it is hit twice by the same player hit by a player and his/her partner successively;

(d) if a player touches the net or intentionally baulks or obstructs an opponent.

A "let" occurs only as a result of any unforeseen or accidental hindrance such a shuttle from a neighbouring court interfering with play, or a shuttle being caught in or held on the net.

If the score reaches 13-all, the player or pair which first reached 13 points has the option of "setting" the game for a further 5 points, or of continuing the game only up to 15. When the game has been set, the score is "love-all" and the first side to score 5 points wins the game. Similarly at 14-all the game may be set a further 3 points. If a side has declined to set the game at 13-all this does not prevent its being set later if the score should reach 14-all. In games of 21-up the score may be similarly set at 19 or 20.

The women's singles game is a shorter one, of 11 points. If a game reaches 9-all it may be set for 3 points, and at 10-all for 2 points. At the commencement of the second or third game, the winner of the preceding game serves, though in doubles only one service hand is permitted. At the end of each game the opponents change ends and remain at the same end of the

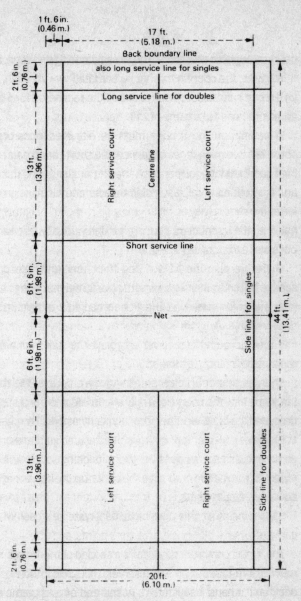

Badminton Court

court throughout that game. The exception to this is when, in a third game, the opponents change ends half-way through, i.e. when one side's score has reached 8 in a game of 15, 6 in a game of 11 or 11 in a game of 21.

In badminton the service must be delivered underhand. There are two main types of service: the short service; and the high service. In the former case, the shuttle just skims the net and is intended to fall just inside the short service-line. In the latter the shuttle may be hit anything up to the full height of the hall with the intention of causing it to fall vertically, as near as possible to the long service-line.

There are also the "drive" and "flick" services. The drive service will cross the net only just above it, and be made to land near the long service-line. The flick service is deceptively high, delivered in exactly the same way as a short service, and it is intended to catch the receiver off guard. The spot from which the service is hit can be varied.

Shuttles do not bounce, so all shots are volleys. The main strokes during the course of a rally are the clear, the smash, the drop, and the drive, all either forehand or backhand. The clear is sometimes called a "lob" or "toss", and is hit high in the air so as to land as near as possible to the back boundary line. Its object is to gain time or to drive the opponent to the back of the court. Maximum depth is of great importance in order to give the hitter the most time possible to deal with the smash which it invites.

The smash is the natural reply to a clear and though it is much more forceful on the forehand, it is also used on the backhand. It must be hit from a position as high as possible in order to obtain a steep angle. The smash wins more rallies than any other stroke. The drop is made from any part of the court and causes the shuttle to fall within a few feet of the other side of the net. It is achieved by a checking of the wrist, and is most effective when the striking action is identical to that of the smash. Its object can be both attacking and defensive, and a surprise top shot will end many rallies.

The drive, both on the forehand and backhand, is a fast stroke with the shuttle only just crossing the net. It is made only from the side of the court but can be directed straight down or across court, and is frequently used in mixed doubles where the woman covers the net. There are many variations of these basic strokes.

The server must stand with both feet entirely within his/her service court, and neither foot must touch the line. Usually s/he stands a few feet behind the short service-line, and as near as possible to the centre service-line so that the shuttle has the shortest distance to travel, thus giving the receiver the least possible time to deal with it.

The receiver stands as near to the short service-line as s/he dares in order to kill the imperfect short service, and yet be able to retreat to deal with a service over their head. Thus a male player will stand with his/her front foot as near as permitted to the short service-line and leaning forward over it, but a woman will need to stand at least 3 or 4ft (1m) behind the short service line in order to avoid being caught by an unexpected high service.

Neither the server nor the receiver may alter the position of his/her feet until the shuttle is actually hit, but after the service has been delivered there is no restriction on the players' movements.

Equipment

Shuttles are made of either feathers (16 feathers, usually goose) or nylon. The feather shuttle is most popular at high level competitions. The racket must be no more than 9in (230mm) in width and 27in (680mm) in length. The stringed area (no more than 280mm long and 220mm wide) must be flat and of a uniform pattern. Frames are generally made of aluminium or graphite and natural gut is the most popular string material.

For doubles play the entire court is used, but the singles court is 3ft (91cm) narrower, the two tramlines being ignored. In doubles, the service court is a rectangle bound by the short service-line, the centre line, the long service-line and the side-line. In singles the service court extends to the back boundary line and to the appropriate side line.

Scoring

Only the server can add to his/her score by winning a rally. Should the receiving side win a rally, the score remains static but the service changes hands. A game of 15-up can therefore consist of many times that number of rallies before it is completed.

Clothing

There are no strict rules but the clothing must allow ease of movement. For a man, shorts and a lightweight shirt are practical, while a woman may replace the shorts with a skirt.

BALLOONING

Introduction

A form of unpowered flight dependent on the inflation of a spherical fabric container with a gas that is lighter than air. The container (balloon) rises, carrying the pilot and passengers in a basket beneath it. Descent is achieved by the controlled release of the gas through a valve in the top of the container, operated by a cord from the basket.

BALLROOM DANCING

Introduction

For many, ballroom dancing might not appear to be a competitive sport. However, it is, and there are regular competitions all over the world under the auspices of the International Dance Sport Federation (IDSF). It may even be included in a future Olympics. The competitions include Standard dances; waltz, tango, Viennese waltz, slow foxtrot and quickstep and Latin American dances; samba, cha-cha-cha, rumba, paso doble and jive.

History

Prior to the First World War there were some competitive encounters in several European Countries but it was only after the 1930s that "English Style" started to take hold of the Continent and international matches occurred more frequently. By 1935 the Federation Internationale de Dance pour Amatuteurs (FIDA) was born and the first members were from Austria, Czechoslovakia, Denmark, England, France, Germany, Holland, Switzerland and Yugoslavia. They were soon joined by Belgium, Canada, Italy and Norway. The first official World Championships were held in Bad Nauheim in Germany just before the 1936 Olympic Games.

Rules

Dancers take to the dance floor and in all rounds of competitions the music played must be more than one and a half minutes for the waltz, tango, slow foxtrot, quickstep, samba, cha-cha-cha, rumba and paso doble. The minimum length for the viennese waltz and jive is one minute.

The tempo for each dance is: waltz, 30bars/min; tango 33bars/min; viennese waltz 60bars/min; slow foxtrot 30bars/min; quickstep 50bars/min; samba 50bars/min; cha-cha-cha 30bars/min; rumba 27bars/min; paso doble 62bars/min; jive 44bars/min and the music must "have the character of the dances" according the IDSF, for example, there must be no disco music in the Latin American dances.

Clothing

For adult competitions the suit must be black or midnight-blue. Decoration on the Latin suits is allowed, but only if it is in the same colour as the suit material. A white shirt may be worn under the suit, provided that the suit has long sleeves. The woman must wear a competition dress.

BANDY

Introduction

Approximates to HOCKEY played on an ice-covered FOOTBALL pitch. The rules of bandy require that it is played by at most 11 players a side, and not fewer than 8. The object of the game, which is started from the centre circle, is to hit the ball into the opponents' goal.

Venue

The rink is roughly the size of an Association Football pitch, and with similar tolerances: i.e. 90–110m long and 45–65m wide.

History

Bandy was born in England between 1790 and 1820 although the exact date is difficult to fix since no records of the game remain in its country of origin, where it has not been played since the early years of the twentieth century. The low-lying districts of Cambridgeshire and Lincolnshire were the home of the sport but its spread to other districts appears to have been slow. It had reached Nottingham by 1865, which saw the founding at the Forest Racecourse of the Nottingham Forest Football and Bandy Club. Originally an outdoor sport, a condensed version known as rink-bandy is played indoors in Holland, but the game proper lives on only in Finland, Mongolia, Norway, Russia, Estonia, Latvia and Sweden.

Rules

The object of the game, which is started from the centre circle, is to hit the ball into the opponents' goal. Skilled players display the speed and agility of skating seen in ICE HOCKEY, but, since bandy is played with a ball and not a puck, even greater skill with the stick is necessary. The great size of the rink, the duration of the match – two halves of 45 minutes each – and the speed at which it is played make top-class bandy a severe test of physical fitness.

The ball may not be touched with the hands, except by the goalkeeper, and the stick may not be raised higher than the level of the shoulders. The ball may be stopped by the skate, but kicking (except by the goalkeeper) is allowed only to position the ball so that the player himself may strike it. Restrictions as to impeding an opponent are similar to those in hockey: neither he nor his stick may be held, struck, pushed, or kicked. Free strokes are awarded for infringements, and serious infringements within the penalty area are punished by a penalty stroke taken 12m (approx 13yds) from the centre of the goal line. The referee may send off a player guilty of a gross infringement, either for a brief period (as in ice hockey) or for the rest of the match.

Equipment

All players must wear ice skates and all except the goalkeeper carry curved wooden sticks similar to field hockey sticks and the length measured along the outside of the curve must not be more than 1.2m. The ball is hard, usually red, and 6cm in diameter (about half-way between a golf ball and a hockey ball). The goal cages are almost exactly the same size as in hockey: 2.1m high and 3.5m wide.

BASEBALL

Introduction

Baseball is a nine-a-side game played with a bat, ball and glove, mainly in the USA. Teams consist of: a pitcher, and catcher, called the battery; first, second, and third basemen, and shortstop, called the infield; and right, centre, and left fielders, called the outfield. The two teams compete to score runs (points) by players moving around the four bases. The team with the highest score wins.

History

Baseball can be traced back to the English game of STOOL BALL, played in the Middle Ages. Here a batter tried to hit a pitched ball before it reached an upside-down milk stool. If the ball was hit, the batter ran around three stools and back to the "homestool". By the seventeenth century, this evolved into ROUNDERS, which had a diamond-shaped field with bases on the corners. After the colonists arrived in America in the 1700s, rounders became known as town ball because every village seemed to play with their own rules.

Venue

The game is played on a field containing four bases (home plate, first, second, and third base), placed at the angles of a 90ft (27.4m) square (often called a diamond). Two foul lines form the boundaries of fair territory. Starting at home, these lines extend past first and third base the entire length of the field, which is often enclosed by a fence at its farthest limits.

Rules

The object of each team is to score more runs than the other. A run is scored whenever a player circles, counter-clockwise, all the bases and reaches home without being put out. The game is divided into innings, in each of which the teams alternate at bat and in the field. A team is allowed three outs in each half-inning at bat, and must then take up defensive positions in the field while the other team has its turn to try and score. Ordinarily, a game consists of nine innings; in the event of a tie, extra innings are played until one team outscores the other in the same number of innings.

The players take turns batting from home plate in regular rotation. The opposing pitcher throws the ball to his catcher from a slab (called the "rubber") on the pitcher's mound, a slightly raised area of the field directly between home and second base. The rubber is 60ft 6in (18.4m) from home plate, which is 17in (43cm) wide and set flush in the ground. Bases are canvas bags fastened to metal pegs set in the ground.

The batter tries to reach base safely after hitting the pitched ball into fair territory. A hit that enables him to reach first base is called a "single", a two-base hit is a "double", a three-base hit a "triple", and a four-base hit a "home-run". A fair ball hit over an outfield fence is automatically a home run. A batter is also

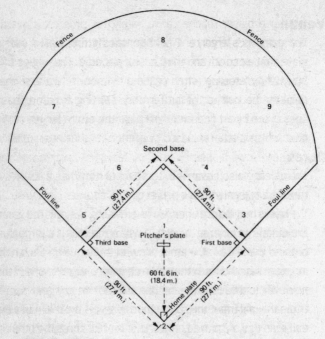

Baseball Field

1) Pitcher; 2) catcher; 3) first baseman; 4) second baseman; 5) third baseman; 6) shortstop; 7) left fielder; 8) centre fielder; 9) right fielder.

awarded his base if the pitcher delivers four pitches which, in the umpire's judgement, do not pass through the "strike-zone", that is, over home plate between the batter's armpits and knees. He may also be awarded his base if he is hit by a pitched ball or the opposing catcher interferes when he swings the bat. To prevent the batter from hitting safely, baseball pitchers deliver the ball with great speed and accuracy and vary its speed and trajectory. Success in batting, therefore, requires courage and a high degree of skill.

After a player reaches base safely, his progress towards home depends largely on his team mates hitting a ball in such a way that he can advance. A base runner may also advance on his own, by "stealing" – running for the next base as the pitcher delivers the ball to the batter and reaching it before he is tagged out by an opposing fielder. A runner may try to move ahead if the pitcher makes a "wild pitch" to the batter, or if the catcher allows a "passed ball" by failing to catch a pitch. A runner may also advance if the pitcher commits a "balk" by making an illegal move or delivery.

Players may be put out in various ways. A batter is out when the pitcher gets three "strikes" on him. A strike is a pitch that crosses the plate in the strike zone, or any pitch that is struck at and missed or is hit into foul territory. After two strikes, however, foul balls do not count except when a batter "bunts" – lets the ball meet the bat instead of swinging at it – and the ball rolls foul. A batter is also out if he hits the ball in the air anywhere in the fair or foul territory and it is caught by an opponent before it touches the ground. He is out if he hits the ball on the ground and a fielder catches and throws it to a player at first base, before the batter (now become a base runner) gets there.

A base player may be put out if, while off base, he is tagged by an opposing player with the hand or glove holding the ball, or if he is forced to leave his base to make room for another runner and fails to reach the next base before an opposing player tags him or the base; or if he is hit by a team mate's batted ball before it has touched or passed a fielder.

An umpire-in-chief "calls" balls and strikes from his position directly behind the catcher at home plate, and one or more base umpires determine whether runners are safe or out on the other three bases. When one umpire is used, he usually stands behind the pitcher in order to call balls and strikes and at the same time to be as close as possible to the bases.

Equipment

The standard ball has a cork-and-rubber centre wound with woollen yarn and covered with horsehide. It weighs from 5 to 5.25oz (148g) and is from 9 to 9.5in (approx. 23cm) in circumference. For softball, a modified form of baseball, a larger ball is used. The bat is a smooth, round, tapered piece of hard wood not more than 2.75in (approx. 7cm) in diameter at its thickest part and no more than 42in (1.07m) long.

Clothing

Originally, fielders played barehanded, but gloves have been developed over the years. First basemen wear a special large mitt and catchers use a large heavily-padded mitt as well as a chest protector, shin guards, and a metal mask. Catchers were at first unprotected. Consequently, they stood back at a distance from home plate and caught pitched balls on the bounce, but the introduction of the large, round, well-padded mitt or "pillow-glove" and the face mask enabled them to move up close behind the plate and catch pitched balls on the fly. Players wear shoes with steel cleats and, while batting and running the bases, they use protective plastic helmets.

BASEBALL, WELSH

Introduction

An 11-a-side team game played with a wooden bat and hard ball, mainly in South Wales and part of north-west England. It differs in several respects, and notably in the matter of equipment, from the more widely-known form of BASEBALL played in the USA.

History

Supporters of this form of the sport claim that the American game came from Welsh baseball. The ancient game of ROUNDERS flourished in the west of England, and almost certainly led to this refinement's building up in South Wales. It spread to isolated pockets, and nationals have been played between two countries since 1908.

Venue

The inner field of play is shaped, as in American baseball, like a diamond, the four points of which are the four bases to which the batsman runs. The batting area (known as the centre peg) is 15ft (4.6m) in front of the fourth, or home, base, which is 100ft (30.5m) from the second base, at the opposite point of the diamond. The first and third bases are 86ft (26.2m) apart. Each base is represented not by a plate but by a pole stuck in the ground, which must be touched by the batsman reaching or passing it. All 11 members of a team bat before the innings is completed.

Equipment

The Welsh baseball bat more nearly resembles a cricket bat than it does a baseball bat. Made of willow, it has a flat striking surface. It may be altogether 3ft (91cm) long, and 3.5in (8.9cm) broad at the base. Unlike that of a cricket bat, the face tapers evenly into the handle, a maximum breadth of 2.5in (6.4cm) being allowed at a point 19in (48.3cm) above the base. The ball is approximately the same size and weight as a CRICKET ball, but covered in white chrome leather. It is delivered underarm by a bowler (not a pitcher) from a rectangle 10ft (3m) long and 2ft

6in (76cm) wide, the front edge of which is 50ft (15m) from the batting point.

Clothing

The clothing worn by the players is much simpler: ordinary football-style shirts and shorts; and either spiked running shoes or lightweight football boots. Catching gloves and other protective gear are not used.

BASKETBALL

Introduction

Basketball is a five-a-side ball game which originated in the USA in 1891 but is now played worldwide. The object of the game as its inventor, Dr James Naismith, conceived it, is for one team to secure possession of the ball and to throw it into the opponents' basket, while attempting to prevent the other team from securing the ball or scoring. A goal is scored when the ball enters the basket from above and remains in, or passes through, the net.

History

The earliest evidence of a game that resembles basketball may be found in ancient Central and South American civilizations. In South America, on the Yucatan peninsula, playing "courts" bounded by stone walls and set among groves of trees, have been found dating from the seventh century BC. Overlooking the courts were sculptures of gods and other religious symbols, suggesting that the game normally took place as part of a religious festival. The game, known as "pok-tapock", was played with a rubber ball filled with sacred plants. The object was to play the ball into the "goal", using only the hips, thighs, and knees. A goal was situated at each end of the court and consisted of a flat stone slab with a hole cut through the centre. In Mexico, in the sixteenth century, the Aztec game of "ollamalitzli", required that the players propel a solid rubber ball through a fixed stone ring. The successful player was reputedly entitled to claim the clothing of all the spectators.

Omar Khayyam, the eleventh-century philosopher, seems to have made the first literary allusion to basketball in one of his epigrams, which translates thus: "You are a ball, played with by fate; a ball which God throws since the dawn of time into the catch-basket."

An engraving made by de Bruys in 1603 shows a precursor of basketball, and Vieth in his *Encyclopedia of Athletics* (1818) details a game played in Florida in which the players attempted to throw the ball into a basket attached to the top of a pole.

Credit for the invention of the game of basketball as played today, however, must go to the Canadian-born Dr Naismith. A leader at the International YMCA Training School at Pringfield, Mass., USA, Naismith was instructed, in 1891, to design an indoor team game. In 1895, the YWCA organization requested a copy of the rules, which were adopted with certain restrictions to make the game more suitable for women. From these rules the game of NETBALL subsequently developed independently.

USA Basketball is the national governing body for the sport in the US and is made up of many different organizations. These include the Amateur Athletic Union (AAU), the National Basketball Association (NBA), the National Collegiate Athletic Association (NCAA), the National Federation of State High School Associations, and the coaches associations for both men and women. The International Basketball Federation

(FIBA) is the sport's world organisation formed by the 176 national groups.

Venue

The court is a rectangular hard surface, free from obstruction and varying according to the level of play: NCAA, 50x90ft; NBA and WNBA, 50x94ft; FIBA, 49ft 2.5in x 91ft 10in; High School, 50x84ft. Its surface may be of any one of a number of suitable materials, but grass-covered courts are not permitted. The court is marked by clearly defined lines, 5cm (2in) in width.

Rules

Each team consists of five players, up to five substitutes being allowed to each side. These usually consist of a centre, two forwards and two guards. A point guard is the primary ball handler; the shooting guard is the top scorer. The ball may be passed, rolled, thrown, tapped, or dribbled as the team with the ball moves towards the goal.

Dribbling allows an individual player to move the ball about the court unassisted. The dribble begins when a player bounces the ball on the floor and then touches it again, without the intrusion of another player. The dribbler may continue to bounce the ball for as long as he wishes or is able, but once he catches it, or allows it to come to rest in his hand, he is not permitted to start another dribble. He must either pass or attempt a shot at goal. A proficient dribbler will be able to dribble using either hand and will not need to look at the ball, thereby enabling him to watch the positions of the players on the court.

The aim of passing and dribbling the ball is to attempt to reach a suitable shooting position. There is no restriction on which players are entitled to shoot or from where a shot may

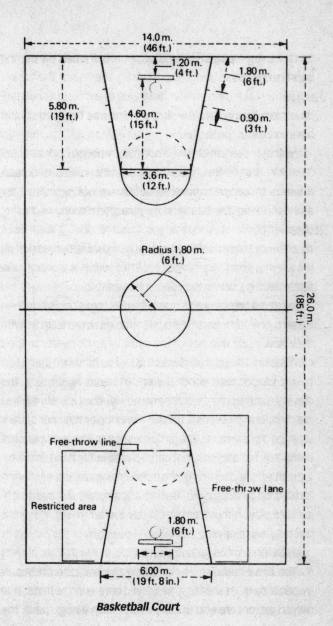

Basketball Court

Basketball

be taken. Any player in possession of the ball within the playing court is entitled to shoot, but naturally the nearer the basket the shot is taken, the greater likelihood of success. A shot may be aimed directly into the ring or it may be bounced off the backboard into the basket.

If a shot misses, the ball will normally rebound back into play from the ring or the backboard and both teams may then attempt to secure control of it. The attacking team may attempt to tip the ball directly into the basket, or, having obtained possession, may attempt another shot. A team must try to shoot at goal within 30 seconds of gaining possession on the playing court. An infraction of this rule is a violation and possession is given to the opposing team.

The game begins with a "jump-ball" at the centre circle. Two players, one from each team, stand in the centre circle, with their feet inside that half of the circle which is nearer to their own basket. The referee tosses the ball up between them, to a height greater than either player can reach by jumping. The players jump upwards and strive to tap the ball, after it has reached its highest point, in such a way that a member of their team gain possession. The jumpers are each allowed two taps of the ball, but they may not catch the ball until it has touched, or been touched by, one of the non-jumping players, the floor, a basket, or a back-board. During a jump-ball, the eight non-jumping players must remain outside the centre circle until the ball has been tapped.

Once a team has gained possession of the ball, its players may advance the ball either by passing it among themselves, or by dribbling it. The ball may be played only with the hands and players are not allowed to carry it more than a single pace. The swiftest and most efficient way of moving the ball about the court is by interpassing. There is no limit to the number of passes a team may make before attempting a shot at goal. It is usual for a team to make several passes before shooting, but there is never any obligation to pass the ball when one is in possession within the playing court.

The play in basketball is fast and free and on the comparatively small court every player must try to avoid personal contact at all times. If such contact occurs, a "personal foul" is charged against the player responsible. A player is, however, entitled to take up a floor position that is not already occupied by an opponent, providing that this causes no personal contact. With this definition of a personal foul the game becomes one in which skill and power are of paramount importance.

If the player who had been fouled was in the act of shooting for goal, and if the shot proved unsuccessful, that player is awarded two free throws, i.e. two unhindered shots at the basket from immediately behind the "free-throw line". This is a line drawn parallel to the end line, 12x19ft, and a semi-circle with a 6ft radius from the centre of the free throw line (NCAA and WNBA); 16x19ft, and a semi-circle with a 6ft radius from the centre of the free throw line (NBA).

A free throw, if successful, is worth one point. The shooter must remain behind the free-throw line until the ball hits the ring or the backboard and no other player is allowed to enter the free-throw line until that time. If the second throw is unsuccessful, and the ball rebounds from the ring, players of both sides may compete for the rebound in the normal way.

The non-offending team may waive its right to free throws, if it so desires, and accept possession of the ball opposite the half-way line. If the official considers that a foul is "intentional" it is treated as having been committed against a player in the act of shooting and thus carries the free-throw penalty.

There is an alternative form of foul, known as a "technical foul", which is charged for an offence not involving personal contact. This is normally an offence against the spirit of the game, and may be committed by a player, by the coach, or by a substitute. The penalty for a technical foul by a player is two free throws, to be taken by any member of the opposition, after which the ball remains in play in the normal way. For a technical foul by a coach, or substitute, the penalty is one free throw, followed by possession of the ball opposite the half-way line.

If a player commits five fouls during a match (NCAA and FIBA) or six (NBA) he is automatically barred from taking any further part in the game. In case of any flagrant infraction of the rules, a player may be disqualified immediately. In either case, a substitute may be introduced in place of the player who has been required to leave the game.

All breaches of the rules not considered to be fouls are known as "violations". Violations include:

Running with the ball ("travelling").

Kicking or punching the ball.

Making an illegal dribble.

Causing the ball to go out of bounds.

Keeping the ball in the back court more than ten seconds.

Not attempting a field goal before the shot clock expires.

Staying in the freethrow lane more than three seconds when a player's own team has possession of the ball.

An opponent crossing the boundary line before the ball does on a throw-in.

Because the goal is 3.05m (10ft) above the floor and the ball must enter it from above, the tall player has a natural advantage in basketball, and it usual for the leading teams to include several players considerably over 6ft (1.8m). There is still opportunity, however, for the skilful smaller player to excel at the sport.

Basketball is a game in which every player on the court is involved in constant action, irrespective of which team is in possession, or of the part of the court in which the ball is located. It is usual for all five players of a team to attack when their team is in possession and to defend when the opposition has control of the ball.

There are no formal positions and teams will attack and defend in whatever formation the coach chooses. The attack employed by a team will naturally depend upon the ability and talents of its players and upon their comparison with the opposition. Such additional factors as the number of fouls already committed by individuals and the local conditions and rules of the competition will also influence the offensive style chosen by the coach.

The method of attack by means of the "fast break" gives a team the opportunity to exploit its speed and skill and to nullify its opponents' defensive tactics. Using the fast break, the team that had been defending, having gained possession, will immediately attempt to advance the ball up court and try to establish a numerical advantage near its opponents' goal. In this way, it is possible to make a worthwhile shot before the defence has time to form.

If it is not possible to use the fast break, or if this is incompatible with the tactics of the team, then that team will normally attempt to establish some form of controlled offence. The scope of offence is limitless but the guiding principles are few. The object is to gain the opportunity for making a shot with some probability of success, but at the same time a team will try to safeguard possession throughout its offensive manoeuvres.

The deployment of players is governed principally by their respective heights and the tactics employed by the defending team. The smaller, more agile, players work mainly in the mid-court area and are known as guards or quarterbacks. These players are usually the most skilful dribblers and passers of the ball. The taller players who normally play at the side or corner of the court, are known as forwards, while the tallest players of all, playing near the basket, are called pivots, centres, or posts. The actual formation employed is at the discretion of the coach. The terminology used to describe the offence is conventionally counted from mid-court, towards the basket.

The one essential tactical restriction governing offensive formation is the need to have at least one guard to bring the ball up court so as to initiate the offence and maintain a suitable position to offer some defence against a possible fast break by the opposition.

The variety of defensive tactics is equally great. The basic defence involves strict man-to-man marking, where each defensive player is assigned responsibility for a member of the opposition. The position on the court at which the defender first assumes this responsibility, and the closeness with which he marks this opponent, will depend upon the overall defensive strategy which his team is adopting.

The alternative principle is the system of "zone" defence, in which each player is responsible for defending a loosely-defined area of the court and assumes responsibility for any attacking player within this area. He will also be ready to assist players in adjacent areas, when necessary. The shape of the zone is defined by a numerical system, counting from the mid-court, e.g. 2-1-2, 1-3-1, 1-2-2.

The defence employed by a team will depend on the personnel involved, the tactics chosen, and the state of the game. It may involve man-to-man principles, zone principles, or a combination of the two. In addition, the defence may be passive or may involve a degree of pressure.

In "passive" defence, the team will defend the area close to the basket, seeking to deny the opposition the opportunity of shooting from this range, thus encouraging the longer shot in the hope that it will be unsuccessful and the defence will obtain the rebound. In "pressure" defence, the defending team make positive attempts to gain possession of the ball and prevent the shot being taken.

An extension to the principle of pressure defence leads to the "press". This is a form of defence in which pressure is applied over an area far beyond that from which a shot would normally be taken. In the case of a "full-court press", pressure is applied over the whole court whenever that team is defending. The "press" may employ the principles of a zone, man-to-man defence, or a combination of the two. In addition to the general scope of offence and defence, there are several facets of the game which require attention. These include jump-balls, free throws and out-of-bounds throws. The coach, who controls the tactics, may be said to be the most important member of the team. He not only orders substitutions and time-outs, but may direct and change the team tactics during these time-outs.

Equipment

The goal consists of a basket made of a bottomless net of white cord, suspended from an orange-painted iron ring of 45cm (18in) inside diameter, and constructed of metal 20mm (approx 0.75in) in cross-sectional diameter. The net is constructed so as to check the ball momentarily as it passes through the basket. The ring lies in a horizontal plane, 3.05m (10ft) above the floor, and is rigidly attached to the backboard at a point equidistant from the two vertical edges and 30cm (1ft) above the bottom edge of this board.

Backboards are made of hard wood, painted white, or of a suitable transparent material of an equivalent rigidity. Each backboard measures 1.80m (6ft) horizontally, 1.20m (4ft) vertically, and has a plane front surface. It is rigidly mounted in a position at the end of the court in a perpendicular plane, parallel to the end lines, with its lower edge 2.75m (9ft) above the floor. The centre of the backboard lies in the perpendicular plane erected 1.20m (4ft) inside the court, opposite the mid-point of the end line. The supporting structures must be carefully constructed so as not to interfere with the playing area or the immediate out-of-bounds area.

The ball used in basketball is spherical and made of leather, rubber, or moulded nylon casing, or similar synthetic material, around a rubber inner bladder. The ball is normally bright orange in colour, with black panel markings.

Clothing

Each team wears a set of matching vests, or singlets, contrasting in colour with those of their opponents, brief-cut shorts, socks, and specially constructed shoes or boots with rubber soles and canvas uppers. Each player is numbered on the front and back of their vest. In international competition, only the numbers four to 15 inclusive may be used. No team mates may wear duplicate numbers.

BATINTON

Introduction

Batinton is a game for two or four players based on BADMINTON with a TABLE TENNIS scoring system.

History

Batinton was invented in 1918 on the instructions of Bombing Officer Pat Hannah, NZ Division on the Rhine. Games for more than 30,000 men in restricted areas, which everyone knew or could learn quickly and which needed little space, did not exist. So, Hannah devised a new game and called it Batinton. It was based on the ancient battledore and shuttlecock. 48 people could play in the area of one tennis court. The game was simple yet skilful. It was so popular that the supplies of shuttles ran out and the game drifted into obscurity.

Venue

The game is played indoors or outdoors or on any non-slippery surface. The standard size of an individual court is 36ft by 12ft but the width may vary between 10ft and 13ft. If only 30ft is available, the back boundary lines may be extended 6ft vertically up the wall or background. It is usual for several courts to be laid out side by side in a hall or gymnasium.

Rules

Doubles, two players on each side of the net, is the most popular form, although singles is often played. The game commences with a service from the right-hand service court into the opponent's right-hand service court. The object is to hit the shuttle into the opponent's court or to force the opponent to hit the shuttle out of court or into the net. The player who achieves either wins the point. Each game is played until one player, or side, has reached 21 points, unless the score reaches 20-all when the game will continue until one side is 2 points ahead.

Equipment

The game is played with a bat similar in construction to a table tennis bat, but longer. The hitting head is of wood covered with cork or plastic. The overall length is 16in (41cm), the head 8.5in (22cm) long and 6.5in (16.5cm) wide. The shuttle is exactly the same as the rubber-nosed plastic shuttle used in Badminton. In 1965, the first plastic bat with cork face was produced and has largely replaced the wooden bat.

Scoring

Each player serves in turn for five consecutive points. Service is taken alternately from the right and left service courts, always commencing from the right-hand court. Once play has commenced any type of stroke may be played to keep the shuttle moving from one end to the other. In doubles either partner may play the shot. The boundary lines constitute part of the court and if any part of the shuttle falls on the line it is in court.

Serving

In service the shuttle must be hit with an under-arm action in order to start play. The bat must be below the level of the elbow and both feet must be in contact with the surface of the service court. The three main strokes are, as in badminton: the drop shot, played either slowly or quickly so that the shuttle just clears the net and drops in front of the opponent's court; the high back-court drive, played high into the air so that it is beyond the reach of an opponent close to the net (i.e. dropping close to the back boundary line); and the smash, played with the bat coming down on to the shuttle in order to hit it as steeply as possible into the opponent's court.

BEACH VOLLEYBALL
Introduction
Beach volleyball is a team game played on either a beach or a large sandpit area, it involves punching a ball over a net and is like VOLLEYBALL.

History
The first accounts of beach volleyball place the sport in Santa Monica, California, USA, where the first volleyball courts were put up on beach at the Playground (Santa Monica). In 1927 beach volleyball became the principal sport in a French nudist camp founded in Francoville (a north-western suburb of Paris). By the 1930s the first two-man beach volleyball game was played in Santa Monica and started appearing around the world: Palavas, Lacanau and Royan (France); around Sofia (Bulgaria); Prague (Czechoslavakia); and Riga (Latvia). Nearly 17 years later the first official two-man beach tournament was held at State Beach in California.

Venue
The playing area consists of a rectangular playing court

measuring 59ft x 29ft 6in and has a surrounding free zone which is a minimum of 9ft 10in wide. The surface of the playing area must be as flat as possible, free of rocks, or any objects that would cause injury. Sand courts are at least 12in. The court has boundary lines which consist of two sidelines and two end lines which mark the playing court. They are made of rope or wide flat bands or tape. The centre line divides the playing court into two square team courts, but is not marked.

The Rules

Beach volleyball can be played with anything from two players on the court per team (doubles), to six per team, i.e. the maximum number of players that should be on the court at any one time is twelve.

The winner of a coin toss at the beginning of a match decides either to select, serve or receive service of the first ball or to choose the side of the court on which to serve. The loser takes the remaining alternative and, for the second game in a two out of three match, gets to select from the above choices.

To win a rally, whenever a team fails to serve or return the ball, or commits any other fault, the opposing team wins the rally. If the serving team wins a rally, it scores a point and continues to serve. If the receiving team wins a rally, it gains the right to serve, but does not score a point. The game is then identical to indoor volleyball (see volleyball).

Equipment

The net must be at least 7ft 1.62in measured at the centre. The ball must be of flexible leather or water-resistant leather-like material with a rubber or rubber-like bladder. Its circumference must be 25.5-26.5ft and its weight 9-10oz. It may be of any colour or multicoloured.

Clothing

A player's clothing has to be presentable and appropriate for the game. Players on the same team may wear different coloured clothing and designs. Players can also wear hats, sunglasses and visors. They may also play barefoot, in socks, or in shoes which can't have spikes. Any objects that would cause an injury to another player, i.e. jewelry, are forbidden.

Scoring

Matches may either consist of a single game, or best two out of three. In a one game match, a team can win by scoring 15 points with a two point margin. For the first or second game in a two out of three, a team can win by scoring 11 points with a two point margin, and in a deciding game in two out of three, a team must win with seven points, by at least one point, i.e. with 7-6.

BIATHLON

Introduction

The term biathlon comes from the Greek meaning "two tests". This is a combined running and swimming event introduced by the Modern Pentathlon Association of Great Britain in 1968. Senior men compete over the same distances as those for the modern pentathalon – 4,000m running, 300m swimming. At its introduction the standards set for the gold badge award of the Association were 15 minutes for the running and 4min 40sec for the swimming.

The sport is designed to produce modern pentathalon performers on the theory that it is desirable to teach swimming at an early age; that a certain proportion of capable swimmers are natural runners and that, if these two abilities are developed early, the other three skills of pentathlon – horse riding, pistol-shooting and fencing – can be acquired later.

(See also BIATHLON, SKIING).

BIATHLON SKIING
Introduction

The term biathlon comes from the Greek meaning "two tests". In this sport, competitors race across country on skis stopping at various stages to shoot at targets with a rifle. Penalties are given for any target missed and the fastest time wins.

History

The sport originates from the times when men hunted on skis for food in the winter months. There are early cave paintings dating from 3,000 BC showing hunters with bows and arrows travelling on primitive skis made of wood.

Venue

When race courses are set there are maximum allowable individual and overall climbs. For instance, in the men's 20km race the longest individual climb must not exceed 75m and the overall amount of climbing within the course must be 600-750m. There must also be a distance of at least 3km between shooting stations and the penalty loop must be in a level area immediately adjacent to the shooting range.

Rules

At the 1998 Nagano Winter Olympics there were six biathlon events: individual races at 20km and 10km for men and at 7.5km and 15km for women; and a 7.5km relay for both men and women. Competitors ski along specially prepared cross-country trails carrying a rifle, firing at targets which are set up at varying stages of each race. Each competitor carries 20 rounds of ammunition (ten for the sprint) in the individual races.

In the 20km race for men, there are four firing stations each with five targets set at a distance of 50m (164ft). Competitors fire from the prone position at the first and third station and from the standing position at the second and fourth. A time penalty of one minute is added for each target missed. The fastest time wins because of the staggered start.

In the men's sprint, or 10km, race competitors have to ski a penalty loop of 150m (492ft) for each of the targets missed. This gives them the option of taking more risks with their shooting, relying on their speed of skiing to make up the time lost. In this race there are two firing stations each of five shots. The first station, 3km into the race, is from the prone position and the second is standing.

Shooting stations of five targets apiece are spaced between the 3km and 12km positions in the women's 15km race. The first and third are tackled in the prone position and the other two in the standing position. A minute is added for any targets missed. The women's sprint is a 7.5km race with two firing stations, the first prone, the second standing, and penalty loops of 150m are skied for missed targets.

Relay teams consist of four competitors each of whom skis 7.5km and fires, once prone and once standing. Each skier has eight rounds of ammunition to hit the five targets. A penalty loop is only incurred if all eight rounds have been fired and a target has still been missed. In the changeover zone the next skier is sent on his or her way with a pat on the back. The winner is the first team to cross the line.

Equipment

Biathlon competitors use skis which are designed for cross-country skiing. These are narrower and shorter than their Alpine counterparts. They have upturned tips and taper towards the rear. It is important that skiers choose the right type of wax for the snow conditions. There are also special cross-country skiing boots which clip into bindings on the ski by the toe only. Each skier carries a 0.22 calibre rifle on his/her back with a special harness. This does not have a telescopic sight and weighs between 3.5kg (7.7lbs) and 4.5kg (9.9lbs).

BICYCLE POLO

Introduction

Bicycle polo is a form of POLO adapted to the use of bicycles instead of ponies. It is a team game in which the players' object is to score goals (the units of scoring) by driving a ball upfield with the long-handled mallet that each player carries, before striking the ball between the goal posts which the opposite team is defending.

History

Bicycle polo was probably invented in Ireland in 1891 by R. J. Mecredy, a former racing cyclist who had remained an active member of the Ohnehast CC of Dublin, and was then editor of *Irish Cyclist*. It was the custom of the club at the period to make a Saturday excursion to Co. Wicklow, 20 miles from Dublin. On 10 October 1891, a report referring to the excursion appeared in *Cycling*, under the heading "Polo on wheels". Of the precious Saturday's club run it said, "the game of cycling polo was inaugurated, and promises to be immensely popular with members". The report continued: "After a few games there were hardly any collisions, and these only occurred when the riders were travelling at very slow pace. One would think that polo is a sport which would peculiarly gladden the heart of the cycle-repairer, but there is not even a bent pedal. R. J. Mecredy is enthusiastic about it, and hopes to get a few matches when it is generally known."

Venue

The regulation pitch is 120yds in length and 60yds in width. Fields of slightly smaller dimensions may be used but the pitch should not exceed 100yds in length and 50yds in width. The goal posts are 4m apart (and at an equal distance from the corners) and at least 2m in height. They must be light enough to break if collided with.

Rules

A game of bicycle polo consists of six 15-minute periods of play (chukkas), separated by intervals of one minute. Teams change ends once, between the third and fourth chukkas. Substitution of players is permitted only during intervals, but a player coming off the field at one interval may return at the next; thus it is customary for the six players in the team to rest in turn. The five players engaged in the game normally take up positions as goalkeeper, full-back, half-back, and two forwards.

At the start of the game or a chukka, or after a goal has been scored, the referee (who is on foot) places the ball on the sprinters' line at the centre of the field. On his signal, one player on either side (referred to as the "sprinter") races to gain possession of the ball from a standing start on the left-hand side of his/her goal. It is an offence for him/her to cross the sprinters' line before either s/he or the opposing sprinter has touched the ball (a ruling that reduces the likelihood of a head-on crash), or for any other player to approach within 10yds (9.14m) of the ball before this has been done.

The team which gains possession then attempts to work the ball up field either by individually driving it through or by interpassing. The ball is normally trapped by blocking with the wheels of the bicycle, but a player is allowed to stop it with his body, including his hand (although he may not catch it), and to kick it, provided that it is in the air.

The most common foul is to lay the ball while dismounted, for playing the ball includes merely allowing it to touch one's body or bicycle, and to be dismounted it is sufficient just to put a foot on the ground. It is not an offence to be dismounted at other times.

The defending player may tackle with his bicycle, shoulder-charge a player in possession, or hook his mallet, and he may ride-off an opponent challenging for the ball. However, he may not slash at the other's mallet, or play round him at a ball on the further side of the machine.

While in his own penalty area, the goalkeeper may not be charged or obstructed, the onus of avoiding him being always on the attacker. Offside is limited to the area between the opponents' quarter-line and goal line, where an attacking player may legitimately receive the ball only if there is at least one defending player nearer the goal line.

For an offence committed by the defending side within its own penalty area, a penalty hit is awarded to the attacking side. This is taken from the centre of the penalty line, and only the goalkeeper may attempt to stop the ball. After any other infringement, a free hit is taken at the spot where it occurred by a member of the non-offending side.

If the ball crosses the touch line, a member of the side not responsible for putting it out of play takes a "hit-on". This he

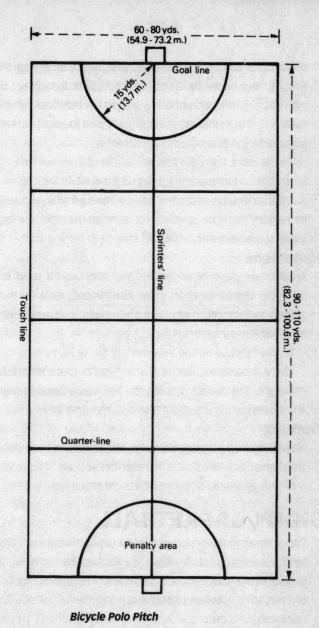

Bicycle Polo Pitch

does with a "back hit" or "cross hit" while facing away from the field. He may hit the ball in any direction. If the attacking side puts the ball over the opposing goal line, a defender takes a "goal hit". If the other side puts the ball over its own goal line, the attacking side is awarded a "corner hit".

This is taken from the junction of the quarter-line and the touch line on the appropriate side of the field. In the case of a deadlock in a scrimmage, the referee takes a "roll-in", i.e. with all players standing at least 10yds away, he rolls the ball towards the centre of the field.

Equipment

An ordinary cycle of any make and size can be used but no cycle should have an extra attachment, such as mud guards, bell, stand, carrier etc., thereby giving a player an extra advantage on the other players.

The ball should not be less than 12.5in or more than 15in in circumference and not less than 170g or more than 182g in weight. The mallet to strike the ball has a wooden head and a cane handle; it is about 32in (813mm) in length.

Clothing

Players wear shots, football jerseys, and protective knee-pads. They must also wear a protective helmet, and facemasks and/or goggles are recommended but not required.

BIDDY BASKETBALL

This is the original version of mini-BASKETBALL. Invented in 1950 by the American youth leader Jay Archer, the game is still played, as biddy basketball, in the USA. It differs in some details of the rules from the international version.

BILLIARDS, CAROM
Introduction

Carom billiards is played on a BILLIARDS table with no pockets. It is played with three balls: red, spot white, and white. A carom, scoring one point, is made when after using a cue (a long wooden stick) to hit a cue ball, it glances off one object ball on to the other. The first player to reach an agreed number of points wins the game.

Venue

Carom billiards is played on a table covered with a green baize and there are no pockets. A carom billiards table can be 10ft/3.05m x 5ft/1.52m, 9ft x 4.5ft, or 4ft by 8ft.

Rules

The break or opening shot is made with the red ball on the foot spot and the white object ball on the head spot. The cue ball is played from the head string, within 6in (centre to centre) from the white object ball. The cue ball must contact the red ball first.

In any shot but a break shot, a player's cue ball may contact either of the object balls first. A player's turn continues until s/he fails to score, when s/he also loses one point if the last shot was not a successful "safety".

If there are more than two players, the order may be decided by lot. If there are two players or two teams, the order is decided by lagging. In lagging, the red ball is placed on the foot spot.

Each player takes a cue ball, and plays it against the foot cushion from behind the head string. One player lags to the right, and the other to the left, of the red ball. Choice of playing order and cue ball goes to the player whose cue ball at the lag comes to rest nearest the head of the table. Cue balls may touch the side rails during lagging. A player loses the lag if their cue ball interferes with the red ball on the foot spot, or is clearly out of line and interferes with his/her opponent's ball. The lag is repeated if both players are in error or if the result is a tie.

All fouls cause the loss of one point and the end of the offender's turn. The following constitute a foul:

Balls in motion: making a shot when any ball is still moving.

Cueing ball: touching the cue ball during "warm-up" stroking. The offender may not claim that the touch was his stroke.

Push or shove shot: making a push or shove shot, which is defined as a shot in which the cue tip remains in contact with the cue ball after the cue ball has struck an object ball.

Double stroke: making a double stroke, one in which the cue hits the cue ball after the cue ball has struck an object ball.

Cue and object ball: touching an object ball with the cue.

Wrong cue ball: shooting the wrong cue ball (the incoming player must accept the balls that are in position).

Foot on floor: not having one foot touching the floor when making a shot. It is a foul if any player causes interference. The offender loses a point and the invoking player must accept the balls in position.

A miscue is not a foul.

Equipment

Balls are red, white, or a white ball with two small spots and must be of equal size and weight, while the cue must be of traditional shape and not less than 3ft long.

Scoring

To score a carom, one point is gained when the cue ball glances from one object to the other. It may do so directly or by way of touching a cushion. A safety shot allows a player to end their turn without penalty. The cue ball must either contact a cushion after striking an object ball, or drive an object ball to a cushion. Safety shots are generally not permitted in consecutive innings.

BILLIARDS, ENGLISH
Introduction
English billiards is played on a special table by two players or pairs. Three balls are used; white, spot white, and red. A player uses a cue (long wooden stick) to hit a cue ball across the table to score points by pocketing balls (hazards) or by hitting both other balls (cannons).

History
Comparatively little is known of the origins of billiards. One source is that Catkire More, King of Ireland in the second century, left behind him "fifty-five billiard balls, of brass, with the pools and cues of the same materials". Another source describes the travels of Anacharsis through Greece, 400 BC, during which time he saw a game similar to billiards. It was well known as a lawn game in the twelfth century. The *Dictionnaire Universal* and the *Académie Des Jeux* ascribe the invention to the English. It was certainly known in ancient England, where it may well have been invented. It was brought into France by Louis XIV, whose physician recommended the exercise. The *Académie* states, "It would seem that the game was invented in England."

In Strutt's *Sports and Pastimes of the People of England* he considers it likely that it was the ancient game of Peillemaille (Pall Mall) (See also croquet), but played on a table instead of on the ground or floor. It was certainly known in the time of Shakespeare where in *Antony and Cleopatra* Cleopatra calls her attendent to join in: "Let us to billiards: come."

Venue

English billiards is played on a table covered with a green baize and though the regular size of table is 12ft/3.66m x 6ft 1.5in/1.86m, scaled down tables are sometimes used.

Rules

The red ball is placed on the spot, and the striker places their cue ball at any point in the "D" and plays the first shot. When their turn is ended, the second player brings his/her cue ball into play. When bringing a cue ball into play, no shot may be made directly at any ball within the "balk" area. If both balls are in this area, the cue ball must strike a cushion outside the balk before it can touch either ball. The striker uses the tip of his/her cue to hit their cue ball in the direction of another ball. Chalk is applied to the cue to improve contact. The cue ball must be struck and not pushed; and at the moment of striking, the player must have a foot on the ground. Balls must not be forced off the table.

Play lasts an agreed length of time, or until one player or side reaches an agreed number of points. A game is known as a "frame", while the shots comprising a player's turn are known as a "break". Each time a player scores from a shot, s/he is entitled to another shot. Only when s/he fails to score does the player forfeit his/her turn. All points scored up to that time are scored for the break. If the striker's ball comes to rest against another ball, the red ball is replaced on the spot. The non-striker's ball, if on the table, is placed on the centre spot; if off the table, it is left off, and the striker plays from the "D".

If the non-striker's cue ball is pocketed during a break, it remains off the table until the break ends. When the red ball is sunk, it is immediately replaced on the spot. When the cue ball is pocketed, the striker brings it back into play by playing from the "D".

Equipment

Balls are white and spot white or red and must be of equal size and weight, while the cue must be of traditional shape and not less than 3ft long.

Scoring

The striker scores points for winning hazards, losing hazards, and cannons. All points accumulated in a shot are counted. To win a hazard, you get two points if the cue ball hits the other white ball into a pocket and three points if the cue ball hits the red into a pocket. To lose a hazard, two points are gained if the cue ball is pocketed "in off" the white while you get three points if the cue ball is pocketed "in off" the red. Only 15 consecutive hazards may be scored, whether winning, losing, or both. To win cannons, two points are scored when the cue ball strikes both other balls. If the cue ball goes into a pocket after a cannon, it scores an additional two points if the white ball, or three points if the red ball, was struck first. 75 cannons may be scored consecutively. The non-striker receives two points for all fouls.

BOBSLEIGH

Introduction

Bobsleigh, or bobsledding, is a winter-sport in which sleds, normally manned by four-man or two-man crews, are guided down a specially prepared, descending track of solid ice with banked bends. In competitive bobsleighs the aim of the bobsleigh is to complete a run down the track in the fastest possible time by having the best push start and by finding the best line through the bends.

History

Although various forms of sleigh-riding on ice have been popular for centuries, bobsleigh – as a recognised sport distinct from TOBOGGANING – originated in Switzerland in 1888, when an Englishman, Wilson Smith, connected two sleighs with a board to travel from St. Moritz to Celerina. This relatively unsophisticated structure was quickly improved and the first organized competition was staged at St. Moritz in 1898 on the Cresta run, which had been built for one-man tobogganing and was not really suitable for the faster-moving bobsleds. A special, separate bob run, the world's first, was built at St. Moritz in 1902.

Venue

Most bobsleigh tracks are artificially constructed, formed from concrete with special refrigeration pipes below the surface of the tracks. Ice is formed by spraying a fine film of water over the course. This layer must be at least 19mm (0.75in) thick before racing can take place.

Rules

Intimate knowledge of the course is of prime importance before participating in competitions. If one's bobsled touches the steep, packed ice banking, one is likely at least to lose a vital split second. At the start, initial impetus is given by members of the crew when they push, while holding rear and side handles, before jumping into their seats.

Arts which help reduce decimal time fractions include the

driver's trick of turning his head before moving into a bend, the pace being too quick to enable him otherwise to realign his sights for the new direction on exit. The skill of weight transference to correct a skidding sled has also to be acquired by trial and error.

The brakeman has to check skids and stop the sled at the end of the run. The official practice runs which usually take place on four of the five days preceding a championship are essential for learning the characteristics of a course.

Equipment

The bobsleigh, originally of wooden construction, is now a precision-built machine of steel and aluminium and moulded from fiberglass and other composite materials. It also has four steel runners – one pair at the front and another pair at the rear which are a maximum of 270cm (8ft 10in) long for the two-man and 335cm (10ft 11in) long for the four-man bob. A bob may have a cowled front end but must be open at the rear (see diagrams). The cowling may be made of Plexiglass, transparent material or any material which will splinter on impact. The bobsleigh has a supporting frame and axles which are made of steel. It has two axles, which two rounded runners mounted on each. The rear axle is fixed and the front one turns for steering. The sled may be steered either by ropes or a wheel. The driver steers a bob by means of steering handles and cords attached to a steering mechanism for the front axle. The driver is the only one who has a clear view of the track and must select the fastest line through the curves. His crew sit crouched behind him, taking care not to touch him. They tilt their heads to help round the curves more effectively.

Clothing

When bobsleighing, crash helmets are compulsory, in addition goggles, elbow guards and gloves should be worn. For racing, teams usually wear skintight racing suits.

BOWL-PLAYING

Introduction

Bowl-playing, or road bowling as it is also called, is almost entirely confined to parts of the south and north of Ireland, although a similar game Klootschien, is played in Holland and some adjacent districts in West Germany.

History

Bowl-playing devotees claim for their game a very ancient origin, but it could not have gained any wide popularity until a permanent road system existed. The heydey of the game was through much of the nineteenth century when traffic was slow and sparse on relatively good clay-and-stone roads. Later, the obstruction caused by bowl-players and their hundreds of followers led to confrontations with the law after the advent of the bicycle and the motor car. The game itself, however, was never made illegal. Nowadays, bowl-playing on tarmacadam or concrete highways is not feasible, so the game has been relegated to the side roads.

Venue

The game is quite simple; two players bowl or throw an iron ball along an ordinary public road, the less busy the better, and the winner is the player who covers a set distance with fewer throws.

Rules

One of the skills of the game is the negotiation of a bend in the road. In the south of Ireland, the players, using a wheel-like swing of the arm, develop great skill in lofting the ball round and over even the sharpest of bends, so that it lands on and continues safely along the roadway. This is essential, since a player is penalized if his bowl lands in or over the road-side fence. In the north, where the under-arm delivery is favoured, the players are extremely skilled at spinning the bowl along the ground round even the sharpest bends.

If a player wins by one throw, he is said to have won by a "bowl of odds". Singles games, known as "single-handed scores", are the more popular, although doubles scores, between pairs, are also common, with each man playing from the spot where his partner's throw rested.

Equipment
The ball, made of solid iron and usually weighs 28oz (790g) – though lighter ones may be used – is called a bowl, but is popularly termed the "bullet".

BOWLS, CANADIAN FIVE PIN
Introduction
Canadian five pin bowling is played by two players or two teams of equal numbers. Each player propels a ball at five pins. Points are scored to the value of the pins knocked down.

Venue
The bowling lane is around 60ft or 18.30m in length and 3ft 6in in width.

Rules
One game of Canadian five pin bowling consists of ten frames. Each player bowls three balls consecutively in each frame, unless they score a strike or a spare.

Equipment

The pins are made of plastic or wood, with a strip of rubber around the middle to deaden the force of the ball. Unlike pins used in TENPIN BOWLING they are smaller and measure 12.5in in length. The ball too is smaller and is made of hard rubber and is 5in in diameter and has no finger holes.

Scoring

Pins have different values: the fifth pin, the head pin, at the top of the pyramid, is worth five points; the two immediately behind it are worth three each; while the remaining two pins at the back of the pyramid are each worth two points. A pin counts as being knocked down when it is hit by a ball before it leaves the lane surface. Pins do not count as being knocked down if they are hit by a ball that has rebounded off any foreign object in the lane, or the channel (gutter).

Clothing

Clothes should be lightweight and loose fitting to allow freedom of movement but special bowling shoes are worn to provide comfort and the necessary slide.

BOWLS, CROWN GREEN

Introduction

In southern England and round the world in countries affiliated to the IBB (International Bowling Board), bowls is played on a level green. In the northern areas of England and Wales and in the Isle of Man, there exists this variation in which the centre of the green is higher than its boundaries.

History

This game has a common ancestry with all other forms of bowls, dating back to the old target-hitting days of 5200BC. It is believed to have evolved through the difficulties once experienced in producing level greens in some of the poorer areas of industrial northern England where small greens abounded behind public houses.

Venue

The game is played on a square area of short grass varying in size from 30 to 60yds (27.4–54.9m) but usually about 40yds (36.6m) square. The surface of the green slopes gently upwards from the sides to a central "crown" which is 8 to 18in (203–457mm) higher than the sides. Unlike the greens used for flat green play (see BOWLS, LAWN), the surface tends to be irregular, adding a further variable to that caused by the crown.

Three points are clearly marked on all greens: (1) the centre; (2) the official entrance, which must be near the middle of one of the sides; and (3) a 4yd (3.7m) distance from the edges of the green, which is indicated by pegs at the four corners.

Rules

The object is to cast each bowl nearer to a smaller bowl – the "jack" – than any or all of the opposition's bowls. Each bowl finishing nearer to the jack than the best opposition bowl scores a point. The standard game is won by the first player or pair scoring 21 but some tournaments are run at anything between 11 and 41 up, the latter figure applying to matches organized by the Lancashire Professional Bowling Association for their panel of bowlers.

A player bowling with their right (left) hand must keep the toe of their right (left) foot in contact with the footer until the bowl or jack has left their hand. A player must use the same hand throughout the game, for both bowls and jacks. A player may not move or use the footer until his/her opponent's bowl has stopped moving. If the footer is moved before an end is finished it must be replaced. A bowl delivered out of turn must be returned or replayed properly. A bowl or jack that may interfere with another game should be stopped and replayed. A leader may set another mark if they are unable to deliver their first bowl because another game is measuring up.

Equipment

Most bowls in use weigh between 2lb 6oz and 3lb (1.1–1.4kg). They tend to be smaller in diameter than those used in flat-green bowls, but there are no restrictions in size, weight, or bias. Some bowls have a bias which causes them to follow a curved path when delivered along a flat green. The bias is imparted by flattening one side of the bowl. The jack is biased and must weigh between 20 and 24oz. The footer is a round mat of between 5 and 6in in diameter.

Clothing

Players and officials wear footwear with smooth rubber soles and no heels. Casual clothing is also worn to allow freedom of movement.

BOWLS, INDOOR

Introduction

The game is an indoor version of LAWN BOWLS. It can either be played by two players or in pairs and points are scored after each "end", when all the bowls have been delivered and one point is scored for each bowl nearer to the jack than the opposition's best bowl. Games are decided by ends or by points.

History

In the form of SKITTLES, bowls has been played at least since the sixteenth century, but not until the start of the twentieth century was any serious attempt made to reproduce the standard International Bowling Board (IBB) outdoor game (see Bowls, Lawn) under cover. At that time, cricketers were practising throughout the year on indoor matting wickets and it was W.G. Grace who exerted the greatest influence over bowls-players, persuading them that indoor play was also feasible for them.

Venue

Indoor championship bowls needs only 7sq yds (6 sq m) per participant, whilst indoor LAWN TENNIS requires 200sq yds (approximately 170 sq m) per player in doubles.

Rules

See Lawn Bowls.

Clothing

Clothes should be lightweight to allow freedom of movement. All bowlers should wear bowling shoes with soft soles so as not to scar the approach surface.

BOWLS, LAWN

Introduction

A lawn bowls match may be one against one (singles), two against two (pairs), three against three (triples) or four against four (now "fours" but once "rinks", a term still used quite frequently). Points are scored after each "end", when all the bowls have been delivered, and one point is scored for each bowl nearer to the jack than the opposition's best bowl. Games are decided by ends or by points.

History

Bowls probably evolved from the earliest days of history when primitive man, in moments of relaxation, threw rocks or large stones at smaller stones or other targets. Its existence as a disciplined game may be safely traced back some 7,000 years to when Sir Flinders Petrie, the great Eygptologist, discovered implements for a game similar to modern TENPIN BOWLING in the grave of an Egyptian child buried about 5200BC.

The ancient Polynesians, including some who emigrated to New Zealand in the fourteenth century, played a version of bowls with pieces of whetstone 3 to 4in (76–102mm) in diameter, about 1in (25mm) across at their running edges, and shaped very precisely into an ellipse. The game spread from Egypt to Greece and Rome, and from there to other regions of Europe during the time of the Roman colonization. Sculptured and painted antiquities of ancient Greece and Rome indicate that games based on rolling bowls or hoops at targets existed several thousands of years ago. There are even suggestions that a version of bowls was played in England during the first century AD, though it was of such a vigorous nature that it might be regarded as a forerunner to throwing the JAVELIN rather than the gentler game of bowls.

Venue

In world competitions it is played on a flat lawn or green, which in championship play is usually at least 40x40 yds (36.6m) in size. The green is surrounded by a ditch approximately 2in (51mm) deep and 12in (305mm) wide and enclosed by a bank sloping at an angle of 35° from the perpendicular. The green is divided by boundaries of fine string into six "rinks", the length of the green, and 19–21 ft (5.8–6.4m) wide.

Rules

A player must make each delivery with at least one foot on or over a mat, towards the jack which has been bowled and then centred on the green at a distance not less than 25yds (22.9m) from the edge of the mat facing the jack. The mat is usually made of rubber and is 24in long by 14in wide (610 x 356 mm). Delivery is said to be complete at the moment the bowl leaves the player's hand.

Bowls which come to rest outside the strings bounding the rink on which play is taking place are deemed "dead", as are those which go into the ditch without touching the jack when first delivered. Bowls that hit the jack on their initial run – whether or not they cannon on to it via another bowl or bowls – become live and potential scorers until completion. They are called "touchers", are marked with chalk, and remain where they are whenever they run or are cannoned into the ditch. Any toucher in the ditch and nearer the jack than the best opposing bowl counts in the score.

A jack cannoned into the ditch and within the strings marking the width of the rink on which play is taking place remains in play. Its position is indicated to bowlers at the delivery end by a "suitable object" – usually a strip of metal painted white – stuck into the bank behind the jack. Touchers cannot be established after the jack has gone into the ditch.

When all the bowls have been delivered from one end of the rink to the jack and the score agreed by the opposing players, the end is said to be complete. The jack and all bowls are then delivered from the mat down the green in the reverse direction, the score is agreed on – and so the game continues.

Equipment

The bowls are made of wood, rubber, or composition, and may be black or brown. Each set must have a maximum diameter of

5 1/8in and a maximum weight of 3.5lb. They may not be weighted. Rubber or composition bowls must be 4 5/8–5 1/8in diameter, and weigh 3–3.5lb. All bowls are biased to move along a curved path. The degree of bias is prescribed, and bowls must be officially tested. The biased side is marked. The jack must be white, weigh 8–10oz, and have a diameter of 2 15/32-2 17/32in.

Clothing

Players and officials wear footwear with smooth rubber soles and no heels, and casual clothing is worn to allow freedom of movement.

Scoring

One point is won for each bowl nearer the jack than the opponents' best bowl. If the nearest bowl from each side is equidistant the end is drawn and not scored. The last player may always choose not to play his last bowl in an end. Either side may claim a maximum of 30 seconds after the last bowl has stopped moving to allow all the bowls to settle.

BOWLING, TENPIN

Introduction

Tenpin bowling an indoor game for individual players or for teams, largely concentrated in the USA, in which a player aims to knock down with a ball ten "pins" placed in a triangle, the apex of which is 60ft (18.29m) away at the end of a "lane" of smooth polished wood.

History

Related games were played in ancient Egypt – a stone ball and nine stone pins were found in the tomb of a child buried in 5200BC – and in the ancient Polynesian game of "ula naika" a player bowled at a target from 60ft (18.29m), the distance between delivery and pin in modern tenpin bowling.

According to Pehle, a German writer on bowls, members of the congregation in Germany would bowl in church cloisters in the third and fourth centuries. The "kegel", which men carried for sport and protection, would be set up as a target, representing "Heide" (the Heathen One) and, if the bowler hit it, he would be judged clean of sin. The term "kegling" or "kegeline" is still used for bowling in Germany and among German-Americans. Luther approved of the past-time and a successful kegeler was said to have "knocked the Devil out of his ground."

The game reached the States when the Dutch brought it over with them during the 1600s, and their legacy can still be noted in Manhattan which has an area known as Bowling Green.

Venue

All modern tenpin bowling is played at specially-constructed or adapted bowling centres or alleys.

Rules

The ball is rolled and if the bowler knocks down all ten pins with his first delivery or after his second delivery, the pins are put up again by an automatic machine, known as pin-spotter and the balls are automatically returned to the bowling end of the lane.

Equipment

The modern pin is 15in (381mm) tall and 14.97in, in circumference. If made of wood, it may weigh between 3lb 2oz and 3lb 10oz, or between 3lb 4oz and 3lb 6oz, if of synthetic material. The ball must not have a circumference of more than

27 in (685mm) and it may not weigh more than 16lb (7.26kg). Its diameter must be constant. It has one thumb-hole and two finger holes.

Clothing

Clothes should be lightweight to allow freedom of movement. All bowlers should wear bowling shoes with soft soles so as not to scar the approach surface. Ideally, shoes for the right-handed bowler should have leather on the left shoe sole, and rubber tipped with leather on the right sole. Heels are made of hard rubber.

Scoring

Scoring is progressive. Ten frames of ten pins make up a game and points are awarded for the number of pins knocked down. If all the pins are knocked down by the first ball, called a "strike", the player is rewarded by a bonus – ten points plus the score of the next two balls bowled.

Thus in a game of ten frames, a player must bowl 12 strikes in succession in order to bowl a perfect game of 300 points. If two deliveries are needed to knock down the pins (called a "spare"), 10 points are awarded plus the bonus of the next ball. When a "spare" is scored in the tenth frame, a third bowl is bowled. A core of 120 would be extremely good for a newcomer to the game and a player who regularly achieves 170 should be good enough for scratch league play.

BOXING

Introduction

Boxing, fist-fighting with gloves worn by two fighters in a roped square, is both an amateur and professional sport with a large international following and widespread participation. Though the majority of world professional champions have come from the USA, many outstanding boxers have been produced in Europe, Central and South America and recently Asia.

History

Boxing may be said to date from the first time a fist was clenched and used as a weapon. The first record of its being practiced as a major sport, however, dates from the ancient Greeks who introduced pugilism into the Olympic Games about 686 BC. The boxers had much in common with their modern counterparts. They wore soft leather coverings for their hands and in training used primitive punching-bags and head-guards. Their technique was not very different save that body-punching and clinching were virtually unknown.

Gradually, boxing became brutalized as spectators showed an increasing taste for blood. The Romans, perhaps influenced by Etruscan interest in gladiatoral contests, developed the cestus, an iron-studded gauntlet which could, if it landed flush upon an opponent's temple, cause death. As the Roman populace demanded ever bloodier circuses, pugilism as such declined and eventually disappeared during the fourth century AD.

Bare knuckle fighting was the style until 1867 when the Queensberry Rules were drafted by Chambers under the patronage and name of the Marquess of Queensberry. They formed the basis of modern glove-fighting as distinct from the earlier bare-knuckle contests and were first used for the World Professional Heavyweight Championship in 1892. The rules called for the wearing of gloves, rounds of three minutes' duration, interspersed with a minute's rest, and prohibited wrestling.

Venue

The ring must be at least 3.66m square (14ftsq) and the maximum size is 6.10msq (20ftsq), measured inside the line of the ropes. The platform must be safely constructed, level and free from any obstructing projections and should be of canvas over an undercover of felt or rubber. It must be fitted with four well-padded corner posts (58in) or otherwise contructed so as to prevent injury to the boxers. The ring needs three sets of steps at opposite corners for the use of contestants, officials and seconds

Rules

Boxing is basically a simple sport though it is sometimes appears complex due to the lack of one authoritative governing professional body. This causes disagreements over rules and, at worst, over who should be world champion.

Boxers may win:

On points – by scoring more blows to the target, defined as "any part of the front or sides of the head or body above the belt."

Due to a stoppage by the referee.

By outclassing an opponent so that he is unable to defend himself – retirement.

By being counted out within ten seconds for a "knock-out".

At the start, the referee first calls the boxers together to ensure that the rules are understood. The boxers then shake hands. In professional contests the handshake is repeated at the start of the final round; amateurs must shake hands at the start of the third round. During the bout boxers must obey all the referee's instructions.

At the knock-down, the standing boxer is ordered to a

neutral corner and the referee takes up the count. If the fallen boxer rises, the count is over (though in amateur and some professional contests there is a mandatory count of eight). The boxers then continue to fight.

In both professional and amateur boxing, if a boxer is given a count at the end of a round, the count must continue either to eight or, if he is unable to resume, to ten, before the gong is sounded for the end of the round. The referee has the power to end the contest if he judges that one boxer is unfit to continue. The referee raises the winner's hand when the contest is over.

Each round in a contest is worth a fixed number of points to the winner of the round. In amateur boxing the round's winner receives 20 points, and his opponent proportionally fewer. When boxers are of equal merit,

Left jab

Left hook

Straight right

Right uppercut

Basic stance

Boxing Stance and Punches

each receives 20 points. Auxiliary points (three of which make up one point) are awarded for scoring blows. At the end of the contest auxiliary points may be awarded for attack, defence, leading off or for style. Similar principles apply in professional boxing. The maximum number of points for a round is 10 in most countries.

Points are awarded for attack, defence, showing initiative and style. If scores are equal at the end, the bout is declared a draw. To score, all blows must be delivered with the knuckle part of the closed glove and must land on the target area.

Boxers need sharp reflexes, speed and the ability to concentrate. The punches include: the jab, a short sharp punch; the hook, which is a heavy blow, usually to the head; and the uppercut which is delivered from below and aimed at the lower part of the face or at the body.

Clothing

Amateurs wear shorts and vest and use 8oz gloves or 10oz gloves if the competitor is over 148lb. Professionals wear only shorts with 8oz gloves. Both wear boots.

BOXING, CHINESE

Introduction

Chinese Boxing, correctly called a Chinese martial art, has been described by people who do not understand it as "shadow boxing". It is far from that. Chinese boxing, with its various forms and styles minutely copied from the movements of animals, was first created and used for self-defence and, in the days of divided kingdoms, taught to and used by soldiers. However, as dynasties changed, Chinese philosophers and boxing masters began a search for a means of using this martial exercise to make man live longer. Thus was born the modern form of the soft school of the martial art – Tai Chi, Paat Kaw and Luk Hop Paat Faat. Today, the Chinese and some westerners are taking this art as a sport, and as a health exercise.

History

Although Chinese boxing is used now solely for self-defence and body-building, in the past warriors and warrior-emperors made their mark in Chinese history because of their prowess in a particular fighting style. Ngok Fei, who lived a century before the start of the Sung Dynasty (AD 1127-1280), was credited with a fighting style, "ying yi", and the use of the lance. Another style, "hau kuen" ("monkey fist"), is linked with a legend dating back to the Tang Dynasty (AD 618-907) in which the goddess of mercy ordered the monkey god to accompany a Buddhist monk, Tong Sam Chong, to Tibet to collect Buddha's scriptures. The warrior-emperor, Kuen Lung Wong, was the third in the Ching Dynasty (1644-1912). A wanderer righting wrongs, he was said to have been trained by the masters at Siu Lam Chi. It was he who burned down a temple while seeking the rebels who were plotting to overthrow the Ching empire in an attempt to re-establish the Ming Dynasty (AD 1368-1644).

Rules

Chinese boxing is divided into two schools: the soft and the hard. "Siu Lam Pai" embraces all the present hard forms, one of which, "Hung Kuen" ("Red Fist"), was adapted by the Japanese and became the popular Karate. The soft school of Chinese boxing was formulated by a scholar called Chan Tuan who lived just before Chiu Hon Yang became the first emperor in the Sung Dynasty (960-1127). The first soft style was "Luk Hop Paat

Faat", from which the other soft styles possibly derived. These include Tai Chi, created by a Taoist monk, Cheung Sam Fung, in the Yuan Dynasty.

BOXING, THAI
Introduction
This is a sporting form of self-defence indigenous to Thailand. Blows with the feet, knees and elbows are permitted, as well as those with the gloved fist used in BOXING under the Queensberry Rules. It is at once a science and an art, and is of deep traditional significance to the Thai people, all the males of whom are expected to master at least its fundamentals.

Rules
Blows may be aimed at any part of the opponent's body above the abdomen, a high kick to the head, carried out with remarkable speed and dexterity, being one of the most common.

An essential skill of the sport is the ability to land a combination of blows in different places: while in-fighting, for instance, a boxer may be upper-cutting (see boxing) with his fists at the same time as delivering a damaging blow to the ribs with his knee. Clinches are frequent, but the throwing of an opponent, while not an offence, is discouraged and may lead to a loss of points. Butting, eye-gouging and smothering are not permitted. The fight is controlled by a referee in the ring and two judges outside it, who award a maximum of five points per round. Matches are made within weight classes similar to those of the Queensberry Rules for boxing.

The incidental trappings of a Thai boxing bout are as vital as the fight itself. Each boxer enters the ring beforehand for a ritual which has its roots deep in the history of their country. It opens with a form of prayer to the sacred objects held in veneration by all Thai people, and a ceremonial salute to the boxer's instructor and trainers, followed by homage to the King. Then comes a demonstration of shadow-boxing, the form of which denotes the area from which the boxer comes. It is intended both to loosen the muscles and to strike fear into the heart of the opponent.

Meanwhile the accompanying music starts and plays throughout the fight as well as the preliminaries. It is provided by a ringside orchestra of: pipe, two long drums, and cymbals. The musicians, under the leadership of the piper, change their tune spontaneously to suit the mood of the fight and sometimes raise the tempo to bring life to a dull bout.

The enthusiasm of the crowd is a major part of the entertainment, which is by far the most popular sport in Thailand. There are two main stadia in Bangkok, each staging a programme twice a week. Queensberry and Thai boxing are often seen in the same evening and many experts in the native sport become excellent international boxers in the lighter weights.

Clothing

Combatants are dressed as normal boxers, except that their feet are bare and bandaged from the ankle to the instep.

BROOMBALL
Introduction

Is a rather exclusive game played mainly in Russia and the CIS, but has started to spread to the rest of the world. It is literally HOCKEY on ice. A similar game "hockey with a ball" is also played on ice in Russia and the CIS, but with hockey sticks. The object of the game is to score more goals than the opposition.

History

Broomball was an organized sport in Canada in the early 1900s and started from early matches where corn brooms hit footballs around the ice. One of the first recorded matches was played in Saskatchewan in 1909, and Ontario in 1911 but there are some indications that it was played as early as the 1890s. There are at least five different stories about how broomball started: a group of footballers were watching a small boy hitting a ball with a toy broom; non skaters wanted to play ICE HOCKEY; tram drivers used to hit a small ball about the ice in their lunch breaks; as a game for women; as a game of the Indians in Eastern Canada called stickball. Whatever the truth of the matter, broomball has progressed and held its first World Championship in 1991.

Venue

Broomball can be played on an ice rink of any size.

Rules

The game consists of six players from each team on the ice: these include a goal keeper, two defenders and three forwards. 14 players can sit on the bench as reserves. The ball is propelled about the rink with the stick and players try to score goals. The game consists of two 20 minute periods. Two referees control the match.

There are various tournaments all over the world which include Athletic Broomball and Moscow (Russian) Style Broomball. This latter is currently played in Finland and Russia and instead of the standard stick used in traditional broomball, players use a shorter stick, with a hockey style hook at one end, made from bound rafia. The game is either played inside or out, on varying sizes of rink. The rules are similar, but kicking is not allowed, nor touching of the ball with the hand. Intramural Broomball is often played between universities and colleges. Rules vary, but may include: no checking; no broomball shoes; and no lifting the stick above the shoulders.

Equipment

The ball is made with a similar material to a basketball but measures about 5in in diameter. The sticks, which used to be straw brooms dipped in water and frozen to provide stiffness, have now been replaced by high-tech paddle-shaped sticks made of rubber with a wooden or aluminium shaft.

Clothing

There are specially designed shoes which have about an inch of soft rubber on their sole. Players also wear ice hockey helmets – which are mandatory – and knee and elbow protection. Some players use padding around the hips and rear, but players all wear protective gloves specifically designed for broomball.

BULL

Introduction

Bull is one of the earliest DECK GAMES, still popular with passengers.

History

See DECK GAMES.

Venue

It is usually played on board a boat.

Rules

Each player has six discs or bags and throws them on the

numbered squares of the board, from a distance agreed on by the players, and in a sequence that may vary slightly according to the custom followed by the ships of different companies. There are twelve squares on the board, made up of four rows of three squares each with the furthest row showing the right-hand bull, the number 10, and the left-hand bull. The remaining numbers (1 to 9) are allocated to the three lower rows such that the aggregate number in each line is 15. The usual sequence of numbers is: 8-1-6; 3-5-7; and 4-9-2. The winner is the person who first completes the full sequence of the board and this usually means covering numbers 1 to 10 consecutively, followed by the right-hand and finally the left-hand bull. The player then returns in the reverse order to number 1.

When a player has thrown his/her six discs, the last division or square s/he has covered in the correct sequence is noted, and the next player takes six throws. Discs must rest in a square without touching the lines, but a disc may be driven completely into a square by another one and, if it is in the correct sequence, count. The rules differ as to what penalty should follow a disc being thrown or moved into the wrong bull square but generally this means going back to the start and re-commencing the entire sequence. A player whose disc or bag falls off the board is penalized by dropping back one number.

Equipment

The playing pieces are either rubber discs or canvas bags filled with sand, as they probably were centuries ago.

CABER, TOSSING THE

Introduction

Tossing the caber is one of the best-known events featured in meetings of Scottish professional athletes, and also practiced in other parts of the Commonwealth.

Rules

The caber is presented vertically to the competitor, who makes a platform of his hands to take its weight, with his arms stretched down in front of him. In the perfect toss, the caber will revolve longitudinally, landing with its base pointing away from the competitor. It should point in the exact direction he was facing at the moment of the throw (known as a "twelve o'clock toss"), and not be angled to left or right.

In competition, the thrower has three trials and is judged on the best, to his satisfaction. There are no restrictions on the length of his run nor the mark from which he makes the throw.

Caber-tossers who compete regularly in the same area become familiar with the individual characteristics of each caber, which, once it has been tossed, must never be cut. One of the greatest challenges in Scotland is presented by the Braemar caber, which weighs more than 120lb (54.5kg) and is 19ft (5.79m) long. It was first tossed in 1951 by George Clark, who was then 51 years old.

A new caber, never tossed, may be shortened if none of the competing athletes is able to toss it successfully.

Equipment

The caber is a tree trunk of unspecified size, but according to the rules of the Scottish Games Association, it should be "of a length and weight beyond the powers of the best athlete to turn".

CAMEL WRESTLING
Introduction
Camel wrestling is popular in all the provinces of the Aegean coast from Canakkale in the north to Antalya in the south. In this region there are an estimated thousand wrestling camels whose prices range from $2,500 to as much as $25,000. A wrestling camel can participate in between 10 and 12 wrestling competitions per year and around thirty camel wrestling festivals are held in Turkey each year.

CAMOGIE
Introduction
Ireland's native field sport for women, is a 12-a-side stick-and-ball game. Since it is a modified form of HURLING, the rules are very similar, but body-charging, or any other unnecessary physical contact with an opponent, is expressly forbidden.

History
Feminism was relatively late in arriving on the Irish sports fields, and it was not until the opening years of the twentieth century that girl members of some of the Dublin branches of the national language movement, the Gaelic League evolved, from hurling, a game all their own, which they named camogie.

The game was first played competitively in public at Navan in the autumn of 1904 and a controlling body, the Camogie Association of Ireland, was founded later that year. Little progress was made outside Dublin city and some parts of Co. Louth, and the game did not receive its first real boost until an annual inter-university competition.

Venue
The pitch is also shorter (100 to 120yds long – 91–110m) and

narrower (60 to 75yds wide – 55–68m) than the standard hurling ground. A distinctive feature of camogie is a second crossbar across the top of the goal posts, which are 20ft (6.1m) high. The goal posts are 15ft (4.6m) apart.

Rules

As in hurling, the ball may be struck with the stick when in the air and may be lifted from the ground to hand by means of the stick, but may not be picked up off the ground with the hand. If a defender "gouls" within her own goal area, the attacking side is awarded a free stroke from a line 30yds (27m) out, at a point opposite the spot where the ball crossed the line.

The team comprises a goalkeeper, full-back, right back, centre back, left back, right wing, mid-field, left wing, right forward, centre forward, left forward, and full forward. Championship games are of 50 minutes' duration, in two halves of 25 minutes each way; a maximum of three substitutes may be introduced and games are controlled by a referee, assisted by two goal umpires at each end and a touch judge on each side line.

The outlawing of physical contact means that success in camogie can be ensured only by complete control of stick and ball, and the game, as played between top class teams, can be both thrilling and artistic.

Equipment

The crooked, broad-bladed stick, called the "camog" – a diminutive of the hurler's "caman" – is lighter and shorter than the hurley, being usually about 3ft (91cm) long in the handle. The ball is similar to a hurling ball, 9 to 10in (23-25cm) in circumference, but lighter.

Clothing

The official dress is a sleeveless tunic, blouse, and black tights, together with light studded boots. Most players also wear short ankle-socks.

Scoring

A point is scored when the ball passes between the crossbars in the upper scoring place (above the second cross bar). A ball driven under the lower crossbar, which is 7ft (2.1m) high, counts as a goal and equals 3 points.

CANOE POLO

Introduction

Canoe Polo is a form of WATER POLO in which the participants are in short, low canoes known as bats and use double paddles. Teams are five-a-side, passing to each other a ball about the size of a football, with the object of scoring a goal by throwing it against a vertical board square on the opposing goal line.

Venue

The game may be played in any convenient area, either in swimming baths or on a roped-off course on open water. In baths, ropes are also used to keep play at least 1m away from the perimeter to avoid damage.

Rules

Deliberate ramming and unseemly use of the paddle are offences, punishable by a free throw, but bumping and brushing of canoes is almost incessant.

A game usually lasts for two periods of seven minutes each.

Equipment

The board square, found on the opposing goal line, is 1m (3ft 3in).

CANOE SAILING

Introduction

Canoe sailing bears little resemblance, apart from the pointed ends of its vessel, to a canoe or kayak. It is more like YACHT RACING than canoeing. However, the craft is a direct descendant of the Rob Roy kayak and is called the international 10sq m sailing canoe (IC).

Venue

The course is marked out on the open water by an equilateral triangle marked by three buoys (1, 2 and 3). Each leg of the course is usually 1.125 nautical miles, giving a total distance of about 10 nautical miles.

Rules

The sailors get into the boat and the course is sailed in a specific order: start, 1, 2, 3, 1, 3, 1, 2, 3, finish. The start and finish lines are between the buoys and the foremost of the race, a committee boat which flies a blue flag.

Equipment

The canoe is usually a 10sq m canoe, which is around 5,180m (17ft) long. The beam is 1.018m. The sails cover an area of about 10sq m, the mainsail area is a maximum of 8.5sq m, and all sails pass through a hoop of an internal diameter of 300mm. The centreboard must not project more than 1m from the underside of the hull. It must be fixed in case of capsize and be capable of being raised. The letters IC in red, the national letter and registered number must be displayed on the mainsail. All boats must be officially measured and receive certificates of conformity to class rules. These aim to make hull and sail areas as uniform as possible. There are no restrictions on deck layout or sail plan.

Scoring

1st place – 0.75 points, 2nd place – 2 points, 3rd place – 3 points and so on. Retirement, maximum plus one point. Non-starter, maximum plus 2. Disqualification, maximum plus three points. The lowest scorer wins. If six or seven races are held, each competitor may discard their score for one race. If less than five races are held, the championship is annulled.

Clothing

The sailors wear life jackets, or other buoyancy aids.

CANOE SLALOM

Introduction

Slalom is the most exciting and spectacular of canoe sports, not only for the paddler but also for the spectator. It is performed on the roughest of rivers, where falls are steep, rapids thunder and boil, and rocks jut from the water.

History

In 1936 Germany requested its introduction to the Olympic Games. With Olympic status, it progressed across the Atlantic. Canoe slalom was only in its early stages but racing the wild water soon caught on in European countries. It was introduced to Britain in 1939 but did not take hold until 1948. Later it was introduced to America, Canada, New Zealand, and Australia. At the 1969 World Championships, the Japanese and Dutch competed for the first time, while the Russians joined in the following at the Zwickau International in former East Germany.

Canoes for slalom and rough water remained open-decked, although the deck was covered by a canvas spraydeck with openings for the paddlers, and the craft were built to touring specifications of wood veneer or planking. With the introduction of fibreglass in the 1950s craft became more specialized, international specifications were agreed and four models of boat were built – C1 and C2 for slalom, C1 and C2 for wild water. The decks were completely covered in, save for rounded holes for the paddlers, hard gunwhale lines became rounded, and small half-seats were incorporated on the rear of the cockpit, but still the basic kneeling position was retained. The canoe became a specialized form of slalom transport with its capability for touring or load-carrying lost.

Venue

The course can be on mountainous rivers, below weirs or on special artificial rings. The water flow must be fast and reach at least 2m/sec. The course should have both artificial and natural hazards, including currents, counter currents, rocks and rapids. Courses have "gates", which are poles strung over the river which dangle down to the water.

Rules

The slalom canoeists start singly at set intervals and race down the half-mile (0.8km) course, the fastest paddler or crew being the winner. The main principles of canoe slalom are borrowed from skiing; snow-covered slopes and skis are exchanged for racing water and fibreglass kayaks. The paddler does not simply race down stream from start to finish, but negotiates a number of "gates" which are hung just above the water. The gate consists of two poles, at least 1.8m (5ft 11in) long with a diameter of 35 to 50mm (1.4-2.0in). The right-hand pole has green and white rings, the left-hand pole red and white.

The gates are adjustable in height and position, and the width of each gate must be from 3.5 to 1.2m (11ft 6in-4ft). Above each gate is a board indicating its number and perhaps the letter "R" for a reverse gate, or "T" for a team gate. A free gate – which may be taken in reverse or forwards from any direction – is marked with black and white rings. The canoeist must pass cleanly through the gates in their numbered order, either forwards or in reverse, time penalties being added for incorrect taking or hitting of the gates. Two separate runs are allowed, the better score only to count.

As the paddler passes through the start gate, an automatic timer is started in the control centre. The canoeist traverses the rough water and goes down through the rough water and goes through gate 1 which is a forward gate in the main stream, followed by gate 2 which is just off the main stream and must be taken in an up-stream direction. This requires a "break-out" (a stroke forcing the craft out of the main stream) whereby the paddler gains the slack water and goes through the gate. If the stern of the kayak clips the right-hand pole a penalty of 10 seconds is marked down by the gate judge.

The canoeist will now ride high into the rough water to allow time to align for gate 3, over the standing wave, through the "stopper" – a term given to rough-water condition. With fast-flowing water falling over rock or a weir, it creates a situation where the water will roll back on itself and is thus flowing both down stream and up stream. Anything passing through this point will be checked or temporarily held – hence stopper. The heavier the water and the bigger the drop, the more severe the stopper. (In the USA, Australia, and New Zealand, this water condition is termed "pressure wave".)

Different skills are called upon for all the various gates, navigating through artificial hazards such as rapids, rocks, weirs, and bridges and picking up time penalties or point penalties along the way for errors and mistakes.

The course must include between 20 and 25 gates, including at least six upstream gates, and are numbered in order.

Equipment

Canoes must be unsinkable, rudderless and fitted with handholds at the stem and stern (toggles or loops, or a cord running the length of the craft).

Clothing

The canoeists wear life jackets, or other buoyancy aids and crash helmets.

CANOEING

Introduction

Canoeing is a sport performed on water in a small craft, pointed at both ends (a canoe or kayak), propelled by one or more persons kneeling or sitting in a forward-facing position roughly in the centre of the boat, using a single-bladed or double-bladed paddle. As a sport, canoeing divides into: SLALOM RACING, WILD WATER (sometimes referred to as down-river racing), LONG-DISTANCE RACING and SPRINT RACING. Further variations include CANOE SAILING and CANOE POLO.

History

As the canoe originated in North America it is now generally referred to as the Canadian canoe, and craft of traditional lines – although of modern materials – can still be obtained today. The origins of the canoe can be traced directly to the North American Indians when early craft were built with birch bark stitched over a light framework. The Indians used their canoes for hunting and the early trappers and fur traders used them for carrying goods, the canoe being the major means of

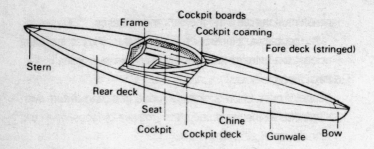

transport in the pioneer days of the New Territories.

The canoe also features in the adventures of missionaries and explorers of North America. The craft was built to varying lengths, commonly around 20ft (6.1m), but much greater lengths were seen in the "voyageurs'" canoes, which were upwards of 35ft (10.67m) and carried great loads and many people.

Although early man may have used a craft similar in dimensions by hollowing out a log, the kayak as we know it today is descended from those used by the Eskimos of Greenland and Alaska at a much later date. The Eskimo kayak was a very light craft, being made of a framework, either of driftwood or bone, over which was stitched a covering of sealskin, greased with animal fat to make it waterproof.

Venue

Courses can be on mountain rivers, other stretches of rivers with natural and artificial hazards (for slalom events), below weirs or on special artificial streams.

Equipment

The term "canoe" is used in Britain to describe almost any craft pointed at both ends in which the paddler faces forward, though the craft may well be a kayak. In the North Americas and on the Continent the terms "canoe" and distinct types of craft: the canoe, pointed at both ends, with the paddler kneeling in a forward-facing position and propelling it with the use of a single-bladed paddle; and the kayak, pointed at both ends, with the paddler sitting in a forward-facing position and using a double-bladed paddle.

CANOEING, LONG-DISTANCE RACING

Introduction

Long-distance canoe racing is to CANOEING as cross-country racing is to ATHLETICS or car-rallying to MOTOR RACING.

History

Long-distance racing was started in Britain about 1947–48 although the first recorded event was in December 1867, when a 12 mile (19km) race was organized by the Royal Canoe Club at Teddington, on the Thames just outside London.

As the sport progressed, the design of the kayaks became more specialized. The racing paddlers demanded more speed, the slalomists more manoeuvrability, and the tourists wanted lighter and faster craft which still retained a good carrying capacity. In 1948 the first cold-moulded wood veneer racing kayaks appeared in Britain – soon to be replaced by hot-moulded craft from Denmark – while in the following decade an entirely new material, glass fibre, was introduced.

Venue

Courses vary a great deal and this seems to be one of the main attractions of the competitions. Weather conditions, too, are variable and the average course of about 12 miles (20km) can provide a testing experience.

Rules

Long-distance racing may take place on any type of river, lake, or open water. The distance is usually 10 to 15 miles (16–24km). Massed starts are used, usually by class or at times by all singles classes or all double classes of senior, junior, or women's events. On many rivers where there is no great width and the entry is large, a good start can almost win the race for a paddler; thus at such events there is much jockeying for position as the starting time gets near. In most races, at least two or three locks have to be portaged (i.e. the craft carried round) and five or six crews arriving at a portage simultaneously create great excitement.

Equipment

Canoes must be unsinkable, rudderless and fitted with handholds at the stem and stern (toggles or loops, or a cord running the length of the craft).

Clothing

The canoeists wear life jackets, or other buoyancy aids, and crash helmets.

CANOEING, SPRINT RACING

Introduction

Sprint Racing for a canoe or kayak is competed on flat water (a regatta course) over a straight distance of 500m, 1000m, or a circuit of 10,000m (574yds, 1094yds, 6.2 miles).

History

See CANOEING.

Venue

Water should be 3m (9ft 10in) deep over the entire course.

Rules

Each race has a mass start (at international events a maximum of nine lanes is permitted), the winner being the paddler whose bow first crosses the finish line. At international regattas, for all but the 10,000m event, each competitor or crew must stay in their buoyed lane and be at least 5m (16ft 5in) away from all other paddlers at any time. This is to prevent "wash-hanging", where a following paddler may contrive to get their kayak to plane on the bow wave of a leading paddler, thereby conserving strength. In the 10,000m event crews must adhere to the 5m rule for the first and last 1,000m. It is not usually possible to provide a straight 10,000m course and the event is then run over a circuit with up to four turns.

Equipment

Canoes must be unsinkable, rudderless and fitted with handholds at the stem and stern (toggles or loops, or a cord running the length of the craft).

Clothing

The canoeists wear life jackets, or other buoyancy aids and crash helmets.

CANOEING, WILD-WATER OR DOWN-RIVER RACING

Introduction

This is the straightforward racing version of rough-water canoeing. Here there are no gates to be negotiated as in Slalom, the only hazards being natural ones in the shape of rocks, fallen trees, bridges, or other obstacles in the river. It is a straight race from start to finish, the fastest man over the course being the winner. Contestants are started in intervals, the course being a minimum of 3km (1.9m) on water not less than grade III.

Venue

A grade III river usually means fast flowing water with rapids, many quite heavy.

Equipment

The canoes and equipment are similar to those used in the slalom event but have no rudders.

CLUB BALL

Introduction

This was an ancient pastime played with a stick and a ball and of "rude and unadulterated simplicity".

History

Its history as a game is obscure but it is important because by at least Tudor times the use of a relatively straight bat (as distinct from the curved sticks with knobs on the end that were used in early forms of HURLING, GOLF, and HOCKEY) and, it seems, the placing of fielders used to catch the ball, were features of the club ball that combined with the use of the stool as a wicket in STOOLBALL to evolve a form of CRICKET in line with the modern game.

At a time when stoolball was a popular rural game in south and west England, the Worcestershire regional name for a low wooden stool, such as would have been used as the wicket in stoolball, was "cricket" and it has been suggested that cricket got its name from this direct association with stoolball.

There seems however to be a wider claim that the name cricket derived from the Anglo-Saxon word "criec" meaning a staff, stick, or club. Nyren in *The Crickets of My Time* (1833) accepted that derivation and at the same time cast doubt on Strutt's earlier contention that the ancient game of club ball got its name from the compound of the Welsh and Danish words "clwppa" and "bol". Nyren preferred to date club ball from the earlier Saxon period.

A game played by hitting a ball with a club is known to have been played at least as early as the middle of the twelfth century, and a sport called "creag" is mentioned in Edward I's Wardrobe Account for 1300 as one of the games played by 16-year-old Prince Edward. Later in the reign of Edward IV (1461-83), club ball was among the games outlawed because they diverted persons "strong and able of bodie" from using their bows. The enactment failed to have the desired effect and most of the games and pastimes were still flourishing some fifty years later. At this point the bowyers, fletchers, stringers, and arrowheadmakers of the reign of Henry VIII, getting short of employment, persuaded the king to authorize the playing of BOWLS and TENNIS within the precincts of their houses.

The common people, despite the new enactment, continued to play club ball, a game that required only a stick and a ball by way of equipment, and an area of open space in which to play. Nyren thought that it had "similar laws and customs prescribed in the playing at it" as trapball that followed it which, he believed, carried with it an air of refinement.

CRICKET
Introduction
Cricket is an 11-a-side bat-and-ball game played in the main in English-speaking countries. The two teams bat in

successive innings and attempt to score runs, while the opposing team fields and attempts to bring an end to the batting team's innings. After each team has batted an equal number of innings (either one or two, depending on the conditions before the game) the team, when in field, that scores the most runs wins.

History

Cricket grew most strongly in England but its precise origins are not known. A reference to its being played is contained in the wardrobe of accounts of Edward I for 1300. An Elizabethan coroner testified that, in about 1550, he and other scholars of the free school of Guilford went to a piece of land in the parish of Holy Trinity and "did runne and play there at creckett". There are regular references to it during the seventeenth century and William Goldwin's Latin poem *"In Certamen Pilai; Anglice,"* *A Cricket-Match* (1706), describes unmistakably the game known today as cricket.

The basic pattern of one person casting a ball at a target – hurdle, gate, stool, or stone – defended by another who tries to hit the ball away with a stick is so simple that it may have origins in different communities; Celtic, Scandinavian, and French origins have all been suggested. It is generally accepted that the English form of the game originated in the sheep country of south-eastern England, where, on the short, down-land grass, a ball of rag or wool, literally bowled – all along the ground – would run truly. The bowler's target was the wicket-gate of the sheepfold as the term "wicket" indicates; and the shepherd's crook which the batsman used to hit the ball away would account for the fact that the earliest known cricket bats were long with a curving blade. In the early seventeenth century Cotgrave referred to a "crosse" as the "crooked staff wherewith boys play at cricket." Some say that its origins are French, having been brought over by French soldiers. This would seem to be borne out by the fact that a version known as "French Cricket" is still played in playgrounds today.

Venue

Cricket is traditionally played on turf, but in some areas matches take place on matting stretched over earth or concrete, or on other artificial surfaces. The ground may be of any shape, but is usually oval, and ranging in size from about 90 to 150m (100-160 yds). The full playing area is contained within a defined boundary line, ideally at least 75yds (68.58m) from the playing pitch. The pitch, which is set as nearly as possible centrally on the ground, is a carefully prepared rectangle of closely mown and rolled grass over hard packed earth, is 22yds (20.12m) long, and is marked out in whiting called creases.

The term "wicket" is also often used as a synonym for pitch or, in the plural, for the number of batsmen dismissed or still to bat: the context indicates the meaning intended. The size of the wicket has carried since it was first set, in 1744, at 22in (55.88cm) high and 6in (15.24cm) wide – with only two stumps supporting one bail. The middle stump was added around 1776. Since 1931 the dimensions of the wicket have been 28.5in (72.39cm) high and 9in (22.86cm) wide.

Rules

Cricket, which has evolved over several centuries, is a complicated game, and those who are not familiar with it as part of their environment often find it difficult to follow. It has been described as "casting a ball at three straight sticks and defending the same with a fourth", but in addition to defending the "sticks" (stumps which form the wicket), the batsman attempts to score a run (the unit of scoring) or runs. The winning team is that with the greater aggregate of runs in a completed match, which may last from a few hours to as much as six days in some Test (international) matches.

The order in which the teams bat is determined by a coin toss. The captain of the side winning the toss may elect to bat or field first. The captain of the side which takes the first innings (the batting side) decides the order in which his/her batsmen will take their individual innings, and the first two start the batting. They each have a bat and will almost certainly wear padded batting gloves, pads for the legs and a protector for the lower abdomen.

One batsman (the "striker") goes to the crease from which s/he will face the bowler; the other ("the non-striker") goes to the opposite crease. The batsman may bat right or left-handed. The two sides of the ground are known as the "on" (or "leg") side (to a right-handed batsman's left as s/he faces the bowler), and the "off" side (to his/her right).

The captain of the fielding side selects his/her first bowler, the wicket-keeper takes up position, and the other nine members of the fielding side are disposed by the captain in appropriate positions, depending on whether the batsman is right or left-handed.

The bowler, a member of the fielding side, bowls, propels, or delivers the ball by hand. Essentially, "the ball must be bowled, not thrown or jerked" – otherwise it is an unfair delivery (or "no ball"). There should be no bending or straightening of the arm at the elbow during the final armswing at the end of which the ball is released.

The bowler may bowl with his/her right arm or left, under-arm, round-arm, or over-arm, although s/he may not change from one to the other without informing the umpire, who will warn the batsman of the coming change. Virtually all bowling nowadays is over-arm. The bowler may also bowl over the wicket, or from the other side of the stumps, called "round the wicket".

A delivery is called by the umpire as a "no-ball" unless, at the moment of delivery, the bowler has at least some part of his/her front foot behind the popping crease, and both feet within – and not touching – the return crease.

Ultimately, the bowler is trying to dismiss the batsman – i.e. to end his/her individual innings.

The batsman may be:

"Bowled" – when, regardless of whether the ball has touched the batsman or his/her bat, it breaks the wicket, i.e. completely removes either bail from the top of the stumps. The batsman is not out if the wicket does not break.

"Caught" – when the ball, after touching any part of the bat or the batsman's hand or glove, is caught and held by a fieldsman before it touches the ground. (NB: If the catcher, either during the catch or immediately afterwards, touches or steps over the boundary, then the batsman scores six runs and is not out.)

"Leg before wicket" (usually abbreviated "l.b.w.") – when a ball would, in the opinion of the umpire, have hit the wicket had it not been stopped, voluntarily or involuntarily, by any part of the batsman's body or clothing except his/her hand (holding the bat). If s/he deliberately pads away a ball outside the off stump (i.e. the stump furthest from the batsman) s/he is out, provided, as always, that the ball would have hit the wicket.

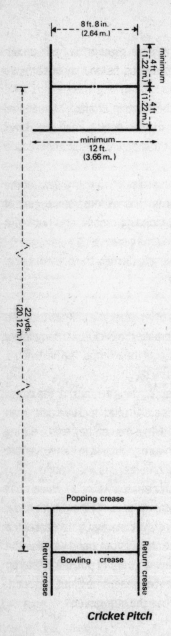

Cricket Pitch

"Stumped" – If a batsman misses the ball and in attempting to play it steps outside his/her crease, s/he is out stumped if the wicketkeeper gathers the ball and breaks the wicket with it before the batsman can ground part of his/her body or his/her bat behind crease.

"Hit Wicket" – This may only rarely be intentional on the part of the bowler, but it is credited to him/her in the score-book. It happens when, while playing at the ball, the batsman breaks his/her wicket with his/her bat or any part of his/her body or clothing.

The batsman is also out (though the dismissal is not credited to the bowler) if s/he:

Is "run out" – when the wicket s/he has left (if batsmen have not crossed) or the one to which s/he is running (if they have crossed) is broken by the ball while s/he is "out of his/her ground" (when no part of his/her body or bat is grounded behind the line of the popping crease).

Handles the ball except at the request of one of the fielding side. This does not include being hit on the hand by a delivery, or any other non-deliberate action.

Having stopped the ball, deliberately hits it a second time in an attempt to score runs. If the ball is bouncing or rolling around near the stumps, the batsman is entitled to knock it away so as to avoid being bowled, but not to score runs.

Wilfully obstructs a fieldsman. This does not include running a path between the fielder and the wicket so that the fielder cannot throw the stumps down with the ball, which is quite legal, but does include any deliberate attempt to swat the ball away; is timed out if a new batsman takes longer than two minutes, from the time the previous wicket falls, to appear on the field.

An appeal (in the words "How's that?" or "Howzat?"), which may be made by any member of the fielding side, covers all forms of dismissal, and must be answered by an umpire in the terms "Out" or "Not out". As each batsman is out, s/he is replaced by the next in the batting order, which the captain may vary at any time.

Equipment

The cylindrical wooden stumps (each 28in/71.12cm high) are set up at the centre of the bowling crease at both ends of the pitch in two groups of three, called the wickets, and surmounted by two bails (each 4 3/8in/11.11cm long) which rest in grooves cut in the tops of the stumps and project no more than 0.5in (1.27cm) above the stumps. (NB: In Australia "stumps" is a term meaning the end of play for the day.

The ball is a hard, cork and string ball, covered with leather. The circumference is between 224 and 229mm (8.81 to 9.00in), and the ball weighs between 156 and 163g (5.5 to 5.75oz). Traditionally the ball is dyed red, with the stitching left white. Nowadays white balls are also used, for visibility in games played at night under artificial lighting.

Scoring

Batting is a complex and precarious skill but its aims are simple – to prevent the bowler and fieldsmen from dismissing the batsman and to score runs.

Runs are scored by a batsman when s/he strikes the ball and s/he and his/her partner both run and make good their ground behind the popping creases at the opposite end from which they started. This they must do before the fielding side can return the ball and break the wicket: thus one run is scored. If they turn, run, cross, and make good their ground a second, third, or any number of times, they score two, three, or other appropriate number of runs. If either batsman fails to make good his/her ground while running two or more runs the umpire will cancel that run by calling and signalling "Short run".

In the case of boundary hits, the batsman need not run to score. If s/he hits the ball and it crosses the boundary line after having touched the ground, s/he automatically scores a "boundary" – four runs. If the ball passes over the boundary line without touching the ground, six runs are added to the striker's score.

"Extras" (called "sundries" in Australia) are added to the team's total, but not to the batsman's individual score for:

A "no ball" – one extra is scored for a no ball unless the

batsman hits the delivery for runs, as s/he may do and count them to his/her score. It is in effect a free hit for him/her: s/he cannot be out in any of the ways credited to a bowler, but only for handling the ball, hitting the ball twice, obstructing the field, or by being run out.

A "bye" – when the batsman misses the ball or allows it to pass, and the wicket-keeper fails to stop it, the batsmen may run, or count a boundary, as the case may be.

A "wide" – if the ball is bowled so high or wide that the umpire considers it to have been out of the batsman's reach, one run is scored; but, if the wicket-keeper does not stop a wide ball, the batsmen may take as many runs as they can, as in the case of byes.

The ball becomes "dead" after its return by a fielder to the wicket-keeper or bowler, and the cycle of play begins again as the bowler commences his/her run-up for the next delivery.

The first bowler bowls an "over" of six balls (eight in Australia), not inclusive of wides or no balls, from the end at

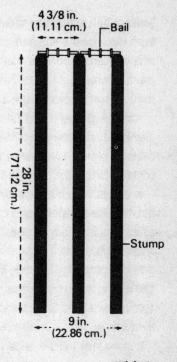

Wicket

which s/he started. The second bowler then bowls an over from the opposite end and, provided overs are bowled from alternate ends, bowlers may be changed as often as the captain of the fielding side desires, except that a bowler may not bowl two successive overs.

An innings may continue until ten batsmen have been dismissed (except in limited-overs matches): the remaining batsman of the 11 is described as "not out" and s/he does not continue to bat when s/he no longer has a batting partner.

A cricket match is won by the team which scores most runs in a completed match. At its simplest: if in a single innings match, team A scores 200 runs and team B, 100, team A wins by 100 runs.

In the same way, in a two-innings match, if team A scores 150 runs in its first innings and 200 in its second, and team B 100 runs in its first innings and 150 in its second, team A wins by 100 runs.

If the team batting second scores enough runs to win without all its batsmen being out (i.e. without losing all its wickets) it does not need to go on batting. Thus, if team A scores 200 runs and team B reaches 201 when only four of its batsmen are out, the scores are said to be: team A 200; team B 201 "for four wickets", and team B is said to have won by six wickets.

To expedite a result a captain may declare its innings closed at any time. If team A has scored 400 runs with only, say two batsmen out, and the captain considers this a probable winning total, s/he may declare the innings closed (or ended). If team B is then dismissed for 300, the final score would read: team A 400 "for two wickets declared", team B 300. Team A wins by 100 runs.

In a two-innings match, a captain may often declare his/her team's second innings closed to achieve a positive result within the time remaining. Then the scores might read: team A 350 and 200 for six wickets declared, team B 200 and 150. Team A wins by 200 runs. Alternatively: team A 200 and 300 for eight wickets declared, team B 200 and 301 for eight wickets. Team B wins by two wickets (i.e. having two of its ten second-innings wickets remaining).

Clothing

All white trousers, shirt, shoes and sweaters (with team colours as a trim) for test matches, coloured outfits for one-day matches. The wicket-keeper must wear leg pads and protective gloves and batsmen must wear leg pads, gloves and protective helmets. Shoes are leather, usually with spiked soles for grip on grass.

For games played with a red ball, the clothing must be white or cream. With a white ball, players usually wear outfits in solid team colours and they can wear a hat or cap to keep the sun off. There are no regulations regarding identifying marks or numbers on clothing.

CROQUET
Introduction

Croquet is a lawn game played with balls and a mallet on a court. The game is for between two and four players. The object of the game is to score points by hitting balls with the mallet through a course of hoops and against a centre peg. The game is won by the side that finishes the course first with both balls or scores most points in an agreed time.

Croquet

History

It is popularly supposed that croquet was played in Pall Mall (Pell-Mell, or Pale-maille) in the early sixteenth century. An account of about this time describes a game "where-in a round box ball is struck with a mallet through a high arch which he that can do at the fewest blows or at the number agreed upon wins."

The precise form of the game is uncertain, but it is reasonable to assume that it had originated in France, because so many of the terms then used were French. The connect of "maille" and "mallet" is certainly indicative and it is thought that a form of the game was played on the sands of northern France with bent willow boughs in which a ball was hit with something like a shepherd's crook and apparently called "croquet". It is said that Louis XIV was fond of playing an open-air game which is the ancestor of modern croquet. It was called "le jeu de mail", the ball being played with a mallet through successive hoops on the ground.

Venue

The court measures approximately 35yds by 28yds (31.95 x 25.56m), on which are set out six hoops and one central peg. The hoops are made of round iron 5/8in (1.59cm) thick and have a square crown, the crown of the first hoops being coloured blue and that of the last, or rover hoop, red. They stand 1ft (30.5cm) out of the ground and the inside measurement between the uprights is 3.75in (9.53cm). Four coloured clips corresponding to the colours of the balls are used to show which hoop each ball next has to make. They are placed on the crown of the hoop for hoops 1 to 6 and on one of the uprights on the return journey.

Rules

As stated, the object of the game is to score all 12 hoops (each hoop in both directions) and the peg point in the correct order with each ball. Four balls are always used; in singles each player has two balls. Blue and black are always partners against red and yellow. The striker strikes with their mallet only one of their balls during any turn. The winner of the toss may choose either whether to play first or second, or which colour balls to play with.

The player starting then places a ball anywhere on the baulk line and strikes it to begin the game. The opposing player does the same. Then two more alternating turns are taken to that all four balls are in play.

The boundary of the court is defined by a white line, the inside edge of which is the actual boundary. The balls are played into the court from either of the baulks, which are part of the yard-line, an imaginary line which runs right round the court 1yd (0.91m) in from the boundary. The A baulk runs from the 1st corner spot to the middle of the south boundary and the B baulk from the 3rd corner spot to the middle of the north boundary.

When all four balls are in play, the sides play alternately but the balls need not be played in sequence. Thus the player of blue and black could play blue for as many turns as they wish. In doubles, each player plays the same ball throughout, but one player of a partnership can play several consecutive turns for their side.

A turn consists of initially one stroke, but this can be extended if that stroke is a roquet – made when the striker's ball hits one of the other three balls – or scores a hoop. A

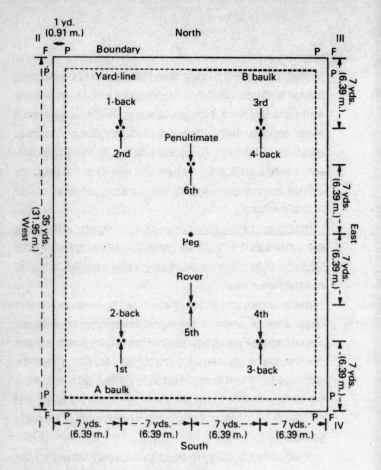

Standard Croquet Court and Setting
P) corner pegs; F) corner flags.

roquet entitles the striker to two further strokes – a croquet stroke, played with the striker's ball touching the roqueted ball, and then one further ordinary stroke, called the continuation stroke. On this continuation stroke, the striker may roquet each ball only once in each turn unless a hoop is scored. Running a hoop entitles the striker to another ordinary stroke and also the right to roquet the other three balls again. Thus, every time a hoop is run the sequence of roquet and croquet can begin again and, by a combination of these strokes and running hoops (called making a break), the turn can be extended even until the peg has been reached. The turn does not end if a ball is sent off the court unless it is either the croqueted ball or the striker's ball in a croquet stroke.

The making of a break follows a basic pattern. In a four-ball break the striker will have one ball (called the pioneer) waiting at his/her next hoop, say the second. Another ball (called the "pivot") will be about half-way between that and the present hoop with the remaining ball (called the "pilot") off which the striker will make their hoop.

The striker approaches the first hoop on the croquet stroke, sending their own ball in front of the hoop and the pilot behind it. They now run the hoop and can roquet the pilot again. The striker croquets this to the third hoop as their pioneer for that, at the same time going to the pivot in the middle. The striker then roquets the new pilot, makes the second hoop in the same way as the first and afterwards sends the pilot ball to the fourth hoop as the pioneer, going back to the pivot and from there to the new pilot waiting at the third hoop.

However perfect a break, its advantage can be entirely wiped out if the leave at the end is not a good one. Normally it should be such that the opponents are separated and the striker's balls are together, but they should lie in such a way that they are strategically placed for their next turn, to play either with that ball or their partner's. At the same time they should not offer the opponent the chance of a break if they should hit.

A good player can frequently leave the balls so that they will have a break in their next turn if they play one or two very good shots. Their opponent therefore may think that, if they shoot at any of the other balls, they will eliminate the necessity for these good shots and decide to go off to a distant corner in the hope that an error will be made and the break will not materialize.

Playing a break, although presenting enough problems in the controlling of all the balls accurately enough to maintain it, is perhaps the easiest part of a turn. More often than not, the break will have to be gathered in, a very formidable undertaking if all the balls are on the boundaries. Frequently, the break will have to be only a three-ball one, played without the pivot ball; sometimes a two-ball break is all that can be managed, and in this case it is unlikely that more than two or three hoops will be made.

Equipment

The peg is made of wood 1.5in (3.8cm) in diameter and stands 18in (45.72cm) out of the ground, exclusive of a detachable portion at the top to hold the clips. The mallet may be any length but the head must be wood. Metal may be used for weighting and strengthening. The balls are made of compressed cork covered with a layer of composition or plastic and coloured respectively blue, red, black and yellow. They must be of even weight, 15.75–16.25oz.

Scoring

One point is scored for sending a ball through its next hoop, and one when it hits the peg at the end of the course.

Therefore, each ball scores 13 points, with a maximum of 26 points per side.

Clothing

Players must wear rubber-soled, flat-heeled shoes. White clothing is usual for competitions.

CURLING

Introduction

Curling is similar to BOWLS except it is played on ice, usually by two teams of four players (a match played by any large gathering is a "bonspiel"), each player using two curling stones and playing them in the direction of their "skip" (captain), alternately with their opposite number. A curler throws the stones over 40yds (36.58m) to circles (the "house") cut on the ice and often coloured.

History

The origins of curling, "Scotland's ain game", are unknown and there is still some doubt as to whether the game started in Scotland or the Low Countries. The case for Holland rests on paintings by Breughel, two of whose landscapes show a game similar to curling being played on frozen ponds. Scotland's claim is supported by references in early literature and by many examples of old curling stones which, over hundreds of years, have been unearthed in digging and salvaged from lochs throughout the country.

Venue

The ice on which curlers play is called the rink (also the name for a team of four players). At either end are cut circles with a radius of 6ft (1.83m), whose centres (or tees) are 38yds (34.75m) apart. Inner circles may also be drawn at 2ft

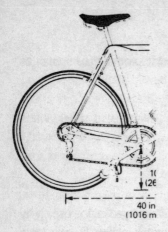

Curling Rink
*Inner circles and centre lines,
shown in fine line, are
optional.*

(60.96cm) intervals. In alignment with each tee, a centre line may be drawn to a point 4yds (3.66m) behind the tee. Four scores are drawn across the rink at right angles to the centre line: (a) the tee; (d) the hog score, one-sixth of the distance between the foot score and the farther tee.

Rules

The object of the game is to place more stones nearer the tee (called the "button" in Canada and the US) than the opponent. A stone which does not pass the hog score, or "hog", is removed from the ice; similarly, a stone which passes the back score is removed. All games are decided by a majority of shots. A team (or rink) scores one shot for every stone of the opposing rink. All measurements are taken from the tee to the nearest part of the stone. Every stone which is not clearly outside the outer circle is eligible to count.

The first player in a team is

called the "lead" and the rotation of play and the system of scoring is the same as for lawn bowls. ("Points" is a version played by individual curlers with a series of different shots.) An end (or "head") is completed when the eight players have played their 16 stones and the players then play the next end on the same sheet of ice in the opposite direction. A game is played by time or a fixed number of ends.

To throw the stone, a curler places their right foot on the hack (a foothold for curlers which is positioned on the foot score) for purchase and adopts a sitting position, with their left foot comfortably on the ice and slightly ahead of them. They grip the handle of the stone in their right hand and hold their broom in the left. With their eye firmly fixed on the skip's broom at the other end of the ice, the curler lines up their shot and, with an under-arm pendulum action, draws the stone back, lifts it off the ice, and brings it forward to release it with a follow-through directed at the skip's broom. During the backward swing, the curler raises his/her body to place all the weight on the right foot, possibly swinging the left leg to the right to counter the weight of the stone on the right side.

Equipment

The stones are round, not more than 36in (91.44cm) in circumference or less than 4.5in (11.43cm) high. They must not weigh more than 44lb (19.96kg) including the handle and bolt. They are concave on the top and underneath. Curling stones, which traditionally come from Scotland, are known as "granites". The stones are fine-grained to provide a strong interlocking quality and have a low water-absorbency and a consistent hardness to give even wear. A bolt through a centre hole screws into a goose-neck handle, which is used to deliver the stone. An iron sheet on which a player stands to throw a curling stone is called the "crampit". It is 3 or 4ft (91.4 or 121.9cm) long by about 12in (30.5cm) wide. Brooms or brushes are used in Scotland, elsewhere in Europe, United States and Canada. Whisk brooms can be made of corn straw, nylon, flagged polypropylene, or horsehair. In the modern sport, two types of broom are used to clear the stones' path. These are a new-style synthetic pad and a "push broom". The "broom" is made of thick hog or horse-hair bristles.

Scoring

When all stones have been played the game is completed and the score is taken. The scoring side gains a point for each stone inside the house and closer to its centre, or tee, than any stone of the opposing team. Measurements are taken from the tee to the nearest part of the stones.

Clothing

Competitors usually wear rubber-soled shoes or boots. Spikes on the footwear, which would damage the ice, are not allowed. Otherwise, dress is usually informal and gloves are a matter of choice.

CYCLE BALL

Rules

Cycle ball is an amateur cycling ball game derived from ASSOCIATION FOOTBALL in which the ball is trapped, driven forward, and shot at goal by the rider manipulating the front wheel of their bicycle. It is played indoors between teams of two riders, and as a field game between teams of six. World championships are held annually.

CYCLING

Introduction

Cyclists race bicycles on road courses or tracks in events of various distances either as individuals or teams. Indoor events can include special track races and stationary races on sets of rollers. The winner is the first to finish, or has the best time or most points based on performance.

History

The first cycle race took place at the Parc de St Cloud, in the suburbs of Paris, on 31 May 1868: it was over 1,200m (1,312yds), and was won by an English resident, James Moore. The first inter-town road race, between Paris and Rouen, followed 18 months later; from 325 starters. Moore was again the winner, covering the 83 miles (133.57km) in 10 hrs 25 min. Yet while these are recognized landmarks in the history of organized cycle racing, informal challenge matches and speed trials date back to the earliest development of the bicycle, the object of each designer being to show that his machine was faster and more reliable than its predecessors.

Venue

For road events this can be a specially constructed cycle track, which is suitable for vehicles. It may be streets and highways, a motor-racing circuit, or a course marked out on an aerodrome or seaside promenade. It may be open or closed to other traffic.

Rules

There are no standard distances in road racing. A road race may cover anything from 20 miles (32km) to more than 3,000 miles (4,828km), and last under an hour or, broken into daily stages, several weeks. At whatever length, the basis of competition remains the same; the riders move off together at the start of the race, or any subsequent stage, and the winner is the person covering the total course in the shortest time. Hence the title, massed-start racing, to distinguish this from time-trialing.

In track events, a track specially constructed for cycling which is symmetrical and approximately oval in shape, but with two straight sections – a back straight and a finishing straight – is used. It is generally banked all round, though far more steeply on the curves than on the straights. The surface of an open-air track is made of concrete, asphalt, shale, cinders or, occasionally, wood.

In the road events, the strongest rider wins by simply outstripping the others, as the strongest runner might in an athletics marathon. Certain physical principles, peculiar to cycling, have led to the development of team tactics which can either nullify or reinforce individual prowess. The basic principle is that it requires less effort to ride in the shelter of another cyclist (either directly behind them, or slightly to the side if there is a cross-wind) than it does to ride alone or in the lead. It therefore follows (a) that the second rider is conserving energy which may enable them to beat a stronger rider in the end, and (b) that if each of two good riders takes it in turn to pace and shelter the other, together they can maintain a faster pace than a single rider of equal, or greater, strength and determination, who is pursuing or trying to elude them. Three good riders working together will be a more potent force than two, and so on, although in practice the maximum advantage is probably gained when the group numbers eight to ten.

As a result, a road race is only exceptionally decided by an all-out individual effort from start to finish. It is rather made up of quiet spells interspersed with attacks, chases, counter-attacks, and regroupings dictated by the tactics of the moment. The riders compete in teams, generally of six to twelve riders. One is the leader, although there may be one or two other protected riders; the remainder are supporting members of the team, or in the widely-used French term, "domestiques".

The job of the domestique is to help close the gap if a rival breaks away; to pace their leader up to the break; to pace them back to the main bunch (or "peloton") if they puncture or drop behind; to exchange bicycles with them if they have mechanical trouble; to hinder pursuit if they escape, by blocking at the front of the peloton and slowing its progress; and in a mass finish, to lead them out in the final sprint.

The moves in a road race are often difficult to interpret because of their constantly changing pattern. Two or three members of rival teams, for instance, may form a temporary coalition in order to establish a break, and not become opponents again until the last few miles. During the course of a race the team may switch its support to a different rider; if the nominal leader is not well placed to win, it will work instead to get its best sprinter into a breakaway. Frequently a domestique, having attached themselves to a strong breakaway on behalf of their leader, will find themselves with no helpful alternative but to contest the finish.

There are exceptional circumstances in which tactics play little part. One is where the race is decided by "selection from behind", usually in an arduous event where the winner does not make a clean break from the field, but sets such a hard pace at the front that the other riders drop behind. Another is on mountainous stretches where, since pace-making is of little value, the rider must strike out for themselves.

A distinctive feature of sprint and motorpaced races is the "repêchage". This is an extra heat in which riders eliminated during the qualifying rounds are given a second chance to win a place in the next stage of the competition.

Sprint races are organized within a knock-out competition, with three riders on the track in the earlier rounds, and two or three in the finals. Each race is held over 1km (or 500m for women), but only the last 200m or 220yds is timed. This is because the first part of the race is traditionally given up to manoeuvres in which the riders switch across the width of the track, slow down, and sometimes stand still in an effort to force each other to take the lead. All else being equal, it is easier to use the other rider as pace-maker and to accelerate from behind them in the final straight than it is to win from the front.

Tandem sprints, although faster over the last 200m, cover the same distance and take the same general form as singles sprints. The front rider in the team controls the racing; the rider behind, who provides the extra power and is often called the "stoker", also acts as lookout if an opposing team is to the rear.

Motor-paced races are the longest track events; the championship distance for professionals is 100km (62.1 miles), while for amateurs the final lasts an hour. Each competitor is paced by a specially built motor-cycle of between 125c.c. and 650c.c., and, riding in the shelter of its driver, they are able to maintain average speeds of 80km/h (50mph) and more.

In the "1,000 metres time trial" the rider has the track to him/herself and from a standing start tries to cover 1km in the

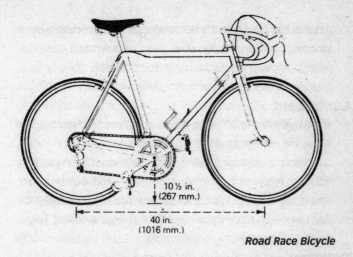

10 ½ in.
(267 mm.)

40 in.
(1016 mm.)

Road Race Bicycle

shortest possible time.

"Individual pursuit" is an event contested by professionals over 5km, by amateurs over 4km and by women over 3km. Two riders take part in each race, starting from stations on opposite sides of the track and attempting to gain on each other. Victory goes to the first rider to reach their home station on completing the distance or, less often, to the rider who overtakes their opponent.

Although following the same principle as the individual pursuit, "Team Pursuit", over 4km, is between amateur teams of four riders. Each rider leads the team for one lap or half a lap, then swings up on the end banking and drops back to the end of the file. Thus, after another three laps or another lap and a half they find themselves leading the team once more. The weakest rider can afford to drop out near the finish as the time is taken on the third rider to reach the team's home station.

While these six events form the basis of the programme at

most indoor or outdoor track meetings, other cycling events include: Madison racing; devil-take-the-hindmost; point-to-point; Australian pursuit; Italian pursuit; omnium; six-day race; grass-track racing; and cycle speedway.

Equipment

The bicycle has to be pedal-driven and moved only by human force; The maximum size is 6ft 6ins in length and 3ft in width but the wheels may be different diameters. There are two different types of bicycle: A road cycle – this has one free wheel, with multiple gears on the rear wheel, and a brake for each wheel; A track cycle has one cog-fixed wheel, a single gear on the rear wheel and no brakes.

Clothing

Cyclists wear a molded protective helmet, a jersey that covers their shoulders and black pants to mid-thigh, or a similar one-piece outfit; white socks are preferred but goggles and mitts are optional, however the goggles must be non-splinterable.

CYCLO CROSS

Introduction

Cyclo cross is a form of bicycle racing practiced in winter on cross-country courses. Interest in the sport is mainly confined to Europe, where its strongest following is in Luxembourg, the Low Countries, and Russia, but it is also found in the USA, especially around Chicago.

History

The origins of cyclo-cross are obscure, although it is thought to have taken shape in France shortly after the turn of the century, and to have been influenced by the use of bicycles in military manoeuvres. Many so-called road races at that time, however, included sections of rough, unmade ground, and there can have been only a difference of degree between these and cyclo-cross events.

The beginnings of cyclo-cross in Britain can be traced back to a cyclists v. harriers race held at Walsall, Staffordshire, from 1921, and its early progress ran parallel with that of motor-cycle scrambling, or Motor Cross, which it resembles.

Venue

The recommended length for a cyclo-cross race is 10-15 miles (16-24km), which, depending upon the severity of the course, will give a duration of 60-70 minutes. Most races are made up of successive laps of a circuit of half a mile to 2 miles (0.8-3.2 km). Since courses, where possible, are left in their natural state, their characteristics vary considerably. No more than one-third of the distance may be composed of metalled road, and usually the proportion is much less. For the rest, organizers are officially encouraged to choose "terrain calling for skilled machine-handling and balance."

Such a terrain will usually include most of the following features: pasture or ploughed field and woodland; steep banks and flights of steps to climb and descend; walls, stiles, gates, fallen trees, streams, and ditches; narrow paths, bridges and gaps where it is difficult for one competitor to pass another. If the landscape does not provide sufficient obstacles, artificial hurdles may be added. Because the cyclo-cross season runs from September to mid-March, rain, snow and ice often create additional hazards.

Rules

All cyclo-cross races have a massed start, which must take place in an area wide enough for the whole field to assemble in not more than two lines abreast. Thereafter the cyclists tackle the course in their own way, riding where they are able and, when the going becomes too rough or steep, or where there are obstacles to cross, carrying their bicycles on their shoulders. Ability in cross-country running and nimbleness in vaulting are therefore required, but generally the advantage lies with those who can keep riding where others are forced to take to their feet.

Apart from basic strength and stamina, the qualities shown by the most successful competitors are dexterity in controlling the bicycle, nerve in taking steep, slippery and uneven surfaces at speed, and judgement in selecting the best line where the course is broad enough to offer a choice. It is characteristic of cyclo-cross that the class of rider is well defined, and that results are more predictable than in most sports.

The rider's initial objective is to make a fast start and be ahead at the first obstacle or narrow section; the leader has a clearer path than those who follow and get in each other's way. Races are often lost, if not won, in the first 200yds (183m). Beyond that the tactics of the sport are rudimentary. There are rarely stretches sufficiently fast and level for pace-making between members of a team and, while situations may occur during a breakaway which can work against an opponent (e.g. attacking and relaxing in turn to break the rhythm of their riding), a rider's effort needs to be self-sufficient.

Equipment

The bicycle used in cyclo-cross is basically a steel-framed road machine (see CYCLING) with its weight reduced by the use of aluminium alloy for handlebars, brakes, and pedals, plastic for the saddle and nylon for the gears. Five or six gears, with handlebar controls, are more common than ten or twelve; the chain-wheel is equipped with a flange or guide on either side to stop the chain jogging off on broken ground.

Clothing

Clothing worn is similar to that in road races, except that the jersey is without pockets and has long sleeves as a protection against the cold and scratches from thorns and branches. Depending on the condition of the ground, a rider may wear football studs or running spikes on their shoes.

DAKYU
Rules

This is an equestrian, ball-and-goal, team game which has been played in Japan for more than a thousand years. It might be described as a form of mounted LACROSSE. The players carry a pole with a metal net at the end: their purpose is to catch the ball in the net and throw it into the opposing goal, which is a circle 61cm (24in) in diameter. The winning team is that which first scores 12 points.

DARTS
Introduction

This is a sport in which players have to throw dart at a circular target divided into different scoring areas. The game can be played by individual players, pairs, or teams of any number. Using three darts, the players aim to reduce a starting score (usually 301, 501, or 1001) exactly down to zero.

History

In pubs and clubs throughout Britain "arrers" has been a popular sport for some time. A Lancashire carpenter, Brian

Gamlin (1852–1903) was responsible for creating the board and the scoring system. Some argue that darts began in France and was a form of indoor archery. Furthermore, it arrived in America with the Pilgrim Fathers in the sixteenth century and was played on the Mayflower. The American Darts Organization was formed in 1933 and the United States Darts Association was formed in 1969.

Venue

The playing area has a dartboard which is hung on a wall, with the scoreboard to one side. The toe line, 2.37m from the dart board, is marked either on a mat or on the floor.

Rules

Each player uses three darts and in the singles games, each opponent throws darts in turn. In pairs or team games, different sides throw in turn, with members of each side playing in the order established at the start. The player has to throw his/her darts from behind the toe-line, which is 2.37m from where the board is hung. For darts to score, only those that stick into the board at the end of a player's turn are allowed. They are not scored if they rebound, stick into another dart, fall out of the board, or are knocked out before the player ends their turn. Re-throws are not permitted.

To finish the game, dart players must end with a double bringing the score exactly to zero but if the player scores past zero, or to one, they go right back to the score before that turn, and forfeit any darts remaining in that turn.

Equipment

The dartboard is usually made of cork, bristle, or elm, with the divisions and various sector numbers marked by wires. The board is hung so that the 20 sector is vertically above the bull.

Scoring

Players start out with a score of either 301, 501, or 1001. Darts score according to their sector number – unless they are within the outer ring, when they score double the sector number, or the inner ring, when they score three times the sector number.

Clothing

There is no set uniform for darts players but they usually wear casual clothes that allow freedom of movement.

DECK CRICKET

Introduction

This is a form of CRICKET first played on board ships, with a tethered ball. Few players found that satisfactory and the bigger ships sought to allocate a considerable area of deck space to the game.

Nets rigged from awning spars to the deck enclosed the playing area, to avoid losing too many cricket balls and as a necessary means of preventing injury to other passengers. The area itself was about 30ft wide and 60ft long (9.1 x 18.3m). A strip of coconut matting was laid the full length of the pitch and the stumps were set in a block of wood. The pattern of play was the same as for the game on land except that scoring was related to the area the ball reached before being fielded.

An area, which stretched the width of the playing space and reached 8ft (2.4m) from a line drawn about 15ft (4.6m) from the stumps, was worth one run. The next area extended for a further 8ft, and was worth two runs. A slightly bigger area extending for a further 9ft 6in was worth 3 runs; and beyond that was the boundary worth 4 runs.

Like most DECK GAMES, deck cricket was appreciated by

spectators as well as by the players themselves, but the game did take up a relatively large amount of the available deck space and needed its special protective netting. It was losing favour, perhaps with shipping companies more than with passengers, even before the 1945. After this time the increase in air passenger traffic persuaded shipping companies to build smaller vessels with a consequent reduction in deck space for the smaller number of passengers. Some passengers may try their own improvised games of cricket but as part of the organized programme of deck games it is out of fashion.

DECK GAMES

Introduction

These are organized diversions and means of recreation for passengers on board ships, particularly those on holiday cruises.

History

The games date only from the 1920s, but games were played aboard ship several centuries earlier and some few of them, like BULL, swinging the monkey, and SHUFFLEBOARD are still played today even though the former two linger on the programme of many shipping lines more for reasons of sentiment than popular demand.

Small sailing ships offered little clear deck space in which games could be played, nor did the conditions under which they lived and worked leave seamen with much time or energy for sport. Before about the fifteenth century there was little enthusiasm for playing games when on board ships.

The situation changed when the fighting ships needed more men. The unwilling landsmen caught by the press gang and forced to serve in the fighting ships from the fifteenth until well into the ninteenth century had been accustomed to playing games in their rural environments and sought to adopt some of them to preserve a link with their previous existence. It is probably not a coincidence that one of the earliest known deck games was called Bull and involved the use of a bag known as a "bull's head". Regular seamen would have given the game a name and symbols with more nautical associations.

One the whole, however, it seems likely that the crews of ships, particularly fighting vessels, were too fatigued with work, suffering, and sickness to play many games – even if space and opportunity permitted. It was probably only the increase in the emigrant trade in the first days of sail that kept alive the deck games that did survive until the post-1918 fashion for cruising ships revived them and established a host of new ones.

The emigrant trade meant the presence of a large number of passengers on board ships which had not been designed for this. The accommodation was wretched, and sometimes intolerably slow. It was then, not from any particular interest in games themselves but to overcome boredom and as a means of keeping a measure of good health, that the emigrants played such games as they could.

The post-1918 extension of passenger traffic on ships coincided with an increase in interest in sports generally that showed itself in the added enthusiasm of most nations for the Olympic Games and the introduction of a world football championship. It was reflected in the demand for more opportunities to play games on the decks of ships, and it was not long before shipping companies acknowledged the situation by allocating additional space for games and by introducing a new term in the plans for passenger vessels – a "sports deck".

Many of the games introduced had a direct connection with the most popular of games played ashore, notably DECK TENNIS, deck bowls, DECK QUOITS, deck golf, DECK CRICKET, and deck croquet. Sea voyages, even cruises, no longer occupied months and apart from the immediate response expected from passengers towards a game they played, or had played, ashore, it was an obvious advantage that deck games had familiar playing terms even if the rules and equipment had to be modified.

Considerations of space, even on the largest passenger vessels, has probably been the main reason for the decline, indeed the virtual demise, of many deck games introduced in the first boom period.

DECK QUOITS

Introduction

The object of the game is simple enough – to place quoits (rope rings) as near as possible to the centre mark (the jack) since the circles closest to the jack attract the highest points.

History

See DECK GAMES.

Venue

This can be played wherever convenient on the deck but, in practice, most ships have brass marks sunk into the deck that minimize the necessity of measuring and chalking before each game.

Rules

Each player has either three or four quoits and the game is won by the player, or pair of players in a doubles match, first scoring 21 points. A match is won by the player or pair winning the most of three games. Opponents stand together at the ends of the pitch in the singles games, and play from each end alternately. In doubles, partners stand at opposite ends, that is to say, each against an opponent.

Scoring

Only those quoits nearer to the jack than the best quoit of the opposite player/pair are counted as scoring. The rules vary slightly but generally they are:

Quoits must be thown backhand and over the centre line.

Women must stand with their feet behind the chalk line, and not outside the ends.

Men must stand with the foremost foot inside the small circle.

Quoits falling short of the dead line (or ladies' line) do not count and must be removed properly.

A quoit touching a circle will score the number of the outer ring.

Bumping one's own or opponent's quoits to further one's own interests is permitted.

"Riding" quoits do not count.

Clothing

Clothing can be casual and should not restrict movement.

DECK TENNIS

Introduction

This is a combination of tennis and quoits, and it has been, since the 1920s, one of the most popular of all deck games. It is played by either two or four people who throw a quoit or rubber ring to one another across a net suspended over the centre of the court, which is divided like a lawn tennis court.

History

See DECK GAMES.

Venue

On board the ship, the size of the courts, whether for singles or for doubles, varies. There are exceptions but generally singles courts are 30–40ft (9.1–12.2m) long, and 10–15ft (3–4.6m) wide. In the faster doubles game, the length may be less, say 28–34ft (8.5–10.4m), but the width should not be less than 14ft (4.3m) and not more than 15ft (4.6m). Whatever the overall dimensions of the court, there must be a neutral space extending for 3ft (0.9m) on either side of the net across the width of the court. Parallel to the neutral line, and 6–8ft (1.8–2.4m) from each end of the court, there are other lines known as back lines. The centre line, making four divisions, extends from the middle of the back line to the middle of the neutral line on each side of the net.

Rules

There are no definitive rules for deck tennis, for the simple reason that a court has to be marked out in whatever deck space is available and often surrounding influences, deck fittings, the convenience of other passengers, and the welfare of players and spectators, have enforced amendments and revision of the more generally accepted rules.

The server stands on the back line of the right-hand court and delivers the quoit over the net to his/her opponent in the diagonally opposite court. The quoit must be delivered in an upward direction for at least 6in (152mm) after it leaves the hand. The server's hand may pass over the back line before the ring leaves it, but the quoit must not be delivered flat and, although "wobblers" are allowed, they are not considered good form. Forehand and backhand deliveries must be given but not overhand ones or deliveries from a height above the shoulder. Feints at delivery or baulking in any form are forbidden. If the quoit touches the net in service it must be played again if it drops within the bounds. Players standing over the neutral line are faulted.

After a serve all four players may run or stand anywhere in the playing area on their own side. Players may stretch their hands over the neutral line but not over the net.

If the quoit touches an outside object it counts against the player delivering it. The quoit must be returned by the player receiving it from the position in the court in which they catch it. If the quoit falls within the neutral space the point is lost. If a player's hand touches, but drops the quoit, the point will count against them. Should the quoit strike a boundary line and pass out of bounds, it is considered to have fallen within bounds. Even if the quoit is already out of bounds, anyone attempting to catch it, and failing to do so, will lose the point.

Should both players touch the quoit, it is a fault. Players must not hold on to a quoit unnecessarily, or use both hands. A quoit touching any part of the body is faulted. Players are not allowed to serve or return the quoit with both feet off the deck.

If the quoit falls on the deck in the proper court when serving, or within bounds in subsequent play, it counts against the player who fails to catch it. A quoit falling untouched out of the proper court when served, or out of bounds in subsequent play, will lose the point for those serving or delivering the quoit.

Scoring

Scoring advances 15, 30, 40, advantage, game. There are six games to a set.

Clothing

Clothing can be casual and should not restrict movement.

DIVING

Introduction

Diving is an individual competitive sport, with separate events for men and women, in which the diver projects himself into the air from an elevated board and executes either a simple header or more complicated somersaults, before entering the water. Competitive diving is divided into separate sections, men's and women's springboard and platform (otherwise known as highboard) events. Divers perform set numbers of dives, each of which is marked by judges. The diver with the most marks in the final is the winner.

History

Until the beginning of the nineteenth century, books on swimming only refer to diving as a plunge from the side of a pool as a means of entering the pool for the purpose of swimming. This eventually developed into the "racing dive" used at the start of some competitive swimming events.

It is not clear when people first dived into the water. The first swimming obviously took place in the rivers and the neighbouring sea in countries near the tropics. The original object of the dive (to enter the water and swim) gave way to jumping and then to diving for its own sake. The challenge and the satisfaction came from the flight through the air and men jumped and dived from greater and greater heights.

In more recent history, professional divers have dived from temporary towers, often over 60ft (18.29m) high, into tanks of water for the amusement of the crowds of fairgrounds and carnivals. People began jumping from bridges in Europe or the USA, later diving head first from them. Indians in Mexico were adept at jumping and diving from high cliffs into the sea. During a visit to Hawaii in the late nineteenth century, Lady Brassey observed how the natives leaped, dived and somersaulted from considerable heights, often into pools at the bottom of waterfalls, for the sheer excitement of it.

By the beginning of the nineteenth century a new form of diving was developing in Europe, mainly in Germany and Sweden where formal gymnastics was popular. During the summer months, gymnastic apparatus was transferred to the beach. The flying rings, the trapeze and the springboard were erected and used from high platforms to enable gymnastics to be performed over the water. This was the beginning of "fancy diving", the name later given to aerial acrobatics over the water. Until this time, most diving was "plain" – the simple forward header with the body held straight and arms extended sideways – known in the early days in Europe as the "Swedish swallow" and later in the USA as the "swan dive". The trapeze and rings were gradually discarded and diving from the platform and springboard incorporating gymnastic somersaults developed as a separate sport, becoming known as springboard diving and fancy high diving.

Venue

The high board is a rigid platform with a resilient hardwood surface, covered with a non-slip surface. It is installed at heights of 5m, 7.5m and 10m (16ft 5in, 24ft 7in, and approx.

33ft) above water level. They are usually mounted on reinforced concrete or steel. The front of the platform must project at least 1.5m (4ft 11in) beyond the edge of the bath, and the back and sides must be surrounded by hand rails. Springboards are installed at heights of 1m and 3m (3ft 3.5in and 9ft 10in) above water level. Regulations require that the springboards be at least 4.8m (15 ft 9in) long and 0.5m (1ft in) wide and covered with a non-slip surface. The depth of water varies for different heights.

Rules

A dive is split into four parts:

1 The starting position on the board.
2 The take-off from the board.
3 The flight through the air.
4 The entry into the water.

In practice the dive is one continuous movement and in competition it is judged as a whole and not in parts.

The starting position for standing dives is at the front end of the board with the body erect, hands by the sides or above the head. For running dives the erect position with hands by the sides is taken up at least four paces back from the front end of the board.

The take-off comprises every movement the diver makes from the time they assume the starting position until the moment their feet leave the board. For running dives from the fixed platform, the run is on the balls of the feet followed by a low hop, to land on the end of the board. From the springboard the "run" is in reality a three-step walk, followed by a high leap into the air from one foot, called the hurdle step, and a landing on the end of the board with both feet together. Before the diver loses contact with the board at the completion of the take-off, three objects must be achieved:

1 The body must be projected upwards with maximum velocity to obtain height, with its resultant gain in time.

2 The body must be set in motion away from the board, for safety.

3 The body movements necessary to produce the forward or backward rotation must be completed. After the diver has lost contact with the board there is little they can do to alter their dive.

The flight is that part of the dive when the body is free in the air and is finished the moment any part of the body touches the water. During the flight the body may be carried in one of three recognized body positions:

1 Straight – the body is not bent either at hips or knees.

2 Pick – the body is bent at the hips (90° or more) but the legs are straight at the knees.

3 Tuck – the whole body is bunched up with the knees together, hands on the lower legs. In each position the feet are together with toes pointed.

The positions are assumed soon after take-off and held for varying lengths of time during the flight, depending on the requirements of the dive being performed. Just prior to the entry the body is straightened. During the diver's time in the air, they are able to control their rate of rotation (angular velocity) within certain limits. The tighter they tuck, the faster they spin and when they stretch out for the entry they are rotating at their slowest.

The entry begins the moment any part of the body touches the water and is completed (as is the dive) the moment the body is totally submerged. From the high platform the diver plummets into the water at about 32.5mph (52km/h). To avoid the shock to the diver's system, they aim to enter the water as nearly vertical as possible, with their body perfectly straight. When entering feet first, the arms are held close to the body, but for head-first entries the arms are stretched above the head, hands close together.

All dives are some form of somersault. The simple header is a half-somersault. This is followed by the single somersault, 1.5 somersault, double somersault, 2.5 somersault, triple somersault, and finally the 3.5 somersault. The single, double, and triple somersault divers enter feet first. All feet-first entries are more difficult to control, the majority of divers select head-first entry dives in competition. The diver takes off from the board whether facing, or with their back to, the water, and there are four basic groups of dives:

1 Forward dive – forward start with forward rotation.

2 Back dive – back start with backward rotation

3 Reverse dive – forward start with backward rotation

4 Inward dive – back start with forward rotation.

There is a fifth group – "twist" – comprising any dive in which the body rotates laterally about its long axis in addition to any somersaulting rotation. There is also a sixth group "arm-stand", used from fixed boards only, in which the diver commences his/her dive from a position balanced on his/her hands.

The men's high-board competitions consists of six basic dives and four voluntary dives. In each section each dive is selected from a different group. The dives may be performed from either the 5m or 10m platform. The ladies' high-board competitions comprise four required dives (forward, back, reverse, and inward dives) and four voluntary dives from four different groups performed from either the 10m or 5m platform. When there are more than 12 competitors, there are preliminary and final contests.

Scoring

Divers are judged on execution only. The degree of difficulty of the dive is reflected in the tariff value allocated to it. The diver has to decide whether to risk a more difficult high-tariff position with a possible low award from the judges if they "flop". The judges' awards are multiplied by the degree of difficulty value to arrive in the final score.

Clothing

Male divers need a well-fitting pair of trunks with an internal tying cord (external belts cannot withstand the impact with the water). Women need a one-piece costume with strong shoulder straps.

EQUESTRIAN EVENTS

Introduction

These are competitive events for horse and rider designed to test the horse's development and training, his jumping ability, endurance, speed and agility and the all-round ability of horse and rider.

History

The training of horses by means of gymnastic exercises has probably existed ever since man began training horses more than 3,000 years ago. Originally dressage was connected solely with the basic training of war horses and unlike the advanced form of equitation known as high school ("haute école"), it was regarded only as a means to an end. The first Olympic Grand

Prix de Dressage had repercussions throughout the equestrian world and, at competition level, dressage has become an end in itself. Since the end of the Second World War, the Olympic test has included advanced movements, which come into the category of high school "airs". Although the precise venue and date of the first show jumping competition are unknown, the sport gained popularity in a number of countries towards the end of the nineteenth century.

Clothing

Male riders at international events wear uniforms affiliated to clubs recognized by their national federation hunt uniform, a red or black coat, white breeches, hunting cap, black boots or black-topped boots. Women riders wear light fawn breeches and usually a riding hat.

• DRESSAGE

The French term for the training of horses, "dressage", has been adopted by the equestrian world generally for a series of movements which test a horse's development and state of training. The Fédération Équestre Internationale (FEI) gives the following definition: "The object of dressage is the harmonious development of the physique and ability of the horse. As a result, it makes the horse calm, supple, and keen, thus achieving perfect understanding with its rider. These qualities are revealed by: the freedom and regularity of the paces; the harmony, lightness, and ease of movements; the lightening of quarters; the horse remaining absolutely straight in any movement along a straight line and bending accordingly when moving on curved lines. The horse thus gives the impression of doing of his own accord what is required of him."

Venue

All tests are judged in areas of 60m by 20m (66 x 22yds). An area of 40m x 20m may be used for less advanced tests.

Rules

Dressage competitions are designed to assess how far the objectives set out by the FEI have been achieved. Thus the tests for international competitions cover standards compiled by the FEI. At the dressage, the competitors carry out official tests incorporating a variety of paces, stops, changes of direction, movements and figures which are graded in difficulty according to the standard of competitors. Each movement is marked individually by the judges and the total marks are then averaged to give each horse's final score.

The tests include: "the halt"; "the walk"; "the trot"; "the canter"; "the counter (false) move"; "change of leg at the canter"; "the collected paces"; "the rein back"; "the submission"; and "transitions" – these changes of pace and speed should all be smooth but quickly made. This also applies to the transitions between the "passage" and "piaffe".

Changes of direction – the horse should adjust the bend of its body to the curvature of the line followed.

Riding corners – at collected paces, the horse must describe a quarter of a circle of approximately 3m radius, at the paces the radius should be 6m.

The passage– this is a measured, very collected, elevated and cadenced trot.

The piaffe – this is a movement resembling the very collected trot on the spot.

Lateral movements – (work on two tracks) comprise two suppling movements, the "leg yielding" and "shoulder-in" as well as the classical movements, "travers", "renvers" and "half pass".

There are also figures that must be completed: "the volte"; "the circle"; "the serpentine"; "the figure of eight"; "the half-pirouette"; "the pirouette" and "position of the rider".

Clothing

Riders can wear service uniforms while other riders wear a dark coat and white breeches, top hat, hunting stock and spurs. No whip is used.

• SHOW JUMPING

This is where a horse and rider jump a set course of fences specially designed and built for each contest. It has three main categories of competition: those which primarily test jumping ability but use time counting in the first round or, more frequently, those which time the first or second "jumping-off". Jumping ability is of prime importance, since time counts only when there is equality of faults and a horse with a slow clear round will therefore beat a fast one with four faults.

Venue

From the start to the finishing line the maximum length in metres is the number of obstacles in the course multiplied by 60. The start and finish lines, and all the obstacles, are marked with red flags on the right and white flags on the left.

Rules

Most competitions come into the category of testing jumping ability alone, with time counting in the first round or, more frequently, in the first or second jump-off. Jumping ability is of prime importance, since time counts only when there is equality of faults.

Faults are incurred as follows, under "Table A" Rules:

Fence knocked down – 4 faults.

One or more feet in the water, or on the landing tape – 4 faults.

Refusals (including running-out or circling)

First – 3 faults.

Second – 6 faults.

Third – Elimination.

Fall of horse and/or rider – 8 faults.

For each second over the time allowed – 1/4 fault.

Exceeding the time limit (which is double the time allowed) – 1/4 fault for each second or part of a second.

Competitors may be eliminated for other reasons, which rarely apply. These include failure to start within 60 seconds of the starting signal, taking the wrong course, and receiving unauthorized assistance.

The competition which tests jumping ability alone is known as a "puissance" and this, too, is judged under Table A rules. In this case there is no recourse to the clock, since the object is to test the horse over "a limited number of large obstacles". During successive jump-offs, the fences are reduced to a minimum of two (one spread and one upright) and these are made progressively more difficult. The FEI imposes a limit of four jump-offs in Puissance competitions and, if there is still equality after the fourth jump-off, the first prize is divided.

Table B is used for hunting competitions. The penalties are scored in seconds and added to the time of the round. The number of penalty seconds for each jumping mistake is calculated in relation to the length of the course and the number of times a horse is required to jump in the round.

Showjumping has been described as a test in which the

course designer is the examiner and the competitors the examinees. Since courses are specially designed for each individual competition, the rider's ability to "read" the problems correctly is vital. These problems relate to the positioning of the fences just as much as to their height and width. Combination fences, which comprise two or more jumps within 12m (39ft 4in) of each other, become considerably more difficult when a distance problem is involved. The FEI lays down rules to which course designers must adhere, but there is still considerable scope for individuality.

• THE THREE DAY EVENT

This is an equestrian competition designed to test the all-round ability of horse and rider. The event consists of three distinct parts, or phases, designed to test both horse and rider: dressage, cross-country and show jumping. The phases take place on three separate days, hence the name.

History

The three day event is also known as a horse trials and, because it originated as a test for officers' chargers, it is still referred to on the Continent as the "Militaire". The name given to the sport by the FEI describes it more precisely as the "Concours Complet d'Équitation".

The Event1

The dressage phase (see above) is designed to test the horse's obedience and state of training, as well as the rider's ability to apply the aids correctly. The test consists of a series of movements at the walk, trot, and canter, which the rider must memorize in advance. Each movement is marked separately by the judges and points are also awarded for "general

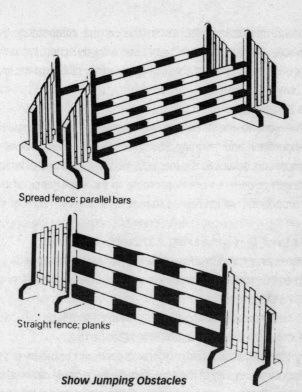

Spread fence: parallel bars

Straight fence: planks

Show Jumping Obstacles

impression". Points are deducted if a rider forgets the test and carries them out in the wrong order.

Scoring

For scoring purposes, the judges' marks are averaged and then deducted from the maximum possible total, to give a penalty score. This penalty is then multiplied by the "multiplying factor" (which can vary between 1 and 2.5) to give the actual penalty points that the competitor will carry through into the next phase. It is through the multiplying factor that the dressage phase can be made to exert "the correct influence on the whole competition". The figure used will vary according to the severity of the second phase and, to a lesser extent, of the final showjumping test.

The Event 2

The second phase, which is designed to test the speed, endurance and jumping ability of the horse, is the most important, as well as the toughest, part of the competition. The length of course varies according to the importance of the competition, which means that riders in the Olympic Games and the world or continental championships cover the longest distance, up to a maximum of 32.3km (about 20 miles).

The course for such an event would be divided as follows:

1) and (3) roads and tracks – in total 16–20km (about 10 to 12 1/2 miles);

2) steeplechase – 3/6 to 4.2km (2 1/4 to 2 1/2 miles);

4) cross-country – 7.2 to 8.1km (4 1/2 to 5 miles).

Though the two roads and tracks sections contribute to the endurance aspect of the test, penalties are rarely incurred on them. There is no jumping involved and competitors can therefore be penalized only by failing to complete each of these sections within the allotted time of 240m (262yds) per minute. Since all riders carry a stop-watch, such mistakes in timing rarely occur.

The first acid test comes on the steeplechase course, for it is here that time bonus marks can be earned and jumping penalties incurred. The time factor calls for a fine judgement of pace, since the horse's energies have to be conserved for the long journey ahead. The maximum bonus (which may vary between 37.6 and 44 points in major international competitions) is obtained when a horse completes the course in a specified time, and it is therefore a waste of effort to go any faster. An alternative method of scoring, which is used fairly extensively, involves translating bonuses into penalties. This means that the horse which would have achieved maximum bonus under the original system is credited with a zero penalty score instead.

After the second section of roads and tracks, there is a compulsory ten-minute halt, during which the horse is inspected by a veterinary surgeon to ensure that it is fit enough to continue. Competitors then set out on the cross-country course, containing between 30 and 35 fixed obstacles, by far the most difficult part of the test.

The height for cross-country obstacles (excluding brush fences where horses can jump through the top 6ins) is limited to 1.2m (3ft11in). This means that the main problems are posed by the shape and siting of the obstacles rather than their size. A typical cross-country course would include one or more jumps into water, obstacles built on a steep down gradient, and several "drop-fences" where the landing is considerably lower than the take-off.

Penalties on the cross-country and steeple-chase courses are incurred as follows:

Refusals (including running-out or circling):

First – 20 penalties.

Second (at the same obstacle) – 40 penalties.

Third (at the same obstacle) – Elimination.

Fall of horse and/or rider within the "penalty zone" which surrounds each fence – 60 penalties.

Second fall of horse and/or rider within the "penalty zone"

which surrounds each fence – Elimination.

Third fall of horse and/or rider within the "penalty zone" which surrounds each fence – Elimination.

Taking the wrong course – Elimination.

It is in the cross-country section that competitors can earn the biggest time bonus. Penalties are incurred for exceeding the "time allowed", at the rate of 0.4 of a penalty for each second over.

The Event 3

On the final morning of a three-day event, each horse which is still in the competition must undergo a thorough veterinary examination. Those which fail to pass are automatically withdrawn. The test on the third day is not an ordinary showjumping competition, nor a test of style or endurance. It is designed with the previous two days in mind and is not a difficult test of the horse's jumping ability.

Show jumping penalties in the three-day event are incurred as follows:

Fence knocked down – 5 penalties.

One or more feet in the water, or on the landing tape – 5 penalties.

Refusals (including running-out or circling)

First – 10 penalties.

Second – 20 penalties.

Third – Elimination.

Fall of horse and/or rider – 30 penalties.

For each second over the time allowed – 1/4 penalty.

Exceeding the time limit – Elimination.

Clothing

Military dress with a helmet or hard hat is permitted for all stages of the event. For the dressage and showjumping competitions civilians should wear hunting attire and for cross-country a polo-necked sweater or shirt, white breeches and black boots. They must all wear some form of protective headgear, which is secured by a harness. Spurs must be worn for the dressage event.

ETON FIELD GAME
Introduction

This is a form of FOOTBALL confined to Eton College, and one of several versions of the game current when ASSOCIATION FOOTBALL evolved in the 1860s. The field game, an 11-a-side game, must be distinguished from the ETON WALL GAME. Whereas the wall game is played only by the 70 scholars and a few enthusiasts from the rest of school, the field game is taught to every Eton boy in his first year. It is still the "official" football game at Eton. There is a school field team, which plays regularly against scratch teams of visitors and masters, and house colours are awarded partially on performance in the field game House Ties, a fiercely contested knock-out competition, which is held every March between 26 houses.

Several features distinguish the field game from other codes of football:

The relatively small size of the goal, with no handling of the ball by any player.

The enforcement of a strict offside rule, which prevents any passing of the ball.

The possibility of scoring "rougues" on the goal line, in addition to kicking actual balls.

History

Football at Eton in some form or another dates back to the Middle Ages. In 1519 the headmaster, William Horman, produced a Latin book based on school life which included the words: "We will play with a ball full of wynde". However, organized football came into existence only during the nineteenth century. In about 1830 hockey was being played concurrently with football, hence perhaps the persistence of HOCKEY-type goals. At this time football was being played at Eton by a number of voluntary "clubs" whose rules varied and were determined partly by the nature of the terrain on which they played. During the same period we find the term "rouge" applied to any episode of violent activity, as in the expressions: "smart and prolonged rouges", "in the thick of every rouge and rally for two hours," or as a verb, "pushing and rouging".

Out of this fluid situation three distinct types of football evolved, the wall game, the field game, and "Lower College", whose scoring in shies and goals suggests that it combined some of the characteristics of both wall and field. Towards the middle of the century football throughout Britain was gradually becoming more organized, and 1850 is a useful rough dividing date between crude less organized sports and compulsory games, which became a characteristic of public school life in the second half. At Eton "Lower College" finally disappeared in 1863, the year of the foundation of the Football Association.

Venue

There is only one "standard" pitch, known as The Field, on which all really important matches are played. Its dimensions are 130yds (from goal to goal) x 90yds (118.87m x 82.29m). It is bounded by touch lines at either side and goal lines at either end, marked in whiting. In the field of play 3yds (2.74m) from each goal line and parallel to it, a dotted line called the 3-yard line is marked. 15yds (13.72m) from each goal line and parallel to it there is a continuous line called the 15-yard line.

Rules

The object of the field game is to propel the ball towards the opponents' goal line and score there.

The chief centre of activity in the field game is the "bully". This is a group of eight of the 11 players on each side, who keep as close together as possible once play has started. Their clustering tendency is due to the rule against passing, which obliges the bully to play as far as possible "as one man". Any bully player who becomes detached from the main mass must take no part in the game until he rejoins the bully. But if a bully player overruns the ball, another immediately behind him may take it on. The three players on each side who are not in the bully are called "behinds", and act as defensive "backs" behind the bully. The bully players are designated as one post, two sideposts, one back-up post (b.u.p.), three corners and one fly (flying man). The binds are called "short", "long", and "goals".

When a "set bully" is formed, the posts, sideposts and b.u.p.s bind together in tight formation. Each side has "heads" in alternate bullies, i.e. has the right to form down first. This means that the front row (post and sideposts) of the side with "heads" put their heads down and together in tight bullies, while the front row of the side without "heads" are obliged to stand upright and so are at a disadvantage in applying pressure and observing the ball. The b.u.p.s on either side bind on behind their posts with their heads down, and, together with their front row, push forward as soon as the ball is put in from the side by one of the corners. The immediate aim of each side is to make ground forwards, or at any rate not lose it. The three corners on either side maintain a fairly loose contact with the more tightly formed part of the bully, ready to pounce on the ball as soon as it appears. The fly informs his bully as to the whereabouts of the ball and directs operations generally, being ready to receive the ball if it is kicked through the bully by the opposing side.

The set bully may in certain circumstances begin a period of play, but on other occasions play may be initiated by the ball being kicked off by one of the behinds. Here the other members of the bully must immediately group themselves together around him, in the manner previously described, if they are to take any part in the game. An individual bully player in normal circumstances will dribble the ball forwards as fast as possible. He ought to be backed up by at least one other member of the bully to take over the ball if he loses control of it, or is tackled. Collectively the bully will normally proceed with heads down and the ball at their feet in what is known as a "bully-rush".

The basic task of the behinds is to stop opposing bully players from getting through the behind's goal or goal line. After tackling an opposing player (in which no use of the arm is permitted) or in any other way gaining access to the ball, the behind's normal task is to return it to his own bully, who ought to be grouping themselves together to receive it. The opposing bully will also join the group, since if they become detached from it they will all be "offside". With as little delay as possible the behind kicks the ball in such a way as, ideally, to fall at the feet of his own bully, so that they may take it on in the direction of the opposing goal. The offside rule does not apply to a behind when he kicks the ball forward towards, or preferable over, the heads of his bully players.

Equipment

It is played on a large number of rectangular pitches, of varying dimensions, throughout Eton. The goals are of uniform size, being the same as that of hockey goals, 12ft wide by 7ft high (3.66m x 2.12m). A round ball is used, similar to a small soccer ball.

Scoring

This may be done by means of goals, which count as 4 points each, or "rouges", which count as 3. To score a goal involves kicking the ball between the goal posts, which is comparatively difficult, since the goal is so small. An alternative method of scoring, somewhat more frequently employed, is to obtain a rouge on the goal line. There are various rather complicated conditions under which a rouge may score, but the principle is always the same, that the ball is touched by an attacker after a mistake of some sort by a defender. Typically a rouge occurs when a defender inadvertently kicks the ball backward over his own line. If an attacker then succeeds in touching it before a defender can do so, a rouge is scored. Similarly a rouge may be scored if the ball is kicked by an attacker, rebounds off a defender backwards over the line, and is touched by an attacker. While "on the line" (i.e. within three yards of the goal line) the ball must be kept in motion by attackers. If it stops, a kick-out is awarded to the defenders. If a "rougeable ball" is touched by the defenders, the attacking side have the choice of scoring 1 point (followed by a kick-off by the defenders) or scoring no points, in which case a bully is formed 3yds from the goal line with attackers' "heads". A heavy or powerful bully who made the latter choice might have a good chance of scoring a rouge.

Once a rouge has been scored, the attackers are allowed to attempt to convert it into goal by means of a "ram". This is a set piece in which the defending bully group themselves in the goal mouth, while a picked body of attackers (usually three or four) form up one behind the other and make an organized rush into the middle of the defenders, in an effort to force the ball through the goal mouth. If successful, they gain an extra 2 points.

ETON FIVES

Introduction

This is a hand-ball game played by pairs in a three-walled court, the design of which is based on an area outside the chapel at Eton College. Here boys have played Eton Fives for centuries.

History

The word "fives" has been used to describe many different games and pastimes in which a ball is propelled either across a net or against a wall with the hand. It has also meant "boxing", the "fives court" for a period being the "ring" of today. The derivation of the word is uncertain, but it is generally accepted that it comes from playing with the five fingers of the hand. Other theories include that scoring was in multiples of fives, that there may have been five persons in a match (four players and an umpire), or that the game may have involved five players per side.

The Eton variation of the game originated outside the chapel at the college where boys waited for roll-call. At the foot of the stairs leading up to the north door of the chapel there was a space between two buttresses, partially obstructed on the left by the end of a stone balustrade known today as the "pepper box". There four boys could play together, two of them between the buttresses, and the other two behind them on a level platform a little lower down. A convenient sloping ledge at a height of 4ft 6in (1.37m) formed the play-line and another ledge about 2ft (0.6m) from the ground formed an additional hazard. The bull's-eye of the court, known as the "dead man's hole", which would make the ball irretrievable, was no more than a drain.

Such was the popularity of the game that in 1840 the headmaster, Dr E.C. Hawtry, instigated, on a more suitable site, the building of he first four Eton fives courts, incorporating the characteristics of the chapel court, but with modifications to make the game easier and faster. Eight more courts were built in 1847.

While footwork is instinctive to natural games players, frequently the game moves so fast that a shot has to be played off the wrong foot. To be able to hit a fives ball equally hard and accurately with both hands is the aim of all players, but particular emphasis is placed on the left hand in Eton fives by the shape of the court which is very much to the benefit of the left-hander. Frequently the ball should be hit no harder than necessary; the modern composition ball is more likely to fall dead if hit firmly but gently into the pepper box. Another basic principle is the necessity for a loose wrist for the majority of shots.

Every effort should be made to avoid getting in the way of opponents as they attempt to make their shots, but such is the speed of the game that it is not always possible to move quickly enough to allow an opponent to play a stroke as he wishes and in every case a "let" should be offered before it is asked for. The spirit of the game is such that an umpire or marker is generally not necessary; nor would an umpire be practical, as the best view of any situation on the court would probably be masked by the players themselves. In the finals of the various championships, however, a marker is usually appointed merely as someone to appeal to if the need arises.

Venue

The dimensions of courts vary, but all have a ledge running across the front wall making a horizontal line 4ft 6in (1.37m) from the ground. Running across the court is a shallow step 10ft (3.05m) from the front wall, dividing the court into an inner or upper court and an outer or lower court. The lower court is 15ft 3in (4.65m) in depth and 14ft (4.27m) wide. At the end of the step, projecting from the left-hand wall, is a buttress (known as "the pepper box").

Rules

One player guards the upper court and his partner the lower court. To start the game, the ball must be served to the opponent's liking. Generally it should bounce to shoulder height and should be lobbed, thrown, or bowled with no spin imparted so that it falls true without breaking. The player receiving ("cutting" or "slogging") has the right to refuse any number of serves if they are not to his liking. The receiver then strikes the ball as the "first cut" to return it above the front ledge within certain limits, aiming to make it impossible to retrieve. If the server or his partner returns the ball, the rally continues until a side fails to hit the ball "up" and the striker and his partner lose that rally. Points are scored only by the pair serving.

The foremost stroke is the "first cut". The laws allow two forms, either that which hits first the right-hand wall and then the front wall above the ledge; or that which hits first the front wall above the ledge between the right-hand wall and the vertical ("blackguard") line. This latter is marked on the front wall 3ft 8in (1.12m) from the right-hand corner.

The purpose of the player on the top step who serves, is to dominate the game. This requires skill, speed, an accurate eye and volleys with either hand. The volley on the top step is the essence of success and delay can cost the rally. Co-operation in partnership, however, is essential, and a volley which would be difficult for the top court player may be possible for his partner. The player in the lower court should back up every stroke by his partner on the top step, who can often miss the ball entirely or change his mind at the last minute.

Equipment

The fives ball is a composition of cork and rubber, painted white, and approximately the size of a golf ball.

Scoring

Game ball is reached at 11 points when the server, apart from still having to provide an ideal service for his opponent, has to place one foot in the lower court and not move until the ball has been hit. A game consists of 12 points, and matches are generally the best of five games. If 11-all is reached, the game may be "set" to three; or at 10-all, to three or five.

Clothing

Dress is usually a white shirt and shorts as in court games, and it should allow complete freedom of movement of waist, arms, and legs. Gloves are of leather and the fingers and palm should be evenly but thinly padded, so that control can be given to placing and "cut". The gloves prevent bruised hands and also protect the fingers and knuckles from injury against the many projections in the court.

THE ETON WALL GAME

Introduction

This is one of the oldest forms of football in existence and certainly one of the oddest of sporting survivals. It is played only on a site at Eton college in Slough, where a red brick wall separates the playing fields from the Slough Road. Originally it was a game for 11-a-side, but after the Second World War the number was reduced to ten. The wall game is quite different from any other kind of football, in that from a spectator's point of view it is mainly static, with only rare moments of rapid movement. These characteristics are largely determined by the site. The object of the game if to propel the ball into the opponent's "Calx" and score there.

History

Eton College was founded in 1440, but the wall game cannot have been played before 1717, which was when the wall was built. It was then not played regularly until the beginning of the nineteenth century. At first it appear to have been merely one variety of FOOTBALL at Eton (though the most formalized and the most popular), which included a wall as a prominent feature of the game, but was played on a comparatively wide area beside it. The technique may have been transferred from "passage football", a familiar pastime in Eton boys' houses at the time, which is still occasionally played.

Venue

Play takes place in a narrow strip, roughly 4 to 5yds wide and 118yds long (3.66–4.57m x 107.89m), adjoining the wall, which is about 11ft (3.35m) high. The surface begins as grass, but in the course of a season becomes reduced to bare earth, dust, or varying consistencies of mud, according to weather conditions. At its left hand end the wall terminates in a cross-wall going off at right angles. 19yds (17.37m) from the junction is a door in the cross-wall, and the goal line is marked in whiting. The goal at this end, 31yds (28.35m) away from the wall, is an old elm tree, with a section of its trunk, approximate in shape to the door, outlined in whitewash. At either end of the wall is a scoring area marked off by a white line on the wall and known a Calx (the Latin for "chalk"). One end is known as Good Calx and the other end as Bad Calx. Somewhat nearer Good Calx than Bad, there is a metal ladder up the wall on the Slough Road side, the bolts of which are visible on the side of the game, and play starts at the ladder.

Rules

The functions of the players is highly specialized, depending on their position, which must be adapted to their build. They are designed as follows: three walls; two seconds; a third; a fourth; a lines; a fly; and a long. Walls are chosen for a combination of tall stature, long reach, and weight. Seconds must be short and stocky, as they play at or under the walls' feet, normally in a crouching position. Third, fourth, and lines are designated "outsides". The third and fourth are sturdy, general-purpose footballers, and play in "line abreast" outside the walls and seconds. Lines must be a quick, agile player with a reliable kick, as he must kick the ball at once if it appears near the touch line.

Finally come the two "behinds", fly ("flying man") who stands behind the main mass (known as the bully), and long, who stands some way back. The eleventh player, formerly employed, is a third behind, called "goals", who had very little to do.

The ball may not be handled, and the only passing allowed is directly sideways – no forward passing or "heeling" of the ball backward is allowed. If a player finds himself in front of the ball he must drop around to the back of his own bully, as he is "offside". An active player may not touch the ground with any part of his body except his hands and feet. Walls and seconds may "knuckle" their opponents with the outside of their "outside hand", but no striking or kicking of an opponent is allowed. Serious injuries are quite rare in the wall game, but if a player feels that he is being crushed into an intolerable position, he is entitled to shout "air", at which the bully breaks up immediately. If the ball is kicked outside the touch line, it becomes "dead" when it stops, or when it makes contact with another player (or spectator). The next bully is formed opposite the point where the ball went dead. To begin or resume play the ball is rolled into the bully by the thirds alternately.

The game consists of two periods of half an hour each, with a five-minute break and change of ends at half-time. On official occasions the game is administered by two umpires and a referee. Normally one umpire is considered sufficient.

The pattern of play varies according to the position of the ball relative to the wall. Ground may be made:

Along the wall, in tight formation.

By "loose" bully rushes.

By kicking.

Equipment

The ball is round and about the size of a child's soccer ball.

Scoring

Once the ball is in Calx the character of the play changes. "Fulking" (heeling, or passing the ball backward) is now allowed, and the object of the attackers is to touch up a "shy", which counts as one point.

This is normally achieved by means of a Calx bully, an elaborate set-piece in which the ball is put in by one of the umpires. Each side then struggles to fulk the ball, so as to get full possession of it. If the attackers manage to touch the ball while it is off the ground and up against the wall, they may claim a shy. If granted, this allows the attackers a free throw at the goal. In practice the goal is very rarely hit (on an average in about one game every two years) and the game is normally won or lost by the number of shies rather than goals scored. If neither side reaches Calx, it is a draw.

A goal may be kicked, rather than thrown, but this is rarer still. A thrown goal is the equivalent of ten shies, and a kicked goal of five. If the defenders gain control of the ball in Good Calx they try to kick it forward and out of Calx. In Bad Calx they may fulk it over the back line, after which they are entitled to kick-out. If they fail to do either of these things, a new Calx bully forms either where the shy was touched up, or (normally) where the ball went dead in Calx.

The mobility, or otherwise, of the game is greatly affected by the conditions. At the beginning of the season, when the ground is firm, movement can be quite free and a decisive score is the rule rather than the exception. Towards the end of a rainy season the mud may be so thick that the ball can only be moved with difficulty. In these conditions Calx may never be reached, so that pointless draws are more common.

The flying man on each side, in addition to playing as a behind, has the duty of reporting on the position of the ball to his side and directing the efforts of his players. Also, a penalty is not normally awarded by the umpire unless a verbal appeal is made to him. In consequence the game takes place amid much shouting by players. The penalties themselves usually consist either of a newly formed bully on the same spot of minor infringement, or an award of 10yds' distance against the offending side for more severe offences.

FELL RUNNING

Introduction

This is an endurance test for both distance runners and mountaineers, deriving its name from the hills of northern England where it is mainly contested, though events also take place in the Midlands, Wales and elsewhere in the British Isles.

Venue

Courses, either "out-and-back" or circuitous, vary from 2 to over 40 miles (3.22–64km), but may not have any formal route. For example, one Scottish challenge is won by the competitor who scales the largest number of peaks in 24 hours.

Rules

One of the more important longer events, dating from 1895, is the Ben Nevis race, a 12-mile (19km) return course then Fort William to the top of Ben Nevis (4,406ft or 1342m) mountain. The nearest equivalent to a national title in fell running is the Three Peaks race, an annual event in north-west Yorkshire since 1954.

Equipment

In tests of extreme severity the overall speed may not exceed a layman's walking pace and, in the event of a fog or mist on the upland sections, a map and compass are often used as in ORIENTEERING. Fell runners have not infrequently lapsed into unconsciousness and occasional fatalities have been reported.

FENCING

Introduction

The dextrous use of a sword for attack or defence has a long and fascinating history with its roots in the traditions of chivalry. Today, it is a sport practiced increasingly throughout the world with three weapons: the foil; the épée; and the sabre.

History

Swords were used before the dawn of recorded history and there are many examples of these weapons dating from the Bronze Age. Fencing, the skilful use of a sword according to established rules and movements, was practiced by all the ancient races – the Persians, Egyptians, Greeks and Romans – not only in war, but as a pastime.

After the fourteenth century, guilds of fencing masters, such as the famous Marxbrüder of Frankfurt, sprang up all over Europe to develop the art of swordsmanship and these fencing schools became very powerful. Early methods were somewhat rough-and-ready and included many tricks borrowed from wrestling.

The Italians are credited with the discovery of the effective use of the point rather than relying exclusively on the edge of the sword. By the end of the sixteenth century, their lighter weapons and controlled swordplay had spread throughout

Foil (for women and men)

Épée

Sabre

The Valid Target

Europe, and rapier fencing was established. From then on, the emphasis was on skill and speed rather than forcefulness. Wrestling tricks were mostly abandoned, the lunge was discovered, and fencing became established as an art.

Venue

Fencing competitions take place on a piste which is 2m (6ft 7in) wide and 14m (46ft) long. An extension of 2m (6ft 7in) to the piste at either end serves as a "run-back" at foil and épée; the piste is 24m (78ft 9in) for the sabre. The piste is marked with lines which indicate the initial positions "on guard" and at which a competitor is warned when they are a certain distance from the rear limit of the piste, having been warned at the warning line.

Rules

Fencing demands quick thinking, poise, balance and muscular control, combined with mental discipline rather than strength. Much practise is required before muscles and mind are trained to carry out complex fencing movements automatically, leaving the brain free to analyse the opponent's game and devise the strategy and tactics necessary to outwit them. Fencing has been likened to a game of chess played at lightning speed.

In a bout, or assault between two fencers in which hits are countered, the fencer takes up a stance, or prepared position – "on guard" – with their arms, weapon, body, and feet so placed as to give them the best possible balance for attack or defence, movement forward or back, or the lunge. When the fencers cross swords they are said to be "engaged", otherwise they are fencing with "absence of the blade". When they are in the "on guard" position, the distance between the two constitutes the "fencing measure". The distance normally maintained is that where each fencer feels safe from a direct attack yet in a position to launch an attack of their own.

The sequence of fencing movements exchanged during a bout is called a "phrase". An attack may be simple, such as straight thrust; or indirect, when it has to pass the point of the weapon to the opposite side of the opponent's blade; or compound or composed, when it includes one or more false attacks – feints or preparatory movements – in order to create an opening for a final scoring movement. The lunge and the recovery from the lunge to the on guard position are known as the "development" and the "return to guard".

A hit is an offensive action which lands the point or edge of the weapon on the opponent. If a hit lands on the opponent's target it is a valid hit, otherwise it is a non-valid, or off-target, hit. A hit made with any part of the front edge or the first third of the back of a sabre is known as a cut. A stop-hit is a form of counter-attack delivered into the oncoming attack, which, ideally, does literally stop the opponent.

A parry is a defensive action which deflects an attacker's blade clear of the target. An important principle of defence in fencing is to oppose the forte of the blade to the foible of the opponent's blade when making a parry.
There are three types of parry:

The simple, or direct, parry, the instinctive reaction moving the sword laterally across the target to protect the line along which the attack is approaching.

The indirect parry, made by moving the sword in a semi-circle from a high-line engagement to deflect an attack into a low-line or vice versa. A circular or counter-parry, made by a

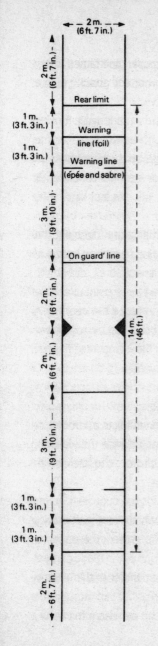

Regulation Piste

2 m. (6 ft. 7 in.)

2 m. (6 ft. 7 in.)

Rear limit

1 m. (3 ft. 3 in.)

Warning line (foil)

1 m. (3 ft. 3 in.)

Warning line (épée and sabre)

3 m. (9 ft. 10 in.)

'On guard' line

2 m. (6 ft. 7 in.)

14 m. (46 ft.)

2 m. (6 ft. 7 in.)

3 m. (9 ft. 10 in.)

1 m. (3 ft. 3 in.)

1 m. (3 ft. 3 in.)

2 m. (6 ft. 7 in.)

circular movement of the defender's blade which gathers the attacker's blade and brings it back to the original line of engagement.

A riposte is the offensive action which follows a successful parry. A riposte may be simple, made with one blade movement (either direct or indirect); or it may be compound, that is, preceded by one or more feints or preparatory movements. If a riposte is parried, the next offensive action from the defender is known as a counter-riposte. A feint is an offensive movement made to draw a reaction from an opponent – usually to change their line of defence, leaving the originally defended line open to the attacker's thrust.

Fencing time – "temps d'escrime" – is the time required to perform one simple fencing movement, such as a single blade movement, an arm movement, or a movement of the foot e.g. a step forward. Fencing time varies according to the speed of reaction of each individual fencer. Counter-time – also called a "second-intention attack" – is effected by draining the opponent's stop-hit or exposing the target during a simulated attack, parrying the stop-hit, and scoring with a riposte.

"In quartana" is an attacking movement made while moving the body out of line with a side-step. "Passata sotto" is the action of avoiding an attacker's blade by ducking below it. "Sentiment de fer" is the term used for feeling an opponent's reactions through the contact of his blades, and thus anticipating his movements.

"Doighte" means finger-play, controlling and directing the weapon by using the fingers only. The first finger and thumb of the sword hand, known as the "manipulators", direct the weapon. The point is raised or lowered by alternately pulling with the thumb and pushing with the forefinger, or vice versa. A circular movement is imparted to the blade by rolling the handle between the manipulators. The remaining fingers, called the "aids", serve to steady the handle.

Equipment

In each case the weapon consists of a blade and mounting. The tang of the blade passes through the mounting to a pommel, or locking nut, which often serves also to balance the weapon. The mounting consists of a metal guard or "coquille" which protects the sword hand.

At foil and épée a small cushion inside the coquille protects the sword hand, and a handle or grip which is the part usually held by the sword hand. At foil and épée a small cushion inside the coquille protects the fingers. The half of the blade nearest to the guard is called the forte; the remainder of the blade is called the foible.

The foil, a light weapon evolved in the seventeenth century

as a practise weapon for the short court sword, was not designed for use in duels. Its maximum total length is 110cm (3ft 7in), and its maximum weight 500g (17 5/8 oz).

The épée is the duelling sword, developed in the nineteenth century to practise in the schools for an actual duel. It is heavier weapon than the foil – maximum weight 770g (27 1/8oz) – though its maximum length is the same.

The sabre is the cut-and-thrust weapon evolved from the backsword and the heavy cavalry sabre. Its maximum length is 105cm (41 3/8in) and its maximum weight 500g (175/8oz).

Scoring

A bout between men at foil, épée, or sabre is fenced for five hits, i.e. the fencer against whom five hits are scored loses the bout. At the women's foil a bout is fenced for four hits. The time limits for a bout are six minutes of actual fencing for men, and five minutes for women.

The competitors are warned when one minute remains for fencing. If the time limit expires at foil or sabre, the fencer who is leading (say 3-2) wins the bout and the hits are brought up to the full number (in this case the score will be 5-4). At épée, if the fencers reach 5-5 (say, by a double hit) before time expires they continue to fence until one has scored a decisive hit. If no decisive hit is scored and time expires, a double defeat is scored.

Clothing

Fencing equipment, in addition to the weapon, includes a mask, jacket and glove. Breeches and stockings complete the outfit. Traditionally jacket and breeches were made of canvas, but nylon is increasingly used today. They must be white.

FISHING
Introduction

In many countries there are governmental rules imposed upon people planning to take fish, wild birds or mammals for sport or food. Trespass laws may be very rigid and in the United States, for example, all wild life is the property of the government. Fish and game are reduced to personal property, however, when the laws and regulations of individual Federal authorities are enforced.

Four different techniques are used: fishing with bait; trolling, bait casting; and fly fishing.

The most common baits for fresh-water fishes are crawlers, earthworms and minnows. The most common salt-water baits are bloodworms, sandworms, shrimp, pieces of soft-shell crabs, pealer crabs, squid, clams, and sea mussels.

History

References throughout history have been made to catching fish. Initially it was a means of obtaining food and it is impossible to pinpoint a time when fishing became a sporting pastime. Homer referred to man "casting his ox-horn lure", the Greek poet Oppian wrote on sea fishing in the third century AD and later in the same century the Roman poet Aelian described the way the Macedonians caught trout with an artificial fly.

• COARSE FISHING

Coarse fishing is a popular sport and usually takes place in a river or lake and often involves the fishing of the following species: barbel, bleak, bream (common and silver), carp (common and crucian), chub, dace, eel, grayling, gudgeon, perch, pike, roach, rudd, ruffle and tench.

Rules

Course anglers must put their line correctly on the wheel. Loading the spool is one of the most important aspects of the sport and when using the fixed spool reel is even more vital. Another important aspect of technique is casting. There are several different styles, all of which are correct, but some popular techniques have been criticized by traditionalists.

On rivers, the cast is usually made across or slightly downstream. If the current is strong enough to impart fishlike motion to the lure by causing it to spin or wobble, the angler does not wind in. In slower water the angler assists the current by winding slowly. The depth at which the angler's lure is "fishing" is also important, and leads may be used to lure down in the current.

Equipment

The simplest pieces of equipment for course fishing includes the "everyman's reel" or fixed spool or threadline. The type and size of the line is dictated by the method of fishing. The circumference of an average fixed spool drum is only about 6in when the spool is brim full. The fixed spool reel is suitable for nearly every type of coarse fishing.

• SEA FISHING

Sea fishing has grown rapidly, especially in the United States where it is estimated that there are approximately 11,000,000 salt water anglers. It can be done either off a boat or dinghy in the ocean, from rocky shore lines, beaches, piers and harbour walls. These all involve different styles, baits and equipment.

Rules

When sea fishing is competitive there are two main classes:

the "Pisces" (bony – cod, whiting, herring etc.) and the "selachii" (the sharks and rays). Other types of fish which feature in sea fishing are: bass, black bream, red bream, brill, coalfish, cod, conger eel, dab, dogfish, the greater and lesser spotted dogfish, spur dogfish, the smoothound, flounder, garfish, gurnard, haddock, hale, halibut, john dory, ling, mackerel, monkfish, mullet, plaice, pollack, pouting, sting ray, thornback, ray, shark, common skate, sole, tope, tunny, turbot, greater and lesser weever, whiting and wrasse. However fish, naturally, do vary over the world.

The four basic methods of fishing (see Introduction) are also used in sea water fishing: fishing with bait, trolling, bait casting and fly fishing. However float fishing is also used. Big game fishing primarily means the members the tuna, shark, swordfish or billfish families. Deep-sea trawling is a highly specialized form of fishing which requires a boat designed to carry heavy-duty tackle for handling very big fish. Game fish are hunted in a number of varied methods. Still-fishing, the simplest and most common form of fishing, is probably the oldest but other methods in modern practice are also of very early origin.

Equipment

Sea fishing equipment can include rods, reels, lines, casting wrights or sinkers, hook, swivels, traces, spinners, feather lures, floats, gaffs and landing nets, prawn nets, spring balances and bait. Also, accessories can include lamps, compasses, knives and protective gloves.

• STILL-FISHING

This is the most common and simplest form of fishing. The

hook is usually baited with natural or live bait, and the line is left resting stationary in the water. Still anglers usually fish from an anchored boat, bridge, pier, or the bank of the stream.

Rules

Along river banks, hand-lines are referred to as "throwlines", so called because about 3ft of the weighted and baited end is given several circular swings and thrown far into the river, while the other end is held in the left hand or tied to a bush on the shore. In the ocean, bay, or deep lake, a long hand-line with sinker and baited hook is used. Bait and fly-casting outfits can also be rigged for still fishing, the reel enabling the bait to be cast farther from the boat than the ordinary pole permits.

FLY BALL

Introduction

This is a bat-and-ball game of the TENNIS type played with a shuttlecock. The racket is the shape of a table tennis bat, and has a net hitting surface; the shuttlecock is like that used in BADMINTON. The court is 7m (23ft) long and 3.20m (10ft 6in) (4.20m–13 ft 93/8in, for doubles) wide. The net is 1.30m (51in) high. Scoring is as in badminton; a game is of 30 points and a match goes to the player, or pair, which first wins two games.

FLYING, SPORTING

Introduction

This embraces all those aspects of flying which have no specific military, commercial, or other working connotation. It has developed in a manner similar to any other sport relying upon a mechanical device for its fulfilment and most countries now have their own aero clubs.

• AIR RACING OR AEROBATICS

Both air racing and aerobatics demand skills in aircraft handling that are not beyond the average person, but their development depends, as in other sports, on enthusiasm and initial aptitude. In both it is possible to enjoy oneself at a basic level without too much specialized equipment. In both, ultimate success depends on considerable financial outlay, constant training, and the selection of the right aircraft.

History

The year 1909, the golden year of the aeroplane, saw the first true competitive international meeting for air racing at Reims (France was the cradle of competitive flying). From then until the First World War, it grew in popularity in France, Germany, Italy, the UK, and the USA, meetings being held every weekend at Hendon, the London aerodrome of Grahame-White.

Equipment

Single-engined light aircraft are usually used. The World Championships and most international competitions are only open to piston-engined aircraft, which have to be capable of performing the required manoeuvres. They are usually 180–360hp and may be biplanes or monoplanes.

Rules

In Britain, handicap races over circuits varying from 12 to 15 miles (19-40km), and longer events over straight or triangular courses continue. Over forty aircraft cross the line in the space of two minutes.

While display flying, that is flying aerobatics of a kind calculated to excite a crowd, is still an important part of the sport, competition aerobatics as an art in itself has entirely taken hold of those who fly this kind of discipline. The basic manoeuvres are: the loop; the roll; the stall turn; and the spin. In competitive work, however, performed before critical judges, the ability of a performer is assessed by his skill in performing sequences of preset free manoeuvres, to a rigid scoring system and within a box of air small enough to tax even the most skilled.

The standard international aerobatic contest consists of three or more sequences, each of from 15 to 30 individual manoeuvres, including a first sequence of pre-set figures, a second sequence of figures shown to the pilots only 24 hours before they fly it, and one or more "free" sequences designed by the pilots themselves to demonstrate their mastery over the machine.

• AIR TOURING

This is the most widely practiced form of sporting flying. It is a continuation of the cross-country training given during instruction for the private pilot's licence and it requires no special skills or aptitudes. In its more deliberate form it takes shape as an organized air rally, but in private flying, where a very large part of the appeal is still simply in flying itself, there is a considerable sporting element in the approach to any but the most prosaic of local flights.

History

The advent of the light aeroplane in the late 1920s was the beginning of air touring. As the aeroplane became capable of overcoming natural barriers such as the English Channel and could reduce the bounds of time and distance, so it gradually became a part of the leisure life of the world.

The sporting element has concentrated more on

competitive events, such as races. In America, air touring has become the latest manifestation of the basic urge to travel, the light aircraft having become the successor to the car, extending the week-end trip – devoted to other sports such as sailing, fishing, and hunting – by hundreds of miles.

Scoring

Under the international scoring system devised by Colonel Aresti of Spain, each manoeuvre has a "difficulty coefficient" between 1 and about 35, which is multiplied by a mark, from 0 to 10, given by the judges according to their assessment of the skill with which each manoeuvre is performed. Total scores in an international contest can be only tens apart, from a possible of perhaps 20,000, such is the equality of skill among top aerobatic pilots.

• RECORD-BREAKING

The setting of records for the fastest, furthest, or highest flight has been part of sporting flying since the first aircraft. It is the most exacting side of competitive aviation, seeking the ultimate in aircraft performance. From the beginning, the FAI has set precise and carefully controlled requirements for the timing and measurement of all official records, since the validity and accuracy of the results must be beyond doubt. Because of the publicity value of breaking records, especially the speed record, these regulations are complex and set to limits of, in the case of measurements and apparatus, 0.1% of error.

Rules

In order to beat a previous record, a fresh attempt must exceed the previous figure by a minimum of 1%. As aircraft have grown more complex and diverse, more different classes of record have been introduced by the FAI record may be set up in any of these classes (from balloons to spaceships), in any of the different categories, the best performance, regardless of class, is taken as a world record.

FOOTBALL, AMERICAN (COLLEGE)
Introduction

This is an 11-a-side team game played with an oval leather ball played on a rectangular field, usually of grass, but often on synthetic turf. The object of the game is to outscore the opposing team. The National Collegiate Association (NCAA), which governs the amateur game, was founded in 1910. The governing body for the professional game, the National Football League (NFL), was founded in 1922.

History

Football in the USA dates as far back as 1609, when colonists from England were kicking an air-filled bladder, as they had done in Britain. It was a crude form of football, really ASSOCIATION FOOTBALL in its most elemental form, and two hundred years were to pass before the sport was taken up in the colleges.

In 1867, the Princeton Rules were drawn up. They were for soccer (association football), with teams of 25-a-side. Rutgers formulated rules about the same time and in late 1867 a patent was taken on the first covering for a football – a canvas layer to go over the rubber bladder. On 6 November 1869, Princeton and Rutgers met at New Brunswick, New Jersey, under Rutger rules, a modification of the London Football Association (LFA).

The Yale Football Association was organized on 31 October 1872, with rules based on those of the LFA.

At Harvard, football was revived in 1871 and what was known as the "Boston game" was played. It was largely soccer, but the round rubber ball could be picked up and the holder could run with it if pursued. Harvard was so taken with English RUGBY that it approached Yale and gained acceptance of "concessionary rules" that established the most famous college football rivalry on 13 November 1875.

Venue

The playing field is 53 1/3 yds wide and 120yds long. The end lines are boundaries at each end of the field, the side lines are boundaries on each side of the field, the goal lines are 100yds apart, 10yds from the end lines, the end zones are 10yds deep, bounded by end, side and goal lines. The end and side lines are out-of-bounds; the goal lines are inside the end zones. The field is marked by horizontal lines the entire width of the playing area and 5yds (4.57m) apart from the goal line to goal line, giving it the appearance of a gridiron. The 50-yard line marks the centre of the field.

Rules

A team advances the ball by running and/or passing it by hand forward and/or laterally until it is brought across the opponent's goal line through a series of plays or in one fell swoop. A touchdown results and entitles the scoring team to try for an extra point by a conversion placement kick through the goal posts or, for an extra 2 points, by running the ball or completing a pass across the goal line. The conversion try, in each instance, starts from scrimmage with the ball placed 3yds (2.7m) from the goal line of the defending team.

The field goal is usually attempted when the advance, by running and/or passing, has stopped short of a touchdown but is within the defensive team's territory so that the goal posts are within range for the kicking specialist. The specialist then boots the ball as it is held on the ground for him by a team mate (a placement kick). A safety is registered when a player in possession of the ball is "downed" in his own end zone.

The team winning the toss usually elects to take the kick-off. It is made from the 40-yard line of the kicking team. The receiving team returns the kick-off or, if the ball crosses its goal line, may elect to down it in the end zone, in which event a "touchback" results and the ball is brought out to its 20-yard line. On rare occasions the ball is run back all the way (100yds or more from the end zone) resulting in the touchdown.

At the point where the receiver of the kick-off is downed (short of a touchdown), the ball is put in play by his side. A scrimmage results. The two lines end up facing each each other, separated by the neutral zone, approximately 11in (279mm) – the length of the ball. The forward line of the team in possession of the ball is crouched low, prepared to block out opponents in solid body contact and open the way for the ball-carrier to advance or to protect the passer, almost invariably the quarterback. He is stationed directly behind the centre in the T-formation. The three other backs (the two halfbacks and one fullback) are positioned two or more yards behind him. Alternatively, one or more may move out, or one may move sideways before the play starts. In addition to the centre, the men in the forward line are the two ends, two tackles and two guards. The forward line of the defending team may vary from four to eight players, occasionally more. They are also in a crouching position or may stand more erect, prepared to break through and try to get to the ball-carrier or passer and suppress him by force.

Traditionally the defence consisted of two ends, two tackles, and two guards on the line, with the centre and a back as "line-backers" directly behind the defensive line, two backs, stationed behind and outside the line-backers, and a "safety" slightly deeper between these backs. The supporting backs and line-backers are prepared to tackle the carrier if he gets through the line. They will also knock or intercept the ball if it is thrown, pursuing the oncoming pass-receivers to intervene between them and the ball, but not laying hands on them before the ball is touched. In a kicking situation, usually on the fourth "down" (play), the defence concentrates on breaking through to block the punt. Some players also fall back down the field and block to open the way for their team mate who catches the kick and runs it back.

Before the team in possession of the ball takes its position for the scrimmage, it goes into a huddle some 10yds (9.14m) behind the spot where the ball is stationed. The quarterback will then tell his team mates what offensive play will be tried and will prepare the players for the start of play at the line of scrimmage by calling out a series of numbers, whose sequence indicates when the centre will move the ball to begin the play. The defensive team usually huddles to prepare an alignment against the play the quarterback is calling. Play then starts when the centre on the offensive team, who is bent over the ball with one or both hands on it, "snaps" or hands it back and up to his quarterback.

To maintain possession of the ball, a team must advance it

10yds by running and/or passing in four downs. If it fails to make the 10yds in three plays, it will usually kick (punt) the ball to the opponent on the fourth down. Each time the 10yds (or more) are made, a "first down" is gained, and the team continues to advance the ball until it scores by a touchdown or field goal, or until it gives up possession by kicking, or failure to make a first down, or through loss of the ball on a fumble or interception of a pass.

A game lasts one hour, divided into quarters of 15 minutes each, with a 15-minute interval between the halves and an interval of one minute between the first and second, and the third and fourth periods. Each half starts with a kick-off, and the teams change ends after the first and third periods. In practice, with the interval, "time-outs" taken for injuries, moving the ball by the referee, penalties, and allowing for television commercials, a game usually lasts two and a quarter hours or more. Each team is allowed three time-outs each half; these are commonly used to slow down offensive drives or to gain extra time for the offence in the closing minutes of a game.

In a game of rugged body contact that may become violent because of the speed with which the players move and may strike one another in blocking and tackling, there are many penalties both for the protection of the men and the enforcement of fair play.

Penalties are most frequently awarded for the following offences, and result in the loss of 5 to 15yds for the guilty team: "offside" (a player, offensive or defensive, penetrating the neutral zone of the line of scrimmage before the ball is played); illegal procedure (usually a back in forward motion or an offensive lineman moving before the play begins) – both 5yd penalties; "holding", in which an offensive or defensive player detains an opposing player by using his hands, the penalty being 15yds on offence and 5yds and a loss of down on defence;

"clipping", in which a player blocks an opponent from behind – 15 yards from the point of the foul;

pass interference, wherein a defensive player (although it may also be an attacking player) actively prevents an opponent from catching a pass, the penalty being the possession of the ball at the point of the foul.

Play is supervised by a referee, an umpire, a lineman, a field judge, and usually a back judge.

Equipment

An oval leather ball is inflated to 12.5–13.5 p.s.i. and weighing 14–15oz (396-425g). It is 11–11.5in long. The yardage chain is 10yds long between two 5ft high sticks. The down marker is a 4ft pole with four flip-over signs numbered 1, 2, 3 and 4. It marks the leading point of the ball at the start of every play and the number of the down.

Scoring

Points are scored on touch-downs (6 points), field goals (3 points), and conversion tries (2 or 1). "Safeties" result in the loss of 2 points.

Clothing

A head guard with a face mask and knee pads are the required protective equipment for each player. Thigh and shin guards, knee braces and show cleats, all conforming to regulations, may be worn but are not mandatory. Jerseys of contrasting colours for the players are required; they carry numbers on the front and back.

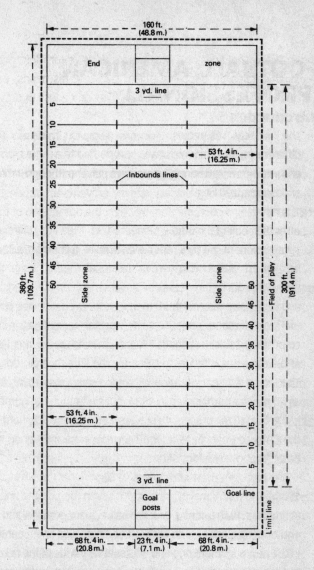

American College Football Field

Broken line surrounding the rectangular filed is the limit line, 5ft (1.5m) outside the playing area. Goal posts are at least 20ft (6.1m) high: the crossbar is 10ft (3.05m) above the ground.

FOOTBALL, AMERICAN (PROFESSIONAL)

Introduction

This closely resembles AMERICAN FOOTBALL (COLLEGE). The differences, most of which have contributed to a more mobile and wide-open (attacking) game between the NFL and NCAA, are summarized here.

History

Although college football pioneered in allowing unlimited substitution of players, specialization of function reached its highest development in professional football from the mid-1950s on. Different sets of players made up the offensive and defensive teams, and there were even special units for kick-offs and punts, called "special teams" or, more colourfully, "suicide squads." These hurtled down the field at full speed as offence, to block for the kick-receiver down. The increased specialization expanded team rosters. As few as 20 players participated in 1934, but since then the number has grown to the present 40 players. Since its development by the Chicago Bears in 1940, the T-formation has remained the basic "pro" offence formation.

The basic offensive and defensive alignments date from the 1950s. The traditional alignment put seven men on the line of scrimmage, with a centre over the ball, a guard, a tackle, and an end lined up close by, one both left and right side of the centre. In the new alignment one end was split very wide of the rest of the line and called a "split end". The other end, who was a more burly athlete, usually weighing about 225lb (102kg), remained close to the line and was used much of the time as a blocker.

He was designated a "tight end". One of the halfbacks was stationed wide of and slightly behind the line, usually on the opposite side from the "split end", and was called a "flanker". The remaining backs, who could line up alongside each other or one behind the other directly behind the quarterback in a "T-formation", were called "running backs".

To counteract this offensive, the defence was realigned. The traditional defensive line of six or seven men, with one or two linebackers, two halfbacks, and safety, changed with the availability of defence specialists.

A general manager will supervise personnel and evaluate scoring information; while the head coach will have assistant coaches for the offensive and defensive lines, offensive backfields and secondaries, often with offensive and defensive "co-ordinators" over them reporting directly to the head coach. Some teams have special coaches for quarterbacks, pass-receivers, "special teams", and/or kickers. Coaching is now a full-time job, with most of the time away from games and practise fields spent viewing films to evaluate the team's players and its future opponents.

The first American professional football game was played in Latrobe, Pennsylvania, on 31 August 1895. In the following years in western Pennsylvania, players like Warner and Heffelfinger emerged. Upper New York state formed teams after 1900 at Buffalo, Syracuse, and some smaller towns. Before 1920, though, the centre of professionally football was Ohio, in towns such as Canton, Massillon, Akron, Columbus, and Dayton. Thorpe first played professionally for the Canton Bulldogs and coached them in 1919-20. At Canton in July 1919 a league, called the American Professional Football

Association, was formed, the precursor to the National Football League (NFL), which began operations in 1922 and has been the dominant force in professional football ever since.

Rules

The dimensions of the field are the same, as are the basic objectives and manoeuvres. The offensive team must make 10yds (9.14m) in four downs or lose the ball. The scoring is the same, except that conversions (extra points) gain only 1 point and are usually accomplished by place-kicks. The conversion try takes place from the 2yd line, and the goal posts are closer together than in college football (18ft 6in–5.6m).

FOOTBALL, ASSOCIATION

Introduction

Football is an 11-a-side ball-and-goal game played at a first-class level throughout the world. It is also known as soccer. The winning team is the one that scores the most goals.

History

Football, as it is now played, began in England in the mid-nineteenth century, but there is evidence that a form of football was played centuries before the birth of Jesus. In China, for example, a game called "Tsu chu" was played 2,500 years ago. "Tsu" may be translated as "to kick the ball with feet" and "chu" as "a ball made of leather, and stuffed". In Sinj on the Dalmation coast of Yugoslavia there is a Roman stele dating from the second century AD that depicts a young man holding a ball made of hexagonal sections, as are many footballs now used throughout Europe.

The Greeks had a word for the game – "episkyros" – and,

although it seems they used a very large ball, they and the Romans when they played "harpastum" and the Chinese, when they played "Tsu chu", agreed that football was a competition between two teams.

In England there are records of football being played in the twelfth century in the fields that surrounded the City of London but it was when the players were forced to use the streets as their pitches that kingly disapproval was first shown by Edward II in 1314, who proclaimed; "Forasmuch as there is a great noise in the city caused by hustling over large balls, from which many evils may arise, which God forbid, we command and forbid, on behalf of the King, on pain of imprisonment, such game to be used in the city in future."

Neither that ban, nor similar edicts of Edward III (1349), Richard II (1389), Henry IV (1401), have stopped the playing of football; but Richard II's act was revealing in that it also decreed that ARCHERY should be encouraged as an alternative. He was less concerned with the noise and "the many evils" than with the disinclination of his subjects to practice archery, a sport with potential military value.

It then developed gradually until the industrial revolution, when the densely populated areas brought people together and football became more popular outside the public schools.

Venue

The football pitch is rectangular and must be 50–100yds wide and 100–130yds long. There is a goal mouth at each end, with a goal area enclosed in the larger penalty area. (See diagram.)

Rules

The fundamental object of the game is for one set of players to force the ball into the goal (a pair of upright posts across which is mounted the crossbar) defended by their opponents.

At the beginning of the match, the choice of ends or the opportunity to kick-off is decided by the toss of a coin, with the team winning the toss having the option of choosing which end of the pitch they wish to defend or to kick-off. The referee gives the signal for the game to start when he is satisfied that every player is in his own half of the field and that every player on the team opposing the player kicking-off is not less than 10yds (9.15m) away from the kicker. Play begins when the ball has travelled the distance of its own circumference and it must not be played for a second time by the player kicking-off until it has been touched or played by another.

Once play has started, no player, except the goalkeepers within their own penalty area, may intentionally handle the ball (unless it is a throw-in). By kicking or heading the ball the players of one team seek to pass it to each other until one of their side is in a position to shoot the ball into the goal of the opposing side with his foot or head.

Opponents can obtain possession of the ball by intercepting passes between members of the attacking side, or by tackling opposing players when they are in possession of the ball. Tackles may be made by the feet, in which case the intention must be to play the ball and force it away from the control of the opponent, or by charging the player fairly, i.e. charging shoulder against shoulder.

Players are penalized if they charge in a violent or dangerous manner, kick or attempt to kick an opponent, trip him, jump at him, charge him from behind, strike, hold, or push him, or handle the ball. The penalty for any one of the above infringements is the award of a direct free kick at the ball by the opposing side from the same place that the offence occurred.

If the place was within the offending player's penalty area, the offence is penalized by a penalty kick. In this case the ball is placed on the penalty spot and all players, except the player taking the kick and the opposing goalkeeper, must be within the field of play but outside the penalty area and at least 10yds (9.15m) from the penalty spot. The opposing goalkeeper must stand on his own goal line, between the goal posts, until the ball is kicked. The player taking the kick must kick the ball forward. He must not play the ball a second time until it has been touched or played by another player. A goal can, of course, be scored from a penalty kick and, similarly, directly from any of the other free kicks awarded against a side for the offences already mentioned.

An indirect free kick is awarded to the non-offending side when the following offences occur: a player charges fairly but when the ball is not within playing distance of the other players concerned; a player intentionally obstructs another player when not playing the ball; or time-wasting tactics are employed. A goal cannot be scored directly from such a kick.

The ball is in play except when it has wholly crossed the goal line or touch line (whether in the ground or in the air) or when the game has been stopped by the referee. The majority of cases when play has been stopped by the referee will involve the award of a free kick and the game is re-started by the taking of a kick. Play is re-started by a throw-in when the ball has crossed the touchlines, or by either a goal kick or a corner kick when it has crossed the goal line.

The corner kick is taken by a member of the attacking side

and the whole of the ball is placed within the quarter circle at the nearest corner flag, which must not be moved, and the ball must be kicked from that position. Players of the defending team must not approach within 10yds (9.15m) of the ball until it is in play, that is to say until it has been kick and travelled the distance of its own circumference. As with free kicks generally, the ball may not be touched or played by another player. A goal may be scored direct from a corner kick.

An attacking side can lose possession of the ball, and thus lose the attacking initiative which then passes to their opponents, by misplacing a pass that is intercepted by an opposing player, by being beaten in a tackle, or by playing the ball last before it passed out of play. Accepting that a shot or header at goal saved by the opposing goalkeeper falls into the same category as that of a misplaced pass, there remains one other circumstance in which an attack breaks down. This is when a player is deemed to be "out of play", as it was first defined in the rules. Later "out of play" became "offside" and the rule of the game affecting this point has ever been among the most discussed of the relatively few laws.

According to the law: "A player is offside if he is nearer his opponents' goal line than the ball at the moment the ball is played unless; (a) he is in his own half of the field of play; (b) there are two of his opponents nearer to their own goal line than he is; (c) the ball last touched an opponent or was last played by him; (d) he receives the ball direct from a goal kick, a corner kick, a throw-in, or when it was dropped by the referee." The penalty for such an infringement is the award of an indirect free kick to the opposing team and there is an addition to the law noting that: "A player in an offside position shall not be penalized unless, in the opinion of the referee, he is interfering with play or with an opponent, or is seeking to gain an advantage by being in an offside position."

When a goal is scored, the game is restarted by a player of the team conceding the goal kicking-off in the same way as when the match itself is started. Similarly, when the game is restarted after half-time, that is to say after 45 minutes of a match (not including extra time added on for injuries etc.) the teams change ends and the kick-off is taken by a player of the opposite team to that which started the game. At the end of the match the team scoring the greater number of goals is the winner; if no goals, or an equal number of goals is scored by both sides; the game is termed a draw. However, in the MLS (Major League Soccer) in the USA if the game is tied after 90 minutes a shot out is held to determine the winner.

Equipment

At its most basic level the only equipment needed for the game is a ball. The goals can, and have, been: chalk marks on a wall; piles of coats; the width of a street; and the respective ends of a town or village square. The dress of the players in such games is optional.

The ball has a circumference of not more than 28in (0.71m) and not less than 27in (0.67m). The goal is 8ft (2.44m) high and 24ft (7.32 m) long.

Scoring

A goal is scored if the ball crosses the goal line under the crossbar and between the posts, provided that the team that scored the goal have not infringed the rules (i.e. offside).

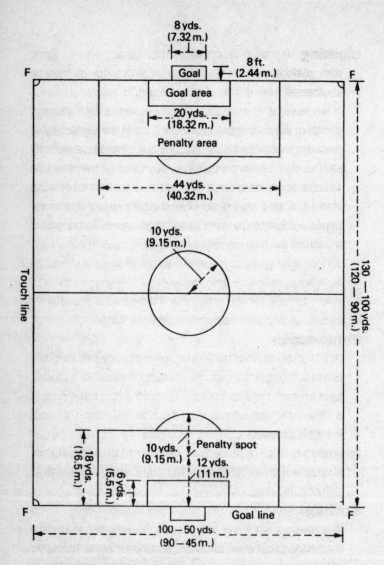

Association Football Pitch

Metric dimensions are those agreed by the International Football Association Board. F) corner flags; optional flagstaff at either end of centre line.

Clothing

The goalkeeper wears different colours to distinguish him/herself from the other players and the referee – often a green jersey. All the other players in the team wear uniform jerseys or shirts, shorts, socks and footwear. Shin pads are also required. The boots may be studded but the studs must be of solid leather, rubber, plastic, or similar material. They must be rounded and have a diameter of not less than 0.5in, or more than 0.75in long. They must not be dangerous to other players. Gloves are frequently worn by the goalkeepers and numbers are usually worn on the back of the shirt.

FOOTBALL, AUSTRALIAN RULES

Introduction

This is a fast-moving game with few rules apart from those aimed at protecting the player. High marking and long kicking (to advance the ball up field) are the main features of the sport, which draws crowds claimed by the Australian National Football Council (AFC) to be the largest in the world *per capita*.

History

Australian football officially dates back to 1858, when H. C. A. Harrison and his cousin T. W. Wills decided to devise a purely Australian game. About this time, Irish garrison troops played their Gaelic football (see FOOTBALL, GAELIC), and the presence of the English game of RUGBY created some confusion. The CRICKET influence in the game probably accounts for the oval shape of the Australian Rules football field. In its early days, the game was played on cricket grounds and controlled by cricket clubs.

The first club to be formed was the Melbourne Football Club, the oldest club in Australia, which celebrated its centenary in 1958. The club was sponsored by the Melbourne Cricket Club as a means of keeping its members during the winter months.

Venue

The oval must have a minimum width of 120yds (110m) and a maximum of 170yds (155m). The minimum length is 150yds (135m) and the maximum 200yds (185m). The ideal playing area is 165m in length and 135m in width.

Rules

A team consists of 18 players with two reserves. A game comprises four quarters of 25 minutes each plus "time on" for delays in play. The teams change ends at each quarter, and there is a 15-minute break at half time and a five-minute break at three-quarter time, when the coaches are allowed to address their team on the field.

A team is made up of three full-forwards, three half-forwards, three centres, three half-backs, and three players known as the "ruck". The ruck consists of two followers and a rover, who moves with the flow of the play to all parts of the ground. The reserves are used to replace injured players at any time, but once a player leaves the ground he is not permitted to return. Play is not held up when a player is injured, and the replacement cannot enter the playing area until the injured player has left it.

The main feature of the game is the long kicking which takes place from player to player. Their chief aim is to kick to a team mate, who though guarded by an opposing player, endeavours to give a "lead out" by breaking away from the opposing player and taking a "mark", which entitles him to a free kick. From the mark, he endeavours to dispose of the ball to another player of the same team (nearer the goal) who is in a position to pass on to the forward line. Goals are often kicked from 60 to 70yds (55–64m). There is no offside rule in the game, nor is there the knock-on rule which applies in rugby. This helps the game flow freely.

At the start of a match the two captains toss a coin for the choice of ends. The field umpire bounces the ball in the centre circle, which is 10ft (3.048m) in diameter. It is here that the rucks, who are usually well over 6ft (1.83m) in height, go for the "hit-out", which sends the ball into play with the rovers, who vie with each other to gain possession of the ball and move it up field towards the opposition's goal. The ball is bounced in the centre circle each time a goal is scored, the ball having been returned by the boundary umpires, who sprint to the centre to maintain the fast pace of the game.

When a ball goes out of bounds but is not kicked out on the full, the boundary umpire stands on the boundary line facing away from the arena and throws the ball high into the air over his head 10 to 15yds (9.1–13.72m) into the arena. The rucks usually go for these throw-ins, but any player can go for a hit-out if the rucks are not up with the play.

A player may run with the ball providing that he bounces it at least every 10yds (9.14m). He may kick the ball off the ground or hand-pass to a member of his team. In hand-passing, the ball must be held in one hand and hit with the clenched fist of the other hand. Throwing is not permitted, and is punished by a penalty free kick to the nearest opposition player.

A "mark" is allowed when a player catches a ball which has been kicked more than 10yds by another player. From the time it is kicked until it is marked, it must not touch the ground or be touched by another player.

Free kicks are given to the opposing side for: (a) throwing the ball; (b) grasping an opponent around the neck, shoulder, or legs; (c) retaining the ball when firmly held by an opponent (a player must hand-pass or kick the ball immediately he is firmly held by an opponent); (e) lying on or over the ball; (f) pushing a player in the back or in the face; (g) tripping (or attempting to trip) or striking (or attempting to strike) an opponent; (h) charging an opponent by rushing at him or pushing him when he is not in possession of the ball; (i) holding or tackling a player who is not in possession of the ball; (j) wilfully wasting time, or wilfully kicking or forcing the ball out of bounds; (k) running with the ball more than 10 yards without bouncing it. In the case of (c) and (d), the player shall not be penalized if, when in the act of kicking or hand-balling, he is swung off balance and his boot or hand does not connect with the ball. The field umpire will give the order to play on.

Play also continues when a player is bumped and the ball falls from his hands; when his hands are pinned to his sides, causing him to drop the ball; when he is knocked on the arm or elbow, causing him to drop the ball. When the ball is held to his body by another player the umpire takes possession of it and bounces it up; if the ground is too muddy he throws it into the air.

A player may not be sent off the field for foul play. However, any of the five umpires on the field may report a player, first having notified him that he is being reported, and taking his number. A report of the offence must be handed to the club officials immediately after the match and the player is then summoned to a tribunal of independent administrators who deal with the matter accordingly. Evidence is given by the umpires and the players concerned, and the tribunal, which may be presided over by a stipendiary magistrate, dismisses the charge or suspends the player for a number of matches.

A player may not be sent off the field for foul play. However, any of the five umpires on the field may report a player, first having notified him that he is being reported and taken his number. A report of the offence must be handed to the club officials immediately after the match, and the player is then summoned to a tribunal of independent administrators who deal with the matter accordingly. Evidence is given by the umpires and the players concerned, and the tribunal, which may be presided over by a stipendiary magistrate, dismisses the charge or suspends the player for a number of matches.

A player is allowed to "check", or block, an opponent from tackling a team mate who is possession of the ball, providing that the checking – which is also referred to as "shepherding" – is done without any infringement of the rules, and that the ball is not more than 5yds (4.57m) away. Shepherding is not, however, permitted at the centre bounce, or at the boundary throw-in. A player can tackle an opponent by "meeting" him with his hip or his shoulder when he is in possession of the ball, and pushing him on the side, or holding him around the waist to retard his progress.

When a behind is scored, the ball is not returned to the centre of the field, but is kicked, by the full-back, or a player from the opposing team, out of the goal square, a 10yd (9m) rectangle immediately in front of the goal posts in the playing area. A ball is also out of bounds if a player kicking for goal fails to sent the ball between either the goal or behind the posts. If it is kicked out on the full a free kick is awarded to the nearest opponent at the spot where the ball crossed the boundary line.

When a player takes a mark, and when taking his kick, his opposite number may attempt to baulk him by jumping in front of him, calling out, or waving his arms. However, if he moves over the mark from which the free kick has been awarded, he can be penalized 15yds (13.72m) and the player taking the free kick can advance that distance nearer the goal. Place-kicking is allowed in Australian Rules football but it is seldom employed as it is regarded as time-wasting.

Equipment

The ball is oval in shape and measures 720–730mm by 545–555mm when firmly inflated. It must weigh 454–82g Before a match the rival captains must approve the quality of the ball, which is shown to them by the field umpire.

Scoring

The scoring consists of "goals" and "behinds". A goal is scored when the half passes through the two centre goal-posts, which are 7yds (6.40m) apart, and 6 points are recorded. A behind is scored when the ball passes outside the centre posts but between a centre post and a behind post (which is situated 7yds to the side of each centre post). When this occurs a score of 1 point is recorded. The ball must be kicked clearly through the centre posts to register the 6 points. If it is touched by any player on its way through the posts, only 1 point is recorded. If the ball hits the goal post, again 1 point only is scored.

Clothing

Players wear jerseys, shorts, socks and studded boots.

FOOTBALL, GAELIC

Introduction

Gaelic football is a 15-a-side ball-and-goal game which, superficially, looks like a combination of ASSOCIATION FOOTBALL and RUGBY. It is played almost exclusively in Ireland, although British and American teams compete in the All-Ireland championships.

History

Despite claims that Gaelic football is as old as HURLING, there is no distinctive reference to the game in the Irish sagas. Indeed, not until 1527 does the first direct mention of football in Ireland occur, when the *Statutes of Galway*, forbade hurling and all other ball games that might threaten the practice of ARCHERY, "except alone football with the grate ball".

Football in Ireland subsequently failed to receive any literary recognition again for more than a century and a half. Then the Gaelic poet MacCurta described a game he had seen in his youth (c. 1660) on the banks of the river Boyne. MacCurta's poem makes clear that the snatching and carrying of the ball were features of the pastime, while wrestling between players was permitted. Wrestling was still a noteworthy part of the game when the English traveller, Dunton, saw football played "according to the Irish style" in north Co. Dublin towards the end of the seventeenth century. Dublin itself is still a stronghold of the game.

Venue

The pitch is usually 150yds (137m) long and 90yds (82m) wide with goal posts at each end 16ft (4.88m) high and 21ft (6.40m) apart, with a crossbar 8ft (2.44m) from the ground.

Rules

A side consists of three full-forwards, three half-forwards, two mid-fields, three half-backs, three full-backs and a goalkeeper. Some important competitions are played 13-a-side, one full-forward and one full-back being omitted. The players are positioned as for hurling, the kindred Irish stick-and-ball game.

If the defending side puts the ball over its own end line, the attackers are awarded a free kick, from a line 50yds (45.72m) out, at a point opposite where the ball crossed the end line. If the ball is driven over the side lines, a free kick is given against the side responsible at the place where the ball crossed the line.

A goal area, based on the end line, 15yds (13.72 m) by 5yds (4.57m) extends in front of the goal posts. If a defender fouls inside this area (known as the "parallelogram" or the "square") a penalty kick is awarded to the opposition from a spot 14yds (12.80m) out and directly in front of the goal posts. All other players, except the kicker and the goalkeeper, must remain outside the 21yd (19.20m) line until the kick is taken. The goalkeeper is allowed to move along his goal line to anticipate the kick, but may not advance until the ball is kicked. When the ball is driven side of the goal posts and over the end line by the attacking side, it is kicked out from the 21yd line.

The rules of Gaelic, as distinct from all other European football codes, include a no off-side rule and allow the players to play the ball both on and off the ground with foot or hand. A player is not, however, permitted to pick the ball directly from the ground with the hand, but can lift it or chip it from the ground into the hand with the foot. This constitutes one of the basic skills of the game. The ball may be caught when in flight or on the bounce and may be passed or punched with the closed fist. Throwing is not permitted. A player in possession of the ball may carry it for four paces, but must then either "hop" (bounce) it – only one hop is permitted if the ball has been caught – or kick or fist it away.

However, the player may "carry" the ball on a solo run in two different ways. He may, hopping the ball every three steps, run in possession as long as he wishes, provided the ball has not been caught. He may also run as he wishes providing he bounces the ball from toe to hand every four steps.

Pulling, pushing, tripping, or elbowing an opponent is a foul, and is punished by a free kick to the opposing side. A rugby-style tackle is similarly penalized, as is a frontal charge or a charge in the back. A fair and square shoulder charge is permitted, however, and is much appreciated by spectators. Any player who kicks or strikes the referee or other officials, is sent from the field and automatically suspended for a period of between one month and two years, depending on the gravity of his offence.

Games are controlled by a referee, who has sole charge of the play, assisted by four goal umpires, two at each end, and a touch judge on each side line. The referee starts the game by throwing in the ball between the mid-field players at the beginning of each half. He is also the sole adjudicator on playing time.

A regular Gaelic football matches lasts between 30 and 60 minutes each half.

Equipment

The ball may weigh between 13 and 15oz (368–425g) and measures 27 to 29in (685–736mm) in circumference. It contains an inflated bladder of rubber, and its cover is of leather, usually horsehide, which is now often plastic-coated,

Scoring

To score a goal, equal to 3 points, the ball must be kicked or punched between the posts, over the crossbar.

FOOTBALL, HARROW

Introduction

Harrow football is an 11-a-side game evolved and played exclusively at Harrow school. The side that scores most bases wins.

History

The game evolved as a form of football that could be played in extremely muddy conditions with few or many players on each side. From the mid-nineteenth century it was played on the present FOOTBALL fields, the rules gradually becoming fixed, with the number of players on each side usually 11. Since 1927, with the introduction of Rugby football in the winter term, Harrow football is been played in the Easter term only.

Though the first XI plays several matches against old Harrovians and one against the masters, the main interest of the season lies in the House matches. There are a few Sixth Form games, for the selection and training of the school team, which are taken by the master-in-charge, but otherwise all arrangements are on a House basis and are entirely organized by boys.

Venue

Harrow Football is played on an ordinary RUGBY pitch, marked only with a half-way line, and with a pair of goal posts 6yds (5.5m) apart at each end.

Rules

There is no crossbar between the posts, and it does not matter how high the ball is when it passes between them. If it is kicked higher than the top of the posts the umpires have to decide whether or not it has passed between their line continued straight up. If it has, a base is scored. A shot that goes straight over the goal post – a "poler" – does not count as a base.

The two features of the game that particularly contribute to its unique character are offside rule and "yards". If a player is in front of the ball when one of his own sides touches it he is offside (except at a throw-in from touch, or when the ball has been put over the base line by an attacker and is being punted back into play by the defending side – a "base-kick"). It is thus impossible to pass the ball forward, and to work the ball up the field a player must dribble it along, preferably with a few of his own side in close support, ready to continue the movement if he is tackled or overruns the ball.

Whenever the ball is kicked in the air, except at a base-kick, any player who is onside may catch it and shout "Yards". The game then stops and he is entitled to a free punt, which will be aimed at the opponents' base if it is within range. The usual method of scoring is to take "yards". This is achieved either from one of the player's own side or by punting the ball through, following a careless kick in the air by an opponent. A base may also be scored by kicking the ball straight off the ground, but this is not easy.

The taking of yards is not limited to potential scoring situations, and a competent player will take yards whenever he can in any part of the field. Even if he is out of range of the base, he can make much ground by punting the ball as far as possible up the field, for preference placing his kick so that the opponents cannot catch it and punt it straight back again. In difficult situations a player near his own base may "known down yards" – i.e. prevent an opponent taking yards: otherwise handling is not allowed.

During play little time is lost for stoppages, for the ball is never intentionally kicked into touch. If it does go out, the side that put it there may easily lose 20 or 30yds from the resulting throw-in, for the ball may be hurled – usually one-handed – in any direction from the place where it went out, and the offside rule does not apply. From a base-kick, up to half the length of the field may be lost, for the ball is punted up the field from the base line, and again the offside rule does not apply. A corner can be conceded (by the defender kicking it out behind his own base line) with impunity, since the attackers have to throw the ball in a direction parallel to the touch line and from the point at which it went out. However, to concede a corner is at best a last-ditch defensive measure, and a more skilful player will attempt rather to bounce the ball out off an opponent, thus securing a base-kick or throw for his own-side.

On wet ground the ball becomes so heavy that it is difficult to kick it 20yds, but in dry conditions a good kicker may well be able to score from the half-way line. The nature of the game thus changes radically with the weather – the heavy slog in the mud of a wet January becomes, on the hard ground of a dry March, a hectic chase after a ball that balloons wildly in the air, is carried by every gust of wind, and is difficult to control.

Most players find that the ball is too massive to be headed, and use their shoulders to stop it in the air. This is called "fouling" the ball, so the cry "Well fouled" is used, without irony.

The 11 players consist of four centres, four wings (inside and outside on the left, inside and outside on the right). The descriptions "top" and "bottom" are sometimes used instead of "left" and "right", because the field is usually not quite level and it is customary for the players to stay on the same side of it throughout the game.

The centres follow the ball wherever it goes and often form a loose scrum round it and, since no heeling is allowed, the ball has to be worked forward. The wings work in pairs and their aim is to dribble the ball rapidly up the field and give "yards". The inside wings will be close to any scrum and almost work in with the centres, while the outside wings are a few feet in support. The backs' aim is to kick the ball farther up the field than their opponents can kick it back again, which can best be achieved by placing a kick where it cannot be caught, and then taking "yards" off the opponents' return.

There is thus much scope for skilful positioning. The centre back is always close behind play, ready to take yards from his own side or stop a breakthrough by the opposition, and the wing back on whose side of the field play is will also be well up. The other wing back stays just far enough behind to ensure that the ball cannot be kicked over his head, since there is no goalkeeper and he is the last line of defence; but when the ball crosses to his side of the field he must be ready to move up rapidly.

There are virtually no penalties and so, in the words of the *Obiter Dicta*, "rules have to be kept for the sake of conscience, and the benefit of the doubt is habitually given to the opposition. If you inadvertently break a rule, stand away at once." If an infringement occurs from which the offending side gains no advantage, the game is allowed to continue. If there is an advantage to the offending side, the umpire stops the game and re-starts it with a "bounce" – throwing the ball a foot or two in the air, with several players from each side standing as near as they wish. They may not touch the ball until it bounces, but as soon as it does the game continues.

The only circumstances in which the umpire may take action which penalizes the offending side are when there is an infringement by the attackers near the base. Whether or not there is an advantage to the offending side, he stops the game and awards a base-kick to the defending side (the phrase "near the base" works perfectly well without precise definition – there is no need for a marked penalty area). A player in a House match can be sent off if he wilfully breaks the rules, but though players have to be reminded of the provision, the threat has seldom if ever had to be carried out.

The players can normally run the game very well by themselves, but in matches it is necessary to have an impartial observer who can determine matters of fact about which there may be a difference of opinion. It is possible for one umpire to control a game with the aid of two touch judges – or even without, if the players are warned that they will have to settle for themselves whether the ball is out or not – but it is better to have two umpires and no touch judges. In this case the umpires take one side of the field each and act as their own touch judges. Their decision is final on matters of fact, but they are at liberty to refer any question of law to the committee of the Philathletic Club if they feel unable to decide it at the time. The umpires do not have a whistle, but they carry a stick (for pointing).

Equipment

It is played with a large ball shaped like a flattened sphere, 10in (25.cm) in diameter in one direction, 11in (27.94 cm) in the other.

FOOTBALL, WINCHESTER COLLEGE

Introduction

Winchester College Football is a 15-a-side or 6-a-side code of football with a unique terminology. It is played exclusively at Winchester College, with a round ball as in ASSOCIATION FOOTBALL. In some other respects it resembles RUGBY.

History

Winchester College football was shaped in isolation by its curious cradle. Until 1790 the school's only playground was a mile away, within the circle of the ancient British camp which crowns St. Catherine's Hill. A Latin poem (c. 2650) mentions football among the games played on "Hills". The Winchester Table of the Laws (c. 1560) refers to going to "Hills" and by this date football was a national pastime. The game played there was the simplest possible – four corner posts, the whole end as goal, and two lines of juniors to keep the ball in play. The rough ground would have produced long kicks rather than dribbling.

Venue

The ground is 80yds long by 27yds wide (73.15 x 24.69m), bounded on the long sides by netting 8ft (2.44m) high (called "canvas"). Parallel to the yard inside the netting is a rope 3ft (91cm) high, supported by nine posts set at 10yd (9.14m) intervals. Between the posts at either end – a distance of

25yds (22.86m) – is a shallow-trenched goal line (though there is no goal in terms of posts) called "worms".

The remaining 2yds of width, one on either side of the goal-line, between the netting and the last post, are called "under-ropes".

Rules

In the 15-a-side game, a team is composed of eight "ups", four "hotwatchers", and three "behinds" or "kicks". In the six-a-side game there are three ups, a hotwatcher, and two kicks. The ups correspond more or less to forwards in rugby, and form the "hot" (or scrum). They pack 3-2-3 or 3-4-1, including one "over-the-ball" in the front row whose duties are similar to those of the hooker in rugby. One "up" may be detached to act as an extra hotwatcher. The hotwatchers act at times like three-quarters and at others like half-backs in rugby, and the kicks discharge the duties of full-backs and three-quarters in rugby.

A game lasts an hour and each half opens with a set hot at the centre of the ground. The fundamental aim of each side is to kick the ball over their opponents' goal line. Progress is made by kicking or scrummaging (known as "hotting"). In the hot, dribbling is allowed, but hard kicking is illegal. The direct opposite is true of open play.

When the ball has last been touched by an opponent it may be kicked to any height (a "flyer"). If a player kicks a ball hard he may follow up and play it again, but such a kick may not rise about shoulder height (an "own-side" kick). Whenever a ball is played, however, any member of his own side who is nearer the opponents' goal line – a back pass – may make an ownside kick. Whenever a ball is played, however, any member of the same side nearer to the opponents' goal line is offside and can take no immediate part in the play without incurring a penalty.

When the ball is kicked out of "ropes" or a kick is deflected by the rope, and if it is caught, only an ownside kick is allowed. Any player may catch a ball kicked by, or bouncing off an opponent but he must then "bust" (punt) it within three strides, unless opponents try to collar him. In this case he may run with the ball until he is brought down or the opposing side stops attempting to bring him down.

The kicks may use their hands to stop the ball. They must then put it down and take an ownside kick. If a player kicks the ball gently, he may "back it up", i.e. stand over it so as to impede an opponent but he must not play it (a dribble).

A player may not go into the space between the rope and the netting ("ropes"), although he may kick at the ball under the rope, kick it into the netting, in which case the rebound is in play.

A goal is scored when the ball passes over "worms" (the goal line) untouched by the defence, at any height from a flyer, but under shoulder height from an ownside kick. Such a goal scores 3 points. If the ball passes over the base line between the last post and "canvas", or over "worms", (1) after being last touched by a defender, or (2) from "ropes", this constitutes a "behind" and the attackers score 1 point. Thereupon, the whole of both sides, except the three players attacking kicks, retire behind "worms". The ball is kicked out from the centre of "worms" by one of the defence and if the attacking side returns it by the first kick, untouched by a defender, over "worms", it scores 2 more points.

The hot differs from a rugby scrum in that the ball is placed between the two over-the-balls. It may not be played until either one side has driven the other back sufficiently for the front row to dribble the ball forward or the ball has been allowed to pass the front row to bring the hot to an end. At this point, the over-the-ball passes it out sideways between the front and second row to the hotwatcher who is waiting at the side of the hot.

A team is penalized for infringement of the rules or kicking the ball out of play ("over canvas") by a hot. This is taken midway between "canvases" and one "post" (i.e. 10yds) towards the goal defended by the penalized side. This means that hots are frequent, and there is little kicking for touch as in rugby. The hot may be used defensibly by dribbling the ball forward, or offensively by passing out to the hotwatcher. The side which controls the hot can open up the play or close it down according to the state of the game and the wind.

Tactically, the side in defence seeks to carry the ball forward by the slow process of driving it along "ropes", whence no goal can be scored. The side in attack seeks to carry it out in a quick rush diagonally forward from under "ropes".

FUTEVOLEI
Introduction
Futevolei, pronounced "foodji-volay", is BEACH VOLLEYBALL played with FOOTBALL rules. You can only use your feet, chest and head to knock the ball over the net.

History
Futevolei was born in Rio in the 1960s and, though it is now played all over Brazil, Rio's beaches are still the place to play. Over the last decade it has grown in popularity and in 1997 the Rio Futevolei Federation was founded.

Venue

The game is played in sandy areas, usually along the beach.

Rules

The game is normally played two vs. two and the rules change only slightly for mixed doubles, in which men can only serve to men because of their stronger kick.

Serving involves a beach ritual similar to a RUGBY player kicking up a grass bound from which to attempt a penalty – putting the ball (which is lighter and softer than a regular football) on a small sandy knoll and then kicking it over the net.

The minimum ball control skills that are needed are heading practise with a high net in the middle and "keepy-uppies". A player needs to be comfortable doing a bicycle kick, placing a ball to an exact spot on the other side, as well as chesting a shot from mid-air to a team-mate two metres away. There is no option to smash so the rallies last longer than volleyball.

Scoring

The scoring is just like volleyball and the game is over at either 12 or 15 points.

Clothing

See Beach Volleyball

GLIDING

Introduction

This is the sport of flying without the use of a motor, by utilizing currents of rising air. Skill is recognised in the awarding of individual proficiency badges, by the breaking of international or national records, and in championships.

History

Hill, or slope, soaring was discovered in 1921, just in time to prevent the new sport from dying because of the tedium of bringing the aircraft back to the top of the mountain after every flight. The first international meeting was held at Iford, Sussex, in 1922, arranged by the *Daily Mail*.

Soaring by using lift under clouds was discovered in 1926 by Kegel and Nehring, and exploited by Kronfeld. Thermal soaring was developed largely by Hirth, the first pure thermal flights being made in America. During the 1930s a great deal of soaring was done in Germany, some in Poland, France, the USA and Britain

Venue

Soaring is the art, or science, of finding and using up-currents, the three main sources of lift being thermals, slope lift, and wave lift. Most cross-country soaring is carried out by using thermals, flights of over 600 miles (1,000km) being made in this way. Thermals are separate rising bubbles of air found in the bottom few thousand feet of the atmosphere, and are caused by the irregular heating of the ground by the sun. Towns, sunny valleys, and dry dusty areas produce better thermals than damp ground or cool, windswept places.

To be of use to a glider, thermals need to be not less than 200yds (180m), preferably up to 800yds (725m), across, and rising at not less than 150ft per min (0.75m/sec). In temperate regions, such as northern Europe, thermals rarely rise higher than 7,000ft (2,300m), but in hotter, continental areas such as Texas or Australia, they may go up to 15,000ft (4,600m), or higher. If the air is moist, condensation take place in the rising, expanding and cooling thermals and a cumulus cloud forms near the top. The small scattered cumulus cloud forms near the top. The small scattered cumulus clouds of a summer day indicate the locations of thermals. The lift continues up into the cloud. If the air is very unstable, the cloud may grow into a thunderhead in which the glider may climb to a height of 33,00ft (10,000m) or more, provided that that pilot is skilled and the glider is equipped with cloud flying instruments and oxygen.

If a glider is properly used in strong thermal conditions, cross-country speeds averaging over 90mph (145km/h) can be made. To achieve this, the glider has to be flown at speeds of over 120mph (193km/h) between thermals and then slowed to about 50mph (80km/h) on entering the next upcurrent. For practical purposes thermals develop only in daytime and are too weak to be of use in winter, other than in the tropics.

Rules

When a glider is flown into rising air it is circled, or otherwise manoeuvred, to stay within the up-current, and is borne upwards. At the top of the lift, the glider is flown, usually fast, in the desired direction, gliding downwards again until another up-current is located. When no further lift can be found, the glider has to be landed.

"Slope soaring" is possible above the windward faces of hills more than 100ft (30m) high, and with a wind speed of more than 15mph (25 km/h). As long as the wind continues to blow up over the hill the glider will stay up if it is flown in the region of this lift. Lift does not normally extend more than 1,000ft (330m) above the crest, and is better over a long ridge than a round hill.

"Wave soaring" is also carried out in lift caused by hills and mountains, but to the lee, or downwind, of them. When air has been forced up over high ground it flows downward again on the lee side and then, under certain conditions, rebounds as a wave or series of waves. The existence of waves may be deduced by the appearance of lenticulars, hard-edged lens-shaped clouds which frequently develop at the crest of each wave and remain stationary in relation to the ground with the wind blowing through them. At a lower level, and near the lee face of the mountains, there may be turbulent reverse flow.

International and national records can be claimed for the following types of flight, provided that the required minimum margin over the previous record has been exceeded:

"Pure distance"– a distance flight in any direction measured as a great circle course between the starting point and the landing place.

"Distance"– to a declared point. A distance flight ending at a point declared before departure.

"Distance to a turn point and back to the starting place"– Evidence of reaching the turn point may be given photographically; the turn point must be pre-declared.

"Gain of height"– the height climbed after release.

"Absolute altitude"– height reached above sea level.

"Speed over a triangular course"– the glider is timed over start and finish lines by an official observer, and the pilot produces evidence that they reached the pre-declared turn points. A triangular course must not have any leg less than 28% of the total distance.

Equipment

Most gliders are monoplanes with long slender wings which are able to make best use of the air currents. The glider, a heavier-than-air machine without an engine, is launched into the air by aerotow, winch, or car-tow, and flies by using gravity, all the time gliding downwards through the air. It is designed to glide at a flat angle – for a high-performance competition glider about 1:48. It will thus travel 48 miles for every 1 mile, or 5,280ft (1,609m), loss of height. The glider is characterised by a large span wing of narrow width, or chord. The ratio of span to chord is termed aspect ratio; for training gliders this is about 15 to 20 and for competition gliders between 20 and 30. Thus a wing span of 20m would have a mean, or average, chord of 1m. The weight of a single-seater glider is 400 to 500lb (180-225kg), and a two-seater about 600 to 800lb (270-260kg), although some big competition single-seaters are above this weight. The wing-loading of a glider is the wing area divided by the combined weight of glider and pilot; for training gliders it is about 4lb (1.814kg) per sq ft and for competition gliders between 5 and 8lb (2.268–3.629kg) per sq ft. The wing span of a training glider is usually about 50 to 55ft (15-17m).

Gliders are made of wood with a fabric covering, or metal – usually aluminium – or fibreglass. Fibreglass gliders are invariably white in colour to prevent their getting too hot in the sun.

Clothing

Since sunshine is needed to provide good soaring weather and the pilot sits in a perspex bubble, suitable clothing for soaring includes: light-coloured, long-sleeved shirt; trousers; sun hat; dark glasses; and boots if the glider may have to be landed in rough country. When training, particularly in winter, windproof clothing and waterproof shoes are essential. Parachutes are also usually worn.

GOLF

Introduction

Golf is a club-and-ball game played throughout the world and to a high level of performance by at least a few players in almost every country. It has been frequently observed that golf is two games in one. It is distinguished from other cross-country club-and-ball games of continental European origin by the fact that, having propelled their ball considerable distances, using as much power as they can command, the golfer must then putt it into a small hole on a prepared surface – a matter of extreme delicacy and finesse. The object of the player is to play the ball from their starting point – the tee – to the hole in as few strokes as possible.

History

The Roman game of "paganica" was played with a bent stick and a leather-covered ball stuffed with feathers. Some golf historians have accepted that since the technique and practice of making balls in this way had such a long and respectable ancestry, it followed that the first golf balls were made in this way; but that assumption is open to some doubt.

No completely convincing evidence has been advanced to prove the origins of golf. Historians have sought to trace the ancestry of the game through other cross-country pursuits such as the Irish SHINTY, or hurly, the Belgian "chole", Dutch "kolven", and French "jeu de mail". Medieval illustrations showing players wielding clubs in more or less golfing postures can be put forward as evidence and, superficially at least, the language of golf frequently appears to have a continental derivation. For example, there are the Dutch words "kolf" (club), "stuit mij" ("it stops me"), and "tuitje" (a pile of earth on which chole players placed the ball to drive off), which suggest "golf", and "stymie", and "tee".

Whether these linguistic signposts prove anything beyond the common root of their English counterparts is open to serious doubt. If the game is defined loosely as hitting a ball across country with a stick or club then it is seen to have some inherited characteristics of the games of continental Europe. If, on the other hand, the essence of golf is the manoeuvring of a ball as a preliminary to putting it into a small hole, then the claim that golf was a pure child of Scotland is strengthened. Assuming that golf sprang unprompted from Scottish ingenuity, conjecture gives way to fact when it comes to establishing its date of birth. In 1424 an Act of James I's parliament forbade the playing of football on the grounds that it interfered with ARCHERY practise. Thirty-three years later a similar Act, under James II, added golf to football as forbidden pastimes. Clearly then, between these two dates golf grew to such proportions as to become a serious diversion from the stern necessity of maintaining a trained citizen army.

Venue

A golf course, usually between 5,000 and 7,000yds (4,572–6,2400m) in length, is divided into 18 separate holes, each one of which may be anything from 100 to 600yds or more long. A hole will normally comprise the following features: a flat teeing ground from which the player makes their initial stroke, or drive in the case of long holes; a fairway of mown grass 30 to 100yds (27–90m) wide extending to the green; the green itself, the prepared putting surface into which the hole of 4.25in (108mm) diameter is sunk and marked by a flag. In addition, each hole will be embellished by hazards such as sand-filled bunkers, ponds, streams, drainage ditches, trees and shrubs, and other natural features sited to impede and penalize an inaccurate shot.

Rules

Golf is played in two main forms. In "stroke play" the golfer counts his/her total number of strokes for the round, or rounds, and the player with the lowest total wins. This is the form of golf used in all the major championships and most professional tournaments: stroke play over 72 holes, or four rounds.

In "match play", the game is contested hole by hole between sides of one or two players, the winner being the side which wins more holes (i.e. takes fewer strokes at each) than there are holes left to play. The widest possible margin or victory in an 18-hole match is therefore "10 and 8", that is, winning the first 10 holes and having only 8 holes remaining.

In knock-out competition, in which an outright winner must emerge to go through to the next round, players tied, "all square" after 18 holes, play extra holes, the first side to win a hole being the winners. Match play is virtually obsolete in the USA where the preference at all levels of the game is for stroke play. Elsewhere, match play predominates among club golfers and stroke play is reserved for organized competitions.

The basic conception of the game is simple – that the ball be played, as it lies, in successive strokes from the teeing ground into the hole, the ball furthest from the hole always to be played first. The complexities in the code arise from the need to provide for all occurrences (such as lost ball, ball out of bounds, ball lying in water, and interference from agencies over which the golfer has no control) which may frustrate straightforward

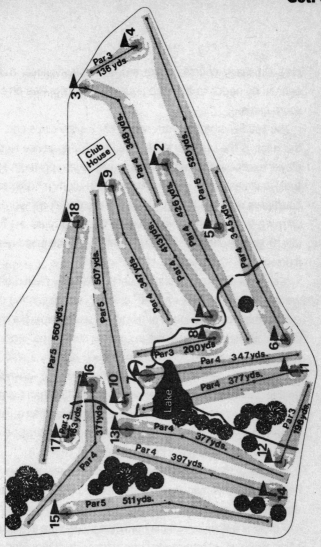

Golf Course

Diagram, from an aerial view of the Portland, Oregon, Golf Club, shows a typical 18-hole course. Par strokes and yardage are shown for each hole. Total yardage for 9 holes: 3,082yds (par 35); for 18 holes: 6,541yds (par 72).

play. On many courses there are also specific local rules, defined by notice in the club house and usually also on the score-cards.

The caddie, or golfer's attendant, carries the clubs and, by the rules, is the only person entitled to proffer advice to the player except in the case of foursomes where partners and their caddies may confer. Among the conventions and courtesies of golf is the cry of "Fore!", the traditional word of warning. When a player, in making a stroke, displaces a turf (divot), golfing etiquette demands that he replace it and tread it down.

It is usual for the first shot at each hole to be played off a wooden or plastic tee-peg ("tee" or "peg") which lifts the ball clear of the teeing ground. "Par" is still the score in which a first-class player should play a hole in summer conditions. "Bogey" is the score that should be taken at each hole by a scratch golfer, i.e. a player with a handicap of below 0. In American golfing parlance it is a score of one stroke higher than the par for the hole. A "birdie" is a score of one shot fewer than the par for the hole, an "eagle" two strokes less, and an "albatross" (in America a "double-eagle") three strokes less.

A player or team is said to be "dormy" when leading in an 18-hole match by as many holes as are left to play. Three up and three to play would thus make the leader dormy.

If there is a tie in stroke play, or when players are all square after 18 holes in match play, the winner is determined by "sudden death", that is to say the players start again at the first hole (unless regulations have been formulated specifying a different order of play) and the first one to win a hole is the winner.

Many terms are used to describe and define the many different vagaries of stroke. To "press" is to try to hit the ball too hard, usually with a resultant mis-hit. To "shank", or "socket", is to hit the ball on that part of the club where the club-head is joined to the neck: as a result the ball flies off at an angle. To "sclaff" is the old-fashioned term for a mis-hit stroke in which the club-head scrapes the ground before coming into contact with the ball.

A "push" is a shot which goes in a straight line to the right of the intended direction. A "slice" is a stroke in which clockwise spin is imparted to the ball, usually inadvertently, causing it to veer to the right. Slice is synonymous with "cut", both words being used as nouns and verbs. When clockwise spin is deliberately applied to curve the ball, the term used for the manoeuvre is "fade". A "pull" is a stroke in which the ball goes in a straight line to the left of the intended direction. A "hook" is a shot in which anti-clockwise spin is imparted to the ball, causing it to veer in flight from right to left. It is known as "draw" when it is used deliberately to obtain greater length – the hooked or drawn ball tends to run further than those sliced, cut, or hit straight – when the sideways movement in the air is controlled. In its most acute and accidental form, when the ball swerves sharply to the left and barely rises from the ground it is known as the "duck-hook".

To "top" obviously is to strike the top of the ball, which sends it scuttling along the ground. An "air shot" or "fresh air shot" is one that completely misses the ball and it counts as a stroke. "Borrow" is the term used for aiming a ball in putting to one side of the hole to compensate for a slope of the green.

The original 13 rules of golf have gradually proliferated to 41 main laws, most of which are further qualified by numerous sub-clauses, a written code of etiquette, 35 definitions, and a considerable body of case-law in the form of decisions which have been handed down by the rules committees in determining disputes.

The rules of etiquette follow the dictates of common sense and good manners, such as remaining still, quiet, and out of the line of vision of a player who is making a stroke; waiting until those ahead are clearly out of range before playing; playing without undue delay and, when held up to search for a ball, inviting the people behind to play through; leaving the course as you find it, by replacing divots and raking bunkers; and by observing the convention that two-ball matches take precedence on the course.

In general, the penalty for breaking a rule is 2 strokes in stroke play and the loss of the hole in match play. As noted above, the player must carry no more than 14 clubs which, like the ball, must conform to specifications. The honour of striking first from the tee is taken by the winner of the previous hole. In friendly games the convention is for the lowest handicap player to take the honour at the first hole. The ball must be teed within the teeing ground, which is defined by two markers and extends backward to a depth of two club-lengths. If the ball falls off the tee it may be replaced without penalty, but if the player makes a stroke at it, that stroke must be counted whether it makes contact or not. All such "air" strokes anywhere on the course must be counted. Having driven off, the player furthest from the hole plays next until the hole is completed.

The player must play their ball as it lies and may touch it only to identify it, after which it must be replaced. They must not move, bend, or break anything fixed or growing to improve their lie, except as may happen in fairly taking their stance and making the stroke. The player is allowed to remove obstructions (anything artificial, or man-made, which is not a part of the construction of the course) in the vicinity of their ball, and they may remove "loose impediments" (natural objects such as stones, leaves, twigs, and fir-cones), except in a hazard. If, in removing such debris, the player causes the ball to move they suffer a penalty of 1 stroke.

If a ball is lost, or out of bounds, or unplayable (and the player is the sole judge of whether their ball is unplayable), the standard procedure is the "stroke and distance" rule. Under this procedure, another ball is played from where the original stroke was made, and 1 penalty stroke is added. Thus, if a tee shot is hit out of bounds, another ball is played from the tee and this stroke is added. In the case of an unplayable ball, the player has two options in addition to the stroke and distance rule. They may drop the ball within two club-lengths, but not nearer the hole under penalty of 1 stroke. Or they may drop the ball behind the point where it lay, keeping that point between themselves and the hole, with no limit to how far behind that point the ball may be dropped.

If the ball is lost in a hazard, another ball may be dropped in the hazard without penalty or, under penalty, outside the hazard, keeping the point of entry between the golfer and the hole. The procedure for dropping is for the player to stand facing the hole and drop the ball over his shoulder. To save time, the rules allow for playing of a provisional ball in cases where it is thought the original ball might be lost or out of bounds. If, on reaching the area, the player finds the original ball is indeed out of bounds or lost, they may continue to play with the provisional ball under the stroke and distance rule. Should the original ball be found and in play, the provisional ball must be abandoned.

A temporary accumulation of water, such as puddles, which is clearly visible after the player has taken away their stance, is "casual water" and a player is entitled to drop the ball without penalty at the nearest spot which avoids these conditions, but not nearer the hole; on the greens the player may not place the ball. Snow and ice may be treated as casual water or as loose impediments at the option of the player.

On the putting green, the player may have the flagstick attended or removed. If the player's ball hits an unattended flagstick from a stroke played on the green, the penalty in match play is loss of hole, or 2 strokes in stroke play.

The foregoing is merely an outline of the main rules. There are many further provisions framed to cover unusual contingencies. For, although golf is basically a simple concept, golf courses, covering large areas of countryside and involving extremes of weather conditions, frequently present the player with problems of procedure. The complexities of the laws reflect the complexity of nature.

The golfer who proceeds on the basis of "play it as it lies" and accepts misfortune as the luck of the game will certainly be observing the spirit of golf and, in most cases, the laws. However, in golf justice and legality are not always synonymous. The obligation to accept relief where the rules allow is no less than the duty to endure penalties.

Equipment

A golf ball, of 1.62in (41mm) minimum diameter (1.68in or 43mm, in the USA and Canada), and 1.62oz (46g) maximum weight, is made of elastic thread and wound under tension around a central core and covered by a plastic casing. To propel it, the player may use a maximum of 14 golf "clubs", "woods" and "irons". Wooden clubs have longer shafts than iron clubs and are used when considerations of distance are paramount; in a normal set of clubs there are four woods. Irons are manufactured in sets numbered from 1 to 9 with the striking faces inclined at progressively increasing angles from 13° to about 47°. The higher-numbered clubs therefore produce a higher trajectory, less distance and greater accuracy. In addition, the golfer carries specialist clubs such as a "putter", a "sand-iron" for bunker play and a "wedge" for short approach shots and for recovering from heavy rough class. The "tee" is a small peg, about two inches long, on which a golf ball is placed before hitting it from the teeing ground.

Clothing

Players dress in active sportswear, with golf shoes.

GRASS SKIING

Introduction

Grass skiing is a sport of individual participation akin to SKIING, but practiced on grassy slopes. The snow skis are replaced by freely-revolving caterpillar tracks or rollers that have more in common with roller skates than with skis. The main centres of the sport are in Germany, Austria, Switzerland and France, though its rapid development has led to a considerable following in other countries with suitably hilly pasture-land, such as Italy, England, Andorra, Australia, Japan and South Africa.

History

Grass skiing originated in Germany in 1967, where a Stuttgart sports goods manufacturer, Kaiser, developed the necessary equipment. It soon spread to neighbouring countries, reaching England in May 1970. The sport's popularity in all countries that adopted it grew quickly, and meets are held throughout the spring, summer and autumn. Skis are usually available on hire at these meets, which often include simple competitions for novices as well as more involved events such as a slalom. Many of the most expert grass skiers in Europe are found in areas already well known for skiing, among them Gstaad (Switzerland) and Lermoos (Austria). The sport is in most cases organized by grass ski committees of the national ski associations.

Rules

Changes in direction are mainly accomplished, as in water skiing or roller skating, by changes in the inclination and emphasis of weight of the body. To attempt a skiing manoeuvre such as snowploughing usually brings disaster, though accidents are seldom serious as long as nursery slopes are being used.

Progress and stability are helped by the use of ski sticks. These need not be of the type used on snow, the points of which are too fine to be helpful in muddy conditions (grass skiing experts sometimes fit plastic bottle-tops to the tips to thicken them). Broom handles, roughly sharpened at one end, are quite suitable. Old clothes are recommended, particularly for the novice.

Grass skiing is restricted to slopes, whatever their gradient, that are reasonably smooth, dry and close-cropped. Long grass tends to clog the tracks and progress at any speed impossible over wet mud. The ground must also be clear of rocks, ruts and bumps, any of which are likely to cause a fall.

Equipment

The essential items of equipment are grass skis, which enable the wearer to move smoothly down slopes. The caterpillar tracks, one to each ski and about 1.5in (3.81cm) wide, are usually formed of rigid plastic studs on a nylon belt, running freely in a steel frame about 4in (10.16cm) high and the same width as the sole of the shoe. The length varies from show length for the recreational skier to as much as 2ft 6in (76.2cm) for top-class racing. A later English model replaces tracks with rollers, 3in (7.62cm) wide and 3.5in (8.89cm) in diameter, five of which are used in each ski. These are not as fast as tracks skis, but are more stable, and unlike tracks permit a small amount of lateral movement. Strong boots, giving ankle support, are the most suitable footwear, and to these the ski frames are strapped or clipped.

GYMNASTICS

(Alloy Rings, Asymmetric Bars, Balance Beam, Floor Exercises, Horizontal or High Bar, Parallel Bars, Pommel Horse, Vaulting Horse.)

Introduction

Gymnastics is one of the most graceful and artistic of sports and is popular all over the world. The combination of strength, dexterity and artistry makes it both a fascinating event in itself and an excellent training for other sports.

Six set exercises exist for men: floor exercises; horizontal and parallel bars; pommel horse; rings; and vault: and four for women: floor exercises; vault; beam; and asymmetrical bars.

History

The origin of gymnastics can be traced back to the ancient civilizations of China, Persia, India and Greece. But it was the Greeks who really started to modernize the sport. Gymnastics derives from the word "gymnos" (naked) and the word "gymnasium" which originally meant a public place or building where the Greek youths exercised. The distinguished physician Galen provided some of the earliest literature on the sport and showed how knowledgeable the Greeks were about its fundamentals. Activities like rope-climbing were included in the ancient Olympic Games and, with the rise of the Roman Empire, the Greek method of physical culture spread.

Among the events the Romans introduced was the wooden horse on which they practised mounting and dismounting. Most of the exercises were used for military preparation, but when the ancient Olympic Games were abolished the sport fell into decline for nearly 1,500 years.

Clothing

Men wear wide long trousers, or shorts, with braces and white sleeveless vests; women are dressed in one-piece costumes. Both sexes wear light slippers. For powerful, heavy movements men often use chalk to assist their grip and sometimes both sexes wear wrist-straps as the strain is considerable.

• THE ALLOY RINGS

The alloy rings is probably the exercise for which most strength is needed and is practiced only by men.

Rules

The gymnast begins by leaping up to clutch the rings, one in each hand, and then performs his routine, concluding by landing on the floor with both legs together. The gymnast with short arms has a tremendous advantage since he can use his strength more easily, but in recent years the swinging skills introduced have given the event even more appeal. During his performance the competitor must hold static positions and execute two inverted positions – handstands – one based on strength and the other utilizing his momentum.

Equipment

The two rings hang from wire cables 0.50m (1ft 7.75in) apart. The cables and rings are joined by looped straps 0.70m (2ft 3.5in) long and 0.035m (1.25in) wide. The inside diameter of the rings is 0.18m (7in). The overhead support which is rectangular is 5.50m (18ft) high and the rings hang at the most 2.50m (8ft 2.5in) above floor level.

• THE ASYMMETRIC BARS

The women use the asymmetric bars as one of their four exercises.

History

Just before the Second World War, the asymmetric, sometimes known as the "high and low bars", were developed, enabling women to take part in bar exercises.

Rules

Emphasis is on suspension and momentary bracing positions and the female gymnast must change bars by turning or executing elegant movements.

Equipment

The bars are still parallel and on the same plane but the upper bar is 2.30m (7ft 6.5in) and the other is 1.50m (4ft 11in) above the ground.

• BALANCE BEAM

The balance beam is used only by women. Routines include spins, twists, held balances, sitting and prone exercises, steps, jumps and turns, all grouped in rhythmic patterns

History

It was originally developed to demonstrate balance but many of the skills of floor exercises have since been introduced.

Equipment

The exercises take place on a slightly rounded wooden beam 5m (16ft 4.75in) long and 0.10m (4in) wide. The beam is 0.16m (6.25in) thick. It is mounted on two adjustable supports and is set 1.20m (3ft 11.25in) above the floor level.

• FLOOR EXERCISES

The floor exercises are usually the first of the events since the give competitors a chance to warm up with movements not requiring tremendous strength. They are probably the most picturesque of all the events but a comparatively new development in the sport.

History

It was fashionable during the nineteenth century to stage massed floor exercises involving hundreds of thousands of performers in displays, but in the 1932 Olympics the individual event was first staged, women entering the event 20 years later.

Rules

Men perform for 70 seconds and women to a musical accompaniment for 90 seconds. Both aim to impress the judges with a sequence of blended leaps, spins and balances, together with the elements of tumbling and acrobatics. Strength movements should be performed slowly and static positions must be held for at least two seconds. Somersaults should be done at shoulder height.

Equipment

The mat on which the gymnasts compete is 12m (13yds) square and is placed inside an area 14m (15yds) square. The mat consists of a soft material 0.045m (1 7/8in) thick. The large mat is comprised of 60 small mats, 2m (6ft 7in) by 1.20m (3ft 11.25in), which are linked together.

• HORIZONTAL OR HIGH BAR

The horizontal or high bar produces some of the most exciting moments in gymnastics. Only men compete on it but women and children use it for training. The whirling actions and swinging movements have made it extremely popular.

History

Jahn introduced the horizontal bar and originated a number of exercises for it. At first a thick wooden bar was used but after a while steel became popular.

Rules

When using the horizontal or high bar any attempt to use strength will interfere with the rhythm of the movement. No held balances are required and any hesitation in the flow is penalized by the judges. The apparatus is mainly concerned with the full extension of the body and a firm hand-grip and gymnastics whose strength/weight ratio is lower than it should be can do well on the horizontal bars. Displays usually last between 15 and 30 seconds.

Equipment

The bar consists of a steel rod 2.4m (7ft 10.5in) long and 0.028m (1 1/8in) thick. It is mounted on posts 2.5m (8ft 2.5in) above the ground.

• PARALLEL BARS

The parallel bars in their original form are used only by men. Skill is now more important than strength and usually the smaller gymnast with supple shoulders is ideal for the event.

History

Jahn invented the apparatus when he discovered that German youth was lacking strength in the arms and for years athletes used them for "pull-ups", "dips" and "press-ups". But as the sport developed, skilled movements involving swinging were introduced.

Rules

Probably the most important exercise is swinging from a hanging position though a somersault into the support position, as this is needed in any voluntary work. The gymnast is required to perform one movement in which both hands release the bars simultaneously and in some routines he may perform movements such as going from a handstand between the bars and then resting again in another handstand.

Equipment

The bars are made of flexible wood and oval in cross section, 0.051m (2in) thick vertically and 0.041m (1.5in) wide. They are 3.50m (11ft 5.75in) long, 0.42m (1ft 4.5in) to 0.48m (1ft 7in) apart and 1.70m (5ft 7in) above floor level. The supports of each bar are 2.30m (7ft 6.5 in) apart and are fastened to a heavy ground-plank.

• POMMEL-HORSE

The pommel-horse is an almost trapezoidal, leather-covered body on which only men compete since it requires great strength in the arms and shoulders.

History

The event probably originated because of the need for soldiers to acquire the skills of horsemanship. Johann Fredrich Ludwig Jahn, a German gymnast, who started a vast number of gymnasiums and funded the German Gymnastic Association, developed it into what is now probably the most fascinating of all exercises for men.

Rules

A competitor grasps the pommels, and then begins a continuous swinging movement, passing one or both legs over the horse, executing forward and backward splits and preferably circular movements to the right and left with both legs. Competitors must swing their legs and not lift them. Even for single leg movements, legs should not be swung individually, one should be used to balance or assist the other. Hands may be placed on the horse as well as on the pommels.

Equipment

The pommel-horse's upper surface is 1.10m (3ft 7.25in) above the floor and measures 1.60m (5ft 3 in) to 1.63m (5ft 4.5in). It is 0.35m (1ft 1.5in) thick. The pommels are 0.12m (4.75in) high and 0.28m (11in) wide. They are centred along the upper surface of the horse 0.40 to 0.45m (1ft 3.75in–1ft 5.75in) apart.

• THE VAULTING HORSE

The vaulting horse is also shared by both men and women. It is probably the simplest of all the events and outsiders have frequently won major international competitions.

Rules

Men vault over the horse lengthways, passing first over the "croup" and then the "neck". Women vault sideways, putting their hands on the middle of the horse which is 1.1m (3ft 7.25in) by 0.6m (1ft 11.75in). The competitor touches the horse and may twist or turn before landing in an upright position. Women are marked for how far they reach after touching the horse. Both sexes are also assessed on the difficulty of the movements they make during the leap and on the smoothness of the effort. Competitors must not stagger on landing.

Equipment

The horse consists of a leather-covered body similar to the pommel-horse, but without the pommels. For men its upper surface is 1.35m (4ft 5.25in) from floor level. The horse is divided into three parts, one 0.40m (1ft 3.75in) long, the next 0.20m (8in), and the third 0.40–0.43m (1ft 3.75in–1ft 5in) long.

HANDBALL

Introduction

Handball is a no-contact game, played either out of doors (field handball) by two opposing teams of 11-a-side or indoors by teams of 7-a-side or 5-a-side (adapted to a smaller court). It is played with one or two hands by catching, interpassing and throwing the ball. The aim is to score, i.e. to throw the ball into the goal.

History

Handball is mentioned in the *Odyssey*. The Urania game of the ancient Greeks is thus described:

"..They took at once in their hands the lovely ball,
which Polybos, with cunning art, had wove from purple wool.
One cast this up to heaven to reach the sparkling clouds,
and caught it nimbly, ere his foot touched the ground again."

Handball as it is played today was first introduced in about 1890 by German gymnastics master, Konrad Koch, but it did not at once become popular. After the First World War, interest was revived by the Germans, Hirschman and Dr Schelenz. It was adapted to ASSOCIATION FOOTBALL rules, and became a regular sport in schools, clubs, colleges, and universities. An "offside" line running across the width of the field was introduced, but as this proved a hindrance to the flow of the game, it was scrapped after some years.

Venue

The playing field for field handball is similar to that of soccer the indoor version (44yds by 22yds, or 40m by 20m) requiring a much more limited playing area.

Rules

A match is started from the centre point, the ball being passed with short or long throws from one player of a team to another, and in this way attacks are built up which culminate in attempts at scoring. Various techniques of throwing at goal can be learned, such as lob, shoulder throw (like putting the shot), falling throw, diving throw. These shots must be executed from outside the goal area, marked by a semicircle drawn 14yds (13m) from the centre of the goal line in field handball and 19ft 8in (6m) in indoor handball. Only the goalkeeper is allowed to be and to move freely in this area, with or without the ball. A goal is scored if the ball has travelled (in the air or on the ground) completely over the goal line between the posts.

An attack can be halted by interception and the defending team can in its turn attempt to mount and attack. This often begins when the goalkeeper, after parrying a shot at goal, makes a "throw-off", for which he may go close to the line of the goal area. During this throw the players whose attack was stopped have to remain outside the free-throw line, which is marked by a broken line 6yds (5m) away from and parallel to the line of the goal area in the large field, and 10ft (3m) in the small court. This line is so called because players of the attacking team, having been awarded a free throw, must stand outside it, facing the goal. A free throw is awarded for various infringements of the rules, which, for ease of recognition, can be classified as:

Faulty handling of the ball.

Faulty movement with the ball.

A faulty approach to an opponent.

A faulty attitude to the referee.

For example, a player is allowed to hold the ball for three seconds only, and must then pass it on or throw for goal. Once the ball has been touched by the hand or any part of the body above the knee, it may not be touched again unless it bounces back from the ground or the goal or returns from another player. The ball may be passed in any direction and even rolled along the ground. Players are allowed to hit the oncoming ball with the fist, but not to throw it up and fist it away.

A player holding the ball may take not more than three steps, and must then either pass it or bounce it with one hand; this

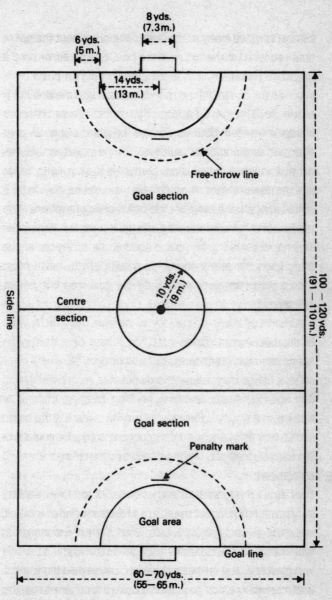

Field Handball Pitch

can be repeated many times. Once the ball has been caught or bounced with two hands, no more bouncing is allowed and it has to be passed or shot at goal within the permitted three seconds. Bouncing with two hands repeatedly is allowed in 11-a-side (field) handball. Passing or throwing with two hands is always allowed, in both versions of the game, but is never as effective, as quick, or as faultlessly on the target as the one-handed action. A player is not permitted to step, jump, or fall into the goal area with the ball in his hand. Yet he may do so, if skilled enough, the moment the ball is clear of his hand. This applies only to overstepping the goal-area line during an attempt at throwing for goal; a spectacular diving technique often gives the player momentum sufficient to reach more than a yard (1m) over and inside the goal-area line before falling down.

As handball is a no-contact game there are many faulty ways of approaching an opponent. While a pass or shot may be intercepted with two hands or head or body (touching once only), a player may attempt to dispossess an opponent with one open hand only. Grabbing, hooking, hugging, tripping, or tackling in any way is forbidden. Carrying or playing the ball in such a way as to endanger an opponent is an infringement of the rules of clean play and is penalized by the referee.

Equipment

The ball is a round inflated leather ball of 23 to 24in (58–60cm) in circumference, about the size of a No.3 Association football, weighing 15 to 17oz (425–480g). For women the weight is 325–400g and the circumference 54–56cm. In the 11-a-side version the goal is an exact replica of the Association football goal, i.e. two wooden goal posts measure 8ft (2.4m) in height, the crossbar 8yds (7.3m) in length, both being inside measurements. The woodwork is 5in (12.7cm) in cross-section. The side of the goal facing the field is painted in alternating light and dark segments, zebra-stripe fashion. In indoor handball the goals measure 6ft 6in (2m) in height and 10ft (3m 7.6cm) in cross-section.

Scoring
A goal is scored when the ball crosses over the goal line between the posts and under the crossbar. A goal is not scored if an official signals to interrupt the game. After a goal, play restarts with a throw off from the centre by the team that did not score. A game is won by the team with most goals when play ends.

Clothing
Players should wear white shirts, shorts, socks and shoes.

HANDBALL, COURT
Introduction
Court handball is ball game played by two players (known as singles) or two pairs (known as doubles) in a walled court. The player hits a ball with a gloved hand and tries to make sure that the opponent cannot return it.

History
The exact origins of the sport are unclear. There is some evidence that a game of this type was played by the Romans; it was definitely played in Ireland about 1000 years ago.

Venue
The court for the four wall game must be at least 20ft (6.10m) wide and 45ft (13.71m) long, and the glass side walls are about 20ft (6.10m) high. The service line is set back 15ft (4.57m) from

the back wall and the service zone is a further 5ft (1.52m) area past that line. At the furthest end of the service zone away from the wall is the short line. 5ft (1.52m) beyond the short line is the receiving area and at least 20ft (6.10m) from the back wall.

Rules

The player or pair that wins the toss serves first in the opening game. In doubles, when the starting player loses, it passes to the opposing pair. Then both players in each team must both serve and lose service before the service passes over to the opposition.

The service may be taken when both sides have been in position for at least one second. It may be taken anywhere within the sevice zone (the area between the short and service lines). The server must have both feet on or within the zone.

Each legal return after the service is called a rally; the player may strike the ball with either the front or the back of the hand. It is a good rally if the player volleys the ball, or hits it after it has bounced once, so that it is returned to the front wall, either with or without touching any part of the court except the floor. If a player strikes at a ball and misses, they may make further attempts to make a good return before it touches the floor for a second time. In doubles, both members of a team may attempt to return the ball, and may make one or more attempts to strike it before it touches the floor for a second time.

Except for the player making the return, any player touching the ball before it has bounced twice on the floor is penalized by an "out" or point against them. In doubles, if the offending player is the server's partner, the server loses the service.

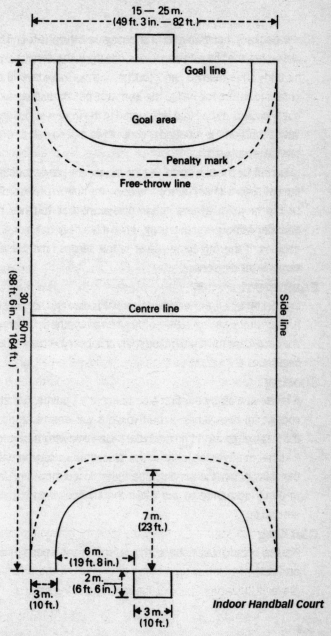

15 — 25 m.
(49 ft. 3 in. — 82 ft.)

Goal line

Goal area

— Penalty mark

Free-throw line

30 — 50 m.
(98 ft. 6 in. — 164 ft.)

Centre line

Side line

7 m.
(23 ft.)

6 m.
(19 ft. 8 in.)

2 m.
(6 ft. 6 in.)

3 m.
(10 ft.)

3 m.
(10 ft.)

Indoor Handball Court

A bad rally results in a point or out against the offender if the player: hits the ball with two hands; hits the ball with any part of his body other than his hand; touches the ball more than once; or fails to return the ball to the front wall but instead strikes it out of court. Any ball that is returned to the front wall but goes out of court on the rebound is considered a dead ball, and the service is replayed.

Except for the player making the return, any player touching the ball before it has bounced twice on the floor is penalized by an out or point against them, unless the ball touches the offender without first bouncing, when it is a dead ball hinder. In doubles, if the offending player is the server's partner, the server loses the service.

Equipment

In court handball, the standard handball is blue and spherical. It has an outer casing either of leather or synthetic material, the outer case must not be too shiny or slippery. Gloves should be a snug fit.

Scoring

A game is won by the first side to score 21 points. A match consists of two games. If the two sides win one game each, the first side to win 11 points in the tie breaker wins the match. Points are awarded only if the side that is serving wins the rally. When the serving side either loses a rally, or fails to serve according to the rules, the service passes to the other side.

Clothing

Players should wear shirts, shorts, socks and shoes of any colour.

HANDBALL, IRISH

Introduction

The Irish version of HANDBALL is very closely related to Spanish "pelota" and English FIVES (see ETON, RUGBY, WINCHESTER). Matches are between two players (singles) or four players (doubles). Each game is won by the first player to score 21 aces, or points, and a match is decided by the winning of three out of five games.

History

(See also Handball)

Handball was originally played against a blank wall or gable-end, but the game soon progressed to three-wall and four-wall alleys. From the middle of the nineteenth century, Irish emigrants took the game with them across the Atlantic, where it attained tremendous popularity.

Venue

The game is played in a four-walled court or alley 60ft (18.3m) long by 30ft (9.14 m) wide. The front wall is 30ft (9.14m) high, while the height of the back wall must be at least 9ft (2.7m). For international championships the court is much smaller, 40ft by 20ft (12.2m x 6.1m) with the front wall 20ft (6.1m) high and the back wall a minimum of 12ft (3.66m). The walls are usually of smooth cement, but glass back and side walls, which allow for a greater number of spectators, are in greater use, while maple floors are replacing concrete.

Rules

Before commencing a game, the players toss a coin to decide first service. The server bounces the ball, from between the "short" and "service" lines, off the front wall. If the receiver, who may take the ball either on the volley or first bounce, fails to get it back to the front wall before it again touches the ground, an ace is credited to the server. Similarly, if the server fails to return the ball after it has been played off the front wall by the receiver, a "hand out" results, and the receiver takes over as server. In doubles, players on each team serve alternately.

Fast rallies are a feature of handball, but the most spectacular skill is the ability to hit the ball hard and low almost off the very base of the front wall so that it comes back along the ground and cannot be retrieved. This tactic is known as the "butt".

Kicking the ball is not allowed, nor is the use of both hands to scoop up the ball.

Equipment

In Ireland, two different types of ball are used, each producing a very different game. Soft-ball is played with a rubber ball and is easily the more popular. Hard-ball is a far faster game, since the ball, which is much smaller, is made of hard rubber covered with goatskin. The hard ball, popularly known as the "alley-cracker", is more difficult to control and return, and calls for greater speed, strength and stamina. Hard-ball games are not played outside Ireland.

Clothing

Although the wearing of a soft glove, or leather band, is permitted, most players prefer to use the bare hand.

HARE AND HOUNDS

Introduction

Hare and Hounds is a form of cross country foot race which became popular in English public schools in the eighteenth century. One or two runners, known as the hares, are given a short start and the rest, known as the hounds, set out to over take them within the distance appointed for the race. Hare and Hounds is still run by schools but it has never been a championship sport in the formal sense. Many athletic clubs, called Harriers, owe their names to this sport. It is similar to paper-chasing.

HOCKEY, FIELD

Introduction

Field Hockey is a stick-and-ball game, and is played in over seventy countries and on all five continents. It is a major sport in Pakistan and India and is widely played in Great Britain, South Africa, Australia, Germany, the Netherlands, and many English-speaking countries. Hockey is usually played in two teams of 11-a-side, though there are 5, 6, and 7-a-side. A team consists of a goalkeeper, two backs, three halves, and five forwards.

History

The name "hockey" (spelt thus) was not given to this ancient stick-and-ball game until the eighteenth or nineteenth century, but without a doubt, hockey has descended from the earliest civilizations. There is, however, no concrete evidence of where it started. History confirms that early man carried a club, staff, or stick and it is a basic instinct to hit at movable objects.

Early hockey historians thought the sport descended from polo but the reverse seems much more likely. This was confirmed in the early twentieth century when studies were made of drawings on the ancient tombs in the Nile Valley. On a wall in Tomb No. 16 at Beni-Hasan, near Minia, there are drawings of six sports, one of which shows two men holding implements that, with their curved ends, closely resemble early twentieth century hockey sticks. The men in the drawing are standing square to each other and between their "sticks" is a round object which may have been a hoop or ball. The stance suggests either that they were carrying out a bully or that one was trying to prevent the other hitting the round object. This tomb was built about 2,000 BC, so it is fair to assume that men have been playing a form of hockey for at least 4,000 years, probably much longer. Hockey is thus the forerunner to all modern sports played with an implement.

Before the Christian era, different variations of stick-and-ball games were being played in many parts of the world, as written and pictorial evidence shows. The Arabs, Greeks, Persians and Romans each had their own version. The Romans played a game called "paganica" in which a ball, which was filled with feathers, was propelled with a club.

One of the most comprehensive records of an early form of hockey comes from Argentina. The early sixteenth-century European settlers recorded the habits and pastimes of the Araucaño Indians. They played a game called "cheuca" ("the twisted one") which took its name from the stick with a twisted end used by the players. Their ball had a leather case. The size of the field depended on whether four, six, or eight players took part, though it was usually in the region of 100 paces in length and ten paces in width, the back line at either end being the goal line. The Araucaños considered cheuca to be an important feature of their lives because it kept them healthy and in good physical condition for war.

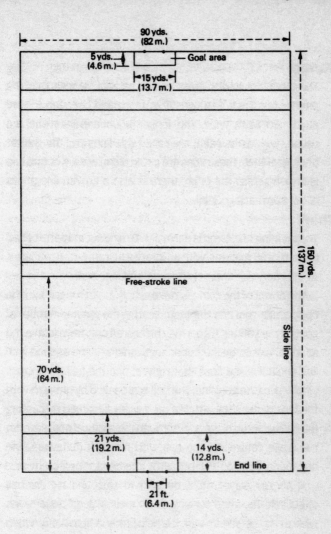

- 90 yds. (82 m.)
- 5 yds. (4.6 m.)
- Goal area
- 15 yds. (13.7 m.)
- 150 yds. (137 m.)
- Free-stroke line
- Side line
- 70 yds. (64 m.)
- 21 yds. (19.2 m.)
- 14 yds. (12.8 m.)
- End line
- 21 ft. (6.4 m.)

Hockey Pitch

Goal post are joined by a horizontal crossbar (not shown in diagram) 7ft (2.14m) from the ground. Flags 1yd (1m) high mark the ends of the goal line, centre line, and 25yd line. Countries playing to the International Federation of Women's Hockey Associations rules use 5yd (4.6m) lines parallel to the side lines.

Venue

The game is played on grass in most parts of the world and the pitch is regular. It is 100yds (92m) long and between 55 and 60yds (50–55m) wide. The longer boundary lines (marked usually with white paint) are called side lines and the shorter ones, goal lines. These lines are all 3in (8cm) wide. A centre line is drawn across the pitch; there is also a broken line 25yds (23m) from each goal line.

Rules

The duration of a game is normally 70 minutes, made up of two periods of 35 minutes, with an interval of from 5 to 10 minutes. At the interval (half-time), the teams change ends.

The object of the game is, quite simply, to get the ball into the opponent's goal and the team scoring the greater number of goals is the winner. A goal may be scored only from within the space enclosed by the opponent's striking circle and the goal line (including the lines themselves) and the ball must cross wholly over the goal line. The ball is propelled by hitting it with the face of the stick. Attacks are usually launched by passing the ball between players, or through the ability of one player to run while controlling the ball with his stick (dribbling). The opponents try to obtain the ball by interception or tackling.

A hockey player must be able to stop and hit the ball effectively. The good player will use their stick efficiently even when it is reversed. The stick is held firmly in both hands when playing the ball, the left hand above the right. When making a hit, the hands are close together; for other strokes, such as the push, flick, or scoop, the left hand grasps the stick firmly near its top and the right hand is moved to a comfortable position further down the handle.

The feet are always astride so that the player is balanced and their body weight can be transferred easily.

The push stroke is intended to keep the ball on the ground; the flick stroke is a push, with a wrist flick added, to make the ball rise. The scoop is used to lift the ball over opponents. Bigger distances can be achieved with the left hand moved down below the right and the head of the stick laid right back. A hit, flick, push or scoop is permitted provided that no part of the stick rises above the players' shoulder level and the ball is not undercut, or played in a dangerous way.

Equipment

The goal, placed in the centre of the goal line, consists of two perpendicular posts 4yds (3.66m) apart, joined together by a horizontal crossbar 7ft (2.13m) from the ground. The ball can enter the area encompassed by the netting only from the field of play. The goals are completed by the fixing of three boards, not exceeding 18in (46cm) high on the ground inside the netting. Two are placed at right angles to the goal posts and the third parallel to the goal line. The ball is solid plastic, weighing 5.5–5.75oz with a circumference of approximately 9.25in.

Scoring

A goal is scored when the whole ball has passed over the goal-line between the posts and under the crossbar, provided it has been played by an attacker from within the striking circle.

Clothing

Hockey players wear shirts, boots and either shorts or a skirt. The boots must not have metal studs, spikes or nails. Goalkeepers wear a face guard, gauntlet gloves, pads, kickers, headgear and elbow pads.

• UK FIELD HOCKEY

The game is started with a centre "bully". The ball is placed on the ground at a spot approximately in the middle of the centre line and one player from each team, usually the centre forward, takes his stance; the two men/women face each other, square to the side lines, with the goal they are defending to the right. Each of them must simultaneously tap with their stick, their opponent's stick above the ball. This is done three times before the ball may be played, when each player tries to obtain the ball for their side.

Until the ball has been played, all other players must remain nearer to their own goal line than the ball and not within 5yds (4.6m) of the ball.

• US FIELD HOCKEY

The match begins with a pass back (a non-defended pass from one team-mate to another at mid-field). A unique rule in field hockey is the obstruction rule. In virtually every other sport, shielding the ball with one's body is an integral part of game strategy. However, this is not allowed in field hockey. All players have an equal chance to gain control of the ball as it is dribbled or passed down the field.

Other infractions include advancing (other than the goalkeeper, no player may use the ball with any part of the body), dangerous use of the stick and hitting the ball in a manner which could lead to dangerous play. For a breach of rules, an umpire may award a free hit, penalty corner or penalty stroke. The majority of scoring opportunities in each match come from penalty corners.

A penalty corner is a free hit by an offensive player from a point on the goal line at least 10yds from the goal. All attackers must be outside the circle before the hit is taken. A maximum of five defenders may be behind the goal line while the remaining defenders must be positioned beyond the centre line.

HOCKEY, INDOOR
Introduction

This is a game adapted from FIELD HOCKEY for teams of up to seven players indoors. It is known in parts of Europe as "Hallenhockey".

History

Hallenhockey started in the 1950s in West Germany, which has always been regarded as its leading exponent, and has become increasingly popular especially in Europe where outdoor hockey is restricted by the weather in midwinter. Other countries with a thriving indoor game are Belgium, Denmark, France, Netherlands, Spain and Switzerland. It is also played in a few centres in Britain. Germany introduced national championships in 1962 and these are now held for men, women, boys and girls. The game proved so popular that the German Federation limited their indoor season from December to February for fear that it might become more popular than outdoor hockey.

Venue

Although normally played indoors, the game can also take place outdoors provided the surface available is flat and hard. The rules are laid down by the International Hockey Federation. The ground is between 40 and 50yds (37–46m) long and 20 to 25yds (18–23m) wide, and is divided into two equal parts by a line drawn from one side line to the other. Down both side lines are wooden boards 4in (10cm) high, off which the ball may be played. As in outdoor hockey, the two goals are placed in the centre of the goal lines but the posts are only 3yds (3m) apart. The striking circle is also smaller, having a radius of 10yds (9m). The penalty-stroke spot is 8yds (7m) in front of the goal.

Rules

The game is played by two teams of six players (usually a goalkeeper and five field players) but each team is permitted a maximum of six substitutes. Substitutions may be made without informing the umpires but only at specific times, i.e. at half-time; when a goal is scored, when the ball has crossed one of the goal lines, or if the game has been stopped because of injury to a player.

The game is usually in two periods of 20 minutes each with a 5-minute interval, but shorter periods are played at tournaments and by women and juniors. The timing is kept by a timekeeper to whom the umpires signal all stoppages.

There are certain major differences between the rules for indoor and outdoor hockey. In the indoor game it is forbidden to hit the ball, which may only be pushed. It may be raised off the ground only when an attacker, in the striking circle, is attempting to score a goal.

The game is started with all members of each team in their own half. A member of the side that lost the toss makes a pass, which must not be forward. The game is re-started in the same manner after half-time and after a goal has been scored.

There are no corners, but at penalty corners all the players of the defending team (except the goalkeeper) must be behind the goal line on the side of the goal opposite to that from which the penalty corner is being taken. Another important difference is that there is no offside rule. Rules vary for the women's game and are sometimes more akin to the women's outdoor rules.

Equipment

This is similar to that used for outdoor hockey. The ball must be white and standard sticks (or sticks specially manufactured for indoor hockey, such as those with a plastic cover) are authorized. In some parts of Europe it is necessary to bind sticks with tape in order to avoid damaging wooden floors.

Clothing

See Hockey, Field.

HOLANI

Introduction

Holani is a very old game, similar to the early forms of HOCKEY, still played in Turkey. The "holani" is a wooden cylinder or wedge which is hit by sticks. It is larger than a tennis ball and very hard. The sticks used are rough-and-ready. There are no rules governing the game, no time limits, field specifications, nor restrictions on the number of players. The aim is to hit the ball through the opponents' goal. Games sometimes start at daybreak and end at nightfall.

HORSE RACING

Introduction

Organized horse racing is of two kinds: "across the flat", flat racing and "over the sticks" or jumping, the latter being subdivided into steeplechasing and hurdle racing.

History

The precise origin of horse racing is lost in time, but it is evidently derived from warfare, chariot racing and the chase. One of the earliest references to rough-and-ready races at Smoothfield is given by the secretary to Thomas Becket, Archbishop of Canterbury in the reign of Henry II of England (1154-89).

In 1377 the Prince of Wales, later Richard II, raced against the Earl of Arundel "owners up", and most of the early accounts of horse racing consist of descriptions of "matches" between two "running horses", where the owner of a "horse of price" wagers that his steed is faster than that of another knight-at-arms, issues a challenge to his rival, and the matter is put to the test over a course of some miles before the king and court. The most celebrated match in the history of the turf was that between The Flying Dutchman and Voltigeur at York in 1851 over a course of 2 miles (3.2km) for a stake of 1,000 guineas, which the former won in 3min 55sec, after a desperate struggle between the two equine champions.

The first permanent racecourse with an annual fixture was established on the Roodee at Chester in 1540, and the Newmarket Gold Cup was first competed for in 1634. By 1660, when "a hound and hawk no longer shall be tokens of disaffection, a cock-fight shall cease to be a breach of the peace, and a horse-race an insurrection", Charles II made Newmarket the headquarters of the turf, and "Newmarket's glory rose, as Britain's fell"; the king himself winning the plate on 14 October 1671.

Venue

The style of the venue varies according to the country. The

surface can range from grass, dirt or packed snow while the layout can be a simple oval or a complex layout with various starting points. Some courses can accommodate flat and steeplechase/hurdle racing.

Rules

Before the race itself the horses are ridden in front of the stand and usually no preliminary jumps are allowed before a steeplechase or hurdle race. The start is usually from starting stalls, but sometimes from a starting gate or flag, with the horses started in a straight line as far as possible.

A horse is considered to have started once it has come under starter's orders. A false start may be declared and the race restarted if there is a problem with the starting mechanism. In steeplechase or hurdle races, if the horses fail to return after the recall signal, the race is void. If one horse returns, it is awarded a walkover.

If a jockey is dismounted they may remount but where they fell. The jockey may be helped catching and remounting the horse, but the horse will be disqualified if it receives assistance from anyone apart from the jockey in jumping a fence or refusing a hurdle. The horse will also be disqualified if it misses a fence or hurdle, passes the wrong side of a direction marker and does not return and ride the course correctly, or if the rider rides recklessly, or jeopardizes another horse's chances. It can also be disqualified, or its placing altered, if, in the steeplechase or hurdle race, it crosses or interferes with another horse on the home run or at the final hurdle/fence. In a flat race the same penalty may result from one horse crossing or interfering with another in any part of the race.

Equipment

For steeplechases all fences, except for the water jump, are at least 4.5ft high. The water jump is at least 12ft wide, and guarded by a fence not more than 3ft high. In each mile long race there has to be at least one ditch, usually 6ft wide, on the take-off side of the fence guarded by a bank and rail not more than 2ft high.

Clothing

Jockeys wear riding hats, which are compulsory, shirts in the colours of their owners, breeches, boots and spurs. They also carry a whip. In steeplechases and hurdle races, riders must wear body protectors.

HORSESHOE PITCHING

Introduction

This is a game of old English origin, now popular in the USA, the object of which is to pitch, or, more accurately, swing, the shoe through the air so that it lands encircling ("ringing") a short stake, driven into the ground.

History

Horseshoe pitching probably began at the time of the Roman occupation of Britain, when officers played quoits and the men copied them (without cost) by throwing horseshoes at stakes. Both games were taken to America by the early English settlers, but it was horseshoe pitching that prospered. It could be played at any point on the trail to the West where there was a blacksmith's shop.

Venue

The standard court is 6 x 64ft with a pit at each end.

Rules

The game may be played by two people (singles) or two pairs (doubles), each player standing within the box to pitch two shoes at the stake before changing ends. The ground surrounding the stake is usually of clay, to reduce skidding of shoes to a minimum.

Scoring

A ringer scores 3 points, unless it is cancelled by an opponent's ringer. If no ringers are scored, the player or pair whose shoe is nearest the stake, provided it is within 6in (15.2cm) of it, scores 1 point; two shoes nearer the stake than an opponent's shoe score 2 points. Games are played to either 12 or 50 points.

HURLING

Introduction

Certainly the fastest of all team games, hurling is played 15-a-side with sticks and a ball. Traditionally a pastime of the Celts, it is still the national game in Ireland, where it is popular in many areas, including the Antrim glens, where the style of play has much in common with the SHINTY of the nearby Scottish highlands. The object of the game is to drive the relatively small ball with the broad-bladed stick (the "hurley" or "caman") through goal posts erected at opposite ends of a playing pitch.

History

Hurling is first mentioned in a description of the Battle of Moytura (c. 1272 BC), in which the Tuatha de Danaan invaders defeated the resident Firbolgs, first in a hurling match and then in a subsequent battle for the lordship of Ireland.

200 years before Jesus it was recorded that a child, Lowry Loingseach, who was to become king of Ireland, was dumb.

While playing hurling, he sustained a sharp blow of a "caman" (stick) to the shin and, in his agony, spoke for the first time. What he said is not recorded. In the *Red Branch Tales*, Cuchullain, the super-hero of Ulster, was as supreme in hurling as he was in every other knightly exercise.

As a small boy, he attracted the attention of Conor the king, by defeating, single-handedly, the whole 150 of the boy-warrior corps in a hurling game on the green before the royal palace at Armagh.

By the fourteenth century, hurling seems to have spread back across the Irish Sea to England where Wat Tyler's rebellion is referred to in *Gregory's Chronicle* as "the hurlying time", i.e. a time of tumult or commotion. Back in Ireland, so futile had the Statute of Kilkenny proved that another was passed at Galway in 1527, which again forbade the "hurling of the little ball with hooked sticks or staves".

Venue

The playing pitch is usually 150yds (137m) long and 90yds (82m) wide. The goal posts stand 21ft (6.4m) apart in the centre of the end lines and are usually 21ft high. There is a crossbar 8ft (2.4m) from the ground.

Rules

The ball, when in play, may not be lifted off the ground with the hand. It must be raised with the hurley, and may then be struck direct, on the volley or half-volley, or may be caught in the hand. The quick and deft lifting of the ball with the stick is an art in itself. The ball may be caught when in the air, and may be struck with the hand, or kicked. But a player who catches the ball may not throw it, nor may he carry it in the hand for more than three paces. A player is permitted, however, to run with the ball

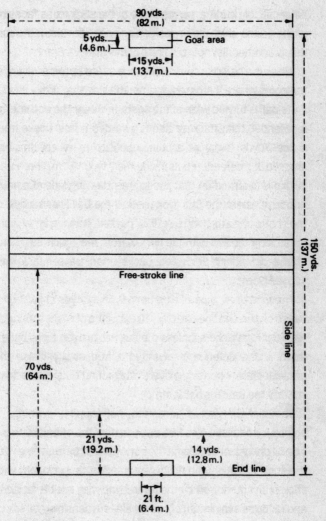

- 90 yds. (82 m.)
- 5 yds. (4.6 m.)
- Goal area
- 15 yds. (13.7 m.)
- 150 yds. (137 m.)
- Free-stroke line
- Side line
- 70 yds. (64 m.)
- 21 yds. (19.2 m.)
- 14 yds. (12.8 m.)
- End line
- 21 ft. (6.4 m.)

Hurling Pitch
*Goal posts are usually 21ft (6.4m) high, with a crossbar 8ft (2.4m) from
the ground.*

balanced, or hopping, on the blade of the stick for as far as he wishes, or as far as the opposition permits. This tactic, the solo run, is another distinctive feature of the game.

When the ball crosses the side line a free stroke is given, at the point where it crossed, against the side that drove it over. If the ball is turned wide of the posts, and over the end line, by a defender, the attacking side is awarded a free stroke from a line 70yds (64m) at a point opposite to where the ball crossed. If a defender fouls inside the 21yd (19.2m) line, a free stroke is awarded on that line to the attacking side at a point opposite where the foul took place. If the ball is sent wide of the goal by the attacking side, it is "pucked" (the technical word for striking the ball with the hurley) from the goal area by one of the defenders. Such goal-pucks often travel more than 100yds (91m).

The goal area, a parallelogram 15yds by 4yds (14 x 3.6m), based on the end line directly in front of the posts, is forbidden territory to attackers, unless the ball has arrived there before them. If the defence is awarded a free stroke inside the parallelogram, opposing players must stand outside the 14yd (12.8m) line until the ball is struck.

Shoulder-charging is permitted, but tripping, pushing, or pulling is penalized by a free puck against the offender, as is a frontal charge, or any dangerous swinging or backlashing with the stick. A player who deliberately strikes an opponent with stick or fist is sent off by the referee; he may not be replaced and receives a minimum of two weeks' suspension.

Teams are composed of a goalkeeper, six defenders, two mid-field players, and six forwards. A maximum of three substitutes may be introduced in the course of a game.

The basic skills of hurling are:

The ability to control and direct the ball both on the ground and in the air.

The power to drive the ball far and accurately.

The ability to stop the ball in flight and flick it away from an opponent's stick. Dexterity in avoiding an opponent's stick when players clash in their endeavours to secure or drive the ball.

Equipment

The wooden hurley or caman is usually 3.5ft (1.07m) long in the handle, and has a crooked blade which is some 3in (7.6cm) across at its broadest. The ball, often called by its Gaelic name, "sliothat", may be from 9 to 10in (22.9–25.4cm) in circumference and from 3.5 to 4.5oz (100–130g) in weight. To facilitate handling, a ridge of hard leather is stitched round the outside of the cover, which is usually of horsehide. The inside is of thread or yarn, tightly wound round a core of cork.

Scoring

A goal, equal to 3 points, is awarded when the ball is driven between the goal posts and under the crossbar. A point is scored when the ball is driven between the posts but over the crossbar.

Clothing

Players wear shirts, socks, shorts and boots. Helmets are optional.

ICE HOCKEY

Introduction

Ice hockey is a six-a-side team game played with sticks and a rubber puck on a rectangular sheet of mechanically-frozen or natural ice, called a rink, measuring, ideally, 200ft (61m) long and 85ft (26m) wide, and surrounded by barrier boards. The game is won by the team which scores the most goals. Hockey Rules come in a wide variety of variants. In the USA there are NHL, International, USAHockey, NCAA, Minnesota High School, and a number of others.

History

The origins of ice hockey date back to the second century. Its historical roots are Canadian, despite the fact that it is generally thought to stem from a game played by Englishmen on the frozen expanse of Kingston Harbour, Ontario, in 1860. This is the first time that a puck, as distinct from a ball, was used and so is usually accepted as the origin of the game with a recognized identity separate from field hockey. Most of these pioneer players were Crimean War veterans in a regiment of the Royal Canadian Rifles.

Subsequently, Montreal became the central point of the game's early progress. In the summer of 1879, W. F. Robertson, a student at McGill University, Montreal, visited England and watched field hockey matches. As a skating enthusiast, he wondered how the game could be suitable adapted so that it could be played on ice. When he returned to Montreal he told R.F. Smith, a fellow student, of his idea. Robertson and Smith then devised rules and regulations, adding a few original ideas to what was basically a combination of field hockey and rugby. A square rubber puck was used, with nine players each side.

From these humble beginnings the first recognized team was formed in 1880 and called McGill University Hockey Club. The game was introduced to Ottawa five years later by one of the original McGill team members, A. P. Low.

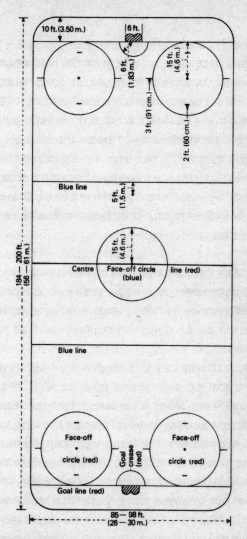

10 ft. (3.50 m.)

6 ft.

6 ft. (1.83 m.)

15 ft. (4.6 m.)

3 ft. (91 cm.)

2 ft. (60 cm.)

Blue line

5 ft. (1.5 m.)

15 ft. (4.6 m.)

Centre   Face-off circle (blue)   line (red)

Blue line

200 ft. (61 m.)

184 (56 m.)

Face-off circle (red)

Goal crease (red)

Face-off circle (red)

Goal line (red)

85 — 98 ft. (26 — 30 m.)

Ice Hockey Rink

Dimensions are those specified under International Ice Hockey Federation rules. Goals are 4ft (1.22m) high, with nets not less than 2ft (60cm) at the base. Under National Hockey League rules the goal crease is rectangular.

Ice Hockey

Venue

The game is played on a sheet of ice (the rink), which usually measures 100ft wide by 200ft long. The ice is enclosed by a wall, and the boards must be no more than 4ft (1.22m) high nor less than 40in (1m). The rink is divided in two halves by a red line across the centre of the ice. The rink is also divided into two thirds by the blue lines, forming two end zones and one neutral zone. In each end zone there is a goal cage and a red goal line, which runs the width of the rink. There are also nine face-off spots, four in each half of the rink and one in the middle.

Rules

Each team may have six players on the ice at one time – three forwards, two defenders, and one goalkeeper. In addition to the players on the ice, each team keeps extra players on the bench to use as substitutes when on-ice players get tired, penalized or injured.

Play is commenced at the beginning of each period, and after a goal has been scored, by a "face-off". The puck is dropped by the referee in the centre of the rink between the sticks of the opposing centre-men (centre forwards), who must stand approximately one stick-length apart, squarely facing their opponents' end of the rink, and with the full blades of their sticks on the ice. No other player is allowed within 10ft (3m) of the two face-off players. Play is re-started at other times of the game by face-offs on the nearest of the other eight marked spots to the point at which a mis-play occurred.

The puck stays in play whenever or wherever it hits the barrier boards, including behind the goals, and thus becomes dead only when hit over the barrier or when the whistle is blown for an infringement. A goal is scored when the whole of the puck passes over the goal line between the goal posts after being driven fairly by a stick.

A goal is not allowed if an attacking player kicks or throws the puck into the goal or if an attacking player is in the goal crease when the puck passes over the goal line. Goal judges positioned behind each goal signify when a goal has been fairly scored by switching on an overhead red light behind the goal concerned.

A "shut-out" occurs when a goalminder concedes no goal during a match. The expression is also used to describe one of the 20-minute periods of a game in which the goalminder does not concede a goal, or with reference to the duration of time, perhaps covering more than one match, during which a goalminder has remained unbeaten.

A player may stop the puck with his hand, body, or skate at any time and in any position. But he cannot hold the puck with his hand for more than three seconds, nor push the puck forward except with his skate or stick. "Stick-handling", or retaining possession of the puck while in motion, is the equivalent of "dribbling" in Association Football.

"Icing" is called when a player shoots the puck from his own half of the ice across the opponent's goal line provided it does not pass through any part of the goal crease. It is not called when a team is short-handed or when a player could have touched the puck before it went over the goal line.

The two blue lines divide the playing area into the three zones – defence, neutral (centre), and attacking zones. Only three players may be in their own defence zone when the puck is outside that zone.

A player may enter the attacking zone only in line or behind the puck or puck-carrier. He may not take a pass from a team mate who is, at the moment of passing, in another zone. When an attacking player precedes the puck into the attacking zone or when the puck travels over more than one line, play is halted and re-started from a face-off. In all instances in deciding an "offside", the position of the player's skates and not that of his stick is the determining factor. Thus, a player is offside when both skates are completely over the outer edge of the determining line involved in the play. To stay "on side", a player can pass the puck only to a colleague in the same zone (also to anyone in his own half if he is his defence zone).

If an attacking player is tripped or pulled down when in a scoring position in front of goal and having no players between him and the goal other than the goalminder, the referee can award a special penalty shot from the blue line of the defending team. The penalty shot is a clear shot at goal with only the goalminder allowed to defend. The time taken for a penalty shot is one phase of play in a game which is not included in the regular playing time. After a penalty shot which fails, a goal cannot be scored from a rebound.

Ice hockey is fairly described as the fastest team game in the world and, because of the pace and frantic action involved, players are penalized for infringements of the rules by being sent off the ice for two or more minutes, according to the severity of the offence. The team of suspension is served in a special penalty box.

Minor penalties of two minutes are imposed for such offences as charging, elbowing, tripping, body-checking (pushing a player deliberately on to the barrier boards), high sticks, and intentionally shooting out of the rink or falling on the puck (excepting the goalminder in the latter case). If the team which has consequent player advantage scores, the absent penalized player is allowed to return immediately. When a goalminder incurs a minor penalty he is not required to leave the ice but, instead, a team colleague is withdrawn by the coach.

A major penalty of five minutes can be imposed for fighting. When both teams incur major penalties, substitutes are permitted while two offenders are off the ice. A goalminder incurring a major penalty, instead of being sent off, has a penalty shot awarded against his team.

A misconduct penalty of ten minutes is imposed for deliberately injuring, or attempting to injure, an opponent. In such a case, a substitute can be allowed after the first five minutes but the offender cannot play in any future match before his case has been dealt with by a disciplinary committee. An offending goalminder must serve a match penalty himself and his place in goal has to be taken over by another member of his team.

Equipment

The puck is made of vulcanized rubber, and is 3ins in diameter and 1in thick. It weighs about 6oz. In the norm, the stick extends in length from the ice to the player's chin (with skates on).

Scoring

A team scores one point for each goal. For a goal the puck must legally and completely cross the goal line, between the goal posts and below the crossbar.

Clothing

It is compulsory to wear helmets in British ice hockey, junior players (under 21) and all netminders must also wear faceguards. All players wear gloves, shoulder, elbow, shin and knee protection. Goalkeepers also wear chest protection. All protection apart from helmets, gloves and goalie pads must be worn completely under the player's uniform.

ICE SKATING

Introduction

Competitive ice skating takes a number of forms, each with its own setting and equipment. Ice speed-skating and long-distance skating often take place in the open air; ice figure-skating and ice dancing are performed on indoor ice arenas.

History

The modern word "skate" is believed to be derived from the early German "schake" (meaning a shark or leg bone) "schaats" in Dutch – and the early English word, "scatch". The first skates were made from the shank or ribs of the elk, ox, reindeer and other animals, well before the discovery of steel, and there still exist in some museums bone skates believed to be 20 centuries old.

An offshoot of SKIING, primitive skating undoubtedly first developed in Scandinavia out of necessity, as a means of transport. Not surprisingly, skating has been widely practiced on the canals of Holland since the Middle Ages. The first known illustration of the sport – and early evidence, incidentally, of female participation – is a Dutch wood-engraving printing in 1498, depicting St. Lydwina of Schiedam who, in 1396, fell and broke a rib when skating at the age of 16. She died in 1433 and subsequently became the patron saint of skaters.

The sport was mentioned by Samuel Pepys who, on 1 December 1662, described in his diary the canal in St. James's Park, London, "where first in my life, it being a Great Frost, [I] did see people sliding with their skeetes, which is a very pretty art." 21 years later, Pepys danced on the ice with Nell Gwynne during the Great Frost of 1683.

Equipment

Skates and boots are the only essential equipment for the average racer. The correct skate for ice speed-skating and long-distance skating is appreciably longer than that used for ice figure-skating and ice dancing. The best steel blade is as thin as 0.22in (0.794mm), reinforced above the steel tubing for lightness and strength. It is straight, usually 12 to 18in (304.8–457.2mm) in length and is designed to travel on straight, or nearly straight, lines. Because of its speed potential, it is usually not permitted during public skating sessions at ice rinks. The boot for speed-skating is lighter in weight than that for ice figure-skating, made of thin leather with lower heel supports, more like a shoe than a boot in appearance.

Clothing

Skaters, for competitions, specifically the ISU, the International Skating Union (not including speed skating), must wear costumes which are modest, dignified and appropriate for athletic competition.

● FIGURE SKATING

This is a sport for solo and pair-skaters which tests style as well as technical skill. For figure skating the five separate disciplines, or divisions, in competitive figure skating are as follows: men's singles; ladies' singles; pairs; ice dancing; and precision team skating.

History

The administrative pioneer in figure-skating was Vandervell, who invented the bracket, the counter, and the rocker figures. Free style technique in Vandervell's time was subordinated to figures, the development of new turns into a restrained and dignified science with pride in accuracy of execution in an era of unwieldy Victorian dress. In the late nineteenth century, the English and the freer Viennese styles became separately recognized until the latter eventually became the international style adopted for all major championships. Ice figure-skating for men, women and pairs became Olympic events when the summer Olympic Games were held in London in 1908, 16 years before the first separate Winter Olympics.

Venue

The rink area for free skating and short programs should be rectangular. The maximum size is 60m x 30m and the minimum 56m x 26m.

Rules

Figures demonstrate a skater's skill in mastering total control of motion, speed, balance, precise movement and skating edges. Each figure consists of two or three circles forming a variation of the figure 8. There are a total of 41 figures plus the Waltz Eight that skaters learn.

The ISU (International Skating Union) voted to eliminate figures from all international competitions and ISU Championships beginning with the 1991–2 competitive season. Since that date, figures have been skated as a separate medal event in some competitions, such as the US Championships and the Junior Olympics.

In these events, a group of three figures is drawn from four pre-designated groups. Each skater traces each figure twice on each foot. The two or three circles that make up the figure should be perfectly shaped and of the same size. Different from singles, pairs and dance, judges only give one mark for each figure skated.

• ICE DANCING

Ice dancing is a relatively modern offshoot of ice figure-skating and is a sport in its own right, with movements based largely on those learned in figures. Unlike pair skating which features overhead lifts and jumps, ice dancing, as its name implies, is based on the difference aspects of dance. The emphasis in ice dancing is on rhythm, interpretation of the music and precise steps.

An ice dancing competition is made up of three parts: two compulsory dances, a two-minute original dance and a four-minute dance.

History

Despite references, by people such as Pepys, to dancing on ice in the seventeenth century, seriously organized ice dancing dates from the waltz-minded Vienna Skating Club's activities in the 1880s. There is evidence that the waltz was skated on ice at Halifax, Nova Scotia, as early as 1885 and that a waltz was demonstrated at the Palais de Glace, Paris, in 1894. The first organized set-pattern dance for skaters was the ten-step, which later became the fourteen-step. It was originated in 1889 by a Viennese, Schöller. The kilian, invented by Schreiter, also emerged from Vienna in 1909. The European waltz was established by this time, though its inventor and exact date have never been ascertained. Ice dancing became more fully organized through its rapid development in Britain during the 1930s.

• PAIRS

Pair skating is essentially free skating performed in unison by partners. Whether the partners are together or apart, their movements should be synchronised with matching body lines, gestures and footwork. The pairs short program consists of eight elements which include overhead lifts, side-by-side solo jumps and solo spins done in unison, footwork, pair spins and a death spiral, all performed to music of the skaters' choice. The short program is 2min 40sec in length. The program consists of technical and artistic moves choreographed to best display the skaters' strengths, skills and ability to perform as a team.

Moves include: the axel lift; the split lutz lift; and the catch-waist camel (arabesque) spin.

• SINGLES

Each competition is composed of two separate parts: the short program is skated first, followed by the free skating program.

The short program counts for 33.3% of the skater's total score for the competition. It consists of: three jumps, three spins and two fast step sequences.

Jumps include:

The "axel": a jump involving one and a half turns in the air, named after its originator, Axel Paulsen. The take-off begins from an outside forward edge of one skate. A double axel is the same jump with two and a half mid-air revolutions.

The "flip": a toe jump, taking off from the back outside edge of the skating blade assisted by the toe-point of the non-skating blade of the free foot, rotating in mid-air before landing on the back outside edge of the original non-skating blade.

The "lutz": most jumps entail counter-clockwise rotation in the air, but a notable exception is this difficult toe jump, in which the skater takes off from a back outside edge, helped by the toe-point of the free foot, rotating clockwise in mid-air before landing on the back outside edge of the original free foot.

The "salchow": a jump named after its originator Salchow, in which the skater takes off from a back inside edge, rotating in mid-air before landing on the back outside edge of the opposite foot.

There are other variants of the jumps and such further advance jumps as the double, triple or quadruple salcow, loop, axel and lutz, their names indicating the number of mid-air rotations involved.

The set moves for the season may be done in any sequence within a two-minute, 40-second time limit, to music selected by the skater. The judges award two marks, one for required elements and a second for presentation, which evaluates the overall programme.

The long program

The free skating program is worth 66.7% of a skater's total score for the competition. The free skate has no required elements, and has a length limited of four minutes, 30 seconds for men and four minutes for ladies. Here skaters select their own music and theme, and choreograph the many difficult jumps, spins, footwork, and interpretative moves to best display their technical and artistic skills. As in the short program, two marks are given: the first for technical merit, the second for presentation.

• SPEED SKATING

For speed skating two skaters, or more, race around a track. Races for men and women are held over varying distances. Points are given in relation to the skater's time in each event and the distance winner is the skater who achieves the fastest time. The overall winner is the skater who has the lowest total of points.

History

Ice speed-skating began to develop in Holland around the beginning of the nineteenth century and the Dutch soon took the sport to their closest neighbours, Germany, France and Austria. The Frieslanders of North Holland introduced it to England in the area extending from Cambridge to the Wash known as the Fens, where recorded competitions in Fenland Skating date from 1814.

The first international speed-skating competitions was in Hamburg, Germany, in 1885. World championships for men, though first held in 1889 at Amsterdam, Holland, were not officially recognized until 1893, when Eden (Netherlands) became the first title-holder.

Skating was first introduced to the Olympics in 1924 and short track speed skating appeared later, probably in the 50s or 60s. Short track speed skating made its entry into the Olympics as a demonstration sport at the 1988 Winter Games in Calgary and became an official sport in 1992 in Albertville.

Venue

Long track speed skating is done on a 400m oval (usually outdoor, but there are a few indoor ovals in the world) which is separated into two lanes.

Rules

When starting an event the skaters must stand still in an upright position between the pre-start line and the starting line. Their skates must not be over the starting line. On the command of "ready" they adopt their starting positions, and are started by a shot or a whistle.

The way in which the skate blade strikes the ice in speed skating is very important. The toe is pointed almost straight down in sprints, to get more ride out of the blade. For distance races the blade is placed on the ice at a 10-degree angle. The upper body relaxes above the leg over which it glides. So, when the skater pushes off their right skate they collapse their upper body over their left thigh. The angle of legs is almost straight to the ice – and the straighter the line on skates, the better.

A skater may only overtake if they do not impede the leading skater. When a skater has been overtaken, s/he must remain at least 5m behind opponents. Any form of pacemaking – in front, alongside, or behind the other skater – is forbidden. Skaters finish the race when one skate reaches the finishing line.

In the Olympics, two skaters can compete against each other. As the outer lane is a longer track than the inner lane the skaters switch lanes once every lap, so that at the end of the race, they have covered the exact same distance.

In mass starts or group races around 6 or 8 skaters use the same track at the same time. As there is only one 400m lane this induces tactics and wind drafting.

In relay races a skater may be replaced by another member of the team at any time except during the last two laps. The incoming team member is not in the race until they have touched, or are touched by the skater who is being replaced. The replaced skater must leave the track without impeding any of the other skaters.

In short track speed skating peloton races, i.e. several skaters racing against each other on the same track, is common. For this, tactics are vital and due to the number of skaters on the ice competitors wear helmets, knee pads, neck protectors, gloves, shin pads and occasionally protective eye gear. The track is only 111m long, considerably smaller than the long track, which means that the straights are shorter and the corners a lot steeper.

When overtaking, the leading competitor has right of way and may be passed on the outside, providing they keep to the inside of the track or may be passed on the inside if they keep to the outside of the track. The responsibility for any collision or obstruction is with the skater who is overtaking. A skater who has been, or is being, lapped may be instructed by the judges to move to the outside of the track to allow the oncoming skaters the right of way.

In the marathon, which is held either on frozen canals and rivers, or on 400m ovals, the distances vary from a few kilometres to a few hundred.

ICE YACHTING
Introduction

Travelling and racing across ice in specially adapted boats with sails propelled by the wind, had been practiced primarily in those parts of North America and Europe with suitable ice and wind conditions. The most favoured North American areas have been near the Atlantic coast between Long Branch, New Jersey, and Portsmouth, New Hampshire, and the Great Lakes basin, from central Wisconsin, eastward to Buffalo, New York, and Toronto, Canada. In Europe, the sport has been most practiced in northern Germany, southern Sweden, the Netherlands, and the Baltic coasts of Estonia, Finland, Latvia, and Lithuania.

History

Ice yachting has been practiced by the Dutch since the middle of the eighteenth century. In 1768, a drawing of a Dutch ice yacht was published by Chapman in the *Architectura Navalis Mercatoria*. The sport is also known to have taken place during the eighteenth century on the frozen bay at Riga, Latvia, and in the Gulf of Finland. In 1790, Booth sailed in a primitive, box-like craft, the first ice boat recorded in North America, on the frozen Hudson River at Poughkeepsie, New York, USA.

In the late nineteenth century in the Hudson River valley, the Poughkeepsie Yacht Club was formed in 1865. The Hudson River Ice Yacht Club, was founded five years later, in part as a result of the active interest of Commodore Roosevelt. The early Hudson River craft were heavy and cumbersome by later standards and in 1970 Roosevelt's "Icicle" was the largest ever built, at 69ft (21.03m) long with 1,070sq ft (99.40sq m) of sail.

Speeds exceeding 100mph (160km/h) were achieved in 1885 by the "Scud" on the Navesink River at Red Bank, New Jersey. In 1907, the "Claret" reached 140mph (225 km/h) along the Shrewsbury River at Long Branch, New Jersey. Ice yachtsmen were then the fastest travelling humans in the world. A long-standing world record, determined over 30 miles (48km), was set in 1907 by "Wolverine" at Kalamazoo, Michigan. Its time of 29min 50sec remained unbeaten until 1953, when Perrigo's "Thunderjet" took 29min 4 sec. A highest speed of 143mph (230km/h) was credited to Buckstaff in 1938, in a stern-steerer on Lake Winnebago, Wisconsin.

The sport was transformed from a rich man's recreation using expensive craft when, in the mid-twentieth century, much cheaper, smaller and lighter boats were introduced and the bow-steering Skeeter class became the most popular, prompting the formation at Chicago in 1939 of the International Skeeter Association, to supervise race organization of this rapidly growing class.

Annual European championships, using stern-steering craft, were held until the Second World War, after which participation diminished but remained particularly popular in Sweden.

Rules

The technique corresponds very much to that of sailing on water. The potential speed of an ice yacht is approximately four times that of the wind velocity.

Equipment

Built usually for only one or two occupants, ice yachts for competition purposes are classified simply by sail area. The most popular craft nowadays is the bow-steering Skeeter class, limited to 75sq ft (7sq m) of sail. A 22ft racing Skeeter, weighing about 300lb (136kg) can be dismantled for transport on a car roof or light trailer. It has sharp-edged steel runners, normally 4.5in high and 40in long (114.3mm x 1.01m).

IN-LINE ROLLER HOCKEY

Introduction

Two games of six players wearing skates use sticks to try and gain possession of a puck or ball and thus score in their opponents' goal. The side with the most points wins.

History

The first in-line skates (with the wheels one behind the other) were patented in France in 1819. Around 1984, Rollerblade Inc. introduced a modern in-line skate with a brake and wheels permanently attached to the boot. As rollerblading became a popular recreational activity, the benefits of the use of in-line skates for roller hockey were quickly recognized; especially their mobility and control, as found in ice hockey. In-line roller hockey is expected to become an Olympic sport.

Venue

An indoor or outdoor skating rink needs to have a smooth, level playing surface of wood, asphalt or cement. It should be a minimum size of 65ft x 130ft and a maximum size of 100ft x 200ft. The ratio of length to width must be 2:1. The surface needs a barrier around it to keep the puck in play. The goal crease area is a semicircle of 6ft 2in from the centre of each goal line. Two face-off spots are marked in each end zone and one at the exact centre of the rink.

Rules

After a coin toss, the game begins with a face-off. One player from each team stands on their own side of the center face-off spot with their stick held to the surface of the rink. All the other players stay in their own half of the rink until the referee drops the puck/ball and play begins.

There are six players on the rink, which includes the

goalkeeper, a centre, two forwards and two defenders, but the team may have up to 14 players which can be substituted onto the rink.

The team with the puck/ball try to pass through the oppositions' defence to take a shot at goal. Whenever play is stopped, it is restarted by a face-off and no player can make physical contact with an opponent until the face-off has been completed. All face-offs can take place at the centre spot or the four other face-off spots on the rink. The location selected depends on where the puck/ball was in play when the face-off was called.

The puck/ball can only be played with the stick, which cannot be raised above shoulder height. A player cannot kick, pick-up, carry, push or pull the puck/ball with any body part or skate.

The game is played in two periods of 10, 12 or 15 minutes, depending on the age group.

Equipment

The goal cage (around 44in x 76in wide) is set on a goal line, 9–11ft from each end barrier. The sticks similar to ICE HOCKEY sticks and the puck is a hard plastic disk of 2.5–3in diameter. The ball, often made from synthetic material, is of approx. 2.5in diameter and may be fluid-filled. The skates have all the wheels in a row with brake pads at one end. No skates that are detachable from the boot are allowed.

Scoring

A goal (one point) is scored whenever the puck/ball has completely crossed over the line between the two vertical posts of the goal.

Clothing

Players on the same team wear jerseys, trousers, pants and socks that match in style and colour. Players also wear helmets with a chin strap, a face mask, hockey-type gloves and shin guards. A mouthpiece is optional but recommended.

JEU PROVENÇAL

Introduction

This is a ball-and-target game similar to LAWN BOWLS, CROWN GREEN BOWLS, and the game which sprang directly from it, PETANQUE. It is played in Provence, where it originated in its present form, and also in other parts of France.

History

Anciently played in Provence, jeu provençal is directly descended from the Greek and Roman forms of bowls which have elsewhere produced lawn bowls, crown green bowls, and pétanque. In this century it has developed from a folk and regional sport to one in which individual, doubles and team championships are played within national organizations.

Venue

Jeu provençal has never called for the specially prepared turf links of lawn bowls or crown green bowls but throughout its long history has been played on rough, stony, or paved surfaces. At serious levels however it is now played on pitches officially selected by the umpire who controls the game, or a local society. These pitches are 3 to 4m wide and at least 25m long (approx. 4 x 27.5yds)

Rules

The chief differences between pétanque and jeu provençal are the length of the pitch – jeu provençal is often called "le longue" – and the fact that the bowler is allowed a run-up in jeu provençal but not in pétanque.

The players in singles, or members from teams, toss for the right to choose the bowling point, throw the target ball and bowl the first bowl. The winner then selects and marks out a circle between 35 and 50cm (approx. 13–19in) in diameter and 1m (1.094yds) from the nearest edge of the circle; 1m sideways and 3m (9ft 10in) in depth from any obstacle; and visible to a player standing within the throwing circle.

The winner of the toss has three chances to throw the jack within valid range; if s/he fails to do so the option for three attempts passes to the opposing side; but that does not deprive the original winner of the toss of the right to throw the first bowl.

The bowler must begin with one foot placed inside the circle. S/he is entitled to take one step while aiming and three in throwing; but s/he must not put foot to ground outside the circle until s/he has delivered his/her bowl (though players disabled in the leg or over 65 years old may bring the front foot from outside the circle, back to the other).

The bowler's aim is to land his/her bowl as closely as possible to the jack. To do so s/he may employ any one of four tactics. The first called "plomber", consists of tossing the bowl high in the air so that it drops close to the hack and stops dead. The second – "rouler" – consists of bowling it all along the ground, as in lawn bowling. There is then the "pointer" – landing a bowl inside the opponent's nearest ball, and the "tir" or "tirer" – consisting of knocking the opponent's winning ball away. At its best this last tactic will, by striking the winning ball at a precisely ideal point, not only knock it away but drop into its place; this last is called "carreau" and is the most spectacular move in the game.

Thus most teams carry an expert in plomber, pointer and carreau. A "clean sweep" shot is not allowed. A tir bowl is disallowed if it pitches more than 1m from the jack or the opponent's ball which it strikes. If it pitches further away, or if it knocks the opponent's bowl or the jack more than 4m (13ft) from its previous position, the bowl is void and everything disturbed by it must be replaced.

The players continue alternately, using any of the three tactics – pointer, tirer, carreau – often in changing circumstances because the jack has been displaced in the course of play, until each has delivered his two, three, or four bowls. Then the player whose ball is nearest to the jack scores 1 point; and if his team has two, three, four, five, or six bowls nearer the jack than any of their opponents they score 2, 3, 4, 5, or 6 points. This single end, to use a term from lawn bowls, is known as a "méne". The second méne is started from a circle about the point where the jack stood in the first game; and subsequent ménes are also played from alternate ends of the pitch.

A match usually consists of three games, each of 13 or other agreed number of points; traditionally the first is called "la partie", the second "la revanche" and the third "la belle".

Equipment

The jack – "cochonnet" (Provençal "lé" or "gari") – or target ball is of light-coloured or white-painted wood, and measures 25–35mm (1–1 1/8in) in diameter. The bowls of metal (usually steel) are between 7.05 and 8cm (2.75–3.13in) in diameter, between 0.62 and 0.8kg (22–28oz) in weight, and are made by officially approved manufacturers without weighting or bias, to a specific density.

Scoring

Jeu provençal is played in singles (three or four bowls per player as decided in advance), doubles (three balls each), or trebles (two bowls each). Points are scored by nearness to the jack after all bowls in each game – or méne – have been bowled: 1 point for the player or team for each bowl nearer to the jack than any on the other side. A game consists usually of 13 points, but, according to local or competition decisions or tradition, may be 11, 15, 18 or 21 points.

JOUSTING

Introduction

Jousting was a medieval form of combat between horsemen armed with lances. A major feature of a joust and indeed the entire tournament in which it took place was that no one under the rank of knight could take part. They were thus distinguished from other military-based sports, such as riding at the Quintain, in which all might participate.

History

Many martial exercises were popular in the medieval period but jousts and tournaments were the most exclusive. The two forms differ in that only two men fought in a joust whereas at a tournament there might be any number on either side. Occasionally single combats were held during a tournament, or a joust in which several pairs of knights had competed might end with a miniature tournament, but for the most part the two forms were separate and distinct.

Not every joust was bloodless. "Joute a plaisance" was a

contest with blunted arms, to display the skills of the contestants. A "joute a l'outrance" was a combat in which sharp weapons were used, when men might be maimed or killed.

Jousting possibly has its roots in a Roman pastime called "Ludus Troiae" which is described by Virgil. Fitzstephen records that, in the reign of Henry II, "every Sunday in Lent...great crowds of young Londoners mounted on war horses... exhibited the representation of battles." Henry III later set up one of many Round Tables, its purpose being to encourage jousting, which would then be followed by dining. During the reign of Edward I, Roger de Mortimer established a Round Table at Kenilworth and Thomas of Walsingham tells of a tournament in which Edward himself took part, held when the king was returning to England via Savoy. The whole affair was not a success, and ended in a near riot.

After the Tudor revival, the popularity of tournaments and jousts declined. Tournaments were a relic of the days of courtly chivalry, and when there was no longer such a convention, they were regarded merely as traditions.

Rules

Strict rules governed both events. The officer-at-arms had to be sure that a prospective contestant was in fact "a gentleman of name and of arms" and only when this had been ascertained was he allowed to appear in the "lists" (the place of combat, including the pavilions). The weapons and armor used, the mode of fighting, and the number of attendant servants and squires were all controlled, and any knight transgressing the rules was excluded from the field. Arms were not always blunted, and the aim was to break an opponent's spear so that he was unhorsed or unarmed and could not go the next course.

Jousts were occasions of great social importance. The ladies of the court provided inspiration for the combatants. Every knight had a lady-love, and it was for her favour that he fought. He wore his lady's glove or sleeve. It was the ladies who decided who were the winners in these contests, and one of them (the Queen if she was present) presented the prizes.

The word "tournament" comes from the French "tournoi" – the wheeling motion of the competitors as they turned and returned to enter the lists. The principal weapon used in jousting was a spear without a head, although in a hand-to-hand encounter a blunt, two-handed sword was wielded.

Scoring

Viscount Dillon in the *Archaeological Journal* records the rules for jousting. If a knight broke a spear between the saddle and the fastening of the helmet to the breast, he scored 1 point; if it was above this he scored 2; if he struck it twice he lost 3 points. If he struck his opponent's horse or back, or his opponent when disarmed, he was disqualified.

JOUTES LYONNAISES

Introduction

This is a traditional and localized French form of JOUSTING on water. Competitors are armed with wooden lances and carry wooden shields on their left arms. They are mounted on platforms raised above the stern of boats which are propelled towards one another and pass at close quarters while each competitor attempts to knock the other off his platform by the impact of the lance against the shield.

JUDO
Introduction

Judo, literally, "easy way", is a combat sport which developed primarily in Japan but now has world-wide appeal and received Olympic recognition in 1964.

History

Judo was developed in Japan from the ancient schools of JU-JITSU by Dr Kano, who combined their outstanding features into a method he called Kodokan judo. Kano opened his first dojo, the Kodokan, in 1882. He called his first method judo rather than ju-jitsu for two reasons: firstly, ju-jitsu had fallen into disrepute because some experts were staging exhibition fights; secondly, a number of ju-jitsu schools had got a reputation for dangerous techniques.

For some time judo was regarded as just one of a number of ju-jitsu schools, but in 1886 the Kodokan gained a lead when the Tokyo Metropolitan Police Board held a tournament between the Kodokan and Totsuka, the biggest of the ju-jitsu schools. Each team entered 15 men and the Kodokan inflicted a crushing defeat on the opposition, winning 13 bouts and drawing 2. From that date interest in judo increased greatly in Japan and ju-jitsu diminished in importance.

The technical formula of the Kodokan was completed in 1887. The major difference between Kodokan judo and ju-jitsu may be summed up, in the words of Kano, as "the elevation of an art to be a principle". Kano declared that judo made the maximum use of mind and body and ju-jitsu was nothing but an application of this principle to the methods of attack and defence. In studying judo, he felt it was essential to train the body and to cultivate the mind through the practice of the methods of attack and defence. He summarized his teaching in the slogans "maximum efficiency with minimum effort" and "mutual welfare and benefit".

Ju-jitsu lacks the sporting aspect of judo but Kano also introduced something completely new, tskuri-komi, taking a fighter off balance in order to throw him. His opinions were respected by the Japanese Ministry of Education who adopted judo as a sport.

Kano, however, was not content to popularize judo only in his home country. He visited Britain in 1885 and one of his outstanding pupils, Yamashita, began teaching in the USA in 1902. By 1905 judo had reached France and was being taught to French police. Judo was became a truly international sport when the first world championships were held in 1956. It became part of the Olympics in 1964.

Venue

The competition area is on a mat which must be a minimum of 14m (15yds) square and a maximum of 16m (17.5 yds) square. It must be covered by tatami or a similar acceptable material and is usually green. The competition area is divided into two zones. The area between these two zones is called the "danger zone" and is indicated by a red area, approximately 1m (3ft) wide, parallel to the four sides of the competition area. The area within and including the danger zone is called the "contest area" and must be a minimum of 8m (26ft) square or a maximum of 10m (33ft) square. The area outside the danger zone is called the "safety area" and must be 3m (10ft) wide. A red tape and a white tape must be fixed on the centre of the contest area 4m (13ft) apart, to indicate the positions at which the contestants must start and end the contest. The red tape must be to the referee's right and the white to the referee's left. A free zone, a minimum of 50cm (19.5in), must be maintained around the competition area.

Rules

The two contestants must stand facing each other on the contest area at the red and white tape according to the belt they are wearing. They must make a standing bow and take one step forward. The referee announces "jajime" to start the contest.

Shiai (contests) are conducted by a roving referee and two judges who sit at opposite corners of the mat. The tatami (mats) are made of compressed straw with a tight canvas covering and usually measure 2m x 1m (6ft 7in x 3ft 3.5in).

The referee calls out any decisive score (waza-ari and below) and may also penalize either competitor for an infringement of the rules. The referee's Japanese terminology includes the following:

Hajime: Begin

Matte: Break

Sono-mama: Do not move

Yoshi: Carry on

Jikan: Time out

Hantei: Decision

Sore-made: That is all.

An ippon is scored when a competitor is hurled on to his/her back with some force. When the throw is less definite and the competitor has not landed completely on his/her back, a waza-ari is awarded.

Most top-class contests are difficult to judge and many decisions are controversial. If there has been no score and neither competitor has received any warning for infringements, the judges award the contest to the fighter who has scored the most knock downs, but these are ignored if a competitor scores a wazari-ni-chikai waza (a decisive knock-down). This is sufficient to win him the contest in the event of no better score.

All infringements count for slightly more than scores. Thus if a fighter has scored a waza-ari but suffers a keikoki and there are no further scores in the bout the verdict goes to his/her opponent.

In hold-downs a competitor must trap at least one arm and hold the opponent for 30 seconds (25 seconds for a waza-ari). The referee will call "osaekomi" (holding) and if the fighter escapes s/he will shout "toketa" (broken).

Competitors seek to gain the maximum from a slight advantage. If one goes ahead on a knock-down (or chui) s/he will usually assume the defensive while his/her opponent will launch an all-out attack. Some fighters specialize in groundwork and attempt to lure their opponent on to the mat so that they can use their strongest techniques.

Fighters grip each side of the opponent's jacket, usually on the sleeves or lapels. They grapple for grips but often attempt throws with only one hand on the jacket or dive at their opponent's leg in a bid to gain a point. Most major throws are derived from kata (a series of regularized movements). The basic groups are: hand throws; leg throws; shoulder throws; and sacrifice throws.

Although strength is needed in judo, it is most successful when correctly applied, at an opponent's weakest point. Thus if a fighter moves forward, his/her opponent will seek to use that momentum in order to throw him/her.

A contestant wins the contest if they score an ippon. If no one scores an ippon, the contestant with the highest score wins the contest.

Scoring

Points are not cumulative (except for a waza-ari). An ippon scores ten points, and wins the contest. A waza-ari scores seven points, and two waza-ari achieve an ippon. A judo scores five points, and a koka scores three points.

Grades

The grades are divided into "Kyu" (pupil) and "Dan" (degree); a beginner wears a while belt:

5th Kyu – yellow belt (in Japan, white)

4th Kyu – orange belt (in Japan, white)

3rd Kyu – green belt (in Japan, brown)

2nd Kyu – blue belt (in Japan, brown)

1st Kyu – brown belt (in Japan, brown)

1st Dan – black belt

2nd Dan – black belt

3rd Dan – black belt

4th Dan – black belt

5th Dan – black belt

6th Dan – red and white belt

7th Dan – red and white belt

8th Dan – red and white belt

9th Dan – red belt

10th Dan – red belt

11th Dan – red belt

12th Dan – red belt

Bow

Inner thigh throw

Changing hip throw

Shoulder throw

Strangle

Judo Throws and Holds

Clothing

All judoka (participants) wear the judogi (judo suit) which resembles a loose-fitting western suit. There are no buttons or pockets, to minimize injury, and feet are left bare. The jacket is fastened by a belt, the colour of which indicates the competitor's standard.

JU-JITSU

Introduction

Ju-Jitsu (or Ju-Jutsu) is the Japanese method of self-defence which Dr Kano studied and developed into the modern sport of JUDO. Both KARATE and AIKIDO include many features of ju-jitsu.

History

Ju-jitsu began to take on a systematized form in the latter half of the sixteenth century and most of the major schools were developed from the seventeenth to the beginning of the nineteenth century. Some references, including the Kikushoji document, state the ju-jitsu was introduced into Japan by a Chinese monk, Chen Yuan-ping, at the start of the seventeenth century, but evidence shows that such Japanese ju-jitsu masters as Hitotsubashi-Joeken and Sekiguchi-Jushin thrived before 1627.

There were many schools, each distinguished by its individual features. According to the *Bu-jutsu-Ryusoruku* (Biographies of the Founders of the Various martial Exercise Schools) there were 20 Ryu of ju-jitsu such as Takenouchi, Kyushin, Kito and Tenchin-Shin'yo, the last two of which were closely studied by Dr Kano.

When, however, the ordinance of 1871 forbade the samurai (knights) to carry swords, ju-jitsu fell into disrepute as experts used its devastating methods on ordinary members of the public, and the expansion of judo further reduced its popularity. It still exists, however, in Japan and in other parts of the world.

Rules

The techniques of ju-jitsu, which was rather a ruthless method of self-defence rather than a sport, included throws, strangleholds, arm-and wrist-locks, kicks, chops with the hand and punches. Many of the different ryu (schools) were based on the principles of the Chinese strategist Hwang-Shihkon: "In yielding is strength", the use of an opponent's force and movement to destroy him/her.

KABADDI

Introduction

Kabaddi is a traditional team pursuit game, played in India, requiring the players to run and hold their breath

History

There is no record to indicate exactly when Kabaddi was first played but it must have been centuries ago. India being a multi-lingual country, the game has been known by different names in various regions until its present name was universally adopted. It has been called hututu, kapati, do-do-do, bhadi-bhadi, wandikali, chedu-gudu, zabar gagana, saunchi-pakki, and kabardee. The game was not played in an organized form until 1923 when the Hind Vijay Gymkhana, Baroda, framed the rules of hurutu, as Kabaddi was known in that part of the country. A similar attempt in 1885 at Poona had failed.

Kabaddi has three varieties:

1 Sanjeevani, where a player once out could be revived.
2 Amar, where a player put out remained on the field, an entry

having been made in the score-book.

3 Ganimi, where a player once out cannot be revived.

When Kabaddi was standardized, the first system – sanjeevani – was adopted, but the rules framed at Baroda covered only one region of the sub-continent. It was not until 1944 that the Indian Olympic Association adopted the rules of Kabaddi to cover the whole of the country. Six years later the Amateur Kabaddi Federation of India, which is now the governing authority of the game, was established. The Federation is an autonomous body and is responsible for the administration and organization of the game in the country.

Since its inception, the game has become well organized. There are now thousands of clubs all over India. Though the years the game has gained in importance and stature. It has become one of India's national games and reflects a philosophy of simple living and high thinking. The simplicity of its nature and organization and its negligible cost makes it easily accessible to the great but poor masses of India. It develops physical strength and creates team spirit. Kabaddi is also played in Pakistan, Burma, Ceylon and China.

Venue

It is played on a rectangular field 13m by 10m (42ft 6in x 33ft) (11m x 8m – 36ft x 26ft for women and juniors) which is divided into two halves by a line drawn across the middle. Each half, called the "court", has a line parallel to the centre line at a distance of 3m (9ft 10in) – 2.5m (8ft 3in) for women and juniors – known as a baulk line.

Rules

A team consists of 12 players but only 7 take the field; the rest remain as reserves on the "waiting blocks" which are drawn

2m (6ft 6in) away from the end lines.

The team winning the toss sends a player into the opponents' court. This player is called the "raider", the opponents being known as the "anti-raiders" or "antis". Only one raider may be sent at a time, and each team sends one alternately until the end of play. Before crossing the centre line, the raider must begin saying loudly and clearly the word "Kabaddi". He repeats it rapidly, without taking a breath, until the raid is completed. This process is called the "cant".

The raider is deemed to have lost his cant if he pauses between his repetition of "Kabaddi" and is therefore out. While on the opponents' court the raider tries to touch one or more antis before retreating. He may touch either by his hands or any part of his body. But he must, at least once, cross the baulk line. If he succeeds in both, i.e. crosses the baulk line and touches one or more antis and returns to his own half, without losing his cant, all the antis touched by him are out. On the other hand, the raider is out if he loses his cant while still on enemy territory. He is out also when he is caught by one or more antis and is prevented from returning to his court. The antis may not resort to unfair means such as trying deliberately to stifle the raider's cant by shutting his mouth or wilfully pushing him over the boundary line. Such tactics are punished by the umpire and the raider is considered to have returned home safely. If, in trying to free himself from the antis, the raider throws himself on the ground and touches his own court with any part of his body, he has made a safe return. A raider, however, is not compelled to touch an anti. If he returns home without touching anybody, but holding on to his cant, neither side loses a player. When a player is out he must leave the field and go on to his waiting block. He is "revived" or re-enters when an opponent is out, in the same order as he was out.

While a raid is in progress all the antis must remain within their own court. If an anti goes over the boundary line or steps into the other half he is out. The raider's captain or team mates may not shout advice while he is away. At the end of the match the team scoring most points wins. If it is a tie an extra ten minutes is allowed. Should it prove to be a deadlock again, the side scoring the first point is declared the winner. A representative match for men has two halves of 20 minutes (15 minutes for women and juniors) with a 5 minute interval.

Equipment

Kabaddi is one of the very few games where no equipment is needed.

Scoring

A team scores 1 point for each player put out by them. They score a "lona" – a bonus of 4 points – if they put out the entire opposition and the game continues by putting all the players of both sides back into their respective courts.

Clothing

A player's kit consists of a jersey, shorts, canvas tennis shoes with plain soles and socks. Their jerseys must be clearly numbered at the back and front and their nails closely clipped. Their bodies and limbs must be free of any greasy substance.

KARATE

Introduction

In exhibitions and training sessions karate – literally "empty hand" fighting – assumes a variety of forms. Exhibitions are normally as follows: "jiu-kumite" (or free-style fighting); "kata"

Karate Stances

The 'cat' stance (*neko-ashi-dachi*)

The 'reclining dragon' stance (*gargu-kamae*)

The *jion* stance

(or training dances); and "tamashiwara" (or wood-breaking). Training sessions also include "kihon" (basic technical training). Each of these forms is described below, as are the unique breathing methods and their relationship with Zen Buddhism, the peculiarity of the stances, and the great variety of body parts used for striking. Technical terms in karate are always in Japanese. A person who practices karate is known as a "karateka".

History

Modern karate is a product of the twentieth century. Its roots, however, can be traced back through the centuries to before the time of Jesus, and Okinawa, China, and India, as well as Japan, have all contributed substantially to it development.

Yoga originated in India and through its diaphragmatic

breathing methods has exerted a substantial influence on the many combat techniques of the Orient and ultimately upon karate. Karateka place special emphasis on the need for powerful diaphragms and utilize strong exhalations of air to assist muscle contraction, thereby increasing power. Also, as the disturbing effect of emotions, such as fear, upon breathing are well known, karateka exploit the relationship to ensure a state of mental calm. This they do by the use of controlled breathing which itself has a calming effect upon the emotions.

Legend has it that at the end of the fifth century AD, a Zen Buddhist priest named Bhodidharma travelled to China to instruct at the monastery of Shaolin-ssu. The aim of Buddhism is the salvation of the soul but, as the body and soul are inseparable, in order to attain true enlightenment, it is necessary to impose severe physical as well as mental discipline. Bhodidharma found that the imposition of such discipline caused many of his student monks to collapse from sheer exhaustion. In order to improve their physical condition, he blended his knowledge of yoga and Indian fist arts with indigenous Chinese "kempo" (fighting) and used it as a form of physical training.

Although Shaolin-ssu kempo spread throughout China it gradually assumed different forms according to local conditions. Combat techniques known simply as "te" (hand) had existed for many centuries in Okinawa, but with the unification of the country in 1470 and the imposition of laws against carrying arms, te received a substantial boost. Later, with the assistance of Chinese kempo masters who fled from China in times of political upheaval, this developed into an early form of "kara-te" (empty hand). At first the new techniques became known as Tang Hand, to indicate their Chinese origin – Tang being the name of a Chinese dynasty, the symbol for which later became associated with China in general. It was not until after 1922, with Funakoshi Gichin, that Tang Hand or Okinawa-te was first introduced to Japan and, incorporating certain aspects of Japanese JU-JITSU, acquired the name of karate.

The name was chosen to convey the Zen concept of emptiness and the student karateka is required to empty his/her mind of all though, especially over-concern with tactics or strategy, and emotions such as fear, in the pursuit of his/her "budo" (martial way, or way of the fighter). An incorrect mental attitude would inevitably have a deleterious effect even upon the most skilled technician, and the karateka therefore trains to the point of automatic reactions where external considerations do not intrude into his/her mental state of impassivity or emptiness.

Karate involves a training of the mind as well as the body and apart from being a system of defence and a sport, it is a physical manifestation of Zen Buddhism. Karate is action and Zen is meditation.

Following the Second World War, and partly due to the presence of many western servicemen in Japan, karate gradually acquired devotees in Europe and the Americas. During the late 1950s and the 1960s this process accelerated and by 1970 this sport was practiced throughout the world.

Venue

In Jiu-kumite the two teams take up their positions on opposite sides of the contest area, 8m to 10m (26-32ft) square. The centre is marked with a cross, on either side of which the individual contestants stand, with an initial distance of 2m (6ft 6in) between them.

Rules

In karate, as in JUDO, a belt system is used to evaluate merit and progress. The two basic categories within the system are "Kyu" (student), and "Dan" (graduate). The requirements for each level vary according to the style and standards of the instructor conducting the grading examination. The number of levels also varies according to style, but the general pattern is as described below.

In most styles there are six grades rising from 6th to 1st Kyu, plus the novice grade. (novices wear a white belt). The requirements for promotion include competence at the style's basic fighting forms (kihon), fitness, and the basic training dances (kata). An able student may be able to gain promotion from the white-belt stage in three or four months of intensive training, but a large proportion of students leave karate before gaining promotion from white belt as they find the training too rigorous.

Kata: The general publication of combat techniques in book form is a very recent innovation; they were originally passed down by word of mouth and personal example and treated with great secrecy.

A kata is a fixed sequence of basic defence and attacking techniques designed for practise, and takes the form of imaginary fighting with several attackers approaching from different directions.

There are approximately 30 different katas but in all the choreography is highly stylized and appears like a strangely beautiful training dance. Unlike dancing, however, the aim is not primarily beauty, but sharpness and combat utility. The beauty lies in the expression of a martial spirit, the smoothness of line, and the economy of movement.

Each movement has a specific meaning and each sequence embodies the concentrated experience of numerous karate masters. The more comprehensive and advanced katas incorporate quick changes of technique, slowness and quickness, maintenance of balance, stretching and bending of the body, correct breathing, body shifting, combinations of hand and foot techniques, and instantaneous tensing and relaxing of the muscles to facilitate the application and withdrawal of power.

Jiu-kumite (free-style fighting) contests are always between two individuals irrespective of grade. Team contests consist of a series of individual contests, the team with the greatest number of winning members being the winner. Each team normally consists of five karateka and each bout normally lasts two minutes, or three minutes in the finals. Time is allowed for stoppages.

Before the contest the karateka perform a standing "rei" (bow) and the referee then calls "Hajime", begin. All instructions are in Japanese. The waiting position is one of watchful, though relaxed, preparedness.

The actual sparring consists of a free exchange of blows, blocks and counter-attacks until one player gets a fully focused blow to one of a number of defined areas on his opponent's body. If the blow is delivered with the proper posture and stance, from the correct distance, and is spirited, an "ippon" (full point) will be awarded and the contest is over. A "wasari" (half-point) can be awarded for a well-timed punch which is weak or a punch slightly off the target with the opponent unguarded. If both contestants score simultaneous points they cancel each other out. If a half-point is awarded the contest will continue until one player obtains a full point or two half-points.

Another means of determining a contest are by "hanteigachi" (win by decision), "hansokumake" (loss by disqualification), or "hikiwake" (draw).

Jiu-kumite is undoubtedly the most popular and exciting aspect of karate and is of Japanese origin. Originally fights were often to the death, but the development of Jiu-kumite with the imposition of combat rules and regulations, and the strict discipline required of karateka, enabled a potentially lethal activity to be enjoyed as a sport.

Tamashiwara: (wood-breaking) is a subject about which there is a difference of opinion within karate. All exponents would agree that karateka should be capable of such feats of strength and that it is the natural outcome of techniques properly executed, but some believe that its public performance is merely flashy showmanship. Such showmanship might include breaking a stack of twenty roofing tiles or three or four 1in boards with the hand, foot, elbow, or head. Other demonstrations might include throwing a water-melon into the air and thrusting the fingers through it as it descends, or chopping off the top of a bottle with the bare hand while leaving the bottle standing.

The advocates of tamashiwara would claim that it is an integral part of karate and that it is a physical, psychological, and even spiritual necessity. Their arguments would include the following: the various striking parts of the body possess quite remarkable power, but this power can be released only when the karateka has rid himself of the fear of striking something hard. Breaking, or destruction as it is sometimes called, is therefore a psychological as well as a physical ordeal, especially in public, and its successful execution gives self-confidence and self-knowledge. The word tamashi in fact means "trial". These styles therefore require their members to demonstrate before being upgraded as proof of their physical and mental ability.

The other argument for breaking is more esoteric, even religious. The self-discipline required is such that the strike at wood is more a strike at oneself. The total commitment to the blow is a discipline which requires the karateka to transcend his normal nature and enter the Zen world of nothingness, where he is momentarily united with the universe. The essence of tamashiwara is therefore enlightenment through a single blow in what amounts to active Zen meditation.

Kihon is basic training in numerous blocks, strikes and kicks with special emphasis on correct stance, balance, breathing and focus. Kihon may be practiced individually or in groups. When practiced in groups it is normally accompanied by semi-hypnotic chanting from a leader who thereby controls the timing and effort involved.

Many different stances are used with a variety of foot and hand positions, each of which is linked to certain appropriate moves. Stances with a wide foot base and a low centre of gravity are very stable and suited to powerful punching; others are designed for mobility and speed of action. A good karateka will command a variety of stances and vary them according to the circumstances. For example, in the "jion" position, the foot position is wide, the centre of gravity low and stability is great.

The arm position appears to invite a strike to the head but it is in fact only provocative. The head and upper body are easily defended and set attacks can follow. The "reclining dragon" ("gargu-kamae") stance emphasizes protection of the vital parts of the body from attack and the front of the body is turned away from the opponent. In the "cat" ("neko-ashi-dachi") stance 90% of the body weight is on the rear foot and the front foot is poised for kicking. This stance facilitates very rapid change of position and posture.

Focus is the art of concentrating all one's physical and mental energies on a specific target in an instant. It is rather like a person trapped in a blazing room being able to produce on demand the strength to knock down the door in a way he would normally find quite impossible. It is said to involve a spontaneous explosion of the life force ("chi") which flows from the pelvic region to the extremities and points of contact. To generate maximum speed, the striking limb is kept relaxed until immediately before impact. On impact the body tenses and the karateka emits a "kiai", or yell, which is propelled by the muscles of the lower diaphragm. This psychologically assists a total commitment to the punch and the muscular effort involved adds to the power produced. The object is to transmit, via the correct use of stance, breathing and timing, the muscular power of the whole body down a striking limb moving at maximum speed, to focus on a given object.

In karate the whole of the body, and in particular the bony parts, are used as weapons. An experienced karateka can utilize even a single finger, suitable strengthened, as a highly effective weapon. In fact, other things being equal, the smaller the area of contact the more effective the blow will be. A rigid finger, if strengthened to withstand impact, would have an effect similar to that of a sword point.

The hand can be used in a great variety of ways for punching and striking. The contact points include: the fist ("seiken"); the inverted fist ("uraken"); the fist edge ("tettsui"); the knife hand ("shuto"); the palm heel ("shotei"); the wrist ("koken"); the fingertips and the thumb or chicken's beak ("keiko"); and the half-clenched fist ("hiraken"). The elbow and forearm can also be used.

The variation in the use of the foot is not as great as that of the hand, but includes the following: the knife foot ("sokuto"); the instep ("haisoku"); the heel ("kakato"); and the ball of the foot ("chusoku"). The knee and head may also be used in in-fighting.

Clothing

Kata: The traditional garb of the sport is called Karatege and consists of a pair of loose white trousers and a jacket. The jacket is fastened with the coloured belt, which indicates the grade of the karateka wearing it. Hachimaki, or sweatbands, worn around the head, are also sometimes used. For jiu-kumite one contestant will wear a red belt and the other a white one.

KARTING

Introduction

Karting is the sport of racing karts. It is a form of MOTOR RACING.

History

Karting and karts are American inventions dating from August 1956 when the first tiny tubular-framed vehicle, which we would now call a kart, was built. Its conception stemmed from a commercial failure on the part of McCulloch, a chainsaw and outboard motor manufacturing company which, in trying to diversify its interests, designed a rotary lawn mower and bought some 10,000 West Bend 750cc. engines to power them. Unfortunately, the mowers proved unreliable and, to safeguard their good name, McCulloch discontinued the range and were left with about 8,000 of the engines in store. Ingels, a mechanic working with the Kurtis Craft racing car company in Glendale, California, built his minuscule tube-framed vehicle that August and a neighbour named Borelli bought one of the engines to power it. At first the 2.5h.p. engine was too underpowered to carry the "kart" and its driver up inclines, so Borelli modified the unit until it could propel the 15-stone (95kg) Ingels with ease.

The two men used the cart for joy-riding off the road, but in September 1956 the operators of a car-silencer business saw the kart and set to work building two replicas. Interest was enormous and led Ingels and Borelli to go into business laying down an initial batch of six machines. Surplus engines from McCulloch provided the motive power, and by early 1957 the dozen or so kart-owners were meeting at week-ends and searching for suitable car parks or other open areas in which to run their vehicles. To call these meetings races would be an exaggeration, but police disapproval soon led these early karters to find a safe site in the Rose Bowl car park at Pasadena. Many inquiries came from the public who stopped to watch the proceedings and in spring 1957 the Go Kart Company was formed by Wineland, Livingstone and Desbrow, as a subsidiary of their silencer business. Production of these McCulloch-powered karts quickly reached 500 per month. Meetings at the Rose Bowl got out of hand, the movement lost their informal venue, and on 14 December 1957 the first meeting of the Go Kart Club of America was convened.

The sport quickly developed in Britain, proving cheap yet fast and extremely exciting. Karting subsequently became established throughout Europe, the USA, Australia, New Zealand, Japan and many other Asiatic nations.

Venue

Kart circuit venues vary, but sections of airfields are popular in Great Britain, Australia and parts of America and Europe, while other temporary sites include car parks, sea-fronts and even full-size motor racing circuits, whose permanent facilities offer greater spectator attraction. Some of the best-equipped kart circuits in the world are to be found in Italy, the home of the dominant rotary-valve engines, where several fine permanent facilities have been developed and used purely for kart racing. Tracks should have a minimum width of 20ft and track edges must be marked in an approved manner. Track markings must not constitute a hazard.

Rules

In Australia karting is governed by the National Karting Association (NKA), which in turn is affiliated to the national motor sporting authority, the Confederation of Australian Motor Sports (CAMS). European and American rules are generally similar to the British ones, and international competition ensures that there is a close parity in the equipment used.

Race meetings are normally held on temporary short-distance courses marked out for the occasion by straw-bale barriers. Due to their small size, a large number of karts may be started on a narrow and quite short circuit, and such competitions lead to the development of split-second timing and intense concentration on the part of the drivers.

The methods of starting a race differ. The Class I direct-drive karts, lacking a gear-box or clutch, are drop-started by helpers who lift the tail end of the kart, with the driver already aboard, push it forward a few paces, and then drop the rear wheels on to the road in order to start the engine. They will then take up a grid formation as they complete a slow lap of the circuit, passing the flag in a flying start. The clutch and gear-box karts are sometimes push-started, the clutch being released to fire the motor; motor cycle kick-starts are sometimes fitted. Grid positions are normally allotted by ballot, and the clutch karts are formed up in a stationary grid formation, making a clutch start as the flag falls.

Equipment

The kart is a tiny wheeled vehicle, usually consisting of a bodiless tubular frame with a small-capacity single-cylinder two-stroke engine mounted towards the rear, and providing a single seat for the driver. Pneumatic tyres are obligatory and have a diameter of 9–17in. Bumpers are compulsory at both front and rear and four-wheel brakes are compulsory for all gearbox karts. The engine must be officially homologated. Supercharging is prohibited.

Clothing

Drivers wear an approved style of crash helmet with goggles or a visor. Drivers also wear a leather or heavy-duty polyvinyl chloride (PVC) suit and gloves. All clothing must be securely fastened at the wrists and ankles. Boots and shoes that cover and protect the ankles are recommended.

KENDO
Introduction

Kendo, literally, "sword way", is the Japanese art of sword fighting. It is very popular in the country of its origin, partly because of its tradition; but during the twentieth century it has spread to most parts of the world, including Europe and North and South America. Apart from Japan; the USA, Canada and Brazil are the nations with which it is most popular.

History

Kendo developed from "kenjutsu" (swordsmanship) which was essential for survival in medieval Japan. The "Samurai" (knights) needed a method of training which was not lethal and so kendo, which uses a bamboo fencing stave rather than the original razor-sharp sword, was developed. Its tiring training, need for self-discipline, and close links with ancient Japan, have made kendo both physically and mentally beneficial.

The origins of kendo go back more than 1,500 years. The first references to "kenjutsu" are in the three volumes of the *Kojiki*, a medieval history. These deal with the period from the mythological ages to the Empress Suiko (AD592–628). The 30 volumes of the *Nihon-Shoki*, from the mythological ages to Empress Jito (AD686–97), also contain references to kenjutsu. Japanese historians use these two reliable documents to cover all aspects of ancient history. It is in these that there is a mention of a school of swordsmanship – "Choisai Iizasa"; another reference is to Kunimatsu no Mahito, who was a direct descendant of Amatsu Koyane no Mikoto, a highly respected swordsman.

The earliest reference to any non-lethal practise weapon is about AD400 – the "bokken" which was a wooden sword whose weight, length and balance was approximately the same as a real one. This was followed by the skill of "tachikaki", now known as "iai", the art of drawing swords. The Samurai practiced many styles and types of cutting. When one was found to be effective in battle, a swordsman would absorb this into his style – so the various schools of were originated.

Like the other Japanese martial arts, kendo has innumerable "ryu" (schools). The earliest of these was "nen-ryu", founded in 1350. These is some dispute as to who originated the style; some authorities say Kamisaka Yasuhisa and some Somashiro Yoshimoto. This style was taught until the eighteenth century by the Higuchi family but has now disappeared. There were probably earlier schools, because under the feudal system each "daimyo" (lord) kept a fencing master.

The Meiji government (1868–1912) changed many of the Japanese customs and kendo was in decline for many years, despite numerous exhibitions which initially proved very popular with the public. The ordinary people had not been allowed, under the shoguns (chief ministers), to learn kendo or even watch it, but these exhibitions briefly aroused a new interest. However, with the people becoming more interested in western culture, kendo and other established customs came to be considered old-fashioned and out of place.

The Tokyo Police Bureau maintained their interest in the sport and men like Yamaoka, who died in 1888, kept it alive. Yamaoka was regarded as the outstanding "kendoka" in the era when the sport was in decline. His pupils, particularly men like Nakata, made great efforts to keep kendo going, but it was not until the start of the twentieth century that the sport began to flourish again.

Venue

The contest area is between 9m (29ft 6in) and 11m (36ft) square and is made of smooth, highly-polished wood. The boundaries are marked by white lines and the centre of the area by a white cross. The participants' starting lines are drawn 1.5m (4ft 11in) from the centre so that the competitors begin 3m (9ft 10in) from each other.

Rules

Kendo makes great physical demands but, equally importantly, gives mental benefits. The kendoka (those who practice the sport) gain much from the discipline it instils in its pupils. In addition, many kendoka absorb the background of Japanese history on which much of modern kendo is based. Kendo is probably closer to its origins than any of the other outstandingly popular Japanese martial arts such as judo, karate and aikido. As an international sport it has flourished only comparatively recently – the first world championships were staged in 1970.

The ultimate aim of the kendokai dates back to the Samurai age when a good swordsman would wait until his opponent was about to attack and then launch his/her own cut. By anticipating an attack, s/he chooses exactly the right moment, since his/her opponent in this split second can neither defend nor anticipate the attack.

Kendoka begin each session with exercises before putting on the armour. The practice commences with "suburi", then they move on to "kiri kaeshi", when they perform a series of cuts and the other kendoka parries. Competitors also practice "kakarigeiko", in which they attack openings as the opponent makes them. Kendoka spend much time in "keiko" (free practise) in which contest situations may be freely practised without the fighter feeling obliged to win, as in a competition.

Kendoka may be penalized for infringements such as leaving the area, forcing an opponent from the area, striking illegal blows and throwing an opponent deliberately to the ground. For the first offence a competitor receives a "cui" (caution) and for a further offence he is disqualified.

The judges' expressions include: "Hajime" (begin); "Yoshii" (carry on); and "Tame" (halt). When the referee wishes to announce a decision he calls out the appropriate term, such as "menari" (cut to the head), "kote-ari" (cut to the arm), and "tsuki-ari" (thrust to the throat), and signals the scorer of the point by pointing his flag at the successful fighter. After this, the referee announces, "Nihomme" (Second point). If both contestants have scored, the referee calls, "Shobu" (Match point). When one of the contestants has scored two points, he calls, "Shobu-ari" (There is a match point) and indicates the winner of the bout.

There are eight target areas:

1 "O-shomen", centre of the head.
2 "Hidari-men", left side of the head.
3 "Migi-men", right side of the head.
4 "Hiari-kote", right forearm.
5 "Migi-kote", right forearm.
6 "Gyaku-do", left side of ribcage.
7 "Migi-do", right side of the rib cage.
8 "Tsuki", throat.

All are attacked by cuts except the throat which can be threatened only by a lunge. Competitors often use only one hand on the shinai in attempts to obtain extra distance, but the majority of the powerful blows are performed with two hands. In contests the areas most frequently attacked are the right forearm and the centre of the head. Individuals tend to favour a particular cut or combination of cuts.

The "kiai" (shout) is even more important in kendo than in other martial arts. A score cannot be registered without the yell that accompanies the blow. The kiai has three functions: it emphasises the point to be attacked; helps with the mental and physical co-ordination; and is used to unnerve an opponent.

The usual starting position in either contest or practise is for the two fighters to stand opposite each other with their right feet forward and the shinai held with the left hand at the bottom of the hilt and the right hand just below the sword guard. The points of the sword overlap about 25mm (1in). The left hand is placed just below the navel. The elbows are kept close to the "do" but relaxed, and the shinai is pointed at the opponent's throat. The basic starting position, which must be strictly adhered to, is called "chudan-n-kamae" (perfect distance).

All blows are "kiri" (cuts) in which a kendoka attacks his/her opponent with the cutting edge of the shinai – the side opposite to the cord joining the handle to the tip. The left hand is used to impart power and the right acts as a fulcrum. The basic cut – o-shomen – (to the centre of the head) – is taught to all kendoka and a considerable amount of training is devoted to "suburi" (empty cutting). Here the kendoka aims to achieve control and accuracy.

All cuts emphasise correct posture. In particular, when striking the target, the arms should be fully stretched, the hips remaining square to the target. The feet should be parallel and the shoulders turned to allow the right arm to straighten freely. After striking, the shinai should slide freely up the target without being disengaged.

There is no defence for its own sake; any parry is used as preparation for an immediate counter attack. Feints are sometimes used but a kendoka will often knock an opponent's arm or sword away before landing a powerful blow to the head. All blows are accompanied not only by a kiai but also by a rapid series of short steps. The cut lands as the right foot comes sharply to the ground and the steps continue as the slicing movement of the shinai goes over the target.

The ultimate aim of the kendoka dates back to the Samurai age when a good swordsman would wait until his/her opponent was about to attack and then launch his/her own cut. By anticipating an attack, s/he chooses exactly the right moment, since his/her opponent in this split second can neither defend nor anticipate the attack.

Equipment

The kendoka holds a "shinai" (practise sword) – four selected, polished staves of bamboo held together by a long sheath which forms the handle. There is a small leather cup at the tip and a cord from the tip to the handle holds the "sword" together. In addition, leather binding, a third of the way from the point, prevents the staves from opening. A piece of tough hide is placed round the handle as a sword-guard. The shinai is up to 1.18m (3ft 10.5in) long and weighs approximately 0.40kg (16oz). But for "kata" (forms), a series of regularized movements, the kendoka dispenses with the body armour and wears only the "hakama" and "keikogi" and holds a "bokken" (a wooden imitation of the real sword). For important demonstrations a real sword – a "katana" – is often used, making the exhibition more lifelike and spectacular.

Clothing

All kendoka wear traditional dress of the Samurai period. The feet are left bare. "Hakama" (flowing trousers) are worn together with a "tare" (an apron, or groin protector). The "keikogi" (kendo jacket) is similar to the one used in judo but worn tucked into the trousers. The hands and forearms are protected by a "kote" (heavily padded glove) and the chest is covered by a "do" (breastplate), which is held in place by cords fastened round the shoulders. Finally the "men" (a head-guard consisting of a steel visor and padded cloth) protects the head, throat and shoulders.

Owing to the vigorous nature of the sport, a "hachimaki" (a piece of towelling) is wrapped round the head to prevent perspiration from falling into the kendoka's eyes during practise or competition. Frequently special towels are given to competition in contests, while leading clubs invariably have their own designs.

The colour of keikogi denotes the competitor's grade. There is less emphasis on grading than in other martial arts, but it is still a valuable method of assessing achievement and serves as a valuable guide to the pupil's ability.

KICK-BOXING

Introduction

Kick-boxing is a combat sport which mixes the foot techniques of KARATE and the fist techniques of BOXING. There are four different types of combat competitions: Semi-Contact, Light-

Contact, Full-Contact and Low-Contact. Musical Forms is the fifth type of competition.

History

Some people argue that kick-boxing's origins can be traced to South East Asia: evolving in Burma, Cambodia, Malaysia, Laos, Thailand and the Philippines. Others say that it developed from karate in the west. During the mid-1970s various American tournament karate practitioners became frustrated with karate and wanted to find a system by which they could apply kicks and punches to the knock-out and they developed "full-contact karate". The first bouts were held on open matted areas, just like ordinary karate. Later events were held in regular-sized boxing rings.

Venue

Kick-boxing usually takes place in a hall on mats to protect kick-boxers from injury. Equipment similar to JUDO and karate is often used.

Rules

The World Kick Boxing Association sanctions three disciplines of contact sports: Full Contact, Kick-boxing and THAI BOXING. Although the rules of each discipline are different, bouts are scored in the same way. Three judges score the fight on a 10 point must system, which means the winner of each round must receive 10 points and the loser less than 10, depending on how badly s/he loses the round. If the round is drawn each fighter receives 10 points. The fighter can also win a bout by knock-out. If a fighter is knocked onto the canvas with a kick or a punch s/he has 10 seconds to stand and fight on. If s/he cannot beat the count s/he loses by knock out.

The original rules system created by the WKA allowed

fighters from the West (USA and Europe) to compete with fighters from the East (Japan and Thailand) under rules that both sides found acceptable. Fighters competing under kick-boxing rules wear shorts and boots. Full contact fighters must fight kicks above the waist only and wear long trousers and boots.

Clothing

Kick-boxers wear protection for the feet and head, and shin guards, safety gloves, mouth guards, groin guards for men and chest protection for women.

KITE-FIGHTING

Introduction

Kite-fighting, in which each of two opponents tries to bring down, destroy, or cut adrift the other's kite, may seem an unreal event to the European child trying to get his/her square of paper airborne at the seaside. But elsewhere it ranges from a vicious pastime to a serious, adult, competitive sport. The means of sabotage vary in the three main regions in which it is practiced.

History

The origin of kite-fighting, like that of kite-flying, is lost in time, but almost certainly has ritual, religious, and possibly sexual, significance. It was a pastime popular for centuries in Japan, where kites were sometimes as big as 1,000sq ft (93 sq m) and needed the entire village to launch them.

Rules

In India, where the kites may fly nearly a mile (1.6km) high, each one has two strings: one is to control the kite; the other, covered in powdered glass, is manoeuvred by its operator to cut through his opponent's string. Several South American countries enjoy the sport, and there the armoury is more lethal: razor blades embedded in the framework of the kite, that may either sever the opponent's string or rip holes in his kite. But it is not until Thai kite-fighting is studied that the subtleties of the sport can be fully appreciated.

In Thailand the kite-fighting season lasts from February to June, when leagues operate as hotly contested as any major sport. Competitions are between the "male" kite, "chula", a star-shaped affair that may be 7ft (2m) across and require several men to launch it, and two "female" kites, "pakpao". These are diamond-shaped, and may not be half the size of the chula, but have the edge on it for speed and manoeuvrability. The chula is armed with bamboo slats tied on its string, with which the operator hopes to entangle the tail of a pakpao, while the opponent tries, for instance, to catch one of the points of the star in a large loop of string under the pakpao and drag it down.

KNUR AND SPELL

Introduction

Knur and Spell (also knurr, nur, nor and spel), or "poor man's golf", is an ancient bat and ball game with mainly northern and, above all, Yorkshire associations. The object of the player, "laiker", or "tipper" is to strike the "knur", or round ball, furthest with bat and stick in an agreed number of attempts or "rises".

History

The game has had a wide geographical distribution, from the Midlands to the north-eastern counties, with countless variations especially among children. It has similarities to trap ball, dag and trigger (from East Riding in Yorkshire), buck and stick, tipcat, billet, and nipsy, peculiar to the Barnsley area, where the sticks are pared-down pickaxe handles, with heads made from wood of mangle rollers. Billet players used a stick with a longer head than is usual in knur and spell, striking a piece of wood the size of a man's finger, sharpened at one end; again, hits are measured in scores of yards.

In Lincolnshire the bat becomes a "kibble": other regional names are "trevit", "tribbitt", "primstick" and "gelstick". Yet almost everywhere the names of the implements give evidence of Teutonic or Old Norse origins. Spell is Old Norse "spill", a game or play; knur, German "knorr", a knot of wood, from which the earliest projectiles were undoubtedly made – hence, "spell a knor", play at ball. The ball play – "nurspel" – of the Norsemen and Icelanders is almost certainly the ancestor of knur and spell.

The game reached the height of its popularity in the early part of the twentieth century, when it was said that every other Yorkshireman was a laiker. For matches players would meticulously prepare a level, sure foothold with a spirit level, shovels, and ashes. By mid-century, the game had almost vanished, but since then there has been a rebirth, hastened by commercial and television sponsorship.

Venue

The field of play is marked out with pegs set in lines every 20yds (18.29m), radiating fanwise from the line upon which the spells and pins stand. The length of a rise is measured from hit to resting place. Not the least remarkable facet of the game is the ability of the players to mark the flight of the knur over long distances (hits of 200yds – 182.88m – are common) and, with the help of the down-wind spectators, to find the knur in rough ground and use it throughout a contest of, say, 15 rises a side.

Rules

The chief methods by which the knur, about the size of a large marble, is set up for striking are as follows:

By throwing it up from a spell – a spring trap.

From a pin – a gallows-like arrangement, from which the knur is suspended.

Out of the hand – a less common method is to balance the knur in a hole on top of the bat head, flicking the knur up before striking.

Played down-wind on waste ground or moorland, the game has two main forms. It is usually contested between individuals, not teams, and is almost exclusively a male preserve. In a match the winner is the layer with the biggest aggregate of hits, measured in scores of yards (i.e. 20yds – 18.29m). Fractions of a score do not count in a match. In a "long knock" the biggest single hit is decisive.

Equipment

The bats or sticks have shafts of ash, hickory, or alder of between 2ft (61cm) and 6ft (1.83m) – usually 3ft 9in (1.14m) to 4ft (1.22m) – with fabric or rubber grips. Steel golf shafts have been tried, with no great success; they lack the necessary whip. The striking head or pommel, round-backed with a flattened striking surface 2–3in (5.08–7.62cm) wide, is often of boxwood, hornbeam, sycamore, or maple. The wood used for the striking surface is compressed to half its natural volume in a steel frame, the club-maker screwing down the frame a little each day over a week or so. The wood is then heated to produce the desired finish, and glued to the club head. A match knur weighs 0.5oz (14.17g). It is made of smooth pot, called in the northern countries a "pottie". Knurs were formerly of wood, or lignum vitae, with hand-carved surfaces, and bore a striking resemblance, save in colour, to the modern dimpled golf ball. Horn knurs weighted with lead were also used.

The spell is a metal or wood frame about 2ft (61cm) long, staked into the ground. The knur is placed in a cup mounted on the end of an adjustable sprung arm. It is released into the air by the player tapping his stick head against the catch holding down the sprung arm. The flight of the knur from the spell can be exactly controlled. Players use pegs to mark the spot at which the knur falls from the spell to ensure that the spell throws up the knur exactly into the plane of their swing with the stick.

KORFBALL

Introduction

Korfball is a type of handball of Dutch origin, usually played out of doors between teams of mixed sexes. The object of the game is to score goals and to prevent the opposing team from scoring. The team with the highest number of goals at the end of the match wins.

History

Since 1900 few outdoor games with a practical purpose have been invented. Korfball is one of those few. The initial aim was to create a game that could be played by both sexes. Shortly after 1900, Nico Broekhuysen, a schoolmaster in Amsterdam, outlined such a game, and in 1902 the pupils of his co-educational school began to play it.

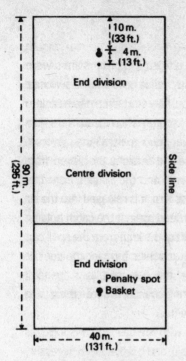

Korfball Pitch

This game immediately aroused great interest, and other schools adopted it. Not only were the pupils participating in the game, but also teachers and parents were playing it and forming their own korfball clubs. By 1903 so many clubs were in existence that Broekhuysen founded the NKA (Nederlands Korfbal Association), which in 1938, on its thirty-fifth anniversary, was granted the prefix "Royal" by Queen Wilhelmina.

Korfball was demonstrated in Antwerp during the 1920 Olympic Games. In 1921 the Belgian Korfball Association was formed: it was also granted the prefix "Royal", in 1950. Since then, the game has spread to Indonesia, Surinam, Germany, Spain, New Guinea and England.

Venue

The ideal playing area, called a pitch, is a rectangle 90m by 40m (295ft x 131ft), level and of short grass. A feature of the game is the marking of the outside, or boundary, lines and the two cross-lines, which divide the pitch into three, by white tapes pinned to the ground. The use of tape means that Korfball can be played anywhere, for the pitch markings are easily laid out, and after the game can be rolled up and carried away.

Rules

Six men and six women form a team and players are divided between the three areas of play called divisions, i.e. two men and two women in each division. Play starts from the middle of the centre division and a goal is scored when the ball falls from the top of the basket. After every two goals, all the players in the centre move into one of the end divisions, the players from that end move to the other end, and the players from that division move into the centre, so that, after six goals have been scored, all players are back in their original division. A game lasts 90mins with an interval of up to 15mins.

The ball is out as soon as it touches: a boundary line; the ground; or an object outside the field of play. A penalty, awarded for the loss of a scoring chance, is a free throw and direct scoring from this is permitted.

The rules preclude running with the ball (and this includes running along, bouncing the ball), and it is therefore necessary for players to pass the ball to their partners in order to ensure that the ball reaches the attack players. Following a mistake in passing the ball, or an interception, the opposing team gains possession and endeavours to pass the ball among its members, and so achieve a goal-scoring opportunity.

The word "party", derived by the Dutch players from the French word "partez" (meaning "break") is the call used to attract the attention of the rest of the team when a successful interception has been made and the defending team has gained possession of the ball. It serves as an instruction to defending players to become attackers.

Although korfball is a team game, demanding that the players of each team co-operate in order to succeed, each player is directly opposed by one of the same sex from the other team. This introduces individual competition as well as the overall team competition.

Although no physical contact is allowed between players, and this is extended to prevent players of one sex opposing players of the other sex, a player is permitted to hinder his or her opponent by making it difficult for the thrower to pass the ball in the desired direction. The result of this permitted hindering is that players are encouraged to run into a free position where the ball is more easily caught and passed, yet at the same time the defender is encouraged to watch his or her attacking opponent so that these opportunities may not be gained. The element of surprise always remains with the members of the team in possession of the ball, and quick passing combined with fast running will ultimately lead to an attacker achieving a free position, anywhere within the end divisions of the field, from which a shot can be taken. Defended shooting is not permitted by the rules; that is to say all goals must be scored from a free position.

The movement of players from division to division, in the prescribed manner, means that all players must be able to shoot, to defend, and to move the ball swiftly through centre. No team can rely on one star performer to score all its goals. This also helps develop mental agility as players have to change tactics and techniques according to the division in which they find themselves.

Equipment

The goals are baskets fixed at the top of posts firmly planted in the grounds in each end division. Each basket faces towards the centre division and its top edge must be 3.50m (11 ft 6in) above the ground all round. The baskets are cylindrical, without a bottom; they are 25cm (10in) high and have an inner diameter of 39–41cm (15 3/8–16 1/8in). Korfball is played with a round ball which consists of a rubber bladder in a one-coloured leather outer casing, with a circumference of 68–71cm (2ft 3in –2ft 4in). It is inflated hard and closed in such a way that it cannot be held by any protruding part. It must not be less than 425g (15oz) or more than 475g (17oz).

KUNINGASPALLO

Introduction

Kuningaspallo, literally "kingball", is a Finnish team bat-and-ball game akin to long-ball, and one of the ancestor games of Pesäpallo. It was played, in various forms, throughout Finland until the end of the nineteenth century.

Venue

The game can be played on any level open space of 20–30m wide by 60–80m long (22–33 by 66–87yds), with a fist-size ball and a bat similar to a baseball bat.

Rules

Teams might number 8 or 9, 17 or 22 players. Each ordinary player could bat three times; the server – or pitcher – four times; and the "king" or best batsman, six times. The ball was served or lobbed high upwards so that it dropped towards the batsman who, whether he hit it or not, could run immediately towards the distant "out-goal" or safe area some 40–50m (44–55yds) away. Alternatively, he could step aside into the safety of the "waiting box" for the opportunity to run when someone else – usually the "king" – made a safe hit. A player caught and "burnt" or "tagged" – i.e. touched with the ball either thrown or in hand – short of the safety of the box or out-goal, was out; and fielding and batting sides changed.

Refinements included a "rescue" rule by which the "burnt" or tagged batsman could throw the ball immediately at the fielding side to "burn" or tag them and so allow his team mates to reach the out-goal or return home safely while still retaining the advantage of batting.

Scoring

It was a lively game but eventually its lack of a definite scoring system rendered it redundant.

LACROSSE, MEN'S

Introduction

Lacrosse is a ball-and-goal field game played with a netted stick by teams of ten a-side. It is played in America, Australia, Canada, England and Hong Kong. Like many other games, it is played (separately) by men and by women but respective rules vary.

History

It is said that lacrosse was born of the North American Indian, christened by the French, but adopted and raised by the Canadians. The Indians called the game baggataway and the earliest use of the word "crosse" applied to the tribal game was made by a Jesuit missionary in 1636 when he saw the Huron tribe playing baggataway in the area now known as Ontario. It was carried south and played among the Huron and Iroquois tribes and later spread to the west. Some form of the game was played by at least 48 tribes scattered throughout southern Canada and parts of the United States.

The French gave lacrosse its name, derived from the shape

of the primitive form of racket which vaguely resembled a bishop's crosier, the French word for which is "crosse". The North American Indians used a cross 3 to 4ft (914mm – 1.219m) in length, the stick of which was curved at one end so as to form a loop or rough circle some 4in (102mm) in diameter. A loose net was constructed within the looped end of the stick in which a primitive ball made of deerskin, stuffed with hair, and sewn with deer sinews, was carried.

The game had a religious significance and was also played as a means of training tribal warrior. Matches lasted for two or three days with the goals, marked by trees, some 500yds (457m) apart.

By the turn of the century, the laws had been modified, the playing area reduced, and the duration of matches fixed at 90 minutes. International, national and regional trophies were competed for, many of them featuring silken flags, a reminder of the days when marker flags were placed on the top of the upright goal posts.

The early 1930s saw a decline in lacrosse in the USA and Canada. In the hope of arresting this, the Americans introduced ten-a-side lacrosse with an offside rule, time-out penalties, and the substitution of players during a game. Canada adopted box lacrosse in 1931, and these measures had the desired effect as the game regained its former popularity.

Venue

Lacrosse is played on a rectangular pitch, 110yds (100.58m) long and 60yds (54.86m) wide, with lines marked in white. Soft flexible cones are placed at each corner, at each end of the substitution gate and at the end of the halfway line which is opposite the bench area.

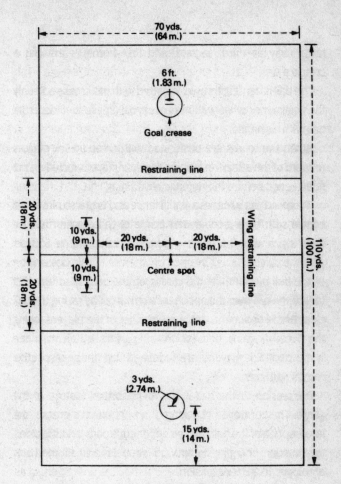

Men's Lacrosse Ground

Rules

The ten-a-side team consists of a goalkeeper, three defences (historically known as point, cover point and third man), a left wing defence, a centre, a right wing midfield (known historically as right wing defence), and three attacks (known historically as third, second, and first home) – the last a crease man.

The ball is carried, thrown or batted with the crosse and only the goalkeeper, while within his own goal crease, can touch the ball with his hands.

When the teams are positioned with three attack players forward of the attack restraining line, four players, including the goalkeeper, behind the defence restraining line, and the wing men behind the wing restraining lines, play is started from the centre spot by a face-off. The frame of the crosse must be touching, and parallel to, the ground. On the whistle to start play, the players taking the face-off attempt to gain possession of the ball by clamping the crosse on the ball, by attempting to flick the ball over the opponent's crosse, or by raking the ball clear of the opponent. Until one or other of the players taking the face-off gains possession, all players other than the wing midfield players are confined by their respective restraining lines.

Possession of the ball is the all-important feature of the game. The controlled checking of an opponent's crosse, the interception of the ball from an opponent's pass, and shoulder-to-shoulder charging in ground scuffles are all methods employed to gain possession.

The laws of lacrosse are simple and few in number, with fouls classified as either technical or personal. The former, in the main, deal with territorial infringements such as off-side (when fewer than three players are in the attack zone or fewer than four in the defence zone), while the latter deal with such offences as slashing with the crosse, tripping, striking an opponent on the head, illegal charging and unsportsmanlike conduct. Penalties include loss of possession of the ball where this applies, a free position is given whereby the offending player is placed behind his opponent) or, for more serious infringements, the suspension of the offending player, for varying periods of time, this being known as a "time-out penalty".

A player in possession of the ball may run, dodge, swerve, feint, pass the ball, or shoot it into the opponent's goal by means of the crosse. A feature of the game is fast accurate shooting, and, because of this, the attack players particularly must be expert stick-handlers.

The tactics employed in lacrosse are basically the same as those used in other field games, such as football and hockey. Positional play is all-important, with players performing a definite task in the pattern of play. It is the function of the attack, for instance, to score goals and to manoeuvre the opposing defence into such a position that the midfield players may break through to score. To achieve this, the return pass, the rapid switching of the line of approach, swerving, dodging an opponent, and beating him by speed, are some of the methods employed when the defence is in possession of attack, to mark out the defenders with the object of preventing a defence clearance.

Equipment

The goals are two vertical posts joined by a crossbar, painted orange and fitted with a pyramidal shaped cord netting. The posts are 6ft (1.83m) apart and the crossbar is 6ft from the ground. Each goal is 15yds (13.72m) from each end line and inside the circle (the goal crease) of radius 9ft (2.74m). For the lacrosse stick itself there are different lengths and head sizes.

A short stick is 40–42in (101.16–106.68cm), a long stick is 52–72in (132.08–182.88cm). Apart from a goalkeeper's stick, only four long sticks per team are allowed. The head of the stick must measure of 4–10in (10.16–25.4cm) at its widest point. The head of the goalkeeper's stick may measure up to 15in (38.1cm). This stick may be any length. The ball is either white or orange rubber, 7.75–8in (19.9–20.32cm) in circumference and 5–5.25oz in weight.

Scoring

Each team attempts to score by getting the ball into the opposition's goal. Each goal scores one point and the team with the most points wins.

Clothing

All players must wear protective gloves and a helmet with a face mask and chinstrap. Jerseys are the same colour for the whole team and should feature players' numbers on the front and back.

LACROSSE, WOMEN'S

Introduction

See LACROSSE, MEN'S

History

See Lacrosse, Men's

Venue

There are no measured boundaries for the playing area although an area of 110 x 60m (120 x 66yds) is desirable. There is a goal circle (2.6m/3yds radius) at each end of the field and a centre circle (9m/10m) in the middle of the field, with a 3m (3.5yds) centre line marked in the middle of this, parallel to the goal lines.

Rules

The team consists of twelve players, six attacks (first, second, and third home, right and left attack, centre) and six defenses (goalkeeper, point, cover point, third man, right and left defense), spaced from one goal to the other, each being closely marked by an opponent. When in possession of the ball, the opposition is in defense. The main duty of the attack is to get the ball as quickly as possible into a position from which a shot at goal may be attempted. The aims and tactics of both attack and defense are similar to those in men's lacrosse.

In theory the game is played in the air. In practice the ball may have to be fathered off the ground into the crosse, but there is no continual stooping. In fact the women's game is one of skill, elegance and finesse, and no body contact is allowed. There is a continual flow of movement up and down the field. From the moment the ball goes into play each player must use her speed, ingenuity and initiative to outmanoeuvre her opponent.

There are very few rules, and these are aimed at controlling the game and protecting the players. There are no boundaries nor off-side rules in the women's game so that it is played at great speed and with few interruptions. Close marking in the women's game makes for speed, accuracy in passing, and the skilled techniques of stick-handling.

The block does not exist in the women's game, but the body check (the placing of the body between the player with the ball and her objective) is designed to impede her movements, to force her to pass, or to force her off her direct path to goal. Crosse-checking (the controlled hitting of an opponent's crosse when she is in control of the ball, in an attempt to take it

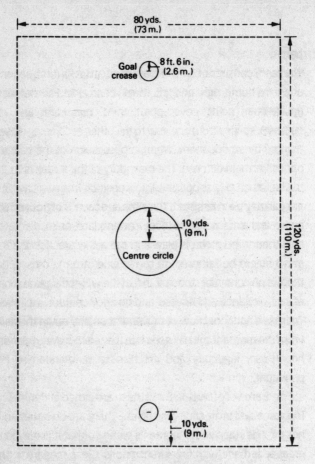

Women's Lacrosse Ground

from her) is allowed but if the umpire considers it rough, it is penalized.

The "draw" (the face-off in the men's game) is executed by the centre players who each stand with one foot toeing the centre line. The crosses are held in the air about hip level, wood to wood, angle to collar, and back to back. The ball is placed between the crosses of the players by the umpire. On the words, "Ready, draw" from the umpire, the two opponents draw their crosses up and away from one another. This ensures that the ball goes in the air at the outset of play.

Equipment

Though the centre of each goal circle is a goal line, marked parallel to the width of the field and 1.83m (2yds) in length. The posts of each goal are placed at either end of the goal lines and are joined by a cross bar 1.83m (2yds) above the ground. The posts and crossbars are 5cm (2in) square or in diameter, constructed of wood or metal and painted white. A goal net is attached to the frame and also the ground at a point 1.83m (2yds) behind the centre of the goal line. The ball is rubber, of any solid colour, with a circumference of 20–20.3cm (8in) and a weight of 142–149g (approx 5oz). The sticks can be made of wood, plastic, fibreglass, nylon, leather and/or gut. Only the handle may be constructed of aluminium or graphite. The field player's stick must be of 0.9–1.1m (approx 1yd) and weigh no more than 567g (20oz). The stick head must be 18–23cm (approx 10–12in) in width and 25.4–30.5cm (approx. 7–9 in) in length. The goalkeeper's stick is a total length of 0.9–1.1m (approx 1yd) and must weigh no more than 773g (27oz). The crosse head must have a maximum inside measurement (width) of 30cm (12in) and a length of 40cm (16in).

Scoring

A goal is scored when the ball passes over the line which joins the two goal posts. If any part of the player who makes the shot or any part of her stick goes over the crease (the circle round the goal posts), during or after the shot, the goal is disallowed. The goalkeeper is the only player in the team who may touch the ball with her hand, and this only when she is within the crease.

Clothing

Women wear a shirt, short skirt/shorts and composition or rubber-soled boots/shoes. All of them must wear mouthguards. The goalies wear a helmet with a face mask, a chest or body pad, throat protector, padded gloves, arm pads and leg pads.

LAWN TENNIS

Introduction

Lawn tennis is game of domination, played with long-handled, oval-headed rackets, by two (singles) or four (doubles) players. They seek to collect points by controlling and manoeuvring the ball within the confines of a court.

History

REAL or ROYAL TENNIS was an aristocratic sport. By contrast lawn tennis, which burst into sudden popularity though the reign of Queen Victoria (1837-1901), began as a diversion for the English middle-classes, who adapted the framework of real tennis to the conditions of outdoor play. Hitting a ball over an obstacle and subsequently keeping it within boundaries is an idea which might have amused the energetic in any country at any time.

The French game of "la longue paume" entailed hitting a cork ball over a mound. It is recorded that at Elveham in Hampshire, Queen Elizabeth I of England was entertained by ten men from the county of Somerset, servants of the Earl of Hertford, who played handball in a square court. "In this square they played, five to five, with handball, with bord and cord, as they term it, to

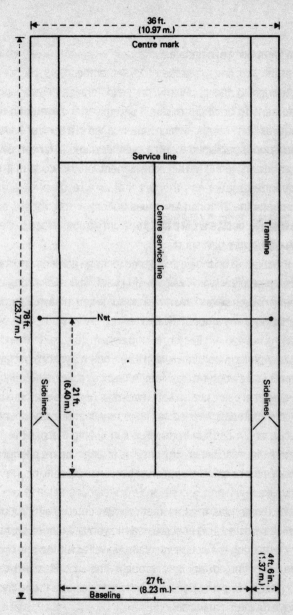

Lawn Tennis Court for Singles or Doubles

the great liking of her majesty."

In the *Sporting Magazine* of 29 September 1793, there is a reference to the popularity of "Field Tennis" ("Field tennis threatens to bowl out cricket") and this may have been the same as "long tennis", which is mentioned in a book of *Games and Sports*, published in 1873. Neither name is far removed from "lawn tennis". The replacement of the cork ball by vulcanized rubber and the fact that as a result of CROQUET's demands the Victorian lawn was no longer soft, mossy, and decorative, but well-rolled and free from shrubs, helped to clear the way for the new sport.

It proved to be the perfect game for large gardens and for a leisured society which was seeking new ways of diverting the young of both sexes. "We have had some very pleasant garden parties and any amount of lawn tennis," Oscar Wilde, who was staying at Bingham Rectory in Nottinghamshire, told a friend in 1876. And as Lyttelton wrote in 1890, only 15 years after lawn tennis had swept into fashion: "A lawn, a racket, a soft ball, a net, a pot of paint, and an active member of either sex, here are all the materials needed for lawn tennis and every country house and most suburban villas can supply them; while for tennis – i.e. real tennis – the pastime of kings, such a panoply is needed that a royal income must be won to provide it."

Unlike real tennis, RACKETS, and (for Victorians, at least) CRICKET, lawn tennis was a game that women could play. Croquet, which it ousted, had accustomed the young Victorian woman to completing against her menfolk. As well as hitting, she could run, and mixed doubles brought the added delight of competing in pairs. Here was a truly social sport, one more move towards emancipation.

Venue

The tennis court measures 78ft (23.77m) long and, for singles play, 27ft (8.23m) wide. The court is divided across the middle into two equal halves by a net 3ft (0.914m) high at the centre and 3ft 6in (1.07m) at the posts. On each side of this obstacle, at a distance of 21ft (6.40 m) and parallel with it, the service lines are drawn. The service area thus lies between the net and the service line, and it is further divided into two sections – the "right" and "left" or "backhand" and "forehand" courts – by centre line, which is 13ft 6in (4.11m) from each of the sidelines. The service area remains constant, even though the width of the court is increased to 36ft (10.97m) for doubles play. The additional areas of 4ft 6in (1.37m) on each side of the court in doubles are known as the "tramlines", or sometimes in the United States as the "alleys".

Rules

A point may be won by one or more strokes. The ball is delivered – or "served" – diagonally from the baseline into the service area on the other side of the net and the object of the game is to force an opponent to hit it into the net or out of court, or to place it in a part of the court where the opponent cannot reach it.

Power and accuracy of service can give a player a considerable advantage. Two deliveries – a "first service" and a "second service" – are allowed. If the server wastes the first by hitting it into the net or outside the service area, he can still win the point with the second. Each wasted service is called a "fault". A "double fault" – i.e. two wasted services – costs the server the point.

After a service the receiver must return the ball on its first bounce. If s/he puts it back into court, shots are exchanged until eventually the point is won. This is called a "rally". Every attempt is made to make the conditions as fair as possible for both players. If a service touches the net but still lands in the correct area (a "let"), the server is allowed to repeat the delivery without penalty.

The service begins in the right court. For the second point of a game the server moves to the left and then back again to the right, and so on until the game is won or lost.

The ball is allowed to bounce only once in a player's court before it must be returned. It must bounce once following a service, but during a rally it need not bounce at all, i.e. if a player returns it with a volley shot. Play is continous. Service alternates between players with each game and ends are changed at the end of the first, third and every subsequent alternate game of a set.

Equipment

The racket is of aluminium, graphite or composite material, various different weights, with a single layer of strings of uniform pattern. The frame must not exceed 29in (73.66cm) in overall length for professional play. The ball is yellow or white with a fabric cover and 6.35–6.668cm in diameter, and 56.7–58.5oz in weight. The net is suspended from a cord or metal cable attached to the tops of the two posts which are positioned 3ft outside each sideline, at the centre of the court. The top of the net must be 3ft above the ground at its centre, at which point the net is also held taut by a vertical white strap.

Scoring

The system of scoring derives from real tennis. The object of the game is to win points for games and sets. A game may be won by the capture of four points – 15, 30, 40 and game. This odd system is based on the habit of using a clock face to record points in the royal days of tennis. The term for zero (no points in a game or no games in a set) is "love", probably a corruption of the French "l'oeuf" (the egg) and is thus related to a "duck" in cricket. A game in which a player does not score is a "love game" and a blank set is a "love set". At the conclusion of each game, service passes to the other player.

The score is given in terms of the server – love-15, or 40-30 – unless both players score three points in a game when they must win two more, a clear head, to take the game. This situation, 40-all, is known as "deuce" from the French "deux", meaning two more to win. The capture of one point at this stage gives a player an "advantage", which an opponent can nullify by taking the next point. Any number of deuces may be played.

The minimum number of games needed for a set is 6, but here again, if conventional scoring is used, a lead of 2 games is required. A set may be won by 6 games to 4, but 5-5 can lead to 9-7, 11-9, or even 15-13 and more.

Clothing

Players wear a shirt and shorts or skirts, clothing is usually white, although colours are permitted.

LOGROLLING

Introduction

This is one of the simplest of sports, and yet one of the most difficult for a novice to master. Two opponents stand facing each other at each end of a large floating log, usually at least 1ft

(30.5cm) in diameter. Wearing "staggers" (shortened overalls or jeans) and ribbed or spiked boots, each one tries to spin the log in such a way that, by changes of speed and direction, the other loses his footing and is thrown into the water. Two falls out of three make a match, which may be over in a few minutes or even a few seconds, though in 1900 one pair were said to have held on for more than three hours. The first contests were held in Canadian lumber camps around 1840, and later spread to Maine and other New England states in the north-east of America.

A related sport is birling, which was developed even more directly from the duties of a river lumberjack, who has to be adept at riding logs downstream from the felling area to the sawmill, clearing log jams as he goes, with a pole. Birling is basically racing in this manner over a measured course, using the pole to steer the log clear of obstacles and through the best run of the river. The first public birling contest was in 1888, and a world championship was held in Omaha, Nebraska, ten years later. Competitions are seldom held in North America now, but the trick riding skills of professional birlers are often seen at riverside fairs and exhibitions.

MARATHON

Introduction

The marathon is the longest race to figure in the programme of events for all major athletics championships.

History

The marathon derives its name from the story of Phidippides, a Greek soldier, who was ordered to run from the battlefield of Marathon to Athens, a distance of about 22 miles, to convey the news of the Greek victory over the Persians in 400 B.C. The marathon was, of course, included in the modern Olympic Games first held at Athens in 1896, but the modern distance of 26 miles 385yds was not standardized until 1908 when the Olympic marathon from Windsor to London measured 26 miles, and the runners were required to cover a further 385 yards in order to finish opposite the Royal Box at White City Stadium.

Owing to the wide variation in courses, the International Amateur Athletic Federation does not recognise a world record. A degree of uniformity has, however, been achieved in marathon courses by the practice, now universally followed in major championships, of running an "out-and-back" course. This neutralizes the advantages which might be obtained from prevailing winds or gradients on a "one-way" course.

MOTO-CROSS

Introduction

Moto-cross or scrambling is a specialized form of MOTOR-CYCLE RACING in which competitors race not on metalled roads but around a closed circuit consisting of a variety of rough cross-country terrain, generally including mud, sand, grass, gravel, stones, streams or any kind of natural obstacle.

History

The sport was invented by a group of clubmen in southern England in 1927. They wanted to organize some sort of cross-country riding trial, but without the observed sections typical of the traditional trial; and by making it a form of cross-country race which they suggested would be "a rare old scramble", they originated this new sport. Only after 1945 did it develop as a specialized sport, a French businessman named Poirer commercializing it by staging meetings on the outskirts of Paris. On the Continent it became known as moto-cross, and the Moto-Cross des Nations was inaugurated in 1947 – without its current set of rules, which were not established until 1963. The main protagonists in the early years were Belgium and Britain, the former fading in the mid-1950s with Sweden taking her place as a serious challenger to the British. These two nations have remained the greatest rivals ever since.

Venue

The course may be of any length. Most courses are between one and three miles in length. Races can be held over a set distance, for example, five laps, or a set time, for example 20 minutes. The starting stretch must be long enough for safety and the course should be marked with flags and other indicators of the width and direction of travel.

Rules

Races are started with the competitors astride their machines in line behind a cord, or similar line, which is raised to permit their passage when the starting signal is given. Thereafter the riders attempt to be the first to complete a prescribed number of laps of the course; which usually calls for a high degree of acrobatic riding skill, though there is no penalty for putting a foot to the ground as would be the case in reliability trials over similarly difficult country.

Equipment

Events are usually for 125c.c., 250c.c. and 500c.c.. Handlebars must be rounded or otherwise protected, the gearbox is modified and strengthened and special knobby tires are used to improve traction. They may of any type allowed in the regulations. Chains and non-skid devices are not permitted. There are other specifications that are necessary for the bike the enter a race including looking after the clutch and brake levers, throttle, engine, chain guard, exhaust, suspension and mudguards.

Clothing

The riders' clothing is normally nondescript because it gets covered in mud almost immediately; but a crash helmet, goggles, leather boots, padded breeches, a body belt for abdominal support, and a light knitted jersey are the usual choices.

MOTOR RACING

Introduction

Motor racing is the staging of a competition of speed capabilities between two or more mechanically-propelled land vehicles over an accepted point-to-point course or closed circuit, the competitors running either together or being timed separately over the course. It is a dangerous sport, the driver's skill being expended on controlling a light-weight projectile capable of speeds in the region of 200mph (322km/h) and in taking it round the bends on a road course as fast as possible, balancing power available at the driving wheels with the grip afforded by the tyres.

History

The invention of the motor car led to a direct extension of the many events in which men already competed against each other.

The first race (sometimes called a trial) for cars, held in 1894, was run from Paris to Rouen; it was won by the Comte de Dion in a steam car which covered the 79 miles (127km) at an average of 11.6mph (18.6km/h). During the next nine years many cross-country races followed and the dominant make was the French Panhard; these cars, all powered by internal combustion engines, ranged from the 1.2 litre model which won the 1895 Paris-Bordeaux-Paris race over 732 miles (1175 km) to the 13.7 litre car with a power output of close to 90 b.h.p. which was the victor in the 1902 Paris-Vienna event.

Grand Prix (large prize) racing began in 1906, the first Indianapolis 500 was in 1911, Le Mans in 1923 and stock car racing in 1936 at Daytona Beach. The Federation Internationale de l'Automobile oversees certain worldwide events. In the USA, sanctioning organizations include the Sports Car Club of America/SCAA, the United States Auto Club/USAC, The Indy Racing League/IRL and National Association for Stock Car Racing/NASCAR.

Whatever body has controlled motor sport, it has always come to the conclusion that racing should be kept from getting too fast and for this reason, for 1938, there came into being a new and considerably more restrictive Grand Prix Formula with an upper engine-capacity limit of 3 litres supercharged and 4.6 litres unsupercharged.

Venue

The circuits vary from banked speedways, lapped in under a minute, to 14-mile circuits, with tight hairpin bends. Officials of the appropriate governing body inspect circuits before awarding a racing license and lay down the maximum number of cars allowed to start in a race.

Under the Fédération Internationale de l'Automobile (FIA) regulations, tracks must be at least 30ft wide.

Rules

All the cars start together and their performances on the starting grid are determined by their performances in the practise session.

The fastest are placed at the front on the grid, with the fastest car in pole position (the position which gives the driver the most advantage coming into the first bend). Some races use a rolling start. A pace car leads the field in their grid order, around one lap. It then drives off the circuit and the race begins. A car moving off before the official signal incurs a time penalty.

Road racing is the highest form of the sport, but track racing, over courses in which the corners and turns were banked as on a railway, enabling the cars to negotiate them at speed without much skidding, was popular prior to the Second World War. The Indianapolis 500, the most famous American race, is run over an oval with slightly banked corners, calling for a special driving technique.

A race varies in length according to the number of laps or length of time (e.g. Le Mans 24-hour Race and a Grand Prix). Formula One races (which are over a set number of laps) are arranged to give either 2 hours or 200 miles racing, whichever is the shorter.

Each category of racing offers events for different types of cars based on their design, function, engine size and other race-specific requirements.

Equipment

The cars must: not have more than four road wheels; have a complete floor; have a protective bulkhead between engine and driver's compartment; and be fitted with sprung suspension between the wheels and the chassis. Other requirements are listed under the various formulae.

Clothing

Drivers must wear a crash helmet, goggles or visors, unless the car has a full-width windshield, protective, fire-resistant clothing which covers arms, legs and the torso.

• AUTOCROSS RACES

These are run on uneven, off-road courses of 500–800yds long. All straightaways must be less than 200yds and the first turn must be within 50yds of the start. Drivers can compete alone or against others, racing the clock for the fastest time. International regulations cover classes for production cars, buggies and special cars.

• DRAG RACING

This is held on a drag strip – which is a straight paved track, usually 440yds long plus additional space for stopping. The width of the track must be at least 50ft. There must be a separate road along which cars return to the starting area. Cars compete in pairs. They line up on the starting line and are started by the "Christmas tree" system. (See MOTORCYCLE RACING, DRAG RACING). Different types of cars are raced including pro stock (modified production cars), "funny cars" (fibreglass copies of passenger cars) and "dragsters" (long, narrow-framed single seaters with large rear wheels; often with a parachute to slow the car down after the finish).

Two cars race against each other in an elimination series to determine a winner. If both cars start cleanly it is a direct race to the finish line. If a car crosses into the opponent's lane, it is disqualified. The elapsed time is the factor that decides the winner, though this may be modified by a time handicap system. It is possible for the losing car to record the faster terminal speed. Time handicapping is not used in professional drag racing, but may be used in the amateur categories. Racers compete in a series of elimination races against cars in a similar category to produce the ultimate winners.

• FORMULA ONE

These cars are custom-built according to specifications that govern body design, engine size, equipment and other elements. Grand Prix races are held on road courses up to 200 miles long.

• HILL TRIALS

These are customized and production cars which are driven between markers up a steep hill. One passenger is usually permitted to provide added traction. The winner is the vehicle that climbs the farthest, as measured by the place where the cars stops its forward motion. Cars are penalized for touching markers. Sporting trial cars may use any engine up to 1650c.c. and have independent braking on each rear wheel.

• INDY CARS

These are similar to Formula One cars in many ways but have different engine sizes, chassis (frame) formats and transmission configurations. Races can be 150 miles and longer. The Indy 500 is 200 2.5miles laps (full circuits around the oval track).

• ROAD RALLY

These are raced by production cars, each with a driver and a navigator to chart the route, complete over long distances on public roads. The race is in stages (individually timed segments) which are totalled. The lowest time determines the winning team.

• SEDAN AND SPORTS CAR RACING

These involve both American and foreign-built unmodified production vehicles or customized and modified cars, including two-seaters and sedans. Cars are grouped into classes based on variables such as engine size and overall performance potential. Races are run on all types of road courses. They can be pre-determined distance or an endurance race (most laps completed within a specific time). Apart from the internationally regulated Group C for long distance cars, sports and sedan (or saloon) car racing is largely run on national or even club basis and recognized categories vary greatly from country to country. Other categories are US production racing, Vintage racing, Group N, Group A.

• SINGLE-SEATER RACING

These cars are built to particular specifications and have sleek chassis, open wheels (no fenders), a low seat position, rear engine and spoiler. The race is different to Formula One, in that events are held on oval tracks as well as on road courses. Single-seater can include Formula 3000, Formula Three, Formula Ford 1600, Formula Vauxhall Lotus, Formula Atlantic, Formula Ford 2000, Formula Vee, Formula Super Vee, Formula Libre and CART.

• SLALOM RACING

For this, custom or production cars are manoeuvred forward and partially in reverse on a level course around markers that have been set out in a curved or winding pattern. One point is given for each second taken and 10 for each marker touched; fewest points wins. Many countries have three classes: production open, production closed and specials. The course is laid out with markers.

MOTOR-CYCLE RACING
Introduction

Motor-cycle racing takes a variety of forms, each subject to its own rules and each encouraging the development of specialized machines. As MOTO-CROSS or scrambling it is conducted over rough country, as speedway on dirt tracks, cinders or shale; other events, usually at amateur level and seldom enjoying international status, are run on tracks of grass, boards, sand or ice.

History

The first motor-cycle races were completely unspecialized. Apart from sundry unofficial contests which must have taken place but are not chronicled, racing began in Europe with events that were open to cars (see MOTOR RACING) and motor cycles alike, racing from one city to another along ordinary roads packed with sightseers, devoid of supervision and often still carrying their everyday traffic. These conditions created obvious dangers which were exacerbated by the tremendous clouds of dust raised by the passage of each vehicle over the unwatered roads, and after a few years of misdirected heroism the great inter-city races were abandoned. The last was the

1903 race from Paris to Madrid, stopped prematurely at Bordeaux after several fatal accidents, mostly involving cars rather than motor cycles.

From 1903 to 1914, motor-cycle sport took on entirely new forms and a much amplified importance, 1907 being a critical year. After the ill-fated Paris-Madrid race of 1903, a new type of race was organized over a closed circuit by the Auto Club de France, a race intended for motor cycles only, with an international field arranged by restricting the entries to teams of three from each of the competing nations – Austria, Britain, Denmark, France and Germany.

In 1911 came a most important development in the history of motor-cycle racing. The Tourist Trophy (colloquially the TT) was revised and would in future be staged over the full-length circuit including the stiff climb up Snaefell. Although the speed and power of racing motor cycles had increased greatly in the preceding three years, the new circuit demanded effective variable-ratio transmission; and the mechanical developments thus encouraged set the seal on the practicality of motor cycles. There were still two races, the permitted capacity of the twins now being reduced to 585c.c. in an effort to keep this class comparable in performance with the 500c.c. single-cylinder class.

By the middle 1950s there was rapid progress but motor cycle racing really took off after the flourishing Japanese industry which, lead by Honda, began a tremendous worldwide sales promotion, using road racing at national and international level as a publicity medium. They took the team prize in the 1959 TT in the 125c.c. race, within two years the four-cylinder Honda 250 was in complete charge of the lightweight class, demonstrating the Japanese firm's mastery of the art of designing an engine. Then Honda produced a four-cylinder 125; a two-cylinder 50, a six-cylinder 250 and a five-cylinder 125. From here on in other international companies became involved and motor-cycle racing became a truly international sport.

Speedway probably began in Australia in 1923, but had its true beginning in America in 1910. The American races bore hardly any resemblance to the sport which descended from them, for they were held in TROTTING stadia with varying numbers of riders on an assortment of motor cycles. After a hit-and-miss beginning, events in Australia settled down and from them emanated the basis of modern speedway racing.

Venue

The track should have a non-skid surface if possible. Ideally, yellow or white lines should be painted along the edges of the track if there is a danger that the rider will leave the course. Warning signs should also be placed in advance of any corners on the course. The start line must be on a flat part of the track.

Equipment

Motor cycles are divided into classes according the swept volume of their engines: for historical reasons metric units are employed for these measurements, and the classes accepted internationally for races of world championship status are for machines of 500, 350, 250, and 125c.c., though for other events there are 50, 750, 1000c.c. and larger classes. Engines are usually air-cooled, but sometimes water-cooled.

Clothing

Riders are obliged to wear protective clothing comprising a safety helmet, goggles or visor, and leather overalls, gloves, and boots. These are inspected before a race and if they do not conform to the published standards, the wearer will be excluded. Except in the matter of helmets there is a good deal of latitude allowed and many leading riders wear leathers that are very thin, close-fitting and unpadded so as to streamline the figure and reduce aerodynamic drag at high speeds.

• DRAG RACING

Motorcycle drag racing is similar to car drag racing. Riders race in pairs on specially prepared machines over a straight 440yd long 50ft wide strip. Riders start using the "Christmas tree" light system and the competition proceeds by a process of elimination, the fastest rider in each pair going through into the next round. The "Christmas tree" system is when in the centre of the track there is a pole with a vertical series of yellow, green, and red lights. These operate in sequence starting from the top of the "tree", when the green light comes on, the cars can move off. If a car moves before the green light, a red light comes on and the car is automatically disqualified.

• GRASS-TRACK RACING

This is an extremely simple form of motorcycle speed sport run, as the name suggests, on tracks laid out in suitable fields. No obstacles are introduced, but riders must negotiate the natural hazards of bumps, dust and flying stones. Originally, circuits were up to a mile (1.6km) long, with left and right-hand bends, and 20 or more riders might take part in a race. Grass-track races are short (about 4 laps) and therefore last only a few minutes. Riders are usually started by a mechanical system to eliminate false starts. The only likely causes for disqualification or stopping the race are if a rider cuts corners or if there is a serious crash. Grass-track machines are of extremely simple design. Capacity limits are: 250, 350, and 500c.c. and up to 1200c.c. for sidecar machines. The engines are usually single-cylinder in the solo classes, but twin-cylinder units are favoured for the sidecar class. Grass-track racing is probably the oldest form of motorcycle sport; it is likely that the first races were run in fields or on dirt roads. It is known that grass-track racing took place in England at Brands Hatch, Kent (the present Grand Prix circuit), in 1928 and continued until 1949. Tracks existed all over England during the 1930s and the sport was the major amateur motorcycle pastime.

• ICE RACING

Ice racing motorcycles originated jointly in Russia and Sweden and has spread as far across Europe as France. There have even been attempts to introduce it to Britain. Basically, ice racing, or ice speedway as it is sometimes known, particularly in Germany, is a form of speedway on ice. Machines are rather like speedway cycles and meetings are always held in stadia which bear a striking resemblance to speedway venues. It is quite common for the organizers of a meeting to take over a winter sports stadium – more usually used for ice skating , and lay out a race track which may be between 200 and 400m in length. Motorcycles have steel spikes attached to their wheels to grip the ice surface.

Events are divided into heats, and points are awarded for the first three places in each heat. Teams normally have seven or eight riders and each team is distinguished by its colours. Points are usually awarded to the first three riders in each heat. Ice races are run like speedway, with four riders on the track at a time, covering four laps of the track for a race. The starts are performed with speedway starting gates, and scoring is on the 3-2-1 principle. The bright colours of the riders' leathers and helmets make this is a particularly attractive sport, and like speedway and long-track racing, ice racing is professionally promoted.

• LONG-TRACK RACING

This, the European name for sand track racing, is a major sporting attraction throughout Germany, Denmark, Sweden and Norway. Most meetings are held on tracks which, at some time in their history, have been used for horse trotting. Generally the track is about 1,000m (1,093yds) long, hence the other common name for the sport, 1,000m racing. The tracks are very wide and are often well surfaced with sand. The sport is highly professional and each large meeting can be worth £200 or more in appearance money to popular competitors. Most of the performers are grass-track riders, although it is also popular with top speedway competitions.

The rules are about midway between speedway and grass tracking. There are always eight riders to each race which covers three laps of the track. Riders use machines very similar to only one class (500c.c.). Long-track racing has been tried in Britain but the response was so poor that the attempt was abandoned.

• SAND-TRACK RACING

Sand-track racing is a motorcycle sport now practically dead, at least in Britain, though it enjoyed some measure of popularity in the 1920s and 1930s. Where broad expanses of firm sand were exposed on beaches, impromptu motorcycle races were staged, attention having been drawn to the viability of such beaches by their use for record-breaking attempts by motor cars. Properly organized race meetings then became a regular feature of the summer racing system, but these events were never vigorously promoted and did not generally pretend to cater for riders of high national or international standing. The machines used were commonly ordinary production or sporting motorcycles suitable stripped of non-essentials, the field being enlivened by a sprinkling of speedway or grass-track racing motorcycles.

The principal reason for the success of this form of sport, despite the known mechanical hazards attending the entry of sand into the engine, was probably that the British government (unlike most others) would not close public roads for racing, so that the enthusiastic sporting motorcyclist had to amass experience and take his fun as he found it. With the creation of a number of a number of road racing circuits in the 1950s, sand racing lost what little attraction it ever had.

• SPEEDWAY

Speedway, or motorcycle dirt track racing, is a highly professionalized sport and takes place only at specially licensed tracks. Speedway operates under a rigid set of rules, the basis of which is that four riders race against each other. The winner of the race is awarded 3 points, the second, 2, and the third, 1. Each race is normally over four laps, regardless of the length of track. A track's lap length is of about 350yd. They are usually loosely surfaced with either ash or shale. A special riding technique is needed as the machines have no brakes and riders are forced to broadside their machines through bends at speeds of up to 70mph.

• SPRINTING

Sprinting is acceleration test over a measured distance. Races take place from point to point in a straight line on an approximately level, metalled surface. They are less than one mile in length and held between two or more competitors or individually against time. There are races for solo machines and for sidecar combinations. The start is made from a stationary position with the engine running and the foremost part of the motorcycle behind the start line.

There is some confusion in the vocabulary of the sport. "Drag racing" is an American term that is often taken as synonymous with "sprinting" from a standing start. However, some authorities maintain that sprinting is a race against the clock, whereas drag racing is a race against other competitors on an elimination basis. In either case such events are run in one direction only, and must therefore be distinguished from record-breaking in which two consecutive runs must be completed in opposite directions within the space of one hour.

Superbikes must be of a type that is in production and on sale to the general public. The engine capacity must be between 501c.c. and 750c.c. Engines over 500c.c. and up to 1000c.c. have a maximum of 2 cylinders. Engines over 400c.c. and up to 750c.c. have a maximum of 3 or 4 cylinders.

For Production Motorcycle class (or "Proddie" racing, as it is also known), the rules vary from country to country, but generally machines should be standard.

MOUNTAIN RUNNING

Introduction

This sport is concentrated in hilly or mountainous areas of the world, where facilities for other types of sports may be scarce. Traditions vary from country to country depending on the type of terrain.

Venue

All courses must avoid dangerous ascents or descents. In competitions the courses are marked with checkpoints and flags. Distances may vary from 1 to 25 miles, and the height climbed will also vary.

Rules

The first runner to finish the course is the winner.

Clothing

Competitors wear running shoes which are specially developed for mountain running and normal athletic clothing. Protective clothing is worn as dictated by the weather conditions.

NETBALL

Introduction

Netball is a seven-a-side ball game played almost entirely by girls and women, mainly in English speaking countries. The chief centres of adult netball are Australia, New Zealand, South Africa, and the United Kingdom. The game is also established in Sri Lanka, India, Malaysia, Singapore, the South Pacific islands, Iraq, Malta, East and West Africa and in the West Indies. It is played only sporadically on the continent in Europe.

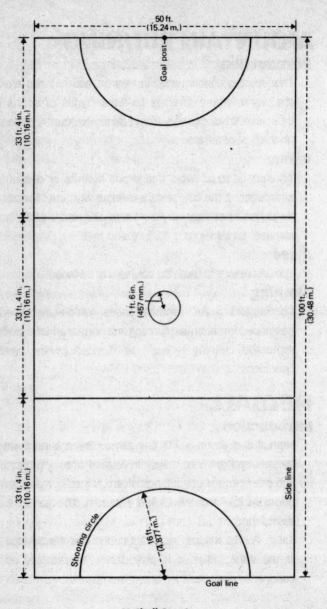

50 ft.
(15.24 m.)

Goal post

33 ft. 4 in.
(10.16 m.)

33 ft. 4 in.
(10.16 m.)

100 ft.
(30.48 m.)

1 ft. 6 in.
(457 mm.)

33 ft. 4 in.
(10.16 m.)

Shooting circle

16 ft.
(4.877 m.)

Side line

Goal line

Netball Court

History

Although the game of netball is of comparatively recent origin, three games popular with the Greeks and Romans are still used as lead-up games for beginners and as practise for experienced players to improve footwork and ball control. "Trugon" was a Roman game for three players, mentioned by Martial and Horace, now used to improve ball-handling; "phainmida" (Greek) and "harpastum" (Roman) were useful for control of footwork and ball-handling; and the Greek "episkyros", mentioned by Hesychius, is a team game excellent for developing dodging and marking, especially in a confined space.

BASKETBALL was invented in the USA in 1891, and by 1897 an American woman paid a visit to the Physical Training College in England, and taught the game as it was then being played by women in her country. Then rings were introduced instead of baskets, a larger ball was introduced, the ground divided into three courts, and American rules were adopted.

The Ling Association, founded in 1899, set up a special sub-committee in 1901 to draft and publish an official set of rules, in an edition of 250 copies, adopting many changes from the latest American rules. These included the scoring of points instead of goals, 1 point if the goal was shot from the first court or from a free throw, 2 points if shot from the centre court. And, to avoid wild shooting from long distances, the shooting circle was reintroduced.

The size of the ball was reduced from 31in (78.7cm) in circumference, as used in America, to 27in (68.5cm), which was the size of the regulation football, thus avoiding the manufacture of a special ball. The goal ring was also reduced from 18in (45.7cm) to 15in (38.1cm) in diameter, and the height of the goal post raised to 10ft (3.05m). As the baskets had been replaced by rings and nets, the name of the game was changed to netball.

Venue

The court is small, being only 100ft long and 50ft wide (30.48m x 15.24m), and is marked with lines painted in any clearly distinguishable colour, or laid with adhesive tape. It is divided into three equal areas, with a semi-circle at either end facing the goal line, and a small circle in the centre.

Rules

A netball side consists of a goal shooter, goal attack, wing attack, centre, wing defence, goal defence, and goalkeeper, each of whom plays in limited areas of the court. The term "offside" does not mean the same in netball as in other ball games. A netball player is offside if she enters any area other than that assigned to her position, whether she holds the ball or not. To enter an area means to land on, or touch with any part of the body, the ground beyond the line marking the boundary of the playing area.

The game is started with a centre pass, the team that wins the toss having the choice of making the first centre pass or selecting the goal they will attack during the first period. (Thereafter the opposing centres alternate in making the centre pass that follows each goal and each interval.) The umpire blows the whistle to start the game when the centre making the pass is in the small circle in the middle of the court, and her opponent is in the centre third. All other players start in their own playing areas in that part of the goal third in which they line up. They are free to move, but, until the whistle is blown, only in that area.

The ball is thrown in any manner from player to player. At least two passes must be made before a goal can be scored and the ball must be thrown by one player to another either in the same or the adjacent third of the court. A goal is scored by throwing the ball above and through the ring on the goal post from any spot within the shooting circle. As goal shooter and goal attack are the only attacking players allowed in the shooting circle, only these two can attempt a shot for goal.

Netball is a throwing and catching game and strict rules disallow other ways of using the ball, such as kicking, striking, throwing or tossing it to oneself to make a double catch. A player may not carry the ball down the court as in RUGBY FOOTBALL, or run while bouncing the ball as in a basketball dribble. Having clearly caught the ball, a player must obey the footwork rule, and throw the ball within three seconds of catching it. In netball no player is allowed to make an attacking movement down the court with the ball in her possession or attempt to score. Attacking is a team effort. One player is dependent upon another to progress the ball to the goal.

A player may receive the ball with one foot grounded or jump to catch and land on one foot. She may then (a) step with the other foot in any direction, lift the landing foot, and throw or shoot before she regrounds that foot; b) step with the other foot any number of times, pivoting on the landing foot, lift it, but release the ball before she regrounds it; (c) jump from the landing foot on to the other, and jump again, releasing the ball before regrounding either foot; or (d) step with the other foot and jump, but again throw or shoot before regrounding either foot. If a player catches the ball while both feet are on the ground, she may follow the rule given above, but may select either foot as the moving foot. A player may not hop while she is holding the ball, neither may she drag the landing foot along the ground.

In attempting to score a goal, the goal shooter or goal attack must be completely inside the shooting circle when she catches the ball, and while she holds it; she must obey the footwork rule and the rules governing catching and throwing. She may attempt to score as often as she can retrieve the ball from the opposition after making a shot at goal. The opponent may attempt to intercept the shot, but if she deflects it and the ball is netted, a goal is scored against her side.

No personal contact with an opponent which interferes with her play is allowed in netball; neither is a player allowed to remove the ball in any way from an opponent, nor may she push or touch an opposing player, with the ball while she holds it. The rules define the physical actions and attitudes which a player may employ in her efforts to defend an opponent. Beyond these limits a legitimate action becomes a foul – known as "obstruction".

The skill of defending an opponent is divided between (a) defending a player who holds the ball, and (b) defending a player who does not hold the ball. In the first case, the defender may attempt to intercept the ball when the opposing player has made her throw or she may attempt to make it difficult for the player to throw the ball in the direction or in the manner she wishes.

The defender must play herself at a distance of at least 3ft (914mm) from the opposing player with the ball, the distance being measured from the nearer foot of the defender to the first landing foot of the catcher if she jumps to catch the ball and lands with it, placing one foot on the ground followed by the other. Should the catcher lift that foot, or jump from it, the distance is still measured from the place on the ground where she first landed. If the catcher lands on two feet and stands still, the distance is taken to the nearer foot of the catcher. Should the catcher be standing on two feet and then move one, the distance is measured from the foot not used for stepping as before. So long as this distance is correct a defensive action may be employed.

A player defending an opponent without the ball may stand close to her, but not so close that she cannot move. The defender may not raise her arms; any movement of the arms other than those involved in natural body balance is deemed to be obstruction and is penalized by the umpire. The penalty for obstruction is a penalty pass, or if against a shooter in the shooting circle, the choice between a penalty pass and a penalty shot for goal.

All contact with or obstruction of a player carries the penalty of a penalty pass. If the goal shooter or goal attack is contacted or obstructed in the shooting circle she is awarded the choice between a penalty pass and a penalty shot. When either of these several penalties is awarded, the infringer must stand beside the thrower until the ball leaves the thrower's hands. All other infringements of the rules carry the penalty of a free pass, that is to say the opposing team is given the ball and takes a throw which may be defended.

When the ball goes out of court, a player in the opposing team to that which last made contact with the ball on court throws it. The thrower must stand outside the court, at a point close to the line, and opposite the point where the ball went out. She must throw within three seconds of the word "Play" from the umpire.

Equipment

The goal posts, made of steel or wood, with a metal ring projection horizontally 6in (152mm) from the supporting pole, are placed half-way along either goal line. The ring, 15in (381mm) in diameter, is provided with a net open at both ends. The post, which is 10ft (3.05m) high, may be supported by a socket in the ground or by a metal base. The ball used is similar to a size 5 Association football, which is of 27–28in (68-71cm) in circumference and 14–16oz (397–454g) in weight.

Clothing

Players wear shirts or blouses, shirts or shorts, socks and shoes which must not be spiked.

NINE MEN'S MORRIS

Introduction

Nine men's morris is an indoor form of QUOITS, also known as merels, the basic equipment for which is a flat board marked out with three squares, with 24 holes, or "stations" in it. In addition to the board, there are wooden pegs of different sizes and sometimes colours. Each player has nine pegs and the aim is to get your own pieces into rows of three. When pegs are so placed that they cannot be taken, the opponent meanwhile would try and take their pieces before they formed rows.

History

The outdoor version of this game is probably the most ancient. The rules are basically the same but it has the advantage, for its humbler players at least, that it can be played virtually anywhere. The proper name for the board was a "pound" and merels pounds have been found carved on the benches of cathedral cloisters and in porches of old churches. Pegs were an unnecessary refinement in the open air, where the stones could be used.

The game persisted in many districts and is probably still played in one form or another. Like so many widespread folk sports it was known by a variety of names according to where it was played. In Lincolnshire this game was called "Meg Merryleys", in Derbyshire "nine men's marriage", in Cambridgeshire "murrels", in Cornwall "Morrice", and in Oxfordshire "ninepenny".

ORIENTEERING

Introduction

Orienteering is a sport akin to cross country running, but staged in less open terrain, in which runners compete in navigating routes between isolated control points set up at defined positions within the area of competition. In most types of event, controls must be approached and visited in the correct sequence and the winner is the competitor completing a full circuit in the fastest time.

History

Though it is known that "chart and compass" races were held in the sports meetings of British army units in the early years of the century, orienteering is generally recognized as being of Scandinavian origin. It was first introduced in 1918, in Sweden, by an enterprising youth leader, Major Killander, who used it in an attempt to attract young men back to competitive running.

Participation in track ATHLETICS was showing a decline and, to add interest to the labour of running, Killander set courses in Sweden, issuing maps and compasses to all competitors. Whatever the immediate effect on track athletics, the new concept of a competition involving route-findings and cross-country running proved attractive to all who took part, and it grew rapidly as sport in its own right, to the extent that by 1949 a leading Swedish athletics coach considered it a threat to the future of middle-distance running.

The International Orienteering Federation was established in 1961 with Sweden, Norway, Finland, Denmark, Switzerland, East Germany, Czechoslovakia and Hungary as its founder members. By 1964 this had increased to 11 countries with the addition of Austria, Bulgaria and Poland and so the sport developed throughout Europe.

Venue

Events are staged in rugged country of a wooded, hilly, or moorland nature, preferably unknown to all runners.

Rules

From a common starting point competitors set out separately at intervals of up to five minutes to make their way across country to each control in succession. The positions of controls are obtained from master maps displayed at the start which show the complete area of the course. Competitors mark these positions as accurately as possible on individual copies of the map issued to them by the organizer and, after careful study of the course, set off for the first objective.

The minutes spent in studying and copying the master map are included within performance time and although accurate copying is vital to a runner's navigation during the race, it must be carried out under the pressure of competition. The runners' choice of route depends upon his/her skill in reading from the map the nature of the terrain confronting them and selecting the route which will require the least time. In making their choice, competitors must take into consideration the general configuration of the land, the type of vegetation they will encounter, the nature of the surface under foot, and their own particular athletic capabilities. All these will affect their speed of progress and shrewd route selection will enable a slow runner to record a better time than a fast runner on a less satisfactory route.

Equipment

Competitors use specially drawn maps and a control card. The card is issued to each competitor and stamped when s/he reaches a control point. It is used to calculate start, finish and elapsed time. The orienteerer also uses a compass which should have orienteering lines, a direction marker, magnifying lens, distance marker, safety cord, transparent base plate and rotating compass housing.

Clothing

Runners can wear any style of athletic clothing, provided that it gives full body and leg protection against cuts and abrasions. Studded athletics shoes are the most suitable footwear.

• CROSS-COUNTRY ORIENTEERING

This is the most highly developed form of the sport. It is conducted as described above and results are judged on a time basis. Two other types of event are judged on timing, both of which place particular emphasis on accurate map-reading.

• LINE ORIENTEERING

In this, the master map shows a set circuit which all competitors must follow. Along its course are a number of undisclosed controls, all of which must be visited, the location of which will be discovered only by following the defined route with great accuracy.

• ROUTE ORIENTEERING

This tests skill by requiring competitors to mark on their own maps the exact position of controls passed on a route which is marked continuously on the ground but not shown on the map.

• SCORE ORIENTEERING

This is a different form of competition. In a selected area a large number of controls is set up. Each is allotted a points value – a high value for those furthest from the start, or difficult to locate, a lower value for those nearest or easier to find. Competitors locate as many as possible within a set time limit, scoring points from each control visited. Penalties are applied for late return. Controls may be visited in any order and results are judged on points accumulated. The maximum score, i.e. the total value of all controls, is impossible within the time-limit set.

Attached to each control is a device for stamping an identifying mark to record a competitor's visit. This is done on the control card, which also serves as a check on the safe return of all runners.

Orienteering is normally carried out on foot but can also be organized for skiers, cyclists, canoeists and horse-riders, though these variants are little developed, with the exception of ski-orienteering in Scandinavia.

PADDER TENNIS

Introduction

Padder tennis is bat-and-ball game played "singles" and "doubles", which in its modern, regulated form has evolved from LAWN TENNIS. Its main advantage over the parent game is that it does not require such a large area for playing.

History

Lawn tennis was, for long time, enjoyed only by the few who could play it on courts in the large grounds attached to private houses or by membership to private clubs. It increased considerably in popularity after the First World War, as local authorities accepted their responsibility to increase recreational facilities available to citizens by providing grass and hard courts that could be hired at reasonable charges. The extended coverage of tennis and inclusion of the game in various schools further increased its popularity.

For years, and perhaps particularly on cruising ships (see DECK TENNIS), efforts were made to produce a substitute for tennis that offered the same satisfaction, the same degree of skills, employed the same scoring, and used more or less the same rules, but which could be played in a much smaller area. The answer was padder tennis.

Venue

With the exception that no provision is made for the "tramlines" of a lawn tennis court, so that in padder tennis singles and doubles are played to the same lines, the court is marked out in a similar way. Some free space at the sides and ends of the court, which measures 39ft by 18ft (11.9 x 5.5m), is obviously necessary but a total area of 55ft by 25ft (16.8 x 7.6m) is adequate. It can be played either outdoors or indoors, providing that the surface allows a reasonably true bounce to the ordinary tennis ball which is used. When played indoors, an overhead clearance of about 10ft (3m) is sufficient.

Rules

Although experience, as in lawn tennis, will show individual players how best to strike the ball, the strokes and technique required for padder tennis are virtually the same as those required for the parent game.

The virtue of the game is that the much smaller area needed for a padder tennis court has given the opportunity for more people to lay out their own courts, and for local authorities, particularly those catering for visitors at seaside resorts, to provide a larger number of courts. The experience of introducing these public padder tennis courts has revealed a further potential appeal to what is still a relatively new game. First impressions were that public padder tennis courts would cater almost exclusively to young children patting the ball over the net. In fact, people of all ages derive enjoyment and exercise from the small-scale tennis game.

Equipment

The wooden padder bat, weighing about 8oz (226g), is the essential implement that has made it possible to enjoy a fast exciting game of tennis on such a comparatively small area. Just as in BADMINTON the featured shuttle, hit by a strung racket, rapidly loses speed as a tennis ball similarly struck would not, with a wooden padder bat it is impossible to send the ordinary tennis ball very far. The ball, however, may be hit really hard either from the baseline or when serving, by a good player, without going beyond the far baseline, or of being a fault by overhitting or going into the net during service. By trial and error, the height for the net was found to be best at 2ft 3in (685mm), even an inch higher or lower impeding sustained play. Marking lines should be no less than 1.5in (38mm) wide. The height of the net at the posts is 2ft 6in (762mm).

PADDLEBALL OR PADDLE TENNIS

Introduction

This is a bat-and-ball game played, chiefly in the USA, with a sponge-rubber ball and a laminated wood bat (paddle) on a court exactly half the size of a LAWN TENNIS court. The object of the game is to hit a ball against a wall (or over a net) by serving it and then returning the ball in such a way that the other person cannot return it to the wall before two bounces on the floor. The first team or player to score 21 points wins.

History

Although HANDBALL was popular for some time at the beginning of the twentieth century it caused sore hands and a doctor, named Frank Beale, invented a paddle stick to use to hit a ball against a wall. During World War II, army recruits training at Michigan learned the sport and it eventually spread to other parts of the country.

Venue

For the one-wall court: the court is 20 x 34ft, with no ceiling and the wall is 16ft high, the short line is 16ft from the wall, and defines the front court. The long line is 18ft behind the short line, and defines the back court. The service markers are 6in long, midway between the short and long lines. The service zone is the area between the short line and service lines. For the three-wall court the court has the same size and markings as the one-wall court, and has two side walls from the top of the front wall to a point 12ft above each side line at the short line.

When playing on the four-wall court: the court is 20 x 40ft with a ceiling; the service line is 15ft from the front wall; the short line is 20ft from the front wall, midway between the front and back walls; the receiving line is 25ft from the front wall; the service zone is a 5ft area between the service and short lines; and the service boxes in the service zone are 18in from each side wall.

Rules

In most respects its rules are as those for lawn tennis, but only one serve is allowed: if it is a "fault", the point is lost.

The winner of a toss chooses to serve or receive and whoever serves first in the first game serves first in the third game. The server stands in the service zone with both feet inside or on the lines. The paddle may extend over the lines. Singles matches are played by two players. Doubles matches are played by four players.

Equipment

The ball is made of rubber, is 1.9in in diameter and weighs 2.3oz. The paddle is made of wood, with a maximum length of 17.5in and a maximum width of 9ins.

Scoring

Points can only be scored by the serving side. One point is scored when an ace is served (the ball bounces twice before the receiver can return it) or when the serving side wins a rally (the exchange of shots that decides a point). The first side to score 21 points (or another pre-determined score, such as 15,

25 or 30) wins the game. All games must be won by two points. The winner is the first side to score 11 points (or 15 points if agreed).

Clothing

Players usually wear white clothes but dress is basically informal.

PARACHUTING

Introduction

Parachuting for sport and competition is practiced in practically every country in the world and up to 40 nations compete in the biannual world championships.

History

A Frenchman, Garnerin, made the first successful parachute descent, over Paris in 1797. Parachute jumping became show business, however, in the USA in the 1880s, when van Tassel and Baldwin dispensed with the idea of rigidity and began jumping from balloons on a small rectangular trapeze, held by lines to the edge of a circular canvas.

Parachuting contests began in the USA in 1926, but the sport developed far faster in Russia, where in 1936, only six years after their first competition, there were 115 parachuting schools. The first world parachuting championships were held in Yugoslavia in 1951, and were dominated for ten years by European and Asian teams. The world's first para-theatre was built at Orange, Massachusetts, for the sixth championships, in 1962, when the USA provided both men's and women's championships.

Rules

The sporting use of parachutes includes competition sport

parachuting, free-fall relative work, para-gliding, and para-ascending.

• COMPETITION PARACHUTING

Using steerable parachutes to get as close as possible to a target area is called "accuracy jumping". The competitive event where the parachutist carries out a pre-determined sequence of manoeuvres in free fall prior to opening his parachute is called "style jumping".

The target area (specified by the Fédération Aeronautique Internationale) is indicated by an exploded cross of red or orange material in the centre of which is a red disc 10cm (4in) in diameter. The distance from the inside end of each arm of the cross to the centre of the 10cm disc is 5m (16.4 ft).

The competitive parachutist is usually required to leave the aircraft with his/her body aligned with an arrow on the ground. They should then be in a stabilized free-fall position – arms extended sideways, legs apart, body face downwards and parallel to the ground – and within a few seconds will receive a visual signal from the judges on the ground. This will tell them which series of pre-arranged manoeuvres to carry out. The expert parachutist (or skydiver at this stage) can control their body as a pilot can control a light aircraft, putting it into banks, turns, dives and even loops.

• FREE-FALL RELATIVE WORK

In this two or more parachutists may leave the aircraft one after the other, and, by using their arms and legs as elevators and rudders, manoeuvre relative to each other during the free-fall period before opening their parachutes. During this

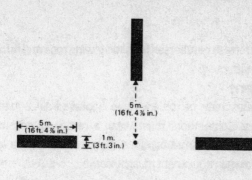

Target Area For Competition Parachuting
In accuracy jumping the parachutist is awarded points for the closeness of his landing to the disc at the centre of he target. Panels are of red or orange material, the disc of red; the disc (not to scale here) is 10cm (4in) in diameter.

"relative work" they may manoeuvre so that they can join hands, pass batons as in a relay race, or merely fall in formation.

• PARA-ASCENDING

This is a long line attached to the parachute harness and, by towing the competitor into wind with a vehicle, they are lifted into the air. The altitude reached is governed only by the length of the rope and the distance which the towing vehicle can travel before reaching any obstruction. When the towing vehicle stops, the parachutist returns slowly to earth at the normal descent speed. The ascender can also elect to release him/herself from the towing rope and return to earth unattached.

Equipment

Parachutes may be of any type approved by a national authority. Competitors must wear a reserve parachute in addition to the main parachute. If the jump takes place above 4500m oxygen equipment must be carried.

Clothing

Each competitor must wear a protective helmet and if the jumps are made over or near water, the parachutist must have suitable life-saving equipment. Generally they wear jumpsuits, goggles and gloves.

• PARA-GLIDING

This utilizes a "family" of parachutes which could more accurately be describe as flexible wings. These "wings", which are carried in a back-pack like a conventional parachute and deployed in the same way, give the parachutist the ability to glide, and, in some circumstances, soar like a conventional glider. The performance of these gliding parachutes has given rise to the sport of cross-country gliding by parachute. The parachutist goes to any altitude s/he requires by aeroplane and then glides to a predetermined landing area.

PATO

Introduction

This is an Argentinian game for horsemen, a cross between POLO and NETBALL, requiring the skills of a circus rider.

History

Pato (Spanish for "duck") was first played in Argentina in the fifteenth century, between unlimited numbers of mounted employees from two neighbouring farms. The size of the field was determined only by the distance between the farms. The ball was a leather basket containing a live duck, and the game was won when one team galloped back to its farm with the duck. Any method – including lassoing – could be used to stop an opponent, who had to carry the basket at arm's length by one of its two handles.

The violence and cruelty of the game did not endear it to the Roman Catholic Church, which at the end of the eighteenth century threatened excommunication to any Catholics involved. In 1822 it was banned by government order, but did not finally disappear from the rural scene for another 80 years.

It was revived with its present unobjectionable rules in 1937, and is played in formal costume of coloured shirt, white breeches and black boots. A handicap system similar to that used in polo is operated by the ruling body of the sport, the Federación Argentina de Pato.

Venue
It is played between two teams of four men on a field 230yds (210m) long and 90yds (82m) wide, with the object of placing or throwing the ball into the opponent's goal, a net that hangs from a 9ft (2.7m) post.

Rules
The ball is thrown into play by the referee, and may be thrown or punched by a player. If it falls to the ground, it may only be picked up by a competitor who is riding at speed. A game consists of six periods of eight minutes each.

Equipment

The ball is like a small football with the addition of six large leather handles. When carried, it should be held with outstretched arm, giving opponents the chance of snatching it away.

PELOTA

Introduction

Pelota (or pilota, or pelote Basque) is a generic name for numerous hand, glove, racquet, or bat-and-ball games adapted originally from the ancient French "jeux de paume" and first – and still mainly – played in the Basque and contingent provinces of France and Spain. Besides these countries, pelota in one or more of its varieties is now played all over the world – in every country of South America, in Belgium, Italy, Ireland, Egypt, Indonesia, Morocco, Mexico, Cuba, the Philippines and in the USA in Florida and California.

History

Pelota in one or more of its several versions is now played in many parts of the world. But it was in France and Spain that it acquired identity as a game with its own characteristics and codes. Thus, a history of pelota is largely the story of its evolution in these countries, more specifically in the Basque provinces of south-western France and northern Spain, where pelota early split across the Pyrenees.

Generally considered to be of Basque origin, pelota was initially no more than an adaptation of one of the most venerable games: the medieval jeux de paume. The Spanish word "pelota" derives, as do "pilota" (Basque), "pelote" (French), and "pallone" (Italian) from the Low Latin "pillata", diminutive of the Roman "pila", "a ball", which in turn derived from the Greek "pilos".

The original game, "longue paume" (long palm, or long glove), was simplicity itself: two or more players beat a ball back and forth to each other across a net or line, using some sort glove, racquet, or bat and any convenient open space as a court. The game, growing more sophisticated as it was urbanized, changed its nature about the middle of the fourteenth century. Lack of space in the towns meant that courts were scaled down, enclosed with walls and sometimes roofed; the new, more confined version of the game was called "courte (short) paume". The English word "court" as applied to tennis and other games, is anglicized "courte".

Venue

The courts used for both categories of game are of three kinds: the "place libre", an open outdoor court of variable dimensions and a single wall; the "fronton", which is a covered outdoor court of varying dimensions with two or three walls; and lastly the "trinquet", a small covered court.

Surfaces of these courts (the Spanish-Basque for "floor" or "surface", "cancha", has by extension come to mean the court itself) vary from the untreated earth of the village place libre, though en tout has rubble and paving, to the high polished cement of the modern fronton known as a "jaï-alaï".

In the United States the game is played on a court which has three walls. The front walls is called the "frontis", the back wall the "rebote", and the side wall the "lateral". The frontis is made of granite blocks; the rebote, lateral, and floor are made of gunite, a pressurized cement. The fourth side of the court has a clear screen through which spectators watch the game. The court is divided into 15 numbered areas. The serving zone is the space between areas 4 and 7.

Rules

The many versions of pelota fall into two distinct categories:

1 "Jeux directs", straight, up-and-down games where the players face each other and the ball (or pelote) flies freely between opponents. In these games scoring is as in tennis – 15, 30, 40, game. The weight and composition of the pelote vary greatly according to the game for which it is made. Pelotes, for "main nue", are handmade and quickly lose their resilience, hence the frequent ball changes during a game.

2 "Jeux indirects", or "jeux de blaid", games where players face a wall against which the ball is hit, either directly or off another wall. In these games scoring is by points. Jeux directs comprise only two games, which are also the oldest, rebot and pasaka. The jeux indirects number 11, which are: "main nue"; "cesta punta"; "pala larga"; "yoko-garbi"; "grand chistera"; "pala corta"; "raquette"; "remonte"; "sare"; and two kinds of "palette".

Pelota's plurality of courts means that some games have two or more versions. Main nue, for example, is played in place libre, fronton, and trinquet; pala in the first; and palette in the last two of these. Rules have been coded for every game recognized by the several authorities but, competition apart, players ignore or modify them at will, improvising as they go along.

More pelota is played with main nue ("bare hand") than with the various bats and racquets. Seventy years ago players were allowed to hold the ball briefly – when taken on the volley – before returning it: that is, the ball was first caught, then thrown. Under modern rules every ball must be hit; there is no way of lessening the force of impact.

• JEUX DIRECTS

Rebot (or Spanish, rebote) from the Old French "reboter", "to reverse", or "to hit back", is a five-a-side form of jeux directs played with leather or chistera-type gloves in the open place libre court.

This is the oldest and most esoteric version of pelota: a survival of the game, derived from longue paume, played before the coming of the rubber-cored ball killed the old order and created the jeux de blaid. Rebot is more than a game: it is a ceremony with its own language and conventions that few but players and initiates can fully understand. It is played only in the Basque provinces, and only in certain villages and towns, among which the best known are Sare, Hasparren, St Jean-de-Luz, St. Ettinne-de-Baïgorry, Ustaritz and Les Aldudes.

The "paso" line divides the players into two camps: a defending, or "refil" side, nearest the wall; and an attacking, or serving side, beyond the paso. Each side alternately attacks and defends, according to the fortunes of the game, but the object of each is to prevent the ball "dying" in its camp, while attempting to make it stop in that of its opponents. In this, the defending side is heavily favoured, for it occupies less than a third of the court.

The spearhead of the attacking side is the server, who hits the ball with his bare hand – the only stroke so made in the game – after bouncing it once on the serving stone. The serve, to be good, must hit the wall in the "barne", either on the volley or first bounce off the barne area on the floor. It is returned by the key player of the defending side, called the "refileur", who guards the barne close to the ball. The ball, thereafter, need not hit the wall.

If, in the ensuing rally, the attackers miss the ball, they lose the point outright; if, on the other hand, they succeed in making it penetrate the barne, either on the wall or on the floor, they win it. Should the defending side miss the ball without letting it enter the barne, or should they let the ball roll along the ground to cross the paso, the umpire calls a "chase".

In the US version the ball must be served against the frontis so that it returns within the serving zone. The ball is then caught in the chistera and thrown in a continuous motion. It may be returned before it bounces or after it has bounced once. The ball must be returned to the frontis and be played within the green areas on the walls.

Points are gained when the opponent returns the ball after it has bounced more than once; misses the ball; does not return the ball on to the frontis; fails to catch the ball and throw it in a continuous motion.

Equipment

Derived from a small wicker fruit basket, the "chistera" or "cesta" was first used tentatively for pelota by French Basques in about 1860. Lengthened and strengthened over the years to attain its present form, it has a curved frame of seasoned chestnut and ash branches and a body of plaited osier twigs. The hand is slid wrist-deep into the aperture, or pocket, which contains the "glove" – actually four leather finger loops in the manner of cricket batting gloves. The whole is lashed to the wrist by laces.

The ball is caught in the "chistera", held for a moment (the "atchiki" – to "hold" or "wait") and then hurled out again. The ball weighs 130g (4.5oz).

Scoring

Scoring is as in tennis, and a match is 13 games.

The US game's scoring is played for a number of points ranging from 7 to 35.

Clothing

Players often wear white trousers, a coloured sash or belt, a coloured shirt bearing a number, white rubber soled shoes and a helmet.

PESÄPALLO

Introduction

Literally in English "nest-ball", but more usually known as "Finnish baseball", pesäpallo is a bat-and-ball team game based on American BASEBALL and certain traditional Finnish games.

History

There is the ball-game tradition of "poltopallo", literally "burnball", in Finland. "Burning" consists of hitting the runner or throwing ahead of the batsman before he can reach the safety of the base. In an early form it was a kind of wall game in which the pitcher threw the ball at a wall 10–15m (33–50ft) distant and, when it rebounded, two batsmen would try to hit it away far enough to score a "run" by touching the wall and returning to their bases before the ball could be returned. Other forms of the game were KUNINGASPALLO, pitkapallo, and ROUNDERS – called in Finnish the "four goals" or in Swedish "brannboll".

Pesäpallo

The creation of Pesäpallo, however, was prompted by the demonstrations of American baseball in Scandinavia after the Stockholm Olympic Games of 1912. The Finns were keen to establish a ball game which would involve sprinting. They felt that the "no hits no runs" paragon of baseball would not suit their national temperament; and they also sought a game which would encourage movement. Hence they did away with the ferocious horizontal pitch of the American game which often confines the game to striker and pitcher while leaving the fielders immobile. They also set increasing distances between bases to reproduce the war situation of football or hockey in which the further the attacking team advances, the stronger grows the defence against it.

After a decade of experiment and planning chiefly by Professor Lauri Pihkala, the shape and rules of Pesäpallo were launched in 1922.

The game was first played, sustained and developed by Finnish volunteer territorial troops largely in smaller population centres.

It grew until, by the 1970s, there were between 5,000 and 6,000 registered teams competing in the five or six most widely practiced games in the country.

Venue

There are spacious bases – with a radius 2.5m (8ft 3in) – which are intended to minimize collisions.

Rules

A match is played between teams of nine players each; scoring is by completed runs from home base to first base, second base, third base and back to home base. The bat and ball are a little lighter than those used in baseball, and there are considerable differences in the pitch on which the game is played, notably in the zig-zag line of running from the strike position to the bases and the progressively increasing distances between them – 20m, 30m and 45m (22, 33, 38 and 49yds).

Another fundamental difference is that when "pitching", or serving, which takes the form of a vertical lob, the ball must rise at least 1m (3ft 3in) above the head of the striker and, if he does not hit it, land on the serving plate. A minimum height is necessary because the batsman is allowed to run to first base as soon as the ball leaves the server's hand. Thus the batsman need not strike the ball at all. Two foul serves entitle him and his team mates on other bases to advance one base without penalty. Each batsman may receive three serves or pitches.

A batsman is out or "killed" if the fielded ball reaches a baseman ahead of the running batsman; if, when running between bases, he is touched with the hand holding the ball; or if he hits the ball beyond the boundary on his third hit.

The sides change from batting to fielding when three batsmen have been put out, or if all nine players have batted but failed to score a single run. If the struck ball is caught, the striker, so long as he reaches the safety of a base ahead of the return, is not out, but is regarded as "wounded"; he cannot score on that run, but he may bat again in his turn if enough members of his team survive. The spacious bases – radius 2.5m (8 ft 3in) – are intended to minimize collisions.

Clothing

Players should wear casual clothing to allow freedom of movement.

PÉTANQUE

Introduction

This, sometimes called "boule", is a ball-and-target game of the same type as LAWN BOWLS, CROWN GREEN BOWLS and its own parent game, JEU PROVENÇAL, which has spread far beyond Provence where it originated and is played extensively in France and as far afield as the USA.

History

It is said that pétanque began in the year 1910. Debate continues as to whether it was at Vallauris, l'Isle-sur-Sorque, or Le Ciotat, when some bowlers engaged in jeu provençal (played on a pitch of up to 21m (23yds), and with a two or three-stride run-up permitted to the bowler) decided – presumably in midday heat – to reduce the amount of physical effort involved. Accordingly they introduced a 10m (11yds) pitch, which made it crucially simpler to succeed at pétanque than at jeu provençal, and the almost stationary delivery.

Since then the game has become immensely popular and has spread far beyond its historical Provençal bounds to cover the whole of France as well as a number of other countries.

Venue

The game does not call for highly prepared turf as in the case of lawn bowls but can be, and is, played on a village street, country lane, back yard, or public square. Official matches, however, usually take place on an accepted pitch, which may be marked out by the umpire, who controls all such matches, or the organizing committee: it should be at least 3 or 4m wide and 15m long (approx. 4 x 16yds).

Rules

The game is played as singles, when each player has three or four balls, as decided; doubles, three bowls each; and trebles, two each.

The players – or deputed members from teams – toss for the right to choose the delivery circle, throw the target ball, and deliver the first bowl. The winner chooses a starting point where s/he marks out a circle 35–50cm (approx. 13–19in) in diameter and at least 1m (1.094yds) from any obstacle. Standing within the circle s/he throws the jack, which must land at a point which – measured from the nearest edge of the circle – lies 5–10m (depending on the age group competing) from him/her. It must also be at least 1m from any obstacle or the edge of the pitch. The player has three chances to throw the ball into an acceptable position; if s/he fails, the option for three attempts passes to the other side: but the right to bowl first does not pass.

Once the target ball is in place, no player may "improve" the pitch by removing or treading down obstructions; though s/he may make good any hole in the ground caused by the landing of an earlier bowl.

To take the example of a single match; the player who won the toss – or any member of his/her team in a team event – delivers the first ball. In doing so s/he must not cross, nor even touch, the line of the starting circle until the bowl has landed (though players disabled in the legs may be allowed to ground one foot or leg outside the circumference). The aim is to leave it as near the jack as possible. He may toss it high in the air so that it lands near the jack and stops dead, which is the technique known as "plomber"; or he may roll it along the ground, as in lawn bowls, which is called "rouler".

The second player then takes up position within the circle

and attempts to place his bowl closer to the jack than the first player's. S/he, too, may employ plomber or rouler; and if his/her bowl finishes closer to the jack it may also block the opponent's approach for his/her second shot. If, however, the first bowl is so close to the jack that it does not leave sufficient space for another between it and the jack, s/he may attempt to throw the next bowl directly on to the winning one and knock it away. This is known as a "tirer". If s/he contrives to hit the opponent's ball flush at the perfect point on its circumference, his/her own bowl will not only dislodge the other, but drop into its place; this stroke – the most spectacular in the game – is known as "carreau".

The players continue, alternately, using any of the three tactics – pointer, tirer, or carreau – until each has bowled his/her agreed three or four bowls, some latterly, perhaps, in a changed position because the jack has been disturbed. The player whose bowl is nearest to the jack scores 1 point; if s/he has a second, a third, or a fourth also nearer the jack than the opponent's s/he will score 2, 3, or 4 points. This unit of the game is called "une méne". In the following méne, the jack is thrown from within a circle drawn round the spot where it stood in the previous round.

A match usually consists of three games of 13 or other agreed number of points; the first is called "la partie", the second "la revanche", and the third "la belle".

Equipment

The target ball or jack – "conchonnet", "petit bois", "ministre" or (Provençal) "lé" or "gari" – is of light or white-painted wood, and 25–35mm (1–1.36in) in diameter. The bowls, made of metal, usually steel, are 7.05–8cm (2.75–3.12in) in diameter.

They may not be leaded or biased, are produced by officially approved manufacturers, and weigh 620–800g (22–28oz).

Scoring

Scoring is at a rate of one point for every bowl of the same player or team which lies nearer to the jack than any of the opponent(s) when all bowls have been bowled. A game is generally of 13 points; but in certain circumstances, and according to some local conventions, it may be of 11, 15, 18, or 21 points.

Clothing

Players wear casual clothing to allow freedom of movement.

PIGEON RACING

Introduction

This is a sport in which the fancier is a combination of owner, breeder, trainer and punter.

History

The modern racing pigeon is descended from the rock dove ("Columba livia") and bears no relation to either the common wood pigeon ("Columba palumbus") or the stock dove ("Columba oenas").

Man has known the rock dove from the earliest recorded times, and at least 5,000 years ago the Egyptians were domesticating them – Pharaoh Rameses III (1198-1167BC) used them to carry messages. Pliny, the Roman historian, refers to the use of pigeons as message carriers during the siege of Matina in 43BC and several hundreds of years later they were employed by the Saracens to the discomfort of King Richard of England, who was frequently surprised at the speed with which his enemy learned of his troop movements.

Other occasions on which pigeons were used include during the sieges of Leyden in 1574, Venice in 1849 and Paris in 1870-71. Reuters, the international news service, was founded on the use of pigeons to carry messages. By the time of the two world wars the modern racing pigeon, capable of sustained flight at high speed over hundreds of miles, had been developed.

The evolution of the modern racing pigeon took place in the latter half of the nineteenth century, with Belgium and Great Britain the pioneers. One of the main centres of development was the province of Antwerp, Belgium, whose fanciers in the early twentieth century would send drafts of pigeons to England for selection by would-be purchasers, after which the pigeons were released on the understanding that if they did not return to their home lofts in Antwerp there was no financial responsibility on the part of the prospective buyer.

It was not until the turn of the century that pigeon racing became an organized sport by the creation of national bodies. The Royal Fédération Colombophile Belge was formed, closely followed in1896 by the formation of the Royal National Homing Union of Great Britain. Other countries throughout the world were not far behind.

Rules

In order to race pigeons, a fancier will belong to a club, the object of which is to provide equality of chance throughout its membership, and each club has a radius outside which membership is barred.

The pigeons are taken to the face point and, prior to liberation, the convoyer will receive, by prior arrangement with a weather bureau, a detailed forecast giving complete information of wind, weather, visibility and cloud height and intensity at the liberation point and along the line of flight to the home end. This is based on an estimated flying speed of 40mph (64km/h). On receipt of the report, the pigeon convoyer will contact the race controller who will himself have obtained reports from fanciers and coast guards along the line of flight. If both agree that everything points to a good race, the pigeons are liberated and the time of the liberation telephoned to the federation secretary, who will in turn inform club secretaries. If the weather is against a good race, the pigeons will be held at the race point until favourable conditions apply.

The speed of flight depends entirely upon the direction of the wind and will obviously be greater with a tail wind than against a head wind. Over a season's racing a reasonable average speed would be in the region of 35–40mph (56–64km/h), but speeds of up to 90mph (145 km/h) have been recorded and verified.

Equipment

The initial equipment can be costly, but less so for the do-it-yourself enthusiast. Undoubtedly the major item is the loft, which may be of wooden or brick construction. If it is wooden, it is customary to have it raised from the ground.

The size of the loft will vary according to the aims and intentions of the fancier, but as a yardstick a loft 12ft (4m) long by 6ft (2m) wide, 7ft (2.1 m) high at the front and 6ft (2m) high at the back partitioned into two halves, is sufficient to accommodate 10 to 12 pairs of old birds in one half, and a similar number of young birds in the other. The pigeon basket or, more commonly, the transporter crate, is another essential item of equipment.

PING BALL

Ping ball is a form of table tennis akin to lawn tennis. It is played on the ground over a net 70cm (27.5in) high, with a racket 28–32cm x 15cm (11–12.5 x 16in), similar in shape to a table tennis bat but with a net hitting surface. The ball is 4cm (1.5in) in diameter. Service passes from game to game and scoring is the same as in tennis.

POLO

Introduction

Polo is a four-a-side team game whose players are mounted on horses and use wooden mallets, or "sticks", to strike a wooden ball in an attempt to score goals. The ball is struck with the side, not the end, of the mallet, and there is no limit to the size of the horse, though one of over 16 hands is not often manoeuvrable enough.

History

The Persian poet Firdausi described a polo match between the Persians and Turkomans about 600BC. At Isfahan are the remains of an ancient polo ground 300yds (274.32m) long with stone goal posts 8yds (7.3m) apart, which are still the correct measurements. The name polo comes from "pulu", the willow root from which the balls were and are made in the East.

The game spread over Asia to China and Japan but by the nineteenth century it survived in only a few mountainous areas in the north-west and north-east frontiers of India, away from the main currents of invasion and disaster. In some of these places, such as Hunza and Gilgit, it is still played in the original form on the small local ponies.

The game was discovered by visiting British officers who,

adopting it with enthusiasm, began to establish polo clubs in India; the first, Calcutta, still exists and celebrated its centenary in 1962. Indian princes soon took up the game and they and the Army were its principal supports in India from that time on.

The first match in England was played in 1871 at Hounslow between the 9th Lancers and the 10th Hussars. The Hurlingham Club was inaugurated shortly afterwards. The Army was the strongest supporter of the game in England as in India; the keenly contested inter-regimental tournaments started in India in 1877 and in England a year later.

Polo was introduced to the USA by Gordon Bennett in the late 1870s and spread rapidly, at first mainly in the east. By 1914 the game was known all over the world, especially where Englishmen or Americans were working, and particularly in countries with plenty of space, sun, and horses – such as India, Argentina and South Africa. In Europe, Spain took second place to the United Kingdom, though a few clubs flourished in Italy, France, Belgium and Germany. Where conditions were suitable, the game was popular; in countries like those of northern Europe with a short summer and an industrial economy, it was confined to being a pastime for the very rich and their friends, and the armed services.

The modern rules of polo were developed first by the Hurlingham Club in London and adopted elsewhere in the same form. Additions and amendments have been made from time to time by the ruling bodies of the major polo countries in consultation with each other.

Venue

The game can be played three-a-side if numbers are short or the ground small. A full-size ground is 300yds (274.32m) long,

200yds (182.88m) wide if unboarded, and 160yds (146.3m) wide if boarded. Grounds are often smaller but these dimension are never exceeded. Boards on the side lines, if used, are 9in (229mm) high and are intended to keep the ball in play. The ground is marked with white lines round the ends and sides and across the field at 30–60yds (27.4–54.9m) from each goal line. There are also crosses or marks of whitewash indicating the centre of the ground and at 40yds (36.5m) from the centre of each goal. There must be generous safety zones behind the goal lines and outside the touch lines, so that players may cross them at full speed and at any angle.

Rules

Any type of horse or pony may be played. There is no limit to size, age, or sex. The horse must, however, be sufficiently well behaved not to constitute a danger to other horses and players, and may be sent off the ground by the umpires if it fails in this respect. The horse must wear boots or bandages to cover the lower leg and fetlock as a protection against blows from ball or mallet. The boots are fitted like gaiters and secured with straps.

The game is divided into periods or "chukkas" of 7 minutes each. The full game is eight periods, but in most tournaments fewer periods are played, many games having only four. In Europe there are no tournaments of more than six periods. A bell is rung at 7 minutes, but the period goes on until the ball goes out of play or the umpire stops the game in a neutral position. In England and the USA, the chukka ends on a second bell at 7.5 minutes, if the ball is still in play. The last period, however, ends on the bell unless there is a tie, in which case the game continues in the normal way until a goal is scored.

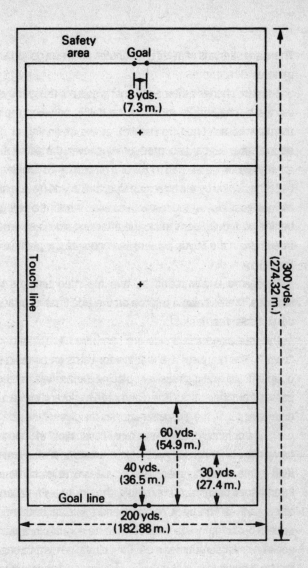

Polo Ground
Dimensions shown are those of a full-size ground including the safety area, which should be at least 5yds (4.5m) beyond the touch lines and 20yds (18.3m) at either end.

There are intervals of at least 3 minutes between period and 5 minutes at half-time.

Ends are changed after each goal is scored. The game is re-started by the umpire throwing the ball in between the two teams, who are lined up parallel, at the beginning of each period, after a goal is scored, or whenever the game stops for any reason other than a goal or a hit behind goal. When the ball is hit behind by the attacking side, the defending side hits it as in a goal kick at ASSOCIATION FOOTBALL. When the ball goes behind off a defender's stick, the attacking side is awarded a free hit from the 60yds (54.9m) line opposite the point where the ball went out.

The game is controlled by two mounted umpires with whistles. There is also a referee on the side lines as arbiter in case of disagreement.

The four players in a side are numbered 1, 2, 3 and 4 (or "back"). The numbers 1 and 2 are forwards and should play optimistically and aggressively, placing themselves to receive passes from their backs. The 3 and 4 are backs and play a more defensive game, the 3 usually acting as the pivot of the side and the 4 as a defensive player who must never allow the opposing forwards a clear run for goal. Polo is however such a fast and fluid game that the members of a team must continually interchange position. For example, the No. 1 may find himself temporarily in the back position, and must play accordingly until an opportunity arises to return to his normal place, while a good back will sometimes meet the ball and go right through to the No. 1 position.

A high degree of teamwork can and should be obtained in polo and a team that has played together and studied this aspect will always, if equally well mounted, defeat a team of four equally good, or better, individualists. One obvious example of teamwork is for a player to pass the ball to a team mate who is already taking up position to receive the pass, having correctly anticipated it. Another is for a player having possession of the ball to leave it for a following team mate to strike, while he gallops ahead to "ride out" (or "ride off", i.e. to push sideways out of the line of play) an opponent who is waiting to intercept. This is a matter of horsemanship and the speed, courage, and training of the horse. Two equal opponents, both correctly anticipating the next position of the ball, will find themselves riding each other off again and again.

A player following the ball on its exact line has the right of way over all other players (whether or not they hit the ball themselves). Any player who crosses or enters the right of way close enough to be dangerous, commits a foul. No player may hook an opponent's stick unless they are on the same side of the pony as the ball.

Dangerous riding or stick-work is not allowed. A player may ride off fairly but must not charge an opponent at an angle of more than about 30°. There is no offside rule.

Each player, as in golf, carries an international rating. A player can rate from -2 (minimum) to +10 (maximum), though in many countries minus handicaps are not used, and a beginner starts at 0.

Equipment

Goal posts are placed 8yds (7.3m) apart; they are about 10ft (3m) high and about 10in (254mm) in diameter. They are not of solid construction but usually of wicker or lath covered with cloth, often in the club colours fixed around a central pole of about 1.5in (38mm) in diameter. This fits into a slot in the ground, and allows a player or horse to collide with the goal post without the certainty of serious injury.

A mallet consists of a handle made of wood clamped to the shaft and bound with rubber, tape, or towelling as a hand grip. The shaft is cane about 0.75in (19mm) thick and 47–54in (1.3–1.4m) long. The head is of wood, about 9in (228mm) long by 2in (51mm) in diameter at the centre, and of cylindrical, oval, or rectangular section. The most common pattern is cigar-shaped with tapered ends. Metal shafts are not used. The design can vary according to the wishes of the player.

The ball is of solid wood, usually willow, bamboo root, or ash. It must not exceed 3.25in (82.5mm) in diameter and must be 4.25–4.75oz (120–135g) in weight. Its life is not long and a considerable number are used in each game.

Clothing

Players wear helmets or caps which protect the head from a fall or a blow. Gloves and leather and rubber knee-pads may also be worn. In matches and tournaments it is customary for players to wear white breeches of a washable material and brown leather-top boots, with a shirt or jersey in the team's colours. Spurs are often worn but sharp spurs or rowels are not allowed.

POLOCROSSE

Introduction

This is a team game played on horseback, created by combining some elements of POLO with some of LACROSSE.

History

Polocrosse was first played at the National School of Equitation in England in 1939, with a weapon formed by splicing a TENNIS racket on to the handle of a polo mallet and replacing the right gut with the loose one. Subsequently special equipment was made, the operative end of which resembled a lacrosse net. Polocrosse resembles the American Indian game of lacrosse, the origin of which dates back hundreds of years to Persia. In England, polocrosse was an indoor exercise to teach people how to ride a horse. The modern game took shape in Australia in the 1930s, and today there are 6,000 players in the world.

Venue

The pitch is much smaller than that of polo, being 160yds long and 60yds wide (146 x 55m). The goal posts are only 8ft (2.4m) apart instead of 8yd (7.3m). There is a penalty line 30yds (27m) from, and parallel to, each goal line, across which the ball may be thrown but not carried.

Rules

The object of the game is to propel a rubber ball into the opponents' goal, by galloping with it or passing it to another member of the team who may be in a better position to score, and by trying to avoid interception by an opponent.

Eight chukkas of eight minutes each are played, with two minutes between each. There are six players to a team, only three of whom may be on the field at one time. The game is regarded as good training for polo, and used to be played frequently by pony clubs.

Equipment

The ball is a soft sponge rubber ball about 4ins in diameter with a latex skin. It is soft and bounces. For the polocrosse racquet the stick is a cane shaft from 30–40in long with a round head that is 7.5in in diameter. The head is fitted with a loose-stringed net. The netting is used to hold the ball as it is scooped up from the ground and carried.

Clothing

See Polo.

POOL

Introduction

Pool is a game played on a special table by two players or pairs. A player uses a cue (long wooden stick) to hit a cue ball across the table to score points by pocketing balls.

History

Pool (or American pocket billiards) is a descendant of BILLIARDS. The Spanish introduced a form of billiards into America in the sixteenth century: the British brought English billiards to New England in the early nineteenth century. (see Billiards).

Venue

The table is a smaller version of an English BILLIARD table. It should be either 4ft x 8ft long or 4ft 6in x 9ft. The playing area should measure 46in x 92in on the 4ft x 8ft table.

Rules

The white ball is placed on the spot, and the striker places his/her cue ball anywhere behind the headstring and plays the first shot. When their turn is over, the second player takes their shot. The striker uses the tip of the cue to hit the cue ball in the direction of another ball. Chalk is applied to the cue to improve contact. The cue ball must be struck and not pushed; and at the moment of striking, the player must have a foot on the ground. Balls must not be forced off the table.

Play lasts an agreed length of time, or until one player or side reaches an agreed number of points. A game is known as a "frame". While the shots comprising a player's turn are known as a "break". Each time a players scores from a shot, they are entitled to another shot. Only when they fail to score do they forfeit their turn.

Equipment

The balls must be equal in size and weight. A standard ball should be 2.25in in diameter and weigh 5.5–6oz. The object balls are numbered 1–15: numbers 1–8 are in solid colours, numbers 9–15 are striped. The cue ball is white, while the cue must be of traditional shape and not less than 3ft long.

Scoring

Individual balls have no points value, a player wins a game if s/he legally pockets the 8 ball, or if his/her opponent commits an offence. A match is won by winning the most games.

POWERBOAT RACING

Introduction

Powerboat racing takes place either inland or on offshore waters, in boats propelled by outboard or inboard motors, and in classes usually determined by the length of the boat.

History

Powerboat racing started in about 1900, and there are now a large number of categories of boat that race on either inland waters or offshore. The first petrol engine was fitted in 1865 on a boat owned by Jean Lenoir on the River Seine.

After the war came the boom in small powerboat racing, mostly on inland waters by craft of 12–25ft (3.7–7.6m) long. The most significant event in the sport since 1903 came in 1959, when a massive offshore race was organized in the USA, from Florida to the Bahamas.

Powerboat Racing

It is a popular sport off the coasts of Europe, the USA, South America, Australia and South Africa, though the price of a suitable boat and the cost of maintenance and transport confine offshore racing to the wealthy.

Small boats, of the kind that usually race on lakes and reservoirs, took to the open sea in 1962, when the first event of its class was held from Putney, on the river Thames in London, to Calais (France) and back.

Even with outboard engines, speeds of more than 100mph (161km/h) are often achieved, and these may be doubled with inboard engines. Many of the fastest craft travel on the hydroplaning principle, whereby the boat rises partially out of the water and skims over the surface. Such boats are usually designed with a hull that is V-shaped, or rounded, at the bow, and flat near the stern where the boat is cut away square. In this way the water displaced by the bow and sides of the boat, which tends to flow inwards again and create suction against the stern, creates less friction and falls away without hindering the boat's speed. The ultimate in such design is the hydrofoil, which at high speed almost flies across the water, touching it at three points only – the propeller and the two thin foils that extend into the water on either side of the craft, lifting the hull out of the water as an aeroplane is lifted by its wings.

• DRAG BOAT RACING

This the equivalent on water of drag racing (see MOTOR RACING) on land, with the additional hazard that the slightest turbulence of the water or the smallest piece of debris, can cause an appalling accident. For this reason it is recognized as one of the world's most dangerous sports.

Rules

Two boats at a time race over a straight quarter-mile (402m) stretch of water. From a slow-moving start, the acceleration is such that speeds of up to 190mph have been recorded over the last 50yds of the course, which may be completed in little over seven seconds.

The boats used are 16–23ft (5–7m) long. There are eight principal classes of competition, arranged according to the style of the hull, type and position of engine (inboard or outboard), fuel (liquid or gas) and method of injection. Drag boat racing began in Southern California in 1956 and is not widely practiced elsewhere.

PUNTING

Introduction

Punting is the propulsion over water, by means of a pole, of a flat-bottomed, shallow, square-ended boat.

History

Though punting may have existed for many centuries, particularly as a means of moving light cargo, the earliest known reference to it as a sport was in 1793. A print of that date shows two Thames watermen in a punt race at Windsor "in honour of the Prince of Wales's Birth Day". Watermen, boat builders, and others employed in river trades raced annually for the professional championship, which was won from 1877 to 1890 by Beasley, the originator of "pricking" (see below). It was his success with this method, while other punters were still running, that established it as the punting style of the future.

Amateurs, who had begun to enjoy punting as a social pastime, took it up as a sport with the foundation of the

Punting

Thames Punting Club in 1885. They drew up the rules for punt racing and instituted the amateur championship for men (1885), men's doubles (1886), women (1927), mixed doubles (1932), and women's doubles (1954). Other later punting clubs on the Thames were affiliated to the Thames Punting Club, which is still the controlling body of punt racing.

Venue

In punt racing, races start and finish at the same point, after a measured course – usually 330yds (302m), 440yds (403m), or 660yds (604m) – has been covered in both directions.

Rules

According to the rules of the UK's Thames Punting Club, probably the only authoritative punting body in the world, a punt must be a craft "without stem, keep or sternpost, of which the width at each end must be at least one half of the width of the widest part". In practice, the pastime is confined not merely to London, but to that part of the river Thames between Kingston and Oxford, and to the river Cam at Cambridge.

The difficulty of mastering punting is seldom appreciated by those who have not tried it. Novices sometimes find the pole stuck in mud, and are faced with having to make an instant decision whether to let go of the pole stuck in mud, as the boat glides on, or to cling to the pole and part company with the boat. Onlookers invariably find the result hilarious whichever the decision.

Until the 1890s there was only one recognized method of punting: to stand at the head of the punt, place the end of the pole on the river bed and walk (or run) to the stern, maintaining firm pressure with the pole and returning to the bow for the next stroke. This is still used for ferry-punting, and for moving light barges and sailing vessels, when it is known as "quanting"; but as punts and poles became smaller and lighter, new techniques were created and "walking" was forgotten.

"Pricking" is a method of punting in which the pole is pushed firmly against the river bed until the angle of the pole to the water makes it impossible to continue, when it is withdrawn for the next stroke. "Bucketing" is the withdrawal of the pole by flicking it out of the water with sufficient impetus to slide it up through the punter's hands ready for the next stroke. "Gathering" is withdrawal of the pole by hand-over-hand method.

Equipment

Punts vary in length from 25 to 35ft (7.6 to 10.7m), and in width from 3ft 6in (1m) for the fishing or shooting punt, to only 14in (36cm) for a racing punt. They can be made of Honduras mahogany or laminated plywood. The craft are propelled by an occupant pushing a pole against the bed of the water in the opposite direction to that in which he wishes to direct the boat. A pole is 13–14ft (4–4.3m) long, ending with a metal fork with which to grip the river bed. Wooden poles are still used for casual punting, but for racing a duralumin tube of 1.25in (31.8mm) diameter is generally preferred.

QUOITS

Introduction

Quoits is an outdoor game in which a ring is thrown at a peg-target.

History

A pastime of considerable antiquity in Britain, it was but one of many variations in different countries of "throwing the discus", one of the five games of the ancient Greek pentathlon. In quoits, however, the merit is not in the distance that the discus (quoit) is thrown but in the accuracy of the throw.

In England quoits was a well-known game from at least the reign of Edward III (1327–77) when it was included among the forbidden sports and pastimes that diverted servants, apprentices and labourers from recreations of an essentially martial character, at a time of recurring wars of conquest against the French. Such edicts were no more successful in stopping the playing of quoits than in stopping the playing of ball games like FOOTBALL that were similarly forbidden. Quoits continued and the game was still being played fairly commonly in parts of the Midlands, Lancashire, and Scotland as late as the 1930s, according to rules that had probably changed little in their essentials over the centuries.

Rules

In a manner of play resembling BOWLS, except that the quoit is thrown in the air. There are two ends about 18yds (16.5m) apart, at each of which an iron or steel pin (known as the "hob") is driven into the middle of a circle of stiff clay 3ft (914mm) in diameter leaving about 1in (25.4mm) of the hob exposed.

Matches are played between individuals, pairs, or teams and for any number of points that has been agreed on, the winner being the player or team that first scores that agreed number of points. Each player, standing not more than 4ft 6in (1.372m) from his/her pin and in line with it, has to throw the quoit such that it lodges in the clay as near as possible to the hob. Expert players are often able to ring the hob and such a "ringer" scores 2 points. Otherwise 1 point is awarded to each quoit, other than a ringer, lying nearer to the hob than that of an opposing player's quoit. All "turned" quoits are foul and not recognized for scoring purposes.

A more sophisticated variant is DECK QUOITS, which developed from the many games played on the long voyages by seamen with quoits they had made of rope. Today rubber rings have taken the place of both the early iron quoits and the seamen's rope ones.

Equipment

The quoit used was an iron ring, nearly flat, of a weight not exceeding 9lb (4.082kg), usually about 6lb (2.72 kg), with a slightly convex upper side, and a niche on the outer rim that could be gripped by one finger in preparation for throwing the quoit. The diameter of the quoit could not exceed 8.5in (216mm), nor be less than 3.5in (88.9mm) in the bore, or more than 2.25in (57.5mm) in the web.

RACE WALKING

Introduction

Race walking is an extended form of walking, now practiced in all the five continents.

History

In the eighteenth and nineteenth centuries with only horse racing and boxing as rivals, walking, or "pedestrianism" as it was then called, was highly popular, with much wagering encouraging men against time, distance and other walkers. Two of the most famous pedestrians were Powell (b. 1736) and Captain Barclay (b.1779) of England. On several occasions between 1773 and 1790, Yorkshire-born Powell completed the 402-mile journey from London to York and back within six days.

Amateur walking became popular after 1860 and a 7–mile

(11km) event was held in the English Amateur Athletics Club's championship in 1866. With working and social conditions allowing a little more time for sport, athletic and walking clubs were formed and town-to-town events became particularly popular. Europe, France, Italy and Denmark were prominent, from 1890 to 1910, in producing outstanding performers over all distances. The USA, Canada and Australia had numerous short-distance experts.

Gradually the sport was accepted in major international sports events such as the Olympic Games (1908), the European Games (1934), and the Commonwealth Games (1966).

Venue

Competitors race on an athletics track over various distances like 10km, 20km and 50km though competitors can race on roads as well as tracks.

Rules

A competitor using the correct method obtains his/her speed by making the fullest use of the mobility of the hips in a lateral rhythm. A maximum range of movement between the toe of the rearmost foot and the heel of the leading foot produces a stride of 40–50in (1.016–1.270m) while the walker maintains balance carried at right-angles to the body. "Heel and toe" was the term used in the nineteenth and early twentieth centuries to describe the action of race walking.

Equipment

Race walking shoes are now mass-produced and differ from ordinary ones in: the flexibility of the soles to facilitate bending; the heel stiffener; and the wide fitting. In the pedestrians' era, ordinary shoes and boxing boots were in vogue, but a lighter shoe, generally hand-made, became popular around 1900. Due to the demands made on them, shoes used for long-distance events are more robust and heavier than those used in track competition. Most competitors use a lining to lessen the possibility of bruising and jarring.

Clothing

Clothing must be clean, non-transparent (even when wet) and designed and worn so as not cause offence.

RACKETS (RACQUETS)

Introduction

Rackets is a racquet-and-ball game played in England, USA, and Canada between two or four players in a court enclosed by four walls. It is held to be the fastest of court games.

History

Although the game, in its modern form, developed in England in the middle of the nineteenth century, its origins may be traced to varieties of HANDBALL played in Italy and France in the Middle Ages. In these games, in uncovered spaces the players struck the ball alternately, endeavouring always to return it themselves but prevent their opponents from doing so. Courts, known as "tripots", were common in French towns and these games were played not only with the bare or gloved hand but also with a bat or "battoir" and, by the end of fifteenth century, with a racket. This implement, was popular enough to distinguish a fashion among ladies in the time of Catherine de Medici when a hair-style, in which the hair was arranged in crossed or plaited bands, was called "en raquettes". A guild of racket-makers, which also embraced ball-making and brush-making, existed in France from the fifteenth century.

Rackets

Venue

The game is played on a court enclosed by four walls, giving a floor area generally 60ft long by 30ft wide (18.3m x 9.1m). The front or main wall, facing the players as s/he enters the court, is traversed by two horizontal lines: the higher the service line, or "cut" line, above which the service must be struck; and the play line, near flood-level and formed by a board fastened to the wall, which determines the lower limit on the front wall to which all returns must be directed.

Rules

As in other court games the ball is hit alternately by opponents until one or other side fails to make a return which is good. In the singles game, the right to serve first having been decided by the spin of the racket, the server takes up his position for starting the ball in play. For this purpose the lines marked on the floor of the court have significance. A line across the floor, known as the short line, divides the rear half of the court from that adjacent to the front wall, and the rear half is further divided down the centre into quarters by the half-court line.

Play starts when the server enters the service box – one of the square areas on either side of the court adjoining the short line – and hits the ball on to the front wall above the service line and onto the opposite quarter of the court. From here his/her opponent makes the return and so produce a rally (or "bully") of alternate shots, which continues until the ball ceases to be in play. This occurs when: the player fails to return the ball above the board; the player fails to return the ball before it strikes the floor for the second time since last struck; the player hits the ball above the area prepared for play; or the player commits some infringement such a hitting his/her opponent.

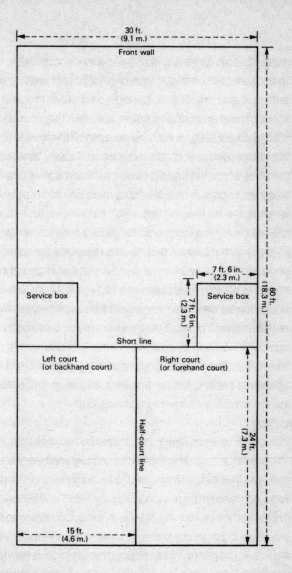

30 ft.
(9.1 m.)

Front wall

60 ft.
(18.3 m.)

7 ft. 6 in.
(2.3 m.)

Service box

7 ft. 6 in.
(2.3 m.)

Service box

Short line

Left court
(or backhand court)

Right court
(or forehand court)

Half-court line

24 ft.
(7.3 m.)

15 ft.
(4.6 m.)

Rackets Court

Plan view shows dimensions of the floor area. The surrounding walls are 30ft (91m) high, and the service line on the front wall is 9ft 6in (2.9m) from the floor.

The doubles game is similar. One partner succeeds the other to the service in each pair, with one opponent receiving in the left court and the other in the right, and rallies proceed with shots from alternate pairs. Rallies are often longer in doubles than in singles, as a sound defence is more readily established, but congestion and obstruction are less easily avoided and "lets", in which the point is played again on appeal, are more frequent. Tactics in doubles make more use of the side walls, whereas the essence of singles play is up-and-down hitting.

Hard hitting is a feature of the game which is often won by sheer pace, but a sound technique is required if the ball is to be adequately controlled and a degree of cut is imparted to the stroke to bring the ball down to an effective length, especially during the service. The cut service can be extremely severe and may dominate a match if the receiver has not sufficient skill, by attacking it, to exploit the server's positional disadvantage. The freedom of server is enhanced, under English rules, by his being allowed a second service following a fault. In American and Canadian courts a single-service is applied.

Scoring

A characteristic of the game, shared by FIVES (see ETON, RUGBY, WINCHESTER) and BADMINTON, is the "in and out" method of scoring. The player who is serving is said to be "hand in" and a stroke or rally won by him scores a point or an "ace". A stroke won by "hand out" earns him the right to serve but does not advance his score. A player continues to serve, from alternate sides of the court, until he becomes hand out or wins the game, usually 15 points.

Each game is 15 up – that is, the player who first scores 15 aces wins the game – excepting that, on the score being called

13-all for the first time in any game, players may, before the next service has been delivered, elect to "set" the game to 5 or to 3; then the player winning 5 (or 3) aces first wins the game (total 18 or 16). Similarly at 14-all, the game may be set to 3 (total 17). Singles matches are mostly best of five games, doubles best of seven.

Equipment

The ball is hollow and pressurized and should be 2.25in in diameter and 1.4oz. The racket head is 13.5in and a maximum width of 9in and the handle may be up to 7in long.

Clothing

Players wear shirts, shorts, socks and shoes of a colour that does not affect their opponents' view of the ball. Players can also wear safety glasses and eyeguards.

REAL TENNIS

Introduction

Real tennis is a racket-and-ball game played in an indoor court. Since the name "tennis" has become an accepted abbreviation for LAWN TENNIS, this ancient game from which lawn tennis was derived is now commonly known as real tennis in Britain, "royal tennis" in Australia and "court tennis" in America. In France it retains its historic name of "le jeu de paume".

History

Ball games are recorded from early times, and the origins of tennis have been variously traced to ancient Egyptians (the town of Tamis or Tinnis in the Nile delta), Homeric Greeks (Nausicaa and her handmaidens), Byzantines (on horseback), Romans (Augustus, Maecenus and Julius Caesar are claimed as players), Persians (the game of "tchigan"), Mexican Indians (the game of "tlatchli"), and Saracens ("racket" is derived from an Arabic word for the palm of the hand). In fact, the game which alone has the distinctive characteristics of real tennis almost certainly originated in France, as much of the nomenclature – dedans, tambour, grille, bisque, bandeau, etc., – suggests. This game was, and still is, called le jeu de paume – literally "the game of the palm".

Starting probably in open fields about 1000 years ago, le jeu de paume was first played in monastery cloisters during the eleventh century. The sloping roofs of the cloisters were retained and the cloisters were themselves represented by the dedans and side galleries. The grille is thought to represent a buttery hatch, the tambour a buttress. Some authorities trace the court's origins to castle courtyards and identify the galleries with cowsheds. There is little doubt that tennis was played in castles at an early date, but it is likely that cloisters had priority over them.

No satisfactory explanation or derivation of the word "tennis" has yet been found. The ancient Egyptian town of Tinnis has been suggested on the grounds that it was famous for linen, which was used for stuffing tennis balls. Another theory suggests a corruption of "tens" (five-a-side) as opposed to "fives", but fives is derived not from two-and-a-half a-side, but from the five knuckles of the bunched fist. The most plausible theory is that tennis is a corruption of the French "tenez", which may have been used for "Play!". Although there is no evidence that "tenez" was called in this way in le jeu de paume, it is significant that in its earliest written form in English tennis is spelt "tenetz".

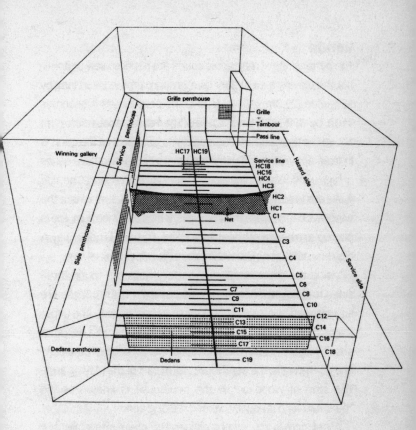

Grille penthouse

Grille

Tambour

Pass line

Winning gallery

Service line
HC17 HC19
HC18
HC16
HC4
HC3
HC2
HC1
C1

Penthouse

Service

Net

C2
C3
C4
C5
C6
C7
C8
C9
C10
C11
C12
C13
C14
C15
C16
C17
C18
C19

Side penthouse

Hazard side

Service side

Dedans penthouse

Dedans

Real Tennis Court

Perspective view looking towards the hazard side. Numbered lines on the service side of the net have the following conventional designations: C1) chase the line; C2) chase the first gallery; C3) chase the door; C4) chase second gallery; C5) chase a yard worse than last gallery; C6) chase last gallery; C7) chase half a yard worse than six; C8) chase six; C9) chase five and six; C10) chase five; C11) chase four and five; C12) chase four; C13) chase three and four; C14) chase three; C15) chase two and three; C16) chase two; C17) chase one and two; C18) chase one yard; C19) chase half a yard. Lines are numbered correspondingly on the hazard side. HC) Hazard chase.

Venue

The dimensions of real tennis courts are not precisely uniform, but the playing area at floor level is approximately 96ft long by 32ft wide (29.3m x 9.8m) (above the penthouses it becomes 110ft by 39ft – 33.5m x 11.9m). The roof is about 30ft (9m) above the floor. Sometimes it contains glass so that the court is lit from above, but it is usual for light to come through a series of high windows running along either side of the court. The side walls are in play up to a height of about 18ft (5.5 m) where the windows begin, while the end walls, which are unbroken, are in play up to a height of about 24ft (7.3m). The roof is not in play. A play line painted on the walls marks the upper limit of play.

Inside the court, internal or battery walls run round three sides to a height of an inch or two over 7ft (2.1m). These are surmounted by sloping roofs known as penthouses. The upper edges of the penthouses meet the walls proper at a height of about 10ft 6in (3.2m). Like the rest of the court below the play-line on the walls, the penthouses form part of the playing area. The strip of wood below the penthouse is known as the "bandeau" and is usually painted red or green.

A net across the centre divides the court into equal but dissimilar halves: the service side (on the right of the entrance), from which service is always delivered, and the hazard side (on the left of the entrance), on which service is received. The net is 5ft (1.5m) high at either side but sags to 3ft (0.9m) in the middle, permitting a lower trajectory for centre-court or cross-court shots than for side-court. The cord supporting the net is called the "line".

The main wall faces the entrance to the court. Unlike the other three walls, it contains no opening, but on the hazard side it projects into the court. This projection is the "tambour". It narrows the court by 1ft 6in (0.5m) for a distance of nearly 14ft (4.3m) from a grille wall, at which point it forms an angle. The face of the angle is 2ft 6in (0.8m) wide. Although the name properly refers to the entire projection it is commonly used to refer to the angle only.

The "dedans" (on the service side) and the "winning gallery" and "grille" (on the hazard side) are the "winning openings". When a player strikes a ball into them from the opposite side of the net he wins a point. The other galleries, on either side of the net, and the tambour are known as hazards.

Rules

Real tennis has affinities with the game of RACKETS, but whereas a rackets court has four plain walls, a real tennis court contains a number of special features, including ingenious hazards. These provide opportunities for a wide range of strokes. Combined with a ball which may be spun, twisted, or cut at will, the peculiar construction of the court makes real tennis a game where experience and subtlety of tactics count for as much as youth and physical fitness. Judgement and anticipation are as important as in other games: in real tennis, it is said, "la balle cherche le bon joueur".

The basic method of play in real tennis is that adopted for lawn tennis. Opponents strike the ball alternately from opposite sides of the net. If the ball passes over the net (or round it, along or above the side penthouse) it must be returned on the volley or after one bounce on the floor. The number of walls struck by the ball is of no consequence, provided that the portion of the ball struck is below the play line, which marks the upper limit of the playing area. Once the ball touches the floor a second time it is dead but, unless the second bounce is in the winning area, a "chase" has been made on the spot where it bounces and the point is not yet won or lost. A chase is a point held in abeyance. If the second bounce is, for example, on the 4yd line "chase four" is made; if it falls on the half-line between 3 and 4, "chase three and four"; if it falls between the two, "chase better than four". Similarly, if a ball enters the second gallery on the service side or falls on the line marked on the floor level with the gallery, it is "chase second gallery'; if it enters the second gallery on the hazard side it is "hazard the line". The best chase is "better than half a yard" – i.e. less than half a yard from the back wall.

Service is always from the same side of the court and does not change with the games as in lawn tennis. It changes only when the players change sides, and this occurs only when chases are played off. If no chase were made, the player who won the toss and chose the service side would continue serving throughout the match. Thus, whether it is finally won or lost, a chase at least wins for the receiver of service the right to serve, and he continues to hold service until dislodged by the making and the playing off of another chase.

Service is said to be the soul of real tennis ("l'ame du jeu"). It is comparable both to the opening gambit in chess and, since length is all-important, to bowling in CRICKET.

The receiver of the service has two choices. S/he can either try to make a chase, and thus win the service end, or s/he can try to win a point outright. The latter can be achieved either by sending his/her opponent a difficult return which will be miss-hit, or by hitting the ball into the dedans, which lies invitingly behind his/her opponent like a goal-mouth. Finding the dedans most often entails a hard "force", straight or "boasted" (stuck against a side wall), like a drive at cricket. This can be volleyed, or if it misses its mark the ball will rebound from the back wall or penthouse and offer an early return.

Equipment

The laws of real tennis place no restriction on the size or shape of rackets. Usually they weigh 13–18oz (369–510g), are 26–27in (660–686mm) in length and have an asymmetrical pear-shaped head which is 7–8in (178–203mm) at its widest. Both the handle and the catgut used for striking are stout because the balls are solid. The racket is normally gripped half or two-thirds of the way down the handle. A leather grip is sometimes used, but usually there is none. The asymmetry of the racket, which is its most notable feature, is said to make for ease in taking balls near the floor. The frame is made from ash, with middle pieces of willow, lime, or beech. Real tennis balls have a diameter of approximately 2.5in (64mm) and weigh 2.5–2.75oz (71–78g).

Scoring

Chases are called by the marker, who stands in a box by the net and also calls the score, faults and passes. Apart from the chases, scoring in real tennis is as in lawn tennis. Four points make a game and the first player to win six games wins the set. Scoring is by 15, 30, and 40 to game, and if both players reach 40, deuces and advantages are played until a lead of 2 clear points is established for the game. At 5-all in games a short set of one deciding game is normally played. In calling the score it is not the practice to give priority to the server, but to call first the score of the player who has won the last point or, in the case of games, the last game.

A marker is necessary to determine the chases accurately. These must be played off within the game in which they are made. When the player on the service side hits a return into the net the point is lost, but if s/he misses the ball completely it is not. If, for instance, the second bounce falls on the 3yd line and "chase three" is called, when either player is within the 1 point of the game, or when a second chase is made, the players change sides and the chase is then played off. The player from the service side is now on the hazard side and he must hit each return to such a length that the second bounce will fall nearer the back wall of the service side than the 3yd line. If it falls further from the back wall, either on the floor or by entering a side gallery, s/he loses the point. If it falls nearer, s/he wins the point. If it falls on the 3yd line, "chase off" is called and the point annulled. When a chase is being played off, the normal rules also apply: the point is lost by a player who fails to return the ball or hits it out of court.

Clothing

Men wear shirts and shorts or trousers, women wear short dresses, or tops with skirts and shorts. Players also wear white rubber-soled shoes.

RHYTHMIC GYMNASTICS

Introduction

The term "rhythmic gymnastics" is applied to all floorwork performed to music with or without small hand apparatus.

History

See GYMNASTICS.

Venue

The mat on which the gymnasts compete is 12m (13yds)

square and is placed inside an area 14m (15yds) square. The mat consists of a soft material 0.045m (1.8in) thick. The large mat is comprised of 60 small mats, 2m (6ft 7in) by 1.20m (3ft 11.25in), which are linked together.

Rules

In the individual events there is a time limit of 1–1.5 minutes. All the exercises, with or without apparatus, must include fundamental groups of body movements including jumps and leaps; balances; and pivots. Other groups of body movements must include various methods of travelling: skips and hops; swings and circles; turns and waves. For group events there is a time limit of 2–2.5 minutes and groups of six gymnasts perform together using either six pieces of identical apparatus; or three pieces of one type of apparatus and three of another; e.g. three ribbons and three clubs.

Competitors are judged on their performance in body movements and certain elements of movement with each specific item of apparatus.

Equipment

This type of gymnastics may involve the use of a rope, a hoop, a ball, a ribbon or clubs. The rope is made of hemp or similar synthetic material without handles and proportionate to the size of the gymnast. The hoop is made from wood or plastic and weighs a minimum of 300g. Its interior diameter is 80–90cm. The ball is made of rubber or similar synthetic material with an interior diameter of 18–20cm, and weighs a minimum of 400g. The ribbon is attached to a stick which is made of wood, plastic or fibre glass and is 50–60cm long. The ribbon is made of satin, or another similar material, is around 6m in length and has a minimum weight of 35g. Clubs are made of wood or a similar synthetic material with a length of 40–50cm, and a minimum weight of 150g.

Clothing

Women dress in one-piece costumes and light slippers.

RING TENNIS

Introduction

Ring tennis, also as tenikoit, is a combination of TENNIS and QUOITS that also closely resembles DECK TENNIS, the most popular of all deck games. It can either be played by two or four players, and, as with deck tennis, it can be played in much smaller area than lawn tennis. It can be enjoyed by players of all ages once they have learnt the knack of catching the ring. It may also be played much more seriously and competitively by skilled players using the familiar tennis techniques of drawing their opponents across the court, and then, quickly and accurately, throwing the ring to unguarded spaces.

Venue

The size of a court is influenced by the space available and the recommended dimensions vary from 10ft x 22ft (3m x 6.7m), through to 12ft x 30ft (3.7m x 9.1m) or 14ft x 36ft (4.3m x 10.97m), to 18ft x 40ft (5.5m x 12.2m). Whatever the size of the court, however, there must be a playing area between the neutral space extending 3ft (0.9m) on each side of the net. The playing area between the neutral space and the base line is then divided into four quarters, somewhat similar to the layout of a lawn tennis court but without tram-lines and with the dividing line extending to the base line. A ring tennis court with the overall dimensions 18ft x 40ft would thus be divided into four areas each measuring 9ft (2.7m) (half the overall width) by

17ft 5.2m long (half the overall length, less 3ft (0.9m), of neutral ground across the centre of the court).

Rules

The duration of a game can be varied to suit the convenience or preference of players but it usually consists of 15 points, except that if the score reaches 14-all the game continues until one player, or pair of players in a doubles game, gains a 2-point lead. Most popularly, three games are played, but again this may be varied by agreement among the players.

At the beginning of each game the first service is taken from behind the base line in the right-hand court, the ring being served diagonally across the court as in lawn tennis. The opponent receiving the service endeavours to catch the ring and to return it across the net to the service side where either player may try to catch and return it.

Play continues until:

The ring is not caught and falls to the ground within the playing area or the ring is touched but not caught by a player.

The ring is caught but is not then thrown back fairly, either going into the net or landing on the ground "out of bounds".

The ring is caught unfairly, that is to say other than with one hand. In such cases, when the play becomes "dead", a point is gained by the non-offending player or pair, except that, if the point is scored by receiving side, the service may be exchanged with no score being recorded or, alternatively, the score may be recorded but the service remain unchanged, according to the decision of the point-winning, receiving side.

No player may stand over the line marking the neutral space on either side of the net, and if the ring falls within the neutral ground, although it has crossed the net in service, it is a fault against the serving side. Since the ring ceases to be in play if and when it touches the ground, the surface of the court, it does not have to give the true and consistent bounce essential for playing either lawn tennis or padder tennis.

Equipment

Factory-produced rubber rings are now generally used and their availability, cheapness and durability have contributed to the increase in popularity of such games as ring tennis.

• BEACH TENNIS

This can be played with the same equipment and to the same rules as ring tennis, but often the only equipment used is the rubber ring. However, even when, as an expedient, the net is dispensed with, a more satisfactory game results from insisting on a neutral space on either side of the centre line, and following the "unwritten laws" of ring tennis or deck tennis. These include that:

A player, having caught the ring, should not hold it unnecessarily. Although both forehead and backhand deliveries are permitted, the ring should not be thrown overhand nor from a height above the shoulder.

The ring should be delivered in an upwards direction for at least 6in (152mm) after leaving the hand.

Feinting at delivery is a form of gamesmanship generally frowned upon.

ROCK CLIMBING

Introduction

Rock climbing requires both mental and physical strength, flexibility, agility and endurance.

History

Contemporary rock or sport climbing has its origins in the mountaineering of the 1800s, as many mountain ascents need a combination of both techniques to some extent. Before this time, religious superstition was a deterrent but with a change in attitude, known as "the Enlightenment", mountains began to lose their mystery.

By the 1950s, specialization took off after there were vast improvements in climbing accessories, and climbers began to concentrate on climbing a specific wall or pitch rather than attempting a mountain. By the 1970s rock climbing expanded and what used to be small communities of climbers developed into a large-scale organized sport. Today climbing walls have been erected in indoor and outdoor facilities worldwide, which means the climbers can achieve increasing levels of difficulty.

Equipment

Basic equipment includes shoes and a climbing harness, a rope, a belay device (such as a figure eight or tube) and at least one carabiner (spring loaded clip).

Clothing

If climbing in the outdoors, a helmet is recommended. When climbing indoors, climbers wear shorts and t-shirts. Outdoors climbers usually wear layers of lightweight thin clothes – mountain weather is unpredictable.

RODEO

Introduction

Rodeo is a competitive exhibition of the riding and other skills of individual cowboys (cattle-punchers). It is now a major sport in North America. There are six principal events at all rodeos;

saddle bronc-riding, bare-back bronc riding, bull-riding, calf-roping, team roping and steer-wrestling. A seventh, barrel racing, is for women, and does not share its origins with the others (ie the practical work of the cowboy). A form of obstacle race on horseback, it belongs more to the gymkhana arena than the rodeo ring, to which it was added as an entertaining gimmick.

History

Rodeo was born in the southern states of America after the Civil War (1861–65), when Texan cowboys, driving their cattle to the north and west in search of new markets, had to find their own amusements. They did so with riding and roping contests, employing those skills which earned them their daily bread.

As towns grew up on the path of the cattle drives, the contests became public entertainment, and in 1888, at Prescott, Arizona, the first admission fee was charged. Now the sport attracts more than 15 million spectators a year in 600 towns of the USA and Canada.

Rodeo-riders are not hired to compete, nor do they work for or through managers and promoters in the way that most other professional sportsmen do. They have retained both individuality and independence, living on what they are able to earn from rodeo to rodeo. The promoters of a rodeo provide the locations, the stock (cattle and horses) and the prize money. The rider comes if he wants to, knowing that he may either win more in a minute than most men earn in a month, or that the pounding hooves of a bull weighing 2,000lb (900kg) may end his career or even his life.

The sport became big business in the late 1930s, after the formation of the Rodeo Cowboys Association (RCA). Founded as a union of professional competitors, the RCA now controls rodeo throughout North America, representing all sides of the business: riders, stock-contractors, and rodeo committees.

Venue

A rodeo may be held in any enclosed space, in or out of doors, that is suitable for the riding of horses and the running of cattle. The most important are staged in sawdust or sand arenas, like large circus rings, with seating for thousands of spectators.

• BAREBACK BRONC-RIDING

Rules

In most respects, this is the same as saddle bronc-riding. The competitor is returned to ride a bucking bronco (a wild or half-tamed horse, or one that refuses to be ridden) in an arena for eight seconds, without saddle, stirrups, or rein. With one hand only, he may hold a suitcase-type handle attached to a cinch, a thick strap around the horse's chest. The free hand must not touch the horse or the cinch. If the rider is not disqualified, he and the horse are marked by judges on the same basis as in the saddle bronc event.

To have much hope of staying on, even for eight seconds, the rider must keep as close as possible to the cinch and the horse's neck. If the bucking of the horse throws him back so that his riding arm is extended, the rider's stability is greatly lessened.

• BULL-RIDING

Rules

This is the most dangerous and the most popular of the six main events of rodeo. The competitor must ride, barebacked, a

Brahma bull that may weigh up to 2,000lb (900kg), the speed and agility of which is matched by the beast's apparently uncontrollable bad temper. The only hand-hold allowed is a loose rope passed round the girth and twisted in the rider's hand.

From the instant the barrier drops and rider and bull storm out of the chute beside the rodeo arena, the bull's energies are directed to ridding itself of the man on its back. It bucks and tosses as fiercely as a bronco, and a rider who loses his grip may be tossed high in the air. Unlike bucking broncos of rodeo, however, a Brahma bull is not satisfied with simply getting rid of its rider; it will also turn to gore him.

• CALF-ROPING

Rules

For calf-roping, the competitor waits, on horseback, outside the rodeo arena. A calf is released into the ring, shortly followed by the rider. He must lasso the animal from horseback, tie the rope to his saddle, dismount, and throw the calf to the ground by hand – an operation made easier if the horse keeps the rope tight. If the calf is already on the ground when the cowboy reaches it, he must let it get to its feet, then throw it down himself. He then has to tie together any three of the animal's feet.

Success in the event depends on precise teamwork between man and horse. They are working against the clock, and in top-class rodeo, fractions of a second separate winners from losers. The moment when the competitor is allowed into the ring after the calf is determined by the barrier in front of him, a rope, being tripped by a length of cord tied round the calf's neck. The roper and his horse try to reach the barrier at speed at the exact moment it is released: if they hit it early, a ten-second penalty is added.

• SADDLE BRONC-RIDING
Rules

This is the classic event of rodeo, in which a competing cowboy must retain his seat on a wildly bucking horse for ten seconds and is marked for the style with which he does so. The horse is held in a chute immediately outside the rodeo arena until the barrier drops; if it is a good bucker, it enters the ring in the air. When its feet hit the ground for the first time, the rider's spurs must be at the high point of the horse's shoulders. From that moment, he should rhythmically spur the bronc from high in front to high behind, a movement known as "lick". Throughout the ride the cowboy must keep one hand free and held in the air, clear of the horse. He is disqualified if he touches the animal with his free hand, changes hands on the rein, loses a stirrup or is bucked off. The rein is a braided rope attached to the halter.

• STEER-WRESTLING
Rules

Also known as "bull-dogging", the competitor must drop from horseback on to the horns of galloping steer and throw it to the ground. Of all the events of rodeo, this one calls for the greatest precision both from the rider (dogger) and his horse.

The horse must gallop within a foot (0.3m) of the steer, usually on the left of it, allowing the rider to lean over and catch the right horn with his right hand. As the horse gallops past, the rider stays with the steer, pulling up the right horn and down with the left. The cowboy's heels must hit the ground ahead of him and away from the steer, acting as a brake and a pivot.

If the operation is accurately carried out, the steer goes into a tight left-hand turn. As its hind quarters swing round, the cowboy tips its head and hopes to throw the steer on to its side. The steer must be caught from horseback. If it breaks loose, the competitor may take only one step to catch it, before being disqualified.

• TEAM ROPING
Rules
This is carried out by two mounted cowboys and should be a fast and efficient operation. One competitor heads off the calf, and throws and ties it after the other has lassoed the animal.

ROLLER HOCKEY
Introduction
See also IN-LINE ROLLER HOCKEY. Roller hockey is a team game played on roller skates with sticks and a ball, adapted from FIELD HOCKEY and ICE HOCKEY, with the object of scoring the most goals to decide the winner.

History
Hockey on roller skates dates back to the early part of the twentieth century as an organized sport. Its earlier history is a little obscure, but is believed that some kind of game with sticks started evolving soon after the first roller skates came to be used around 1870.

The first international inter-club tournament, held in France in 1910 at the Hippodrome, Paris, was won by a British team, Crystal Palace Engineers. The early development was

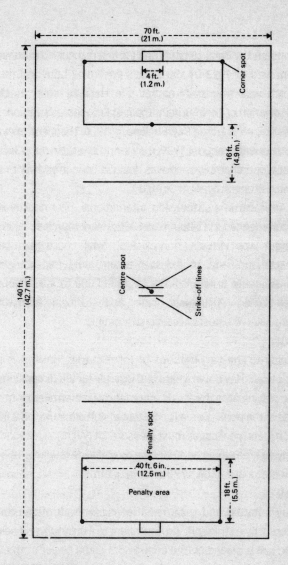

70 ft. (21 m.)

Corner spot

4 ft. (1.2 m.)

16 ft. (4.9 m.)

140 ft. (42.7 m.)

Centre spot

Strike-off lines

Penalty spot

40 ft. 6 in. (12.5 m.)

18 ft. (5.5 m.)

Penalty area

Roller Hockey Pitch

Dimensions given are ideal; actual dimensions vary according to size of the roller-skating rink. The goal cage, 4ft (1.2m) wide, is 3ft (91cm) high and 3ft deep at the bottom.

Roller Hockey

pioneered by British Skaters and the first recognized rules were approved in 1913 by the sport's governing body in Britain, which was eventually named the National Roller Hockey Association of Great Britain. The first European championship was staged at Herne Bay, England, in 1926. Then, and in every subsequent year until 1939, it was won by Britain. In 1936, the first world championship was decided concurrently with the ninth European event at Stuttgart.

After wartime suspension, international roller hockey was recommenced in Lisbon in 1947. The new top-class talent in Britain was virtually non-existent, while Portugal, Spain, Switzerland, and, to a lesser extent, Italy, had advanced considerably. Britain lost her long-held title to a very young, well-trained Portuguese side and Portugal afterwards dominated the post international meetings.

Venue

Owing to the varying sizes of roller staking rinks, it is not practical to lay down a hard and fast rule for the dimensions of the playing area, for this is automatically determined, but the size of the penalty area is constant at 40ft 6in by 18ft (12.5m x 5.5m), and goal cages must measure 3ft (91cm). A reasonable playing area would be 120ft long by 60ft wide (36.5m x 18.3m), but the ideal is 140ft by 70ft (42.7m x 21m).

Rules

Play is started, and re-started after half-time and after a goal is scored, by a strike-off, the equivalent to a bully in field hockey. The ball is placed on the centre spot and a player from each team stands in his own half facing the ball, with the blade of his stick at rest on the ground behind the strike-off line 9in (23cm) from the ball. When the whistle is blown, the ball is immediately in play. There is no off-side, and play continues in the area immediately behind the goals, as in ice hockey. When the ball leaves the playing area, a free hit is awarded to the team opposing the last striker of the ball.

The ball must not be lofted higher than 6ft (1.829m) when a hot is played, the only exceptions being when two players strike the ball simultaneously and when the goalkeeper does so in making a save with his/her hands, legs, or feet. The goalkeeper is the only player permitted to kick or handle the ball, but s/he is not allowed to catch it, nor must the hands or any part of the body, other than the feet, be in contact with the floor when making a save.

Pushing, barging, body-checking, back tackling and tripping are against the rules. Players must not lift their sticks above their shoulders when making a shot. A foul is committed if a player holds the rink barrier with one hand while playing the ball or tackling the opponent with the other.

Equipment

The roller hockey stick is similar in shape to a field hockey stick but flat on both sides of the blade, as it is permissible to hit with either side. It must not exceed 3ft 9in (1.14m) in length, measured from the top of the handle along the outer edge of the curve to the tip of the blade. It must also be possible to pass it through a ring with a diameter of 2in (5cm). The stick, of wood, has no metal fittings, and must not exceed 18oz (510g) in weight. The roller hockey ball is made of composition or compressed cork, weighs 5.5oz (156g) and measures 9in (23cm) in circumference.

Clothing

Players on team wear jerseys, trousers, pants and socks that match in style and colour. Players also wear helmets with a chin strap, a face mask, hockey-type gloves and shin guards. A mouthpiece is optional but recommended.

ROLLER SKATING

Introduction

This is a competitive sport which takes the same principal forms as ICE SKATING, i.e., roller speed-skating, roller figure-skating and roller dancing.

History

Although a roller skate of sorts was invented by a Belgian, Merlin, in 1760, the first practical four-wheel skate was introduced by an American, Plympton, in 1863. The original idea was no more than to provide a means for ice skaters to simulate their sport and practise when there was no natural ice.

In 1866, however, Plympton himself opened the first successful public roller-skating rink at Newport, Rhode Island, USA. Another step forward was the subsequent invention of the more satisfactory Richardson ball-bearing skate in 1884.

A boom on both sides of the Atlantic reached its zenith in 1910, when nearly every town seemed to have at least one rink, and every available floor area, flat roofs included, was used. C.B. Cochran, the impresario, at this time controlled a large rink at the Olympia exhibition in London.

Equipment

The roller skates for the artistic events have a higher boot and larger wheels than skates used for speed skating which are light with a long, low wheelbase.

Clothing

Costumes are similar to those used for ice skating and freedom of movement is a major requirement.

• DANCING

Dancing on roller skates has developed very much on a par with ice dancing. The techniques are as similar as is practical , and the internationally recognized championship dances correspond. The same system is used for judging and marking championships, competitions and proficiency tests.

• FIGURE SKATING

Figure skating on roller skates corresponds in most ways to ice figure skating. The same international schedule of figures is used, the main difference between the two media being that, whereas the skate blade traces the figure pattern that can be seen on the ice, the roller skater performs upon figures painted on the rink floor. The free skating is also similar to that of the ice sport and there are corresponding systems for judging and marking championships, competitions and proficiency tests.

• SPEED SKATING

Speed skating on roller skates is performed at top level on outdoor oval circuits or open road. A more restricted form of the sport is conducted at indoor roller skating rinks which, as in ice speed skating, have area limitations which restrict speed because of the necessarily short straights and constant sharp cornering. Major events are therefore held outdoors. The rules and technique employed on roller skates are fundamentally the same as those on ice.

ROQUE

Introduction

This is a form of CROQUET played in the USA and generally considered to be a more scientific version than the original which it resembles.

History

The National Roque Association was founded in New York in 1889, the name being obtained by dropping the first and last letters of croquet.

Venue

A Roque court is only a quarter the size of a croquet lawn: 10yds by 20yds (9.14m x 18.29m), with the corners cut off to form an octagon. It has a hard surface with a solid boundary wall, and contains ten arches instead of the six of croquet.

Rules

In both cases the object of the game is to hit, with a mallet, hard balls through a series of arches (hoops), endeavouring if possible to help on their way the balls of your partner (if you have one), and to strike aside the opponents' balls. The winner is the first player, or pair, to hit the balls through all the arches and to hit the two posts at each end of the court; or the first to score 32 points, awarded for striking a ball through an arch or for striking an opponent's ball with you own.

Equipment

The arches are both lower and slightly narrower than those used in the original game. A hard rubber ball is used, the diameter of which is only 1/8in (0.32cm) less than the width of the arches. It is struck by a mallet with a 15in (38cm) handle, one head of which is rubber and the other of aluminium or laminated plastic.

ROUNDERS
Introduction

Rounders is an outdoor bat-and-ball game played between two teams of nine players. Though predominately played in Great Britain it is known in many parts of the world and has features in common with BASEBALL. Rounders is perhaps best known as an impromptu leisure game but is widely played in British schools and some adult and youth club leagues.

History

The earliest known literary reference to rounders was in 1744, when *A Little Pretty Pocket Book* included a woodcut of the game and a verse under the name of "Base-ball". In 1829 a description of the rules was included in W. Clarke's *The Boy's Own Book*.

The first governing bodies were established in Liverpool and Scotland in 1889, and in 1943 the National Rounders Association was formed. The game today is not significantly different in concept from the nineteenth-century version. Among changes are the anticlockwise circuit of the running track, introduced in 1839, and the ending of the fielder's ability to put out the batsman by hitting him with a thrown ball.

Venue

Two squares are marked on the pitch, for the bowler and batsman. The running track is indicated by four posts. A line running across the front of the batting square separates the forward and backward areas. The minimum playing area is about 55yds (50m) square, some two-thirds being in the forward area. The posts stand 4ft (1.2m) above the ground. They may stand in bases or, less satisfactorily, be driven into the ground.

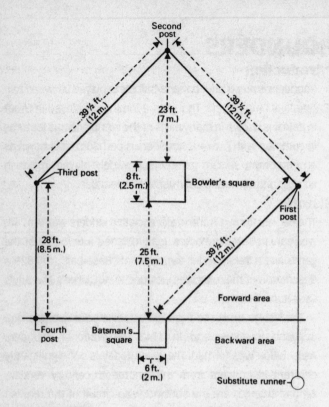

Second
post

39½ ft.
(12 m.)

39½ ft.
(12 m.)

23 ft.
(7 m.)

8 ft.
(2.5 m.)

Bowler's square

Third post

First
post

28 ft.
(8.5 m.)

25 ft.
(7.5 m.)

39½ ft.
(12 m.)

Forward area

Fourth
post

Batsman's
square

Backward area

6 ft.
(2 m.)

Substitute runner

Rounders Pitch
Compulsory markings are the four posts, the two squares, the
substitute runner's position, and the line separating the forward and
backward areas.

Equipment

The ball weighs 2.5–3oz (70–85g) and measures approximately 7.5in (19cm) in circumference. It is hard and covered in light-coloured leather. The bat (known as a "stick") is round and made of wood. The maximum measurements are: length, 18in (46cm); circumference at the thickest part, 6.75in (17cm); weight, 13oz (368g).

Clothing

Clothes are basically informal. Players wear sports shoes, shorts, trousers or a skirt with a shirt or t-shirt.

Rules

The two teams alternate as batting and fielding sides and a match consists of two innings, i.e. each side bats twice. The batsmen try to score rounders while the fielding team attempt to prevent this and to put out the batsmen. The team scoring most rounders wins.

One member of the fielding team is the bowler. The positioning of the remaining eight members is not stipulated but commonly includes a backstop to field balls missed by the batsman, a fielder by each post, and three deep fielders covering the areas behind the posts.

The bowler must use a smooth underarm action and remain within his/her square until s/he has released the ball. The ball must be sent to the hitting side of the batsman, within reach and between the top of the head and the knee. Any movement by the batsman after the bowler releases the ball should be ignored. "No-ball" is called for any infringement.

The batsman attempts to hit the ball as far as possible and to run round the outside of the posts to the fourth post and thus score a rounder. S/he is entitled to received one good ball on which s/he must run at least to first post, having hit or missed. If s/he receives a no-ball s/he cannot be caught out and has the option of running. The last batsman has the choice of three good balls but is out if caught off any.

A batsman may stop temporarily at any post on the way round the track, continuing either before the next ball is bowled or on a subsequent ball. In the latter case he does not score. When the bowler has the ball and is in his square, a batsman may not leave or pass a post. On reaching fourth post a batsman rejoins the batting queue. When all of the batsmen are out, the teams change places.

A batsman who hits the ball into the forward area may score one rounder. If s/he misses the ball or the hit lands in the backward area, s/he may score a half-rounder but in the latter case may not pass first post until the ball is again in the forward area. To score, the batsman must reach fourth post before the next ball is bowled, must not be put out, and at no time when s/he is in contact with a post must the post immediately ahead be touched with the ball.

A half-rounder is awarded if a batsman receives three consecutive no-balls, and for certain cases of obstruction.

A batsman may cause him/herself to be out if:

S/he steps over the front line of the square hitting the ball.

S/he runs inside a post.

S/he overtakes another batsman.

A fielder puts him/her out by catching a hit or by touching with the ball either the post to which the batsman is running or the batsman himself, after he has left the previous post. If all the batting team are on the track, they may be out simultaneously if the ball is thrown into the batting square.

Scoring

Thus, one rounder is scored if the batter hits the ball and runs around the track to touch fourth post before another ball is bowled – unless the batter is dismissed or the next posts is touched by a fielder holding a ball. A half rounder is scored if the batter completes the track as for a rounder but without hitting the ball.

ROUNDERS, IRISH

Introduction

As played in Ireland, this bat-and-ball game is very similar to the SOFTBALL version of BASEBALL. Although rules for the game are given in the *Official Guide* of the Gaelic Athletic Association (GAA), there are no official competitions. Rounders is, however, popular as a recreational pastime in many schools.

Rules

The game, according to the GAA rules, is played nine a side. There are four bases, each 30yds (27.4m) apart. The batter, who stands at home base, attempts to hit the ball thrown by the server from a mark 20yds (18.3m) from the base. Scoring and dismissals are as in baseball.

Equipment

The bat is round, 3ft (91cm) long and not more than 2.5in (6.3cm) wide at its thickest point. The ball is the ordinary HURLING ball, though a semi-solid rubber one may be used.

ROWING

Introduction

Rowing, the art of propelling a boat by means of oars, is practiced as a sport throughout the world wherever suitable stretches of water can be found. It flourishes mainly on inland lakes, canals and rivers, but in some countries coastal rowing is a popular branch of the sport.

History

Rowing dates back to ancient times when it provided motive power for warships before sails replaced galley-slaves. The earliest literary reference to rowing as a sport occurs in the *Aeneid*, in which Virgil describes the funeral games arranged by Aeneas in honour of his father. The sport in its modern form is practiced mainly on inland rivers and lakes and developed in England on the river Thames which, from medieval times, was one of the country's main highways. The wealthy had their own state barges manned by oarsmen and many hundreds of professional watermen plied for hire on the tidal reaches of the river. By the beginning of the eighteenth century there were more than 40,000 licensed watermen active between Chelsea and Windsor. There were frequent contests between professional watermen, and betting on these and on races between barges owned by the well-to-do was a favourite pastime of the gentry in an age addicted to gambling.

Rowing became competitive at Oxford and Cambridge Universities in the early nineteenth century and there were bumping races at Oxford in 1822. The first University Boat Race took place at Henley in 1829 and the interest this aroused eventually encouraged the local townspeople to institute the Henley Regatta ten years later. At about the same time, several leading public schools were rowing. Eton had a ten-oar and three eight-oars by 1811, while at Westminster School the *Water Ledger* was begun in June 1813.

Rowing was also developing at that time in the USA. As in England, the original contests were between professional watermen. The first race of this sort was in 1811 when the "Knickerbocker", manned by ferrymen from Whitehall in New York City, defeated the "Invincible" from Long Island. Two years later, the New York ferrymen were again successful in a race against a crew from Staten Island. In 1824 they defeated a crew of Thames watermen from the British frigate "Hussar" and this contest aroused widespread interest.

In Australia, rowing developed as a sport in around 1830, when it was introduced to Tasmania, the crews of whaling boats competing with crews from shore stations. The Royal Hobart Regatta was founded in 1838. In 1832 a race took place at Port Jackson, Sydney, between four gentlemen and four seaman from the ship "Strathfieldsay". Later the same year there was an amateur single sculling race for a prize worth £20, indicating that competitive rowing and sculling had become established.

Venue

Regattas are held over a stretch of river, lake, coast or artificial course. Head races are held over stretches of river of varying length.

Rules

In rowing, each oarsman/woman holds one oar, as distinct from sculling (see below) in which the sculler has one rather smaller oar, or scull, in each hand. An oar is usually made of wood with a rounded handle at one end and a blade at the other. A collar, called a "button", is fitted to the shaft, or loom, of the oar to prevent it slipping through the rowlock, enabling the oarsman/woman to apply resistance, obtained by the blade in the water to the propulsion of the boat. Adjustment of the button alters the leverage of the oar so that the stroke can be geared to suit the oarsman's physique and skill and the speed required, as well as to compensate for variations in weather conditions, such as head or following wind. The shorter the inboard length of the oar, that is, the part from the button to the tip of the handle, in relation to the outboard length (the distance from the button to the tip of the blade), the more severe the load imposed on the oarsman/woman. This results in an increase in inboard length by the crew if there are, for example, strong head winds.

Modern racing boats hold crews of two, four, or eight oarsmen, and one, two, or four scullers. There are also a few boats for eight scullers, but these are seldom seen. Eights, being fast and comparatively cumbersome, are always steered by a coxswain, but pairs and fours may be with or without a coxswain. In a coxswainless boat, one of the oarsmen/women steers with their foot by means of a pivoting shoe to which the rudderlines are attached.

In an eight, the coxswain sits in the stern section of the boat, but in a coxed pair, and sometimes in a coxed four, it has become usual to place the coxswain in the bows, where s/he lies on his/her back with a small head-rest. This reduces wind resistance and, more importantly, drag in the stern of the boat. The cox steers with lines attached to a small rudder on the stern post or underneath the hull. All racing shells have a small metal fin protruding under the hull near the stern to help stability and steering, and many modern boats have small rudders only a few inches square attached to these fins. The advantage of these is that the cox can steer the boat with more finesse and less drag than with a stern rudder, but even a slight application of a fin rudder can upset the balance, so that more skill is needed by the crew.

The aim during the stroke is to move the boat as far and as fast as possible, and when the blade is out of water, to do as little as possible to hinder the acceleration and the run of the boat. It is possible to get similar results by different methods. For example, a powerful crew rowing a long stroke with a long swing can move their boat at much the same speed as a less powerful few rowing at a shorter stroke at a higher rate of striking, so that the main problem for each crew is to find the optimum length of stroke and rate of striking and to gear the leverage of the oars correctly.

The rate of striking and the gearing will vary with the distance to be rowed. A racing rate for a crew will be between 32 and 40 strokes to the minute for the body of the race; for scullers it is somewhat less. A crew rowing at less than full pressure is said to be paddling, and this is usually carried out at rates of 24–28in – "paddling firm". When the pressure is very light, a crew is "paddling light".

The main source of power is the legs, and a powerful, co-ordinated leg-drive is the hallmark of a good crew. The efficiency with which this is applied to the propulsion of the boat depends on the rhythm set by the stroke and the skill, watermanship and timing of the crew.

Watermanship, which in rowing parlance refers to the skill of handling and balancing boats and oars, comparable to that of professional watermen/women, is vital, since comparatively minor lurches in the boat can upset the timing of the stroke and the speed of the boat. The smaller the boat, the greater the premium on watermanship.

In a racing boat, the oarsman/woman sits on a sliding seat which enables them to obtain a strong position at each end of the stroke. Control of the slide, especially between the strokes, is essential to good performance. At the beginning of the stroke, which is when the blade enters the water, an oarsman/woman must make sure that s/he does not "shoot his/her slide" by driving with the legs before the blade takes the water, as this dissipates the power of the leg-drive. On the way forward s/he must avoid reaching the front-stop of the runners at the beginning, as this will lead to a marked check in the run of the boat.

The oar is turned at each end of the stroke. It is held flat, or "feathered", between strokes in order to reduce wind resistance and to avoid hitting waves, and it is "squared" to a point slightly past a right-angle to the water just before the beginning. The skill with which these turns are made is critical to efficiency. If an oarsman feathers before the finish of the stroke his blade will be caught by the water and the momentum of the boat will result in him/her being knocked flat on his/her back, or even being lifted right out of the boat by the oar. This ignominious occurrence is described as "catching a crab" and usually results in the loss of the race.

Equipment

Modern oars, which weigh about 8lb (3.6kg), are usually between 12ft and 12ft 10in long (3.6–3.9m). Longer oars have been tried, without much success. A scull is usually about 9ft 8in (2.9m) long.

• SCULLING

This differs technically from rowing in that a sculler holds a scull (or small oar) in each hand instead of pulling on one oar with both hands. For all practical purposes, it is part of the sport of rowing, but the skills required for sculling are somewhat different.

Sculling boats are very light and narrow and require considerable skill and watermanship to balance and steer; the slightest clumsiness will destroy the run of the boat. Because of the special skill required, a sculler will generally make a good oarsman/woman, though the reverse does not necessarily follow. Crews made up of good scullers invariably do well and many coaches take sculling proficiency into account when selecting their crews. In single sculling, one person only is responsible for the propulsion of the boat, so that the coach can gauge the worth of each individual.

Quadruple and double sculling in particular require a high degree of uniformity and co-ordination between scullers. A very fast boat, a double sculler, is only marginally slower than a coxed four and a quick, smooth action is necessary to get the best out of the boat. A quadruple sculler is even faster and is second in speed only to an eight.

• SKIFF RACING

This is a special form of sculling which operates under its own rules and for which a special type of heavy boat is used. Special regattas are held, but the sport is restricted to the River Thames in Britain, between Wargrave and Kingston, Surrey.

RUGBY FIVES

Introduction

Rugby Fives is a hand-ball game played with gloved hands in a court enclosed by four walls between two players (singles) or four players (doubles). A small number of courts have been built by enthusiasts in other countries but, generally speaking, the game is confined to the British Isles.

History

The word "fives" has no accepted etymology. Strutt, in *The Sports and Pastimes of the People of England,* accepted the explanation that the word may have come from the fact that a five-a-side game was played in the presence of Elizabeth I in 1591, a suggestion which, though repeated many times, is hardly confirmed by the evidence. It seems clear enough that the game was played between any equal number of people and on any occasion when a convenient wall offered itself.

Strutt unequivocally calls the game "hand tennis" and certainly TENNIS courts were often used, at least until the end of the eighteenth century, for a hand-ball game by then known as fives. There is a public house in London, near Piccadilly, called the Hand and Racquet, and near-by there is an old tennis court, used for many years for a different purpose. Erasmus in 1524, refers to the game played either with the hands or with a racket, and the schoolmaster, Mulcaster, in 1581 adds to our knowledge by explaining that the game is sometimes played like tennis or with a ball made of some "softer stuffe" with the hand against a wall alone.

Venue

The court is rectangular, 28ft (8.5m) long and 18ft (5.5m) wide. The height of the front wall is 15ft (4.6m) and the playing area of the side walls, marked by a painted line, is 15ft (4.6m) for the first 12ft (3.7m), measuring from the front wall, sloping down to 6ft (1.8m) at the back. The height of the back wall is 6ft (0.76m) from the floor, and spans the front wall from side to side. Since the ball is small, white and hard the walls of the standard court are made of a hard composition and coloured black. The floor is usually red.

Rules

A game is begun by a preliminary rally. The side winning that rally becomes the "receiver", and the side losing the rally, the "server".

The game begins when the server throws the ball up for him/herself. If s/he is right-handed, i.e. naturally stronger with the right hand than the left, s/he will throw the ball up into the right-hand corner of the front wall. S/he must do this so that the ball strikes first the front wall above the board and then the right-hand corner of the front wall. If the ball bounces awkwardly on the floor or in any way not to the server's liking s/he may stop it and start again. If s/he wishes s/he may do this over and over again – becoming progressively less popular. Again, if s/he wishes, the server may require the receiver to throw for him/her as was the practice years ago. Some players find it almost as difficult to throw for themselves as they often did for others.

When the ball has bounced once on the floor the server serves by striking the ball first on to the right hand wall, if right handed, and then on to the front wall above the board. The ball is then returned, if s/he is able to do so, by the receiver, either before or after the first bounce, on to the front wall above the board. The shot may be played directly on to the front wall or on to the front wall by way of a side wall. The rally then proceeds, a player from each side hitting the ball alternately with one of his/her opponents. The rally is lost by the side which fails to return the ball on to the front wall above the board before it has bounced twice.

When returning the ball a player may make what use s/he can of the side walls within the confines of the court but s/he cannot hit the ball on to the floor first or on the walls outside the confines of the court including the roof. However, a ball may bounce from the floor on to the back wall and be played from there. Sometimes when serving, a player will hit the ball straight on to the front walls without its touching the side wall first. If s/he does so the ball is called a "blackguard" and may be returned by an opponent who must shout his/her intention to do so before s/he has struck the ball.

Players on the same side in the doubles game usually take one side of the court each but there is a good deal of movement and change of position, and frequent calls of "mine". The fact that all four players are sharing the same playing area inevitably leads to occasional confusion and loss of sight of the ball by one or other of the players. "Lets" are allowed and are usually offered to the players by each other. Umpires are scarce and there is small reliance upon them; accordingly players' efforts to give their opponents a clear view are marked. Because the ball is fast and there is much bending to be done with little respite, styles of play and technique vary. However, the essential abilities are to be able to hit the ball with both hands close to the top of the board, to send the ball close and parallel to the side walls, and to play to a length, i.e. to make the ball die away at the back wall so that an opponent is kept in two minds about when to play the return.

Equipment

The old fives ball, used and preferred by all fives players until its manufacture was stopped in the mid-twentieth century, had a centre of cork round which was wound cloth strips held in position by many yards of thread.

The whole was encased in a leather jacket, put on wet and stitched so that it dried tight. It was mainly a cottage industry and uneconomic for modern times. The present ball is much the same inside but is covered with a thin plastic. It bounces well but lacks the former zip.

Clothing

Players wear on both hands light leather gloves well padded on the face of palms and form at the back, peering over the 6ft wall, or from a gallery.

RUGBY LEAGUE FOOTBALL

Introduction

Rugby League Football is a 13-a-side game of running, passing from hand to hand, and kicking an oval ball. Derived from Rugby Union, it is played by amateurs and professionals in England, Australia, and France, and by amateurs in New Zealand.

History

Unlike most games, the origin of Rugby League can be traced to a precise date. On 29 August 1895, 21 northern clubs, exasperated at repeated refusals by the ruling body to allow them to compensate players for money lost by taking time off from work to play football, divided at a meeting in Huddersfield, Yorkshire, to break away from the Rugby Union. The founder members of the Northern Union (the name was changed to Rugby Football League in 1922) who embarked nine days later on the Lancashire and Yorkshire senior competitions were: Lancashire: Broughton Rangers, Leigh, Oldham, Rochdale Hornets, St. Helens, Tyldesley, Warrington, Widnes, Wigan; Yorkshire: Bately, Bradford, Brighouse Rangers, Dewsbury, Halifax, Huddersfield, Hull, Hunslet, Leeds, Liversedge, Manningham, Wakefield Trinity.

Venue

The rectangular pitch is a maximum of 110yds (100m) long and a minimum of 60yds (55m) wide.

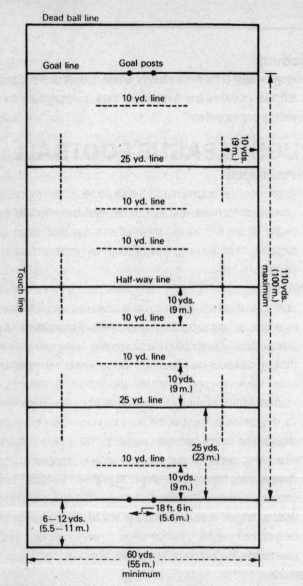

Dead ball line

Goal line   Goal posts

10 yd. line

25 yd. line

10 yds. (9 m.)

10 yd. line

10 yd. line

Half-way line

10 yds. (9 m.)

10 yd. line

10 yd. line

10 yds. (9 m.)

25 yd. line

25 yds. (23 m.)

10 yd. line

10 yds. (9 m.)

Touch line

110 yds. (100 m.) maximum

18 ft. 6 in. (5.6 m.)

6—12 yds. (5.5—11 m.)

60 yds. (55 m.) minimum

Rugby League Pitch
*The crossbar on the goal posts at either end is 10ft (3.048m) from the
ground.*

Rules

Rugby League differs from Rugby Union in the following main particulars: teams are 13-a side instead of 15; the scrum consists of 6 forwards instead of 8; a tackled player is allowed to retain possession of the ball up to a point regulated by the play-the-ball rule; ground gained by a kick to touch (except from a penalty award) does not count unless the ball lands in the field of play before crossing the touch line.

These variations from Rugby Union practice, made at various times over the last 70 years, have been designed to attract spectators by attaching greater rewards to the skills of running and passing. Because the tackled player retains possession of the ball there are no loose mauls. Forwards, as well as backs (i.e. all those players who stand outside the scrum), are free to string themselves across the field in a roughly straight line, leaving only a 5yd gap between one defender and the next.

The forwards are the six players of each side who form the scrum. The front row is formed by the hooker putting an arm round the shoulders of each two prop forwards. The hooker's task is to strike for the ball with his foot when it is put into the scrum by the scrum half, while the props support him against the pushing of the opposing front row. The two second-row forwards pack down behind the front row with their heads on either side of the hooker. Their purpose in the scrum is to help push the opposing pack off the ball The loose forward packs down behind and between the second-row forwards, though in practice he usually detaches himself from the pack when his team is in a defensive position.

The full-back, in addition to being the last line of defence, is an important member of the attack in the modern game. He rarely kicks, but seeks to link up with three-quarters and half-backs in passing movements. The three-quarters and half-backs operate as one unit. As most of the responsibility for scoring tries rests on them, speed and an ability to beat an opponent by swerve and side-step are desirable. The half-backs, who act as a link between forwards and three-quarters, have to be particularly agile because they operate in close proximity to the forwards. Forward play has changed considerably since the days when players were chosen for the weight and strength they supplied to the scrum. Under present-day rules there are fewer scrums and, while the old principles still apply to a large extent to the two prop forwards, no second-row or loose forward can hope to achieve success without handling ability and a good turn of speed, as well as a powerful physique. The hooker is usually of squat build so that he can not only get down low to see the ball as it enters the scrum, but also swing on the framework supplied by the shoulders of his prop forwards.

The game is started with a kick from the halfway line. The side gaining possession attempts to reach the opponents' line by passing the ball by hand or by kicking. The opposition tries to stop them by tackling the player carrying the ball or by intercepting passes. Within this simple framework the rules are complicated (a referee once compiled a list of 30 infringements which can occur in the scrum alone). When the referee stops play he either orders a scrum – in the case of forward passing, knocking-on, one side making six successive tackles, or the ball going out of play – or awards a penalty.

Penalties are imposed for foul play, ungentlemanly conduct, offside, obstruction and technical offences at the scrum and the play-the-ball. A player is offside in general play if the ball is kicked, touched, or held by one of his own side behind him. Offside also applies at the play-the-ball operation to any player (other than the two acting half-backs) who is less than 5yds behind the two players in the play-the-ball operation. Offside players are penalized if they interfere with play.

Equipment

The ball when new is oval in shape, with four panels and the following vital statistics: length in line 280–300mm; circumference (end on) 760–790mm; circumference (in width) 580–620mm; weight 400–440g.

Scoring

Points are scored by touching the ball down behind the opponent's goal line for a try (3 points), and by kicking the ball between the uprights of the goal posts above the crossbar for a goal (2 points). Shots at goal are allowed (a) after a try, (b) from a penalty, and (c) from the field of play, provided that the ball is kicked on the half-volley (drop shot). In international matches a goal from a drop shot scores only 1 point.

Clothing

Players wear jerseys, shorts, socks and boots (studs on the boots must be circular and securely fastened). Headbands or scrum caps may also be worn. Shin guards are optional, and league players may also wear other protective clothing providing it is not rigid.

RUGBY UNION FOOTBALL

Introduction

Rugby Union Football is a ball game, played between teams of 15-a-side, in which the ball may be handled as well as kicked. It is played on a rectangular field with an inflated ball that is oval in shape. The object of the game is to score more points than your opponents. Points are awarded for goals and for tries. A try is scored if the ball is carried or kicked over the defending team's goal line and is then touched down by a member of the attacking team.

History

The early history of the game belongs to England. It was developed at Rugby School, taken up by undergraduates at Cambridge and Oxford, and refined by the Richmond and Blackheath clubs. The game's exact date of birth, however, has not been established. In 1895 a report was presented by a sub-committee of the Old Rugbeian Society which had been appointed "to inquire into the origin of Rugby Football". Its findings were summarized, and perhaps oversimplified, in the working of a plaque later set into the wall of the Close at Rugby School. It reads: "This stone commemorates the exploit of William Webb Ellis, who, with a fine disregard for the rules of football as played in his time, first took the ball in his arms and ran with it, thus originating the distinctive feature of the Rugby game, A.D. 1823.". The plaque was unveiled on 1 November 1923 at a match between England–Wales and Scotland–Ireland to mark the officially recognized centenary. There is only slight evidence, however, to support this account of the birth of Rugby football.

Venue

The field is usually 110yds (100m) long and 75yds (68m) wide. At each end of the field two goal posts are erected 18ft 6in (5.6m) apart, joined by a crossbar 10ft (3.048m) from the ground. The goal posts are extended upwards above the level

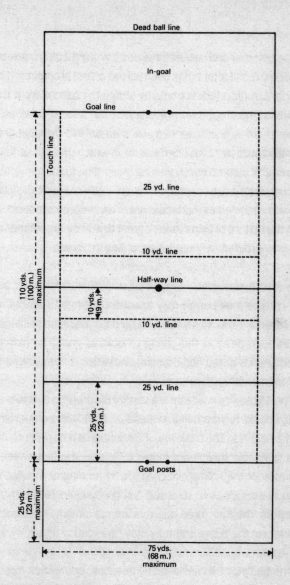

Dead ball line

In-goal

Goal line

Touch line

25 yd. line

10 yd. line

Half-way line

10 yds. (9 m.)

10 yd. line

25 yd. line

25 yds. (23 m.)

Goal posts

110 yds. (100 m.) maximum

25 yds. (23 m.) maximum

75 yds. (68 m.) maximum

Rugby Union Field

Goal posts are 18ft 6in (5.6m) apart: the crossbar is 10ft (3.048m) from the ground.

of the crossbar and between the posts. A place kick is made by kicking the ball after it has been placed on the ground for that purpose. A drop kick is made by letting the ball fall from the hands to the ground and kicking it at the first rebound as it rises. There is also a rectangular area behind the goal line, usually 25yds by 75yds (23m x 68m), in which tries are scored. The field is marked out by whiting. According to the game, the field must be grass-covered or "where this is not available, clay or sand, provided the surface is not of dangerous hardness". In fact the texture of fields varies a great deal at different times of the year in different countries according to climate.

Rules

Play is usually divided into two halves of 40 minutes each, but the referee may permit play to continue longer than that in each half, in order to make up for time lost because of injuries or through delay in the taking of kicks at goal. The players change ends at the half-time interval which is not allowed to last for more than 5 minutes.

The 15 players in a team are usually divided into 8 forwards, 2 half-backs (scrum half and stand-off half), 4 three-quarters, and 1 full-back. The basic job of the forwards is to procure the ball to enable their team mates to attack. The fundamental function of the half-backs is either, by running or kicking, to initiate attacks or to pass the ball on by hand to the three quarters. The four three-quarters are customarily the fastest runners in the team, and they may be joined in attack by the full-back.

The ball may be kicked in any direction, but it must not be passed or knocked forward with the hand. A player carrying the ball may be tackled by an opponent, who is allowed knock him with his shoulder and to grip him with his arms so as to bring him to the ground, but it is illegal to impede anyone who is not carrying the ball.

There are two fundamental set pieces from which the ball is brought into play by a struggle for possession between the forwards of the two teams. These set pieces are the "line-out" and the "set scrum".

Between these set pieces – the line-out and the set scrum – a game of Rugby provides a great deal of loose play, such as when a player carrying the ball is tackled to the ground by an opponent. In such a situation it is the aim of the forwards to arrive on the scene as quickly as possible, to establish possession of the ball, and to feed it back to their scrum half for him and the rest of the team to attack with. A loose situation of this kind, with the forwards struggling for possession, is known as a "ruck" if the ball is on the ground, and as a "maul" if it is not.

Equipment

The ball usually has an outer casing of leather surrounding an inflated inner bladder of rubber. The outer casing is made of four panels, and its length should be from 11–11.75in (27.94–28.575cm). Its circumference should be from 30–31in (76.2–78.74cm) end on and 24–25.5in (60.96–64.77cm) in width. It should weigh 13.5–15oz (382.72–425.25g). Materials other than leather are permissible, and in wet weather the ball may be specially treated to make it resistant to mud and easier to grip.

Scoring

Numerically, the most profitable way of obtaining points is by touching down the ball beyond the opponents' goal line for a try. The try itself is worth four points, and it gives the right to the scorer's team to take a place kick or a drop kick at goal which, if it goes over the crossbar and between the posts, brings a further 2 points, making 6 in all. The kick at goal after a try, known as a conversion, has to be taken from a spot in-field in line with the place where the try was scored. If an infringement of the laws of the game by the defending team prevents a probable try from being scored, the referee may award a penalty try. A penalty try is always awarded between the goal posts, leaving the goal kicker with the easiest of conversions and an almost certain total of 6 points.

There are three ways of obtaining 3 points. The most common of these is by kicking a penalty goal. The referee may award a penalty kick for an infringement of the laws more serious than that which would lead him to call for a set scrum. If the penalty kick is awarded at a spot within kicking distance of the goal, the non-offending team will take a place kick or a drop kick at goal from that spot. Three points are scored if this kick sends the ball over the crossbar and between the posts. Another way of scoring 3 points is by means of the dropped goal. This is achieved when a player, finding himself with room to do so in the course of play, aims a drop kick at goal, and the ball passes over the crossbar and between the goalposts. A further, but rare, method of scoring 3 points is by means of a goal from a free kick. For this a player catchers the ball direct from a kick, knock forward, or throw forward by one of his opponents and, while stationary, shouts "mark". Having done so, he is allowed to make a place kick or drop kick at goal which, if it sends the ball over the crossbar and between the goal posts, scores three points.

Clothing

Players wear jerseys, shorts, stockings, and studded boots. They may wear soft leather helmets to protect their heads and ears, and leather pads to protect their shins, but leather shoulder harnesses and other armour are not allowed.

SAILING (SEE ALSO YACHTING)

Introduction

Sailing as a sport is the art of navigating a sailboat for recreational or competitive purposes.

Rules

In racing, boats are classified according to their sails and masts. The most common types are the sloop (one mast, two sails), schooner (usually two masts and five sails), yawl (two masts, four sails), and ketch (two masts, five sails).

Equipment

Sloops, from 10–70ft (3.05–21.34m) are generally used for racing, and other types usually more than 20ft (6.1m) long, for recreational cruising.

SEPAK TAKRAW

Introduction

Sepak Takraw, a game played with a rattan ball on a BADMINTON court, is widely popular in south-east Asia, being referred to by several names in the various countries (see TAKRAW). In the Philippines it is called "sipak", in Thailand, "takraw", and in Malaysia, "sepak raga". The game was named "sepak takraw" during the 1965 South-East Asian Peninsular Games when there was a deadlock over uniformity. The compromise was the joining of a Malay word and a Thai word – "sepak" (kick) and "takraw" (rattan ball in Thai.)

History

The origin of the game is unknown. The Malays argue that it started in the Malay peninsula, the Thais in Thailand, and the Filipinos in the Philippines. There is a similar game played even in Burma. With British colonization, the game receded into the background and was confined to the Malay peasants in villages, known as "kampongs". It was, and is, the favourite pastime of office boys and chauffeurs, during lunch breaks.

The game was once popular in the royal courts of feudal Malaya. The legendary Malayan hero, Hang Tuah, is often associated with the game in Malay folklore. The rules were simple – the participants formed a ring and the team who kept the ball longest in the air was the winner. Singles matches were also played. Although it was originally played exclusively by men, it is now also popular among women.

Venue

See Badminton.

Rules

The rules are a cross between those of badminton and VOLLEYBALL, and the game has been described as "volleyball played with feet and other parts of the body, except the hands".

Each side has three players. The first, known as "tekong", is positioned inside the semicircle at the baseline. The second player is "apit kiri" (left winger). At the commencement of play the ball is served (kicked) to the centre by the second or third player, both standing within marked positions in the court. The ball must not touch the ground and each side is allowed up to three hits (as in volleyball) before the ball is delivered over the net to the opposite side of the court – except when serving, when there must be only a straight kick. The ball may also be headed over the net (a "balas tandok") but no part of the arms, from the shoulders to fingertips, may be used.

Serving is as in volleyball, but scoring is like badminton; the first side to reach 15 points wins the set. A deuce of 5 points is allowed if the score is deadlocked at 13, and 3 points in the case of a 14-all tie. The game is decided on the best of three sets. There are detailed rules regarded foul services, fixed positions, changed positions, touching the net or the umpire's bench and crossing the opponent's side.

Keeping the ball in the air continuously calls for sharp reflexes and skill, combining the teamwork of volleyball, the dexterity of FOOTBALL, and the speed of badminton.

Equipment

The net is lower than in badminton, 155cm (5ft 1in) off the ground at the top, and the ball is 40cm (16in) in circumference and 298g (10.5oz) in weight.

SHINTY

Introduction

Shinty is the popular name for "camanachd", the native stick-and-ball game of the Scottish Highlands, originally the same pastime as the Irish HURLING. The two games have drifted apart in development and technique through the centuries, but the basis of the two remains the same, the driving of a ball and a stick through a goal.

History

Since shinty was first brought to Scotland by the invading Irish Gaels, the history of the game is shared with hurling until midway through the fourteenth century. But, even from earliest times, there was one very important difference. In Ireland there had always been two types of "caman": the broad-bladed stick, which was more popular in the south, and the narrow blade, which was favoured by the players of the Antrim glens. As it was from Antrim that the Irish colonists crossed to Scotland, the narrow-bladed stick has ever since remained the favoured instrument of the Scottish shinty players.

Down the centuries, shinty, for long more generally known as "camanachd", remained a popular pastime in the Highlands, despite some Lowland laws against the game and continuous efforts to enforce Sabbath observance, which was especially likely to affect shinty since the game was customarily played on Sundays. Eventually, Sunday play died out, but the game itself lived on, surviving both the débâcle of Culloden and the Highland Clearances. Pennant in his *Tour of Scotland* (1769) lists among the ancient sports still practiced in the Highlands "the shinty, or the striking of a ball of wood or hair. The game is played between two parties, furnished with clubs, in a large plain. Whichever side strikes it first to the goal wins the match."

Venue

Modern shinty is played 12-a-side and the ideal measurements of the playing pitch are 160yds long by 80yds wide (146m x 73m). The goal is known as the "hail" so the end lines are the hail lines. The hails themselves are formed by goal posts 12ft (3.7m) wide and 10ft (3.048m) high, with a crossbar. In front of each hail is a 10yd (9.1m) area into which an attacking player is not permitted to enter before the ball. A penalty spot is marked 20yds (18.3m) in front of each hail and a penalty is awarded if a defender fouls within the 10yd area.

Rules

The duration of a game is 90 minutes, the teams playing 45 minutes each way. The game is controlled by a referee who is assisted by hail-judges and linesmen. Goals, or hails, are the only scores. If the ball is sent wide by an attacker, a defender strikes it out from the 10yd area. If the ball is turned over the hail line by a defender, a corner-hit, from which a hail may be scored direct, is granted to the opposition.

A shinty side comprises 12 players. A hail-keeper, a full-back, three half-backs, a centre back, centre-field, centre forward, three half-forwards, and a full-forward. Some shinty teams adjust their line-out as circumstances vary, but the most usual methods of placing the players are:

(1) The "diamond" formation: hail-keeper; full-back; half-back, half-back; centre back, centre-field; centre forward; half-forward, half-forward, half-forward; full-forward.

(2) The "Southern" formation: hail-keeper; right back, left back; right half-back, left half-back; right centre, centre, left centre; right half-forward, left half-forward; right full-forward, left full-forward.

(3) The "Northern" formation: hail-keeper; full-back; right half-back, centre half-back, left half-back; right centre, centre, left centre; right wing-forward, centre forward, left wing-forward full forward.

In direct contrast to hurling custom, only the hail-keeper is permitted to handle the ball. Nor may the ball be caught, kicked, thrown or carried. A player may not hold, obstruct, trip, hack, or back-charge an opponent. All such offences are penalized by a free hit, technically called a "set blow". A referee is entitled to send a player to the line for rough or reckless play, striking an opponent, or general misconduct. If a team deliberately sends the ball over the side line, the opposing side gets a free hit from the place where the ball crossed the line.

Equipment

The stick is called the caman, the same as for Irish hurling, and is likewise crooked at the top. The broad blade of the Irish stick is, however, unknown in Scotland, where the head of the caman must be small enough to pass through a ring 2.5in (6.3cm), in diameter. The Scots caman is wedge-shaped with the broad end at the heel in order to give lift to the ball. The ball itself has a core of cork and worsted, and is covered with leather. Stitched in the same fashion as the Irish hurling ball, it is 7–8in (17.7–20.32cm) in circumference and weighs 2.5–3oz (70–85g).

Scoring

For a goal to be scored, the ball must pass over the goal line between the posts and under the crossbar.

Clothing

Players wear jerseys, shorts, socks and boots without spikes or tackets (hobnails or studs). The goalkeeper must wear a jersey of a different colour.

SHOOTING, AIR WEAPONS

Introduction

All organized shooting with air weapons (known as "pellet guns" in the USA) is with 0.177in (4.5mm) firearms in the standing position without support of any kind.

Standard Targets, Air Weapons

The value of each scoring ring is indicated. Targets are not to scale: the air rifle target is 46mm in diameter and the air pistol target 156mm in diameter.

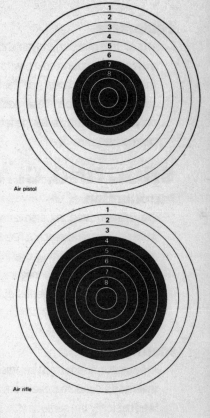

Air pistol

Air rifle

History

Air rifles are mentioned in most of the ancient histories of organized shooting, some dating back to the Middle Ages. The St. Sebastianus Shooting Club in Cologne, which operated a 100 firing points underground range (including 14 point for air rifles) was founded in 1463.

Although air rifle shooting has been popular in parts of Britain and elsewhere since the early 1900s, the International Shooting Union first published rules in April 1965. Three years later they produced rules for air pistol competition.

Rules

The international course of fire is 40 shots in 90 minutes at 10 minutes (32ft 9.75in) range, but some national associations fire a shorter course and, in Britain for example, at 6yds (5.49m) range.

Equipment

The air rifle marksman who shoots from the standing position, unlike their counterpart who fires at greater distances in three positions, does not need a padded shooting jacket or spotting telescope. Once equipped with rifle or pistol, their only expenditure is for pellets at a fraction of the cost of "explosive" cartridges.

SHOOTING, CLAY PIGEON

Introduction

Clay pigeon shooting, also known as "trap shooting", is a sport in which spinning saucer-shaped targets are spring-catapulted into the air, simulating the flight of birds, and fired at with 12-gauge open-bore shotguns. There are two distinct types of competition, the longer-established form known as "down-the-line", "trench", or "Olympic trench" and another event called "skeet".

History

Clay pigeon shooting dates from 1880, when McCaskey, a Scot, invented a suitable target composed of river silt and pitch. This was basically the same as that still used, a combination of pitch and clay or limestone which has the ideal quality of brittleness. Later, in 1880, an American from Cincinnati named Ligowsky developed the first mechanized trap from which the target could be successfully propelled.

The name of the sport derived from earlier competitions near London in which live pigeon were used, from around 1790. These were later made illegal. The participants were nicknamed the "Old Hats" because they kept the pigeons covered with their headgear before releasing them. In a first

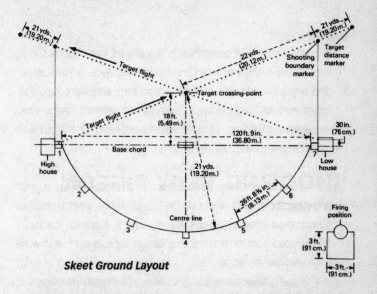

Skeet Ground Layout

attempt to dispense with live targets, hollow glass balls about 2.5in (63.5mm) in diameter were used for a brief period before 1880. Some of the balls were even filled with feathers to add a realistic touch.

The sport has thrived in North America, where the governing body was formed at Vandalia, Ohio, in the 1890s and became the Amateur Trapshooting Association of America in 1924.

Skeet shooting derives its name from an early Norse word for shoot. It was invented in 1915 by Foster, editor of the American magazine, the *National Sportsman*, who originally intended his idea as no more than practise for small-game shooting. But Foster's invention caught on and clubs sprang up all over the USA. The National Skeet Shooting Association of the United States formed in Massachusetts in 1925. The first US national skeet championships were held in 1935. Skeet was introduced to Britain in the mid-1930s.

Rules

In each round of a competition, squads of five shooters at a time stand in a line at fixed firing positions, 3yds (2.74m) apart and 16yds (14.63m) behind the sunken trap, which is concealed in a steel trap house to protect the target-loader. In the senior, more elaborate form of down-the-line shooting 15 traps are used to give a wider variety of target flight.

In a round of 25 single targets, each shooter fires five cartridges at as many targets from each of the five stations. After each member of the squad has shot five times from one stand, they change places, each moving right to the next change position, except the shooter on the extreme right who moves to the extreme left.

The generally approved stance for right-handed shooters is sideways to the direction of firing, with the left foot in front and body well forward, with chin and body weight over the left foot. The heel of the right foot should be slightly raised and the knees should not be bent. An ideal stance is important to counter the effect of recoil.

A major difference from the technique of rifle shooting is the finger action on the trigger. The sensitive shotgun trigger is gently squeezed rather than pulled; there is no second pressure as on a rifle. There is no backsight and, again unlike rifle shooting, it is normal to aim with both eyes open.

The art of swinging the gun smoothly through the target, allowing the correct amount of forward deflection and follow through after firing, underlines the fundamental difference from shooting at a fixed target. The shooter fires a little ahead of the clay pigeon after having swung smoothly through its trajectory. The correct time allowance must be made for muscles and nerves to react, and for the flight of the shot. This is approximately 1/10 second for 40yds. As the shooter does not known at what angle or height each target will travel, the speed of their reaction is an integral part of the skill demanded.

Skeet is a form of clay pigeon shooting designed to simulate almost any kind of bird game-shot that can be had in the field. It appeals particularly to those who like to shoot all year round without the hindrance of game laws or closed seasons, and to many who have never fired a shot in the country.

The shooters, normally in squads of five, start at No. 1 station and fire in turn at one target thrown from the high trap and a second from the lower one. The first resembles that offered by a grouse as it takes flight. The second is an oncoming "bird" which approaches swiftly and directly overhead. The shooters move round to each station in rotation, firing at 2 targets from each of the 7 positions, making a total of 14 singles shots.

Then come the doubles. At No. 7 station, each shooter in turn loads with two cartridges and fires first at the target from the nearer trap. They must then swing back to pick up the other target on its flight in the opposite direction from the farther trap, both targets being released simultaneously. Similar doubles shots are taken at Nos. 6, 4, 2, and 1 stations.

During the shooting of the 24 targets (14 singles and 10 in doubles), each competitor is allowed one extra shot by having a repeat of the first target he misses (or a choice of trap and station for their extra shot if all the other 24 are hits). Thus, a round of skeet for each person consists of 25 targets, each slightly different and every one starting at something like 30mph (48km/h). Two or three rounds usually form the nucleus of a meeting or match.

Equipment

The regulation clay pigeon target is black in colour, weighs 3.5–4oz (99–113g), and has a diameter of 4 5/16in (110mm). On the command "Pull" from the shooter, each target is released at an angle automatically varied by a trap operated by remote control.

Double-barrelled shotguns are commonly used, and there are various secondary clay pigeon competitions which involve the use of a second shot at the same target if it is missed the first time, or "doubles", when the first barrel is used at one target and the second at another.

The 12-bore shotgun usually weighs up to 6.5lb (3kg). A barrel length of 30–32in (up to 813mm) is preferable to the conventional field gun length of 28in (711mm) because of the relatively long range it provides. The cartridge, 2.5in (63.5mm) long is loaded with up to 32g (35.4g in the Olympics) of lead pellets (nearly 400); the manufacture of a single cartridge involves 130 distinct operations. The effective range of the run is up to 40yds (36.6m) and the velocity of the shot about 865ft (264m) per second. The target, which flies at approximately 50mph (80 km/h), breaks only because it is spinning. A similar stationary target cannot be broken at 40yds with the weapon and ammunition used.

SHOOTING, PISTOL
Introduction

The pistol events are considered to be the most demanding in competitive shooting. Competitors stand, free of any support, with the smallest of bullseyes, attempting to score 10 points for a gruelling 60 shots over 2hrs 30min, or they take five shots,

The Rapid-Fire Pistol Target
Value of the scoring rings is indicated; the height is roughly that of a small human figure.

each fired at a different target in the space of 4 seconds. This latter requires the utmost concentration. For the slow-fire pistol event, the classic in this branch of shooting, the same ranges, procedure, administration and tie-breaking as for small-bore rifle events are used (see SHOOTING, RIFLE). A different set-up is necessary for the other three events which include rapid or timed fire.

History

The standard pistol event was introduced by the ISU for the many people who were firing in national programmes with pistols which were unsuitable for the free pistol and the rapid-fire matches.

Competition shooting probably dates from the 1770s when pistols superseded the sword for duelling. There is no record that the crude handguns which came into existence after the invention of gunpowder c.1313 were sufficiently accurate for competition purposes.

Significant milestones in the development of firearms, both rifle and pistol, occurred first in 1805, when the percussion lock (producing the ignition spark) displaced the flint and then in 1816, when the percussion cap was invented. This was the forerunner of the complete cartridge of today. Then came the first breech-loading gun that used a self-contained, rimmed, re-loadable centre-fire cartridge. This was attributed to Pauly, a Swiss gunsmith who worked in Paris and London. It led in turn to the first revolver, in 1835, originated by Col. Colt of Hartford, Connecticut (USA), and the automatic pistol originally manufactured in 1892 in Austria.

The British National Rifle Association (formed in 1860) first staged revolver competitions at their big Wimbledon meeting in 1885. The NRA America (established in 1871) followed the next year at the Creedmore range near New York. That same year representatives of French shooting societies on a goodwill and fact-finding visit to Wimbledon, won several revolver prizes. The British NRA moved to Bisley in 1890 and the use of self-loading semi-automatic pistols was first permitted in 1898.

Venue

The free pistol event, dates from 1900. Sixty shots in 5-shot strings are fired at 50m (54.7yds). A maximum 15 sighting shots are permitted. The target has a bullseye diameter which is larger by 50mm. The 7 scoring ring, which is 200mm (7.87in) in diameter, encloses the black aiming-mark. The score rings (6 down to 1) are printed black on white and the outer ring measures 500mm (19.685in). For the other three international events, which include timed and rapid-fire requirements, the International Shooting Union (ISU) specify how the range shall be designed and furnished, with provision for shooting under cover or in the open. The distance is 25m (27.3yds). An automatic timing apparatus is designed to reveal ("face") the targets for 4, 6, and 8 seconds in one event, for 20 and 150 seconds in another, and for 3 seconds between 7-second intervals in the third event.

Rules

At 25m the 60 shots are fired in 5-shot strings, in 10, 20, and 150 seconds, repeated four times. The term "centre-fire" describes cartridges, usually of larger calibre than 5.66mm (0.22in), which are "rim-fire". In centre-fire cartridges a small percussion cap is inserted into the centre of the base of the cartridge case. When the cartridge is in the breech of the barrel, the trigger mechanism releases a striker which fires the cap. This in turn ignites the propellant. Because of the high cost of manufactured centre-fire cartridges, reloading by individual shooters is widespread. Centre-fire calibres range upwards from 5.67mm (0.22in).

The 60 shots for the centre-fire pistol match are divided equally between a precision, or deliberate, course and a rapid-fire course, both at 25m (27.3yds) range. The precision course is fired at the target for the 50m free pistol event, and the rapid-fire course at silhouette targets. Six 5-shots strings each in six minutes comprise the precision course and six 5-shot strings are fired at a single silhouette target (not five targets as in the rapid-fire event), the target being exposed for 3 seconds for each shot with an edge-on interval of 7 seconds. A maximum of five sighting or practise shots is permitted for each course.

The term free pistol is derived from the freedom from the restrictions which apply to other competition pistols. The grip or stock may be tailored to fit the hand, though it may not also support the wrist. The trigger pressure is not controlled as in most other competition weapons. A hair trigger is standard to free pistols and probably originated in the 1770–1850 duelling era when gunsmiths vied with each other to produce refinements which would favour their clients' survival. In practice the trigger pressure is usually set at 10–15g.

The sights both front and rear are "open" and telescope sights are forbidden, though a sight which incorporated the clever use of mirrors was introduced by the Swiss in 1967 and for a short time was approved for international use.

Pistols for "rapid-fire" event must also be fitted with open sights, are semi-automatic, self-loading and use the 0.22in (5.6mm) short cartridge. "Semi-automatic" means that the discharge of the weapon automatically expels the empty cartridge case and brings the next round into the chamber, and a fresh pressure on the trigger is necessary to fire the next cartridge.

Equipment

There are two types of target, the rapid-fire and the precision. The former is all black, except for a narrow white edging, the size of a small human figure (a remnant of military training). Scoring areas are roughly oval-shaped with the 10-score centre 10cm (3.9in) wide by 15cm (5.9in) vertically. Targets are in banks of five, 75cm (29.5in) axis to axis. Only the first type of target is used for rapid-fire match which is also an Olympic Games event. The 60 shots are fired in 5-shot strings each shot at a separate target in 8, 6, and 4 seconds, repeated four times. The event is usually fired in two half-courses of 30 shots (plus five practise shots in a timing chosen by the competitor) on successive days. The target described for the 50m free pistol event is used in the standard pistol and the centre-fire pistol events for precision, or timed slow-fire shooting, but at 25m (27.3yds) range.

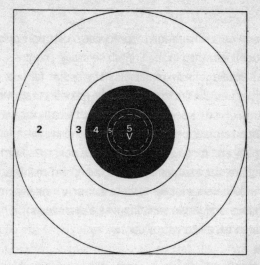

Rifle Target

Scoring:

See Equipment.

SHOOTING, RIFLE

Introduction

Rifle shooting is a pastime and competitive sport, widely practiced, with both full-bore or Service calibre and with small-bore rifles.

History

In England, the change-over from the bow to the firearm began about the middle of the sixteenth century, and it is recorded that matches with muskets took place between marksmen of Bristol and Exeter. It was not, however, until rifling was introduced that the accuracy necessary for shooting at other than very short distances was possible.

This seems to have been appreciated much more quickly on the Continent than in the English-speaking countries, and in Great Britain ARCHERY remained the popular form of target shooting until the firearm became the more accurate medium. Central Europe is generally accepted as the birthplace of rifling, and rifled arms appear to have been in use in Switzerland and Germany and probably other European countries from about the middle of the sixteenth century, but not in Great Britain until nearly 300 years later. Here, there was only a small number of rifle clubs, and target shooting was a pastime which had not acquired any military significance.

Venue

For the 10m range, which can be either indoors or outdoors, the target height is 1.5m above the level of the shooting station and may be adjusted to the competitor's height. For the 50m and 300m range, which again can be indoors or outdoors, the optimum target height above the level of the shooting station is 50cm. Shooting ranges are available for training before the competition, and the target and shooting order are decided by lot.

Rules

The rules governing the positions used in target shooting with Service calibre rifles are more or less universal and framed to permit the firer maximum control of his weapon.

Prone

The shooter lies down forwards on the ground, or on a mat or ground-sheet, the upper part of his body being supported by elbows. The butt of the rifle must be placed against the shoulder or armpit and all parts of the rifle and the arms below the elbow must be visibly clear of the ground and of all other objects. The rifle must be supported by the hands of the shooter only, with the aid of a sling.

Standing

The shooter stands erect on both feet, no other part of the body touching the ground or any other object. The rifle may be supported by the forward hand and held against the shoulder, the cheek and the part of the chest nearest to the shoulder. The upper part and the elbow of the forward arm may rest on the chest and the hip. No form of artificial support is permitted.

Kneeling

British rules simply state that no part of the body may touch the ground or any other object except for one foot and the other leg from the knee downwards. The forward elbow may rest on the knee.

Sitting

The weight of the body is supported on the buttocks, and no part of it above the buttocks may touch the ground or any other object. The rifle may be held in any convenient way, provided the butt is in the shoulder or armpit. The legs may be apart or crossed and may be in front of the front edge of the firing-point.

Back Position

As used in British match rifle shooting, in which it has always been the favoured shooting position, its principal advantages are: (a) the long sight radius; (b) that the rifle is supported for the greater part of its length by the firer's body; and (c) that it allows the firer to sit up and relax between shots.

There are no particular restrictions, the firer lying on his back with his feet pointing towards the targets. Normally, the left knee is raised so that the left foot is alongside the right knee.

The head may be supported with a sling or similar aid. If preferred, the rifle may be held with the right hand only while the left hand supports the back of the head. The butt of the rifle should be firm in the right armpit with the fore end on the bony portion inside the right knee, the left hand grasping the top of the butt.

In the foregoing shooting positions the expressions "left" and "right" should be reversed for shooters firing from the left shoulder.

Equipment

The smallbore rifle has a maximum weight of 8kg and a maximum caliber of 5.6mm. The right-hand grip must not rest on the sling or the left arm. The maximum length of the hook of the butt end is 15.3cm.

The smallbore standard has a maximum weight of 5kg and a maximum caliber of 5.6mm. Bigbore, free and standard rifles have a maximum caliber of 8mm and a minimum trigger weight of 1500g. Any compressed air or CO_2 rifle, of conventional appearance and 4.5mm caliber. No lens, lens systems, or telescopic sights are allowed. Correcting glasses if needed may be worn by the shooter.

Clothing

Restrictions on material, construction, size and thickness prevent any artificial support in the different firing positions.

SHUFFLEBOARD

Introduction

Shuffleboard, or "shovelboard", is one of the oldest DECK GAMES and remains one of the most popular with passengers on most shipping lines.

History

It is an adaptation of the shore game that has been played since the fifteenth century, and possibly before that, and was known variously as shove-groat, shovelpenny, and shove-board and now generally as shove-ha'penny. The game was early adapted for playing on board ship, and is now firmly established as shuffleboard. While the board in the land game has become progressively smaller over the years, on ships it has grown larger. Save in its essentials, shuffleboard now bears only a passing similarity to shove-ha'penny, which may explain why some shipping companies call the same deck game peel billiards or deck billiards.

Rules

The game may be played in singles matches between two players or in doubles by partners, and is usually played for either 50 or 100 up. Each player is provided with four discs, and these s/he plays, alternately with his/her opponent, towards the far squares. In singles, opponents play from the same ends; in doubles, partners stand at opposite ends so that two players, one of each side, are at each end.

The rules vary slightly between shipping companies but they are simple and most include the penalty that any disc that stops short of the ladies' line must be removed from play and not be left as a hazard to the discs subsequently played; that a disc touching a chalk line does not score; that players may knock their own or another's disc into, or out of, any square; and that the score that counts is indicated by the square in which the disc rests when all the discs have been played. Ends are then changed. There is clearly an advantage resting with the player, or pair, who play second in any game since s/he, or they, have the last shot. Generally, therefore, the rules allow that the side with the lower score after the first end must play first in the next.

Equipment

Shuffle-board is played with wooden discs, usually about 6in (152mm) in diameter, which are pushed along the deck with long-handled drivers fitted with a semi-circular shoe that fits the disc. Usually the drivers are painted in different colours to identify the teams. As with BULL, whether the rows of numbers are counted horizontally or vertically they total 15 in each row or column.

Scoring

There is a considerable element of acquired skill in the game although even expert players have different preferences, some aiming for the 10 and then for 5 and 9 to prevent a successful 10-shot being knocked off, others aiming first for their discs higher off the board.

SKIBOBBING

Introduction

Skibobbing is a relatively new winter sport, combining the virtues of the ski, bobsleigh and velocipede in a downhill run.

History

Skibobbing began in Austria. At the turn of the nineteenth century when winter sports had become established, experiments were made to find yet another pastime to add to the programme of attractions. With the CYCLING boom then current the inventive genius of winter sportsmen turned naturally to the creation of a "snow-bicycle". A former Austrian racing cyclists, Lenhardt or Bruck-an-der-Mur, invented a machine on the bicycle principle in 1902 and called it a "mono-slide". However, it resembled more the "hobby-horse" (an early velocipede fashionable at the beginning of the nineteenth century) than the modern bicycle. Its locomotion depended on the use of rider's feet pushing alternately on the ground. The two runners that replaced the wheels were narrow, like sleigh runners, and were ineffective in deep snow.

Venue

A skibob runs varies in length, an average course being between 2 and 3 miles (3–5km) with a drop of about 1300ft (400m). It starts generally with a steep descent down the flank of the mountain, then zig-zags along a wide passage through a forest to finish in the fields.

Rules

Skibobbing, which is practical on any ski slope and in any kind of snow, is performed on a low, elongated vehicle resembling a bicycle with skis in place of wheels, one fixed at the rear, the other mobile in front for steering. The vehicle is fitted with a saddle, and two "patinettes" (mini-skis, or ski-skates) are attached to the feet. The foot skis serve to maintain equilibrium and the skibobber keeps them firmly on the snow.

For a "straight descent" the skibobber sits in an upright position as on a bicycle, keeping his knees near the body and his weight on the foot-skis. For the speedster a "jockey crouch" is employed. If the slope appears too steep for the rider's skill, a zig-zag descent is adopted. Negotiating bumps, known as "bump-riding", is achieved by raising the body slightly above the saddle and pressing on the handlebars and the foot-skis. To stop, it is necessary only to dig in the heels when the metal teeth at the rear of the foot-skis act as emergency brakes.

Equipment

Skibobs are made of wood, aluminium, or plastic, the latter two materials being preferred since wood, though possessing the advantage of lightness, breaks too easily. The prime quality of a skibob is to be springy so that the machine can ride bumps without jolting and thus unsettling the rider. The overall length ranges from 6ft 3in – 7ft 6in (1.90–2.29m). The long ski being faster, the maximum length is generally used for downhill racing; the shorter ski ideal for slalom competition; while an utility model for normal use should not be longer than 6ft 7in (2m). The saddle on some models can be raised or lowered; the average height of the fixed saddle from the ground is 2ft 4in (71cm). The ideal weight for men's skibobs ranges between 20.5lb and 25lb (9.3–11.3lb), and for women's from 17.5lb to 22.5lb (8–10.3kg). Skibobs are sometimes built on a fixed frame or can be dismantled to facilitate transportation. The fixed model is stronger and generally preferred.

The short foot-skis, average 1ft 7in (48cm) in length, are made of wood and metal, and have adjustable bindings. Some have safety straps.

Clothing

Dress for skibobbing is the usual winter sports outfit used by skiers.

SKIING

Introduction

Skiing as a competitive sport is either racing or jumping with feet attached to shaped runners, known as "skis", over snow surfaces of varying angularity. Skiing is divided into two main sections, Alpine and Nordic.

History

Rock engravings of skis go back to 3000BC and there are numerous references to primitive skis before they appeared in their multi-laminated modern forms in the 1930s. Metal skis were introduced generally in 1950, followed in the later years of the decade by fibre-reinforced plastic skis, and then a combination of metal and plastic.

Organized competitive skiing began in the nineteenth century, but skiing as a means of getting from place to place on snow began before the third millennium BC as crude rock engravings in Norway and Russia testify. A dozen skis of the Stone Age have been found in the peat bogs of Scandinavia and Finland. The first recorded written references to skiing are by the Chinese historians of the T'ang Dynasty from the seventh to the tenth century AD who refer to their northern neighbours as "Turks who ride horses of wood". Herodotus, the Greek historian, writes of Abaris the Hyperborean "who is said to have gone on his arrow all round the world without once easing".

An English map of 1280 in Hereford Cathedral shows a man on skis or skates in Norway and a horse-footed man in China. The Norse sagas contain a number of references to skiing, and the Norsemen who penetrated the British Isles brought their skis and techniques with them. Skiing was well known in northern Scotland and in use in Devonshire in the sixteenth century. Weardale miners went to work on "skees" in the seventeenth century and were doing so until the Industrial Revolution brought roads and railways to isolated areas of Britain.

Skiing

Rules

Alpine skiing is racing on skis down steep, prepared snow slopes, one competitor after the other, the fastest time decided the winner. The longest race is about 2 miles (3.2km).

The following procedures are common to all Alpine Events:

The starting order is determined by FIS points: the 15 best skiers going into the first group. Skiers without FIS points go in the last group. In competitions with two runs, the starting order for the second run is determined by the results of the first run; the skier in 15th place goes first, 14th goes second and on down until the first goes 15th.

Nordic skiing includes cross-country skiing, on lighter skis over undulating surfaces with distances from 5km (3.1 miles) to 50km (31 miles), and ski jumping, competitive jumping on skis in which points are awarded for distance and style. There is also a combined competition where the winner is decided on the aggregate of points for cross-country running and jumping.

Equipment

Skis are strips of wood, or composite wood, metal, or synthetic fibre, clipped to the boot so that it is possible to slide or push over snowy or icy surfaces. They are upturned at the pointed fronts so that they will not dig into the snow. Skis vary from 180cm (5ft 11in) to 210cm (6ft 11in) long, and are about 90mm (3.5in) wide at the front end, narrower in the middle by about 15mm (just over 0.5in), and slightly wider again at the ends, though not as wide as the front.

Clothing

Skiers wear warm, waterproof, tight-fitting outfits. Goggles may be used as protection from glare, wind, and snow spray, and to improve visibility in some conditions. Boots are also worn.

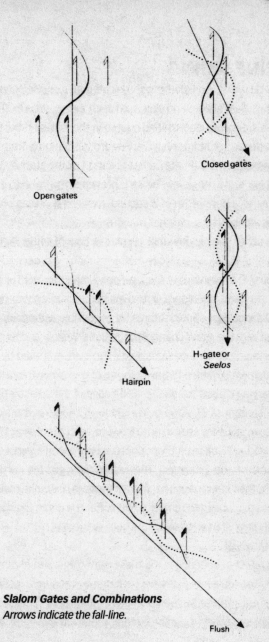

Closed gates

Open gates

H-gate or *Seelos*

Hairpin

Slalom Gates and Combinations
Arrows indicate the fall-line.

Flush

• ALPINE SKIING

Alpine ski racing is divided into three categories or disciplines – downhill, giant slalom and slalom. In each the object is to slide down a steep, pre-determined course in the fastest time, the racers departing at intervals varying from 0.5min to 1min. In top-class races the timing device is set off at the start by the skier's leg, and a magic-eye beam is broken at the finish to give the time to a hundredth of a second, modern ski races often being described by such small margins.

The art of racing downhill on skis is one of anticipation, balance, and flexibility. Most modern teaching preaches an economy of movement of the legs, pelvis, and the small of the back, the head, shoulders, and arms being used only to help keep balance. Skis should slide as far as possible without losing contact with the snow, changing conditions of snow and terrain necessitating constant adjustments. Turns are achieved by up and down weighting and unweighting of one ski or the other, with varying weight put on the inside edge of the ski according to the steepness of slope or condition of snow. As the skier goes downhill, they seek a more forward point of balance. (The term "vorlage" means a pronounced forward lean against the pressure of the bindings.) The faster they go, the further forward their balance will be, though modern boot rake makes this less obvious than formerly. The softer the snow the more weight is transferred towards the back of the skis.

The Downhill

This is a test of speed. It is the most highly regarded of Alpine events. The terrain of a downhill is carefully chosen to include bumps, rolls, gullies, sudden changes of steepness, "schusses" and light and shade. Courses generally follow the fall-line with no sharp changes of direction. Gates, at least 8m (26ft) wide, are used, primarily to keep speed within bounds or to keep the racer away from dangerous obstacles.

Giant Slalom

This was originally intended as a scaled-down version of the downhill which could more certainly be staged because it did not demand so much snow. Basically it tests the racer's ability to find and hold the fastest traverse on courses about 1,500m (1 mile) in length, with a vertical drop of 450m (1,476ft), and through 60 to 70 gates each from 4 to 8m (13–26ft) wide and red and blue alternately.

Slalom

Sometimes called "special slalom" to differentiate it from giant slalom, this has two consecutive runs on different, though usually adjacent, courses. The winner is the competitor with the fastest aggregate time for the two runs. Slalom is primarily a test of control. There are two types of gate, open and closed, and these are varied by a clever course-setter to take advantage of every irregularity of surface to challenge the skier's skill and quickness.

• NORDIC SKIING

Known as "langlauf" in German and "langrenn" in most Scandinavian languages, cross-country ski racing is competitive racing over undulating, pre-arranged snow tracks, the winner being the racer with the fastest time, except in relay events, where the winner is the first to finish. The basic stride is a kick-off from one foot and a gliding step with the other. Kick-offs and glides are alternated between one foot and the other to give a smooth and rhythmical stride. The ski is waxed so that the action is much like a brush on a wet floor and the ski will slide as long as it is in motion, known in Norwegian as "fraspark". The pole in each hand is planted alternately as the leg on the opposite side starts its kick. This is the basic step, to which there are variants. The diagonal stride is similar to that of ice skating, whereby the forward force is gained with a push forward off a slightly angled, edged ski, so that progress is maintained in a series of opened Vs.

• SKI JUMPING

This is a competition based on both distance and style. The jumper takes off down a sloping channel known as an in-run. The distance from the lip of the take-off to the middle point where the jumper's feet touch the snow on landing is measured to an accuracy of 0.5m (or 1ft). Style, or form, is evaluated by official judges. The points for distance and style of the best two rounds of jumping are added together and the jumper with the most points wins. In Nordic combined jumping two best of three jumps are counted. In "ski flying", a form of ski jumping from higher hills, distance alone decides the winner.

During the perfect jump the skier should be in a forward leaning position with straight hips (or bending only slightly) and with his/her arms at his/her side or straight ahead. The ideal for which the jumper is aiming is to remain motionless and in full control throughout the flight. Skis should be parallel, close together, and in roughly the same plane as the upper body. This position is held until just before the landing, when the jumper straightens so that his/her skis are directly under him/her at the moment of impact.

SKITTLES

Introduction

Skittles is a game played with pins and balls, discs, cheeses or other similar projectiles, the aim being to knock pins over with them. There are several varieties of the game, and the dimensions of the equipment vary a great deal between the British Isles and the Continent. Both men and women play.

History

The game began out of doors but is now played mainly indoors. In the main centres, notably the English West Country and Wales, London and the north of England, skittle alleys are attached to inns, public houses, or clubs. In places where skittles is played in leagues, there is frequently also a flourishing complex of friendly teams.

Throwing projectiles at other stationary, but movable, objects with the idea of knocking them down is among the oldest diversions of man. Items similar to present-day skittle pins were found by the Egyptologist, Sir Flanders Petrie, in a child's grave, the burial date being estimated as 5200BC. According to the San Diego Museum, California, the ancient Polynesians played a game called "Ula Maika", where stones had to be bowled at objects 60ft (12.288m) away. This is the length of today's TENPIN BOWLING alleys.

Modern skittles, however, derived from the German peasant's habit of carrying a flat-bottomed club or "kegel" at all times. In the third and fourth centuries, these were used as weapons, and by monks to illustrate simple religious principles. If the club was put on its end, it represented a sin or temptation. In early versions of the game the peasant's right to throw the ball at the clubs was dependent on either praise or admonition from the monks. Gradually this became a pastime enjoyed by increasing numbers of players.

Venue

The run or alley is 3ft wide and must be 21ft long from the front of the first plate (on which the front skittle is placed) to the throwing point. No alley shall be more than 80ft (24.28m) long, or less than 50ft (15.24m) from the "hockey" to the front pin spot. The hockey is a small raised piece of wood at the skittler's end of the alley on which the heel can be rested and some purchase can be gained for under-arm delivery of the ball. The plate on which the nine pins are placed must be about 3ft 6in (1.067m) square and set at right-angles to the centre of the pitchboard. The pitchboard must be of wood 18ft to 24ft (5.486–7.315m) in length and 15in to 18in (381–457mm) in width.

Rules

The game may be played with any number per side, and the variants contain either a series of individual contests, with a final decision based on the number of individual games won, or on the total number of pins knocked down by a team. A fundamental difference in custom is that whereas one game depends on the total number of pins knocked down by a specified number of balls, another version is decided on the number of balls or deliveries required to knock down a set or number of pins.

A typical pattern is a conventional one from the West Country. The pins are set at one end of an alley in diamond formation, with one corner facing the skittler. There will be six, eight, or ten players per side, and usually the team playing at home will begin. The first player throws one ball at the pins and,

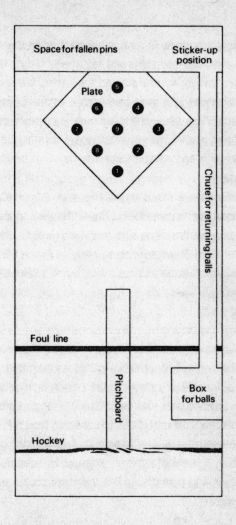

Space for fallen pins

Sticker-up position

Plate

Chute for returning balls

Foul line

Pitchboard

Box for balls

Hockey

Skittles Alley

The pins are shown set up in diamond formation: 1) front; 2) right front second, or quarter; 3) right corner; 4) back right second; 5) back; 6) back left second; 7) left corner; 8) left front second; 9) landlord. The hockey is a thin piece of wood about 2.5in (63mm) high.

providing the throw is legal, s/he waits while the sticker-up clears away the fallen pins and has a second turn. Then, after the balls have again been cleared, the last ball is thrown. All the players of side throw three balls each, then the opposition does the same. This sequence continues until every player has completed his/her "hand" which would normally be a total of 18 or 21 balls, according to local custom.

Equipment

The balls have a maximum diameter of 6.4in (162mm) and a minimum of 1in smaller (137mm). The pins, in this league, must all be of the same size, shape and weight, which is an unusual ruling. The maximum sizes are 12.5in (317.5mm) long, 6in (152.4mm) in diameter at the belly and 3.25in (82.6mm) at the end.

Scoring

If a player knocks down all nine pins with one ball – known variously as a "flopper" or "floorer" – the pins are all replaced and s/he continues as previously. Thus the maximum score per three balls is 27. If a player knocks down all nine pins using his/her first two balls – termed a "spare" – the pins are replaced and s/he takes a throw at the full set again. Thus the maximum for the spare is 18. The maximum in any other case is, of course, 9. In the south-west of England, where pins and balls are larger, and pins placed more closely, scores tend to be much higher.

• DEVIL AMONG THE TAILORS

The most widely known of indoor skittles games is called "table skittles" or, less frequently, "Devil Among The Tailors". This is a compendium of pastimes containing elements of skittles, "ringing the bull", and the maypole. The object is to knock down pins with a small ball attached to a short pole by a wire which swings in an arc. Dimensions vary widely, but a small platform roughly 1ft (305mm) square forms a base for nine pins set diamond fashion, in the middle of an open box. At the side of the box the pole, about 1yd (914mm) high, has a swivelling device at the top which allows the ball at the end of the wire to be swung around and into the pins. Pins and balls are made of hard wood. An interesting departure from the normal scoring is that in some games the domino system is used, where only multiples of three and five are counted. The base of the box, where the pins fall is often covered with baize, to make the game quieter, and a scoring board of holes, in the style of cribbage, is usually to be found at one end of the board.

• HOOD SKITTLES

Hood skittles is an indoor game using nine pins, about 6in (152mm) high, placed in the usual diamond formation at thigh-height from the floor on a table suitably protected with leather pads. Stitched and leather padded "cheeses" are thrown at these pins from various distances, usually in the region of 3yds (2.743m) and scoring rebounds from the sides of the alley or the fallen pins are allowed, adding to the skill of the game. Games are usually played on an individual basis, with three cheeses from each player deciding who has won one "life". Five lives normally decide the game, but in some localities, team totals are used to divide the winners. A usual method is sometimes employed to settle tied lives. To win a replayed life, a player must hit more than his opponent with both his first cheese and his total of three cheeses.

• LONG ALLEY

This most northerly of the popular skittles games is confined largely to Nottinghamshire and north Leicestershire. It is one of the oldest forms, dating from the thirteenth century, and the equipment has long remained unchanged. It has much in common with other versions of the game, but there are differences in detail. Like most very early pins, these are broad-based, and tapered towards the head. They may also be iron-bound for strength. From the bowler's position on the alley, the first eight paces are cobbled but the rest of the area (which is 12yds, or 10.973m, long) is smoothly covered either by a deep crust of slate or heavy boards. This guarantees a true bounce of the cheese. As with most skittles games, there is a trough at the end for the fallen pins, and a chute at the side, down which the setter-up can send the cheeses back to the players. The cheeses are most unusual in shape, like a capsule with rounded ends, weighing in the region of 4lb (1.814kg). When thrown, each cheese must pitch on the smooth-floored section beyond the cobbles and much skill can be used in making the cheese change course from the bounce. Any number of players may take part, but usually six or eight members of a team play individual matches against an opponent. The usual limit of the game is five "legs" of three cheeses each.

• NINEPINS

This is a game with three rows of three pins, set in diamond formation towards the player. This differs markedly from skittles. After the first throw, made from an agreed distance, the player can approach the frame of pins, and "tip", or throw, at the remaining pins from close range. "Dutch-pins" is similar, with higher, more slender pins and with the refinement that the biggest pin – the "kingpin" – could decide the game. Normally 31-pins down is the target, but if the "kingpin" alone is felled, that wins the game.

• OLD ENGLISH SKITTLES

This version is played in London, and has a ruling body, the Amateur Skittles Association, formed in 1900, which runs competitions and keeps records. The equipment used is the same size as that in the south-west, except that the "cheeses" are much bigger than the balls, are in the form of a discus (thickened in the centre), and have a bias. The heaviest weighs more than 12lb (5.4kg) and the pins, made of hornbeam, can be as high as 14.5in (368mm), and 6.75in (171mm) in diameter.

The playing alley, similar to the West Country type, is shorter at 21ft (6.4m), and the frame, or plate, of nine skittles is larger at 4ft 6in (1.37m) across. The area used for play, the run, is often sunk below floor level, and it is an offence to step outside this during play. Also, the back foot must not cross the double line at the end of the run before the cheese is released. The object is to hit the front pin full toss without touching the alley, and almost any shot is possible. The number of throws required to knock down all pins is recorded, and matches are played as a series of individual contests. If a pin is standing after four throws, a penalty of 5 points is given, but by courtesy, if a single pin is standing, it is deemed to be downed by the next throw. Thus is a player gets a floorer, his opponent must do likewise to halve that "frame" or "chalk". Seven frames are usually played in league matches, and eleven in some competitions.

SLED-DOG RACING

Introduction

Sled-dog races are races between harnessed dog teams, which are controlled by a driver. Teams start at intervals, and the team with the shortest elapsed time wins. The number of dogs varies with the distance and terrain.

Rules

There is one driver (also known as the "musher") per team, and drivers often have dog-handlers to help them. Before the race begins their equipment must be inspected and any dog which becomes ill during the race must be carried in the sled. Mushers are not allowied to use the whip unless it is for "snapping".

The sleds usually start at two minute intervals and the time is measured from when the sled's brushbow (at the front of the sled) crosses the starting line to when the first dog reaches the finish line.

Sleds which leave the race trail must return to the point of deviation and continue from there, or they are disqualified

Equipment

The equipment used is a harness, collar, whip and sled. No muzzles or collars hooked as full choke-collars are allowed.

The Dogs

In places like Alaska and Canada most sled dogs are northern breeds which have a double coat to keep them warm. These includes Alaskan, Siberian, Malamute and Greenland huskies. The fur may be quite short, but a thick undercoat and thick, densely-furred ears allow these dogs to lie outside even in the coldest weather.

SNOOKER

Introduction

Snooker may be played by two opponents, pairs or teams. It is usually played one on one. Fifteen red balls, six coloured, and one white cue ball are used. The object of the game is to score points by pocketing balls and by forcing and opponent to give points away through "snookers" and the player with the highest score when all the balls are cleared from the table is the winner.

Venue

Snooker is played on a standard size pocket BILLIARD table.

Rules

The game opens with a "break" which involves playing the cue ball from within the "D" at any red ball. The initial stroke of each turn must have the cue ball hitting a red, while there are still red balls on the table. If the player succeeds in potting a red, they score one point for that ball and continue their break by attempting to pot any non-red ball: they must nominate which ball they are aiming for and they must hit the cue ball against that ball. If they pocket it, they add the score of that ball to their total score.

Red balls that are potted are not replaced on the table; but, at this stage, coloured balls are immediately placed back on the table in their original positions, and the player's break continues. Thus the player pots a red and nominated coloured ball alternately until they fail to score on any stroke. The sum of points in the break is then added to the total score for the game, after which their opponent attempts a break.

The opponent plays from wherever the cue ball (white ball) has come to rest. If the cue ball is pocketed at any time, the break ends, and it is next played from the "D". It can be played from here to any ball.

Play continues in this way until there are no more red balls left on the table. The player potting the last red may attempt to pocket any coloured ball. If he succeeds, that coloured ball is respotted.

Thereafter, the coloured balls must be struck by the cue ball and potted only in strict ascending order of value – yellow, green, brown, blue, pink and black – and once potted they are not put back on the table. A break ends when a player fails to pot the coloured ball of lowest value left on the table.

Equipment

The 22 balls must be of equal size and weight, but English balls are 2.06in in diameter, while American balls are 2.12in. Cues and rests are as for English billiards.

Scoring

Snooker balls score as follows: red, one point; yellow, two points; green, three points; brown, four points; blue, five points; pink, six points; black, seven points. A "snooker" is when a ball that the player is not allowed to play obstructs the ball that is "on". The player must attempt their shot, and will be penalized for missing the "on" ball. If they are snookered by an opponent's foul stroke, they may play any ball they nominate.

SNOWBOARDING

Introduction

Snowboarding is a combination of SKIING and skateboarding.

History

In 1965 Sherman Poppen invented "The Snurfer" for his daughter, Wendy, by bolting two skis together. Five years later a surfer from the East Coast, Dimitriji Milovich, started developing rudimentary snowboards which were based on surfboard design. The boards had metal edges. At the same time, Bob Webber was spending years trying to get a patent for a "skiboard" design. After getting one in 1972, he sold the patent to Jake Burton Carpenter in 1990. By 1975 Dimitrijie Milovich had set up "Winterstick" production in Utah. The metal edges from his early boards were removed and he developed a swallow-tail board based on the same design in surfboards, and, one year later a double-edged design which he got a patented. The first National Snowsurfing Championships was held at Suicide Six Ski Area in Woodstock, Vermont, featuring a slalom and downhill. Snowboarding was included for the first time in the Winter Olympics in 1998.

Venue

In the 1998 Olympics the giant slalom course was almost 1000m (3281ft) long with a drop in elevation of 290m (951ft) and an average gradient of over 18 degrees. The half-pipe course looks like a pipe of snow cut in half. It is 120m (394ft) long and has an average gradient of 18 degrees. The width between the rims is 15m (49ft) and the height of the rims is 3.5m (11ft 6in).

Rules

For the giant slalom event competitors have to negotiate the course through a series of gates, and the snowboarder races against the clock, the one with the fastest time winning. For the half-pipe competition, the boarders ride up and down the U-shaped tube's sides to gain momentum and then launch themselves into the air. The snowboarder performs a series of manoeuvres or "tricks" in the air, which are then judged according to technique, rotation, height, landing and technical merit. The winner is the competitor with the highest total number of points.

Equipment

The most vital piece of equipment is the board itself. It is made of modern composites and/or wood is ridden skateboard style but with fixed bindings. Snowboarders use a slightly different type of board for each discipline. Most ski areas require snowboards to have metal edges, leashes, and secure bindings. A beginner should learn on an all-around or alpine board with high-back bindings and a firmer soft boot or hybrid boot. Hard boots and step-in bindings are not recommended because of the increased difficulties of balancing, turning, skating and using lifts.

Clothing

Some clothing is padded in the stress areas with foam or plastic but normal ski suits can be worn. Ski-suits and helmets are worn by giant slalomists. In the giant slalom the boots are like alpine ski boots but with slightly more flexibility and there is more rubber, allowing for edge control. In the other event, the half-pipe, though boots still come over the ankle, they have to allow a greater degree of flexibility to allow the ankle to move when executing skateboard type manoeuvres. There is a lot of clothing designed specifically for snowboarding. It tends to be reinforced in the knees, backside, shoulders, elbows, palms and fingers.

SOFTBALL

Introduction

Softball is a nine-a-side bat-and-ball game which originated in the USA. The game requires less playing space than its parent sport, BASEBALL, and play is generally faster. Less equipment is necessary (for informal games, just a bat and ball will suffice), and the equipment is relatively inexpensive.

History

Credit for inventing the game of softball has been given to Hancock of the Farragut Boat Club of Chicago, Illinois (USA). In 1887 he foresaw that the then popular American game of baseball could be brought indoors. Indoor baseball, as the new sport was called, became very popular. The name changed to "kitten ball", then to "mush ball", and finally to its present name. The game was soon played in parks and playgrounds in preference to baseball. Alert businessmen became sponsors of favourite teams, furnishing them with uniforms for the privilege of having their names embroidered on them. Already the largest participation sport in America, softball then began to develop as an international sport in the early 1950s. By 1965 it had grown from being a sport that was organized and played by only four countries to being enjoyed in over 50.

Venue

Softball is traditionally played on turf with an infield area skinned of grass. The playing field is in the shape of a diamond, with a home base, and three bases numbered first, second, and third. The home base is at least 46ft (14m) from the pitching point for men and 40ft (12m) for women. Home base and bases one, two and three are 60ft (18.3m) apart.

The playing area of the diamond extends from the home base down two foul lines for approximately 200–275ft (61–84m) which is usually marked inbounds by a line or fence. The outfield area extends from the bases which are stationed

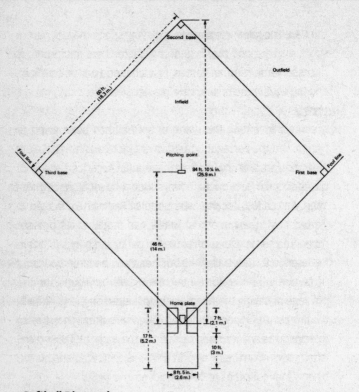

Softball Diamond
The pitching point is 24in by 6in (610 x 152mm). Pitching distance for women is 40ft (12m).

in the infield area to the distance marker that indicates inbounds and out-of-bounds.

Rules

The object of the game is to score runs; the batsman attempts to hit the ball into the fair field of play and having done so, circles the three bases to return to the home base. A run is scored, providing the batsman-runner is not tagged with the ball while circling the bases.

The players in the infield consist of a catcher, stationed behind home base, and a pitcher, stationed on the pitching line. Each of the three bases has a player stationed within the base and one additional player, called a shortstop, who remains within the infield area. The outfield area has three players stationed in each of the areas of the outfield, (1) left field, (2) centre field, and (3) right field.

Each team is allowed three "outs" while taking its turn to bat. An out is recorded when: the third strike (or delivery) is caught by the catcher; the batter has three strikes by hitting at, and missing, the ball; the batter "bunts" foul (a bunt is a legally hit ball – tapped but not swung at – struck softly into the infield) after the second strike; or when a foul ball is legally caught in the field by a fielder before it touches the ground. When three outs have been recorded, the two opposing teams change sides. The length of the game is recorded in innings, one innings consisting of each team having a turn to bat. Seven innings constitute a full and complete game. The team with the most runs at the end of play is the winner.

The basic skills in softball are pitching, catching, throwing, batting and base-running. The fundamentals of the game are the same as baseball. Batting and fielding strategy are similar, though there is an important difference in pitching and technique. The underhand pitch is a distinctive feature in softball. Special skills have been developed in this and the expert pitcher employs a wind-up followed by a release and throw of the ball that achieves a speed comparable to the overhand baseball pitch.

Softball is a more defensive game than baseball, mainly because the softball pitcher has more power over the hitter. The key to successful batting is timing, co-ordination, and reflexes. In softball, the ball is being pitched from a short distance, which results in it coming at the batter at very high speed.

Equipment

The softball is not soft. It is heavier and larger (12in or 304mm in circumference) than a base ball. The centre of the ball is either of a mixture of cork and rubber or of first-quality long-fibre kapok. The bat is of wood, no longer than 2ft 10in and should be not more than 2.25in in diameter (863 x 57mm).

Clothing

Uniforms are similar to those worn for baseball. Gloves may be worn by any player, but mitts may only be worn by the catcher and first baseman. Shoes may have metal plates with spikes a maximum of 0.75in long. Catchers and plate umpires must wear masks. Body protectors may be worn and are compulsory for women catchers.

SPACEBALL

Introduction

Spaceball is a ball game which is played on a trampoline.

History

The game originated and is popular in America and to some extent in England, Germany and Japan. It dates from 1962. Early in that year the inventor of the trampoline began trying to find a game for the equipment. They strung a rope across the centre of a trampoline about 8ft (2.4m) above the bed, with a man either side of the rope passing a ball back and forth.

It was fun, but rather dangerous, since it was an automatic reaction to dive for the ball when receiving and consequently land near the end of the trampoline or indeed come right off it. Obviously to make it safer something had to be erected at each end and thus the backstops evolved. The first idea was the best, an extra half of a trampoline frame, bed and suspension was added to each end. This proved satisfactory since a player landing there was bounced back into the court.

It was decided to make the game like other court and ball games by introducing a single net instead of a rope. It was soon realized, however, that because the court was so small, the ball went out of court if passed off centre, resulting in more time being spent retrieving the ball than playing. The solution was to form a hole in the top of the net, through which the ball would be passed. This would demand skill and help to ensure that the ball was kept central to the trampoline.

Although still at the experimental stage, the game proved enjoyable, but other refinements were necessary. An increase in the height of the backstop prevented the ball, after passing through the hole, from going over the top out of court. An extra net, called the backstop net, opened up the game considerably since the ball would now rebound very quickly into the centre net. This meant that a player would try to catch the ball on the rebound. Finally, it was found that by diving backwards for the ball and rebounding off the backstop net, players frequently collided in the centre of the court. For safety, therefore, the single net was replaced by a double netted gantry, including in it a basket (rather than a hole) which cambered from the centre so that the ball would never get trapped in it.

Nissen, completely enthralled by the invention, set about

selling the game. During the first year, 1963, however, it was not played outside Cedar Rapids, Iowa (USA).

Rules

The server initiates play by throwing the ball through the gantry basket in an attempt to hit the scoring area, complete a double rebound, or cause an opponent to miss or fumble the ball. Either the server or the receiver may score. After the serve, the ball is in continuous play until either side scores or there is a "let" ball (when the ball falls to the scoring area or falls out of bounds after hitting the rebound net). A game is 7 points and a set is two out of three games. The serve always goes to the player who lost the last point; and the loser of the previous game serves first. When a "let" ball occurs, the serve goes to the opposing player.

There is no limit on the number of bounces which may be made by either player. The scoring area includes: the backstop, below the backstop pad; the frame, bed and suspension system; the trampoline bed; and the trampoline suspension system.

Stepping on or crossing the centre line on the trampoline with any part of the body during play results in a point for the opposition. This is so whether or not the infringement occurred during the scoring of a point. Inserting a hand past the middle of the gantry basket; holding on to any part of the gantry net in order to aid the making of a shot; and catching the ball, are all considered to be infringements, and a point is awarded to the opposing player. This rule also applies to hanging on to the backstop, or rebound net. Stepping off the trampoline, either accidentally or intentionally, is also considered to be an infringement and carries the same penalty.

Spaceball may be played as singles, doubles or as a team competition, with up to four players on each side. Initially, one member of each team begins play. As soon as s/he loses a point, s/he is replaced by the next member of the team. The losing team then serves the next point. If the same team loses again, players rotate as before, i.e. the third member of that team comes on to court. At the same time, the other team changes players having won 2 consecutive points, i.e. players change when their team loses a point or wins two points.

Equipment

The apparatus required is an extension of the trampoline. A frame is attached at approximately 75°, on top of which is fixed a rebound net. In the centre of the trampoline is a gantry to divide the playing area into two courts. The gantry, 24in (610mm) deep, has a basket attached to it at the top centre, which is shaped like a two-way funnel so that the ball will always roll out to one court or the other. The backstops, as well as forming part of the scoring area, may be jumped on and used for rebounding. They are made of a woven nylon bed with a suspension of rubber cables in exactly the same way as a trampoline. The nets above the backstops are used to rebound the ball into the centre gantry, which is adjustable in height.

SQUASH RACKETS

Introduction

Squash is one of the newest of the bat-and-ball games to become universally popular, and is usually played between two players. The object is to hit a small ball made of synthetic rubber out of reach of the opponent with a racket similar to, but smaller than, a RACKETS racket.

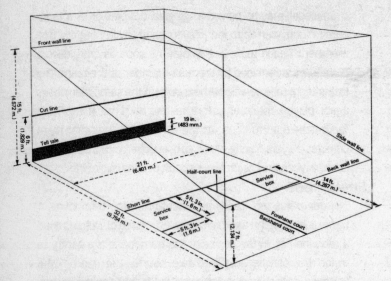

Squash Rackets Court
A flush fitting door in the centre of the back wall below the horizontal line is not shown in this perspective diagram.

History

Squash is derived from the much older game of rackets, and originated at Harrow School, England. It was being played there in 1850 and boys waiting their turn to play rackets knocked a ball about in a confined space adjoining the rackets court. So small was the area that it was necessary to use a softer and slower ball – one which could be squashed with the hand, thus giving the game a name to distinguish it from rackets. In 1929 the Squash Rackets Association was formed. A sub-committee of the Tennis and Rackets Association had laid down rules around 1922, but prior to this a wide variety of balls and courts led to a lack of uniformity which prevented from the growth of the game. By the time war broke out in 1939, over 200 clubs in England alone had become affiliated to the SRA.

Venue

Squash is played in an enclosed rectangular space 32ft long by 18.5ft wide (9.754 x 6.401m) for singles, and 45ft x 25ft for doubles. The international version uses a wider court, and a softer ball, and has different scoring.

Rules

The player winning the toss serves the ball on to the front wall of the court from either of two service boxes, 5ft 3in (1.6m) square, halfway down each side of the court. The ball must rebound into the other half of the court where the opponent hits it so that, after hitting the front wall and bouncing on the floor twice, it cannot be returned by the server. The rally continues until one player is unable to reach the ball and hit it before it has bounced twice, or the ball has been hit outside the lines denoting the boundaries of the playing area. If the player winning the rally is the server, s/he wins a point; if not, s/he then becomes the server.

There are many strokes, the most important being the drive to a length (making the ball "die" in either back corner of the court); the drop, in which the ball is hit softly so that it keeps close to the front wall; and the lob, in which the ball is lofted off the front wall over the head of the opponent forcing him to the back of the court to play the return. Finally, there is a boast, by which the ball is hit on to a side wall before it reaches the front wall, the object being to wrong-foot the opponent.

Equipment

The squash racket has a circular head of wood or plastic strung with gut, and a handle of wood or metal. The overall length must not exceed 27in (685.8mm). The internal stringing area must not exceed 8.5in long by 7.25in wide (215.9mm x 184.2 mm). The ball has an outside diameter of just over 1.5in (38.1mm) and weighs 23.3–24.6g. It is made of rubber or butyl, or a combination of both, and is hollow and "squashy". It is usually black in colour.

Scoring

A game consists of 9 points, except that, if the score reaches 8 points to each player, the player who first reached 9 points has the option of setting the game to 10. If s/he does not exercise this right, the game goes to the first player to reach 9. It is important to remember that a player can score a point only if s/he started the rally as server. A match is won by the player who first wins three games. In the USA, a game is played to 15 points. At 13-all the receiving player may choose his/her call. If the score reaches 14-all without first reaching 13-all, the player reaching 14 first has the option of playing "no set" (game to 15) or "set 2" (game to 16).

• DOUBLES

Rules

The two players on the serving side serve one after the other to the receiving side. The first server serves until his/her side concedes a point and then his/her partner takes over the service. This order is maintained throughout the match. When a further point is lost, the serve passes to the first player of the opposing pair. When they lose a point, the fourth player takes their turn to serve. At the beginning of each new game, however, the serving side loses the right to serve after the loss of only one point. The side winning a game has the choice of serving or receiving at the beginning of the next game. At the start of each game one player from each pair is designated to receive the service in the left-hand court, and the other player in the right-hand court. The receiver may not return faulty serves.

Scoring

The game is played to 15 points, with set calls as for North American singles (see above). If the non-serving side wins a rally, a point is added to its score.

Clothing

Dress is informal but white, or light clothing is often worn and appropriate court shoes are worn which do not mark the court.

STOOLBALL

Introduction

Stoolball is an 11-a-side ball game.

History

Stoolball, because of the simplicity of the equipment involved, began as a sport which the masses could play. It was one of the two older pastimes from which the modern game of CRICKET probably sprang. It was from CLUB BALL that cricket derived the use of the straight bat and of fielders, but the idea of bowling at a wicket, an essential feature in the development of cricket, was borrowed from stoolball where, as its name suggests, the "wicket" was a stool. In the later development of cricket, the target at which a ball was bowled was often the entwined fencing, made of wicker, used by shepherds on southern English downs.

During the reign of Elizabeth I, the Earl of Leicester, with a great number of attendants and country people "went to

Wotton Hill, where he plaid a match at stoball". Stoolball was then a hand game in which the bowler's aim was to strike the stool with the ball, and the batsman's was to defend it with his hand. There were apparently no runs in the sense of the batsman covering the length of the pitch, but if the bowler struck the stool or caught the ball after the batsman had struck it and before it hit the ground, the players changed places, while every time the batsman made a successful stroke, he scored one point.

Venue

The game is played on a pitch 16yds (14.63m) long, with a bowling crease 1yd (0.9m) long at a distance of 10yds (9.14m) from either "wicket".

Rules

The ball is bowled underhand and the bowler must have both feet behind, and within the limits of, the bowling crease at the moment of delivery. The delivery is a "no ball" if the ball hits the ground before it reaches the wicket; if it is thrown; or if it reaches the stake less than 12in (0.3m) from the ground. A "wide ball" is one bowled out of reach of the striker and one run is added to the score of the batting side, although if the striker jumps and hits the ball, it ceases to be wide.

Deliveries are made in "overs" of eight balls each, to each wicket alternately. No balls and wides are not counted as part of the over.

The striker is out if:

The ball, when bowled, hits any part of the face of the wicket (except the stump).

The ball, having been hit, is held clean in the hand, or hands, of one of the opposing team, without touching any other part of

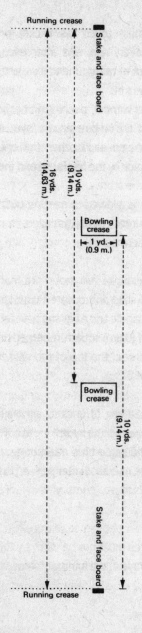

Stoolball Pitch
The striker at the top wicket (i.e. stake and face board) faces bowling from the bottom bowling crease, and vice versa.

the body above the wrist.

While the striker is running or preparing or pretending to run, the ball is thrown by one of the opposite team so that it hits the face of the wicket.

Any of the opposite team hits the face of the wicket with the ball before the bat or hand of either of the strikers touches it.

With any part of his/her person the striker stops the ball which, in the opinion of the bowler's umpire, would have hit his wicket.

A player is not out if: caught or bowled on a no ball; owing to obstruction by a fielder, s/he is unable to touch the wicket; the ball hits the side of the wicket when thrown in by a fielder.

No obstruction at the wicket by any player is allowed. The batsman is counted in his ground if, in the event of dropping his bat, he touches the wicket or stump with his hand. The batsman must touch his wicket on commencing his innings, after every run, and after every attempt to run. A non-striker is out of his ground unless, with his bat in hand, he can touch the wicket.

If a fair delivery passes the striker without touching his bat or person, and any runs are obtained, the umpire signals "bye". If in running the strikers have crossed each other, the one running for the wicket which is struck by the ball is out and the incomplete run does not count in the score.

If "lost ball" is called, the striker is allowed three runs, but if more than three have been run before "lost ball" is called, then the striker scores whatever has been run.

Equipment

The ball, slightly smaller than a ROUNDERS ball (not more than 7.5in – 190mm – in diameter), is solid and covered with kid leather. The bat has a short, stout handle and a flat and bevelled side. The "wickets" are boards, 1ft (0.3m) square, mounted on stakes driven into the running course, the top of the wicket being 4ft 8in (1.4m) from the ground.

Scoring

Scoring and rules are similar to those of cricket, although simpler. The batting side defends the wickets by striking at balls delivered by the opponents, at the same time attempting to score runs by running from crease to crease after striking the ball. One peculiarity of the game is that a "century" is in fact a score of 50 runs.

Clothing

Players wear shin-pads, and gloves must not be worn by the wicket-keeper. Plimsolls are the only form of footwear allowed.

SURFING

Introduction

Surfing or surf riding is the art of planing on the forward portion of a wave as it speeds towards the shore, before it finally breaks in a cascade of white water ("soup"). The movement is performed by the surfer, who should also be a swimmer, with or without the use of a surfboard or other such platform.

• BELLY-BOARD SURFING

This is performed a short-board (a "belly board", made of marine-ply or glass-fibre), an air bed, or a surf mat. Whatever the platform, the surfer rides it grasping the sides with his/her hands and pressing the upper surface close to his/her chest. In this position, his/her legs are clear of the board and can be used for steering. Since it is impractical and virtually impossible to stand up on this type of board, swim fins can be used to great advantage both in paddling out and catching up with the waves. In gentle surf, the belly board can be used as a progression to the long "Malibu" board, but in the more difficult high surf, greater experience is needed.

• BODY SURFING

Body surfing is performed without the use of any kind of board to provide a rigid surface which will plane on a shore-going wave. By rudder-like movements of the limbs s/he can turn on the wave in the same way as the board rider. In high surf even the expert requires considerable skill, whereas, in low or more gentle surf, beginners can achieve reasonable success without too much risk of being precipitated forward over the wave's crest ("taking a purler").

It is a pastime practiced by many swimmers who visit the surf beaches – the strong ones by swimming out beyond the surf and the weaker ones simply by standing in a few feet of water and waiting for the opportunity to join (or "slot in on") the oncoming waves just before they reach their peak. Success can be achieved quite quickly by the bather who is able to swim well, since s/he will have the ability to match his/her forward speed with that of the wave.

The most orthodox body position is a horizontal one, at right angles to the face of the wave, with the surfer's arms above the head. In this position, s/he can change his/her direction by head and limb movements and steer him/herself out of, and away from, the breaking point of a wave, thus prolonging the ride. The surfer takes breath by moving his head forward and upward. This creates a slight breaking action, by lowering the feet, but a few powerful crawl arm and leg strokes enable the surfer to match his/her speed with that of the wave.

• SURF CANOEING

Surf canoeing was practiced by the early Tahitians, and has become popular among present-day canoeists, who use kayaks (see CANOEING). In addition to "surfing in", those who specialize can use the peak of a wave to perform a lateral roll and even a forward loop. In the latter movement the canoe travels though 180° in a forward motion before the canoeist rolls the canoe to the upright plane while still on the wave. Lifeguards who operate from surf beaches also use a type of surf canoe which has flush decks for recovering tired swimmers and bathers. It is designed to plane and can be quickly taken out beyond the surf with the end of a double-bladed paddle.

History

Surfing originated in the primitive societies of coastal areas facing the open sea. Out of necessity the inhabitants built rafts and canoes that were light enough to paddle through the breakers to get to deeper and quieter offshore fishing grounds. With craft designed to plane, the fishermen perfected a form of surfing in order to reach the shore safely without capsizing.

The early Polynesians had a knowledge of seamanship and an adventurous spirit which took them amazingly long distances in the flimsiest of craft and they were masters of the surf when landing. There is much written evidence to suggest that surfing in the South Sea islands, such as Tahiti and Hawaii, was in vogue long before the European mariners made their historic voyages. Captain Cook, in collaboration with his lieutenant, King, and artist-clerk, Webber, made specific reference to the art of surfing in his records of voyages to Tahiti in 1777 and to the island of Oaha in Honolulu in 1778.

He reported seeing a native of the island of Otaheita, as he then called it, paddling a canoe through the surf and apparently looking from side to side waiting for a chance to ride shorewards on a breaker of suitable size. Both paddler and canoe were carried before the racing wave at high speed. After a further voyage to Hawaii, Cook described some of the diversions of these carefree people; how the young men went outside the swell of the surf, lying flat on an oval plank about the size of their own body. Their arms were used to guide the plank, while they waited for the greatest swell, then, pushing forward with their arms to keep on top of the wave, they were driven shorewards with great velocity.

Other references show that the early surfers knew the art of keeping the board straight on its journey and were able to quit the board seconds before it hit rocks.

Rules

Waves that are suitable for surfing occur on long, even, gently sloping beaches that face the open sea. They are formed far out at sea by the action of the wind on the water's surface, while the actual profile of the surf is dictated by the depth of the water and contour of the sea-bed as the waves approach the land. Local tidal streams can also effect the eventual form of the surf, by speeding up or slowing down the main flow of water as it moves towards the shore.

The gradual accumulation out at sea of a number of waves causes a mass of water to form into a rhythmic swell which travels towards the land in one big wheel-like motion. As it travels over undulations on the sea bed, or where the bottom gradually shallows, the "wheel" takes on an elliptical shape and when the bottom becomes too shallow for its forward speed the lower surface of the wheel is held back and the top half topples forward in a cascade of spray.

Surf waves can be classified into two main types, the plunging hollow breaker, or "dumper", which is tall in profile and occurs where the land rises steeply towards the beach, and the rolling breaker which has a stouter profile and flatter crest and occurs where the rise to the beach is more gradual.

Rip-currents are formed when the mass of surf rushing towards the beach makes its own escape route. In a bay, the tip will normally be returning along the two sides, but on an open beach it could be at any point where the pressure increases above the normal backflow. Rip-currents will inevitably affect some part of the surf, whether in a bay or on the open beach, and they need to be treated with caution. For the experienced surfer a rip-current can be a bonus, since s/he can use it to take him/herself out past the surf, but a beginner can easily be upset by its sudden action.

Body surfers and belly-boarders usually equip themselves with fins and therefore their paddling-out speed is achieved with comparatively little effort. The body surfer will also be able to use his/her arms in a crawl stroke while the belly-boarder will rely on paddling movements since his/her arms must also be used to keep him/her in position on the board.

The long board (Malibu) rider also uses his/her arms as paddles in propelling him/herself and his/her board and, like the canoeist, s/he can, with a greater pull on one side, steer the board in that direction. Having slotted in, the surfer takes his/her ride by sliding down the shoreward face of the wave. In this sliding movement, the surfer can increase the hydroplaning effect by flattening the board parallel to the wave's surface. With minimum drag his/her speed will increase. If, instead of planing straight forward, s/he "slides" diagonally across the face of the wave, the length of the ride can be increased.

The body surfer slots in by waiting in a sideways position for his/her wave, then, just as it is about to pass, s/he strikes out as fast as possible, in order not to be overtaken. S/he will increase, and be better able to maintain speed by dropping his or her head between his/her arms, since this will cut drag.

The belly-board rider slots in by paddling ahead of the oncoming wave. Once caught by the surf s/he then stops paddling and hangs on to the sides or rails of the board. In order to turn or change direction in this prone position, the surfer leans on the side to which s/he wishes to turn or simply puts one foot into the water.

The long-board or Malibu rider slots in much the same way as the short-board or belly-board rider but as soon as s/he has joined the wave, s/he grasps the "rails" (edges) of the board and rises to his/her knees, and then quickly to the standing position. While performing this movement s/he has to control the longitudinal and lateral stability of the board by a simple transference of body weight. By weighting and unweighting s/he is able to keep the board in trim and turn it in any direction across the face of the wave. S/he can also reduce forward speed by weighting the stern of the board. The experienced surfer will often walk the full length of the board to effect dramatic changes of direction and speed and then sway to bring about more subtle changes.

A surfer can ride the wave in a straight line to the beach (a "straight-ahead-of-wave ride") or, by weight transference, turn the board to the right or left. The board may be flattened to slide diagonally across and up the face of the wave (a "cut-out" or "cut back") so that s/he is travelling in the opposite direction to the waves.

For a straight-wave ride the surfer, without turning or sliding to either side, balances his/her board evenly, avoiding stern and lateral drag. Speed can be increased if the board is flattened so that as much as possible of its length is brought in contact with and parallel to the surface of the water. The surfer walks to the bow of the board and places five or ten toes over its end (to "hand five or ten"). Too much forward movement will bury the nose of the board in the wave and both surfer and board will be rotated by the oncoming wave.

The board can be turned by moving the feet (a "switch foot") and the body weight to the left or right so that, with a pronounced lean, that side of the board will be depressed in the water. The speed of the turn will depend on the amount of drag produced by the surfer's transference of weight. There are many variations of turn; for example, a slow turn can be combined with a slide, or a fast turn can blend into or be followed by a slide. In fact, a skilled surfer can criss-cross up and down the wave's forward face all the way to shore.

For a straight-wave ride, the surfer stands with flexed joints in a relaxed stance with one foot either side of the lateral and longitudinal centre line. A surfer who prefers to ride with their right foot forward is called a "goofy footer". It is a matter of personal preference whether the feet are sideways or diagonally along the length of the board, but the centre of gravity of the surfer will be slightly astern of a point where the lateral line bisects the longitudinal line.

To finish a ride, the surfer needs to stall the forward speed of the board if s/he is to alight safely and still keep contact with the board. If the ride is finished in the prone position, the body is edged backwards to the stern of the board, and the surfer rises to his/her knees and then into a sitting position. With the stern of the board deep in water and the legs forming a sea anchor the board will stall and wave will pass shorewards. Alternatively, for a faster stop, the prone surfer can pull him/herself forward and, while holding the forward rails, slide off into the water, drawing the board off its forward track.

To "kick-out", the surfer edges to the back of the board in order to stall its forward movement. Then, by a sharp turn, s/he kicks the board out of its forward movement.

In competitions surfers may be required to ride a number of waves. Each performance is scored separately, and points from the best waves are totalled to give a final score. In awarding points, judges take into consideration the degree of difficulty of the wave selected by the surfer and his/her ability to perform, on the most difficult part of that wave, a variety of turning and stalling movements. The surfer judges for him/herself the ideal point at which to join and finally "wipe out" (part company with a wave), since continuing with a poor-quality wave, or one that has lost force, may reduce the degree of difficulty of his/her manoeuvres and the resulting points.

Equipment

The surfboards ("boards") are usually made to the surfer's own individual requirements, according to their weight, experience and the type of surf they wish to use the board on.

Scoring

Surfers in competitions are awarded points for each wave they ride. They may score between 0.1 and 10. Maximum points are awarded for performing in the most difficult part of the wave (selected for quality and size), for the longest time, at the fastest speed, using the widest range of functional manoeuvres, and involving the highest degree of difficulty.

Clothing

Clothes for surfing really depends on the climate. Some wear "baggies" (surf shorts), a full wetsuit with long arms and legs or with short arms and legs made of neoprene rubber.

SWIMMING

Introduction

Swimming is a method of propulsion through water, the value

of which, as a physical activity and as a recreation, is regarded as second to none. In competitive swimming, there are four recognized styles of swimming, of which the fastest is front crawl, known in the rule books as "freestyle". The others are backstroke, breaststroke and butterfly. There are also events in which all four styles are combined in one race, known as "individual medley". There are also team races for freestyle only and for medley, which are known as relays.

History

Although swimming was not in the programme of the ancient Olympic Games, the sport goes back to the great days of early Greece and Rome. It was considered an important part of the training of warriors, not only as an athletic achievement but as a life-saving attribute in times of war.

Bas-reliefs in the British Museum, in London, show fugitives swimming to a fortress, and the crossing of a river by the Assyrian army, both probably dating from 880BC. In each of these, the swimmers are depicted using a stroke very similar to the modern front crawl. One even shows men using inflated animal skins as a form of aqualung.

There were races in Japan in 36BC during the reign of the Emperor Suigiu. The Japanese were the first to organize swimming nationally and an imperial edict in 1603 made it compulsory in schools; there were even intercollege competitions, and a three-day swimming meeting was organized in 1810. But Japan was a closed country and it was left to the Anglo-Saxon nations to lead the world.

Swimming was brought into the programme for the modern Olympic Games at the first celebrations in Athens in 1896, when there were three freestyle events for men and a special race for sailors on ships anchored in the port of Piraeus, where the Olympic races were held. The sport has remained in the Olympic programme ever since.

Venue

The pools vary in length, but in the Olympic Games, a 50m (164ft) pool is used. The 50m pool is 23m (75ft) wide and 2m (6ft 7in) deep. Other pools are often at least 25m (82ft) long and 18m (60ft) wide. The minimum depth is 1.2m (4ft).

Rules

Freestyle, Breaststroke and Butterfly races all start with a dive. On a long whistle from the referee, the swimmers step onto the starting platform, with both feet the same distance from the front. On the starter's command "take your marks", they each take up a starting position with at least one foot at the front of the starting platform. When all the swimmers are stationary, the starter gives the starting signal using a shot, horn, whistle or command.

Backstroke and Medley Relay races start in the water. At the referee's first long whistle the swimmers immediately enter the water. At the referee's second long whistle the swimmers return without delay to the starting position (see below "backstroke"). When all the swimmers have assumed their starting positions, the starter gives the command "take your marks". As above, when all the swimmers are stationary, the starter gives the starting signal.

The rules when a false start occurs are that the starter calls back the swimmers on the first occasion and reminds them not to start before the starting signal. After the first false start any swimmer starting before the starting signal has been given will be disqualified. If the starting signal sounds before the disqualification is declared, the race shall continue and the swimmer or swimmers shall be disqualified upon completion of the race. If the disqualification is declared before the starting signal, the signal shall not be given, but the remaining swimmers shall be called back, be reminded by the starter of the penalties, and start again.

The signal for a false start is the same as the starting signal but is repeated along with a dropping of the false start rope. If an error by an official follows a fault by a swimmer, the fault by the swimmer is written off.

• BACKSTROKE

For backstroke competitions the swimmers line up in the water, facing the starting end, with both hands holding the starting grips. The feet, including the toes, are under the surface of the water. Standing in or on the gutter or bending the toes over the lip of the gutter is forbidden. At the signal for starting and after turning, the swimmer pushes off and swims on their back throughout the race except when turning.

The normal position on the back can include a roll movement of the body up to, but not including, 90° from horizontal. The position of the head is not relevant.

Some part of the swimmer's body must break the surface of the water throughout the race, except when the swimmer is turning, or for 15m at the start of the race and after each turn, when s/he may be completely submerged. By 15m, the head must have broken the surface.

During the turn the shoulders may be turned over the vertical to the breast after which a continuous single arm pull or a continuous simultaneous double arm pull may be used to initiate the turn. Once the body has left the position on the back, there will be no kick or arm pull that is independent of the continuous turning action. The swimmer must have returned to a position on the back upon leaving the wall with some part of the swimmer's body.

When finishing the race, the swimmer must touch the wall while on their back.

• BREASTSTROKE

From the beginning of the first armstroke after the start and after each turn, the body must be on the breast and both shoulders must be in line with the normal water surface. All movements of the arms are simultaneous and in the same horizontal plane without alternating movement.

The hands are pushed forward together from the breast on, under, or over the water. The elbows are under the water, except for the last stroke. The hands are brought back on or under the surface of the water but are not brought back beyond the hip line, except during the first stroke after the start and each turn.

All movements of the legs are simultaneous and in the same horizontal plane without alternating movement. The feet are turned outwards during the propulsive part of the kick. A scissors, flutter or downward dolphin kick is not permitted. Breaking the surface of the water with the feet is allowed, unless followed by a downward dolphin kick.

At each turn and finish of the race, the touch is made with both hands simultaneously at, above or below the water level. The shoulders remain in the horizontal plane until the touch has been made. The head may be submerged after the last arm pull prior to the touch, provided it breaks the surface of the water at some point during the last complete or incomplete cycle preceding the touch.

During each complete cycle of one arm stroke and one leg kick, in that order, some part of the swimmer's head should break the surface of the water, except that after the start and after each turn the swimmer can take one arm stroke completely back to the legs and one leg kick while wholly submerged. The head must break the surface of the water before the hands turn inward at the widest part of the second stroke.

• BUTTERFLY

Here the body must be on the breast at all times, except when executing a turn. The shoulders should be in line with the water surface from the beginning of the first armstroke, after the start and after each turn and shall remain in that position until the next turn or finish. It is not permitted to roll onto the back at any time.

Both arms must be brought together over the water and brought backward simultaneously. All movements of the feet must be executed in a simultaneous manner. Simultaneous up and down movements of the legs and feet in the vertical plane are permitted. The legs or feet need not be at the same level, but no alternative movements are permitted. At each turn and at the finish of the race, the touch should be made with both hands at the same time, at above or below the surface of the water. The shoulders should remain in the horizontal plane until the touch is made.

At the start and at turns, a swimmer is permitted one or

more leg kicks and one arm pull under the water, which must bring them up to the surface.

• FREESTYLE

In a freestyle event, the swimmer may swim in any style, except in individual medley or medley relay events, when freestyle means any style other than backstroke, breast-stroke or butterfly. Also, some part of the swimmer must touch the wall upon completion of each length and at the finish.

• MEDLEY SWIMMING

In individual medley events, the swimmers cover the four swimming styles in the following order: Butterfly, Backstroke, Breaststroke and Freestyle.

In the medley relay events the styles are in a different order: Backstroke, Breaststroke, Butterfly and Freestyle. Each section must be finished in accordance with the rule which applies to the style concerned.

Swimmers are liable for disqualification if they:

Do not cover the whole distance of the race.

Finish the race in a different lane.

Do not make physical contact with the end of the pool or course.

Take a step or stride from the bottom of the pool.

Walk on the floor of the pool.

Obstruct another swimmer by swimming across into their lane or interfering with another swimmer.

Use any equipment, such as fins or flippers, to aid speed and buoyancy.

Appear at the starting block after the swimmers have been

called to the start.

Enter the water while a race is in progress.

Permit any misconduct.

Use abusive language, or fail to follow directions.

Use a relay team member twice.

Fail to complete the designated distance.

Clothing

Costumes should be non-transparent and in good moral taste. Goggles and caps are permitted and no speed or buoyancy devices are allowed.

SWIMMING, OPEN WATER

Introduction

Open water swimming is any competition that takes place in a natural body of water such as a river, lake or ocean. Long distance swimming is any competition in open water of up to 25km in length. Marathon swimming is any competition in open water over 25km.

Venue

The competition is held in water that is subject to only minor currents or tide and may be salt or fresh (sweet) water. The minimum depth of water at any point on the course should be 1m and should have a minimum temperature of 16°C.

Rules

All Open Water competitions start with all the competitors standing or treading water. They then commence swimming on the start signal. All Open Water competitions should be freestyle events and competitors should maintain a 3m clearance from other swimmers except for the first 2km after the start, at the turns, at the finish or where the race conditions dictate otherwise. Competitors can be disqualified if they: walk or jump during the race; get any support from a fixed or floating object; wear any device to aid their speed, endurance or buoyancy; use an excessive amount of grease; or are paced by another person entering the water.

SWIMMING, SYNCHRONIZED

Introduction

This form of swimming, ballet in the water, was recognized internationally in 1952. As well as having the endurance of a trained racing swimmer, the synchronized swimmer must have the skill and artistry of a ballet dancer, and the grace, rhythm, and acrobatic ability of a gymnast, to perform the somersaults, twists, spins and the leg and arm movements, both above and below the water, that are part of the art. There are three types of competition, solo, duet, and team (which consists of four or more members). Each competition has two sections, figure and routine.

Venue

Competitions are held in pools of varying lengths and sizes. The area must be at least 12m square. For compulsory figures it must be at least 3m deep, for routines at least 1.7m deep. The area may be extended but the 1.7m depth must be maintained for a further 8m. The water must be clear enough to see the bottom of the pool and the minimum temperature is 24°C.

Rules

For figure competitions a group of six figures is performed by the swimmer. The draw for the group is made in public, 18 to 36 hours before the event, from 6 groups of compulsory figures. These groups change every four years and have an official degree of difficulty, 3 in each group are 1.8 or under and the remainder are 1.9 or over, at least one figure being from each category and no more than 2 from any one category. Half the figures are of a difficulty of 1.7 or less and half of a difficulty of 1.8 or more.

Usually five or seven judges officiate, awarding marks from 0 to 10. The highest and lowest of these are eliminated before the remaining scores are averaged to one judge.

The moves are judged for their slow, high and controlled movements, and each part of the move should be clearly defined and in a uniform motion. The routine should be judged as united, taking into account the perfection of strokes, stunts and parts thereof; variety, difficulty and pool patterns; and the synchronisation of the swimmers one with the others and with the accompaniment.

For routine competitions, competitors may enter one solo, one duet and one team. International teams consist of eight members.

Scoring

Scores from the figure competition are added on to the routine competition score:

Solo – the sum of the figure marks.

Duet – the average of the figure marks of the two competitors involved.

Team – the average of the scores of each team member.

There are two marks, one for technical merit and the other for artistic impression. Both are awarded by the judges using 0.1 points. The judges marks in both cases are recorded, the highest and lowest cancelled and the remainder totalled. The technical merit mark is multiplied by 6 and divided by the number of judges minus 2, and the artistic impression mark is multiplied by 4 and divided by the number of judges minus 2. The total of the figure score, artistic impression and technical merit marks is the final score for the routine.

A one point penalty is deducted for: exceeding the time limit of 20 seconds for deck movements; or deviating from the time limit for a routine.

Two point penalties are for deliberate use of the bottom of the pool to execute a figure or aid another competitor during the routine. If a routine is interrupted by a competitor during deck movements and a new start is allowed.

If one or more competitors leaves the pool during a routine, the routine is disqualified unless the departure is caused by circumstances beyond their control.

The timing of routines is as follows: Solos – 3.5 minutes; Duets – 4 minutes; Teams – 5 minutes. There is a time allowance of 15 seconds minus or plus the allotted time. The time includes a maximum of 20 seconds for deckwork (movements on the side of the pool).

With figure competitions, contrary to the routine competition, the assistant referee instructs the swimmers when to start and the judges when to show their marks.

Clothing

For the compulsory figures, a white cap and a dark swimming costume must be worn. Routine competitors may choose any design provided it is in good moral taste and it is not transparent.

TABLE TENNIS

Introduction

Table tennis is an indoor game played by two players (singles) or two pairs (doubles) facing each other and hitting a ball with a racket so that it passes over or round a net stretched midway across the surface of a table, striking its surface at each end alternately.

History

No precise date of origin or inventor is known for table tennis, but the game seems to have resulted from efforts to miniaturize TENNIS for the home, undertaken at about the same period of the nineteenth century as the efforts to adapt it for outdoor play on the lawn.

Earliest accounts (from university common rooms and British Army officers' messes) describe improvised rackets and balls with books laid across the table in place of a net. Early names for the sport included "Flim Flam" and "Whiff Whaff" but these names never took off. Equipment for an early manufactured form is mentioned in a sports goods catalogue of F. H. Ayres Ltd in 1884, and a patent for a similar game was taken out by Barter of Moreton-in-Marsh in 1891. At about this date or just after it occurred to Gibb, a noted cross-country athlete and holder of the four-mile record in 1887, to use in domestic play a celluloid toy ball he had picked up on a visit to the USA. The sound made by this ball, first on Gibb's table, on the hollow vellum racket that was then in use, led to the registration throughout the world by his friend John Jacques of the onomatopoeic name Ping-Pong in 1904. Jacques's firm, which had previously called their version "Gossima", later sold the US rights in the new name to Parker Bros.

The monopoly achieved by Jacques meant that equipment became so expensive that Ping Pong fell out of favour until the 1920s when, to evade patent laws, the name was changed to table tennis. The sport appeared at the Olympics in 1988.

Venue

The table is rectangular – 274cm (9ft) in length and 152.5cm (5ft) in width – and the height of its flat upper surface is 76cm (2ft 6in) above the floor. This surface, called the playing surface, and including the top of the extreme edge, is divided by a net across the middle into two equal parts, called "courts"; and the whole is outlined by a line, 2cm (0.75in) broad, along each side and at the ends. A narrower line, 3mm (0.12in) broad, down the centre divides the playing surface's into server's and receiver's right and left half-courts for doubles play. The table may be made of any material so long as a standard ball, dropped anywhere on its surface from a height of 30.5cm (12in) rebounds uniformly to the height of 22–25cm (8.75–10in). The standard colour is green, which is dull so that it does not markedly reflect highlights, and not freshly applied, as it may then come off on the ball. The lines are white. The table should be firm and rigid since, if a player moves it in play, they forfeit the point.

Rules

The grip of the racket is commonly one of two chief styles, the "lawn tennis" or "shake hands" and the "pen holder". In the former, the handle is gripped against the palm by the crook of the last three, or at least the last two, fingers. The thumb is pressed along the forehand side of the blade, the forefinger (with sometimes the second at least partially adjacent) is pressed along the backhand side of the blade. It has the

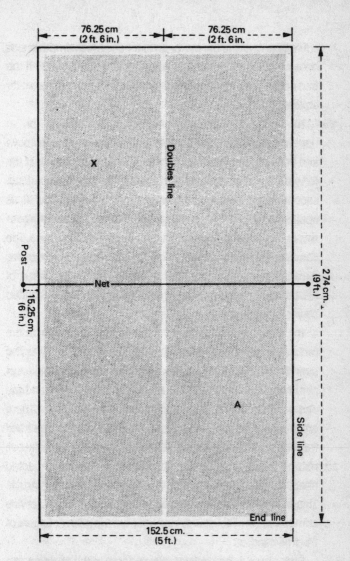

76.25 cm (2 ft. 6 in.) — **76.25 cm** (2 ft. 6 in.

Doubles line

Post — **Net** — 15.25 cm. (6 in.)

274 cm. (9 ft.)

X

A

Side line

End line

152.5 cm. (5 ft.)

Playing Surface of Table Tennis Table

A and X indicate server's and receiver's right half-courts in the doubles game. The side lines and end lines are 2cm (0.75in) wide, and the centre line for doubles service 3mm (0.125in) wide.

advantage of giving the player an extended reach on either side on a wide variety of strokes and angles of direction. With the pen holder grip, only one side of the racket is normally used for striking.

The blade is normally held below the handle, or, at uppermost, in horizontal line with it. The handle projects above and between the forefinger which is pressed back against the forward (striking) surface of the blade to grip it against the second finger, which, the others adjacent or behind it, is applied to the rear (non-striking) side. The tactical advantage of this grip is the instant control it provides for all shots used. The handicap is that mastery of a full repertoire requires exceptional agility and speed to cope with the problems of lesser reach, especially on the left wing of a right-handed player and vice-versa.

The service must be delivered by striking the ball with the racket so that it strikes first the server's court and then, passing over the net, the receiver's court. At the moment of impact of ball on racket in service, the former must be behind the end line and between an imaginary extension of the side lines. There are stringent rules providing that during service the free hand must be held flat, fingers together and thumb free, with the ball resting visibly on the palm, from which it must be projected near-vertically upwards and allowed to fall before being struck. This is to ensure that any speed or spin imparted in service comes from the racket only, and not from the palm or fingers of the free hand.

Each player in turn delivers five services to the other, except that after 20-all the service alternates after each point. In doubles, service must always be from server's right-hand half-court to receiver's right-hand half-court. Only the doubles service is so restricted; in doubles as in singles the return of all subsequent strokes may be to anywhere on the opposite side of the net. Throughout each game the same one of the receiving partners takes each of the five services. The last receiver next serves to the last server's partner, and so on.

Doubles is played according to the same principle, with the proviso that the partners must strike the ball in turn. Thus if there are two pairs, AB and XY, when A serves and X receives, the order of striking must be AXBY throughout A's five services; then XBYA, and so on. This sequence will change only for the next game, when it will become XAYB or YBXA according to who the partners X and Y select to serve first. Volleying is not allowed in either singles or doubles.

Equipment

The net stretched midway across the table is 183cm (6ft) long; it thus projects 15.25cm (6in) on each side of the table. It is 15.25cm (6in) high along its whole length. It is dark green and surmounted by a white tape. It must hang freely from a cord; the mesh must be soft (unsized) and, while not large enough to allow passage of the ball, not smaller than a defined minimum; the tape top must not exceed a maximum width. The ball is now a hollow sphere, of a defined size, weight, material, colour and bounce. The material is defined as "celluloid or a similar plastic". The diameter must be 37.2–38.2mm; the weight 2.4–2.53g (37–39g). The table tennis racket usually consists of a roughly circular or elliptical blade with diameters 125–165mm, with a handle conveniently shaped and balanced to lie comfortably in the palm of the hand or emerge upright between the thumb and forefinger and weighing 6–7oz, in most countries, but sometimes being as light as 4oz. The blade must be made of wood; if it is covered, the cover must either be of pimpled rubber applied directly to the wood (in which case the maximum thickness is 2mm), or with the pimpled rubber as the outside layer of a "sandwich" – the middle layer being of sponge (i.e. cellular) rubber – and both layers together of a maximum total thickness of 4mm.

Scoring

A game is won by the first player or pair to score 21 points; unless the score shall have first reached 20-all, when a two-point lead becomes necessary to win the game. The best-of-five games is the championship course in both men's and women's events. But best-of-three is usual in lesser competitions, junior events and in most team championships.

Clothing

Players can wear clothing of any one or two uniform colours, which usually consists of a shirt, shorts or skirt and flat-soled shoes.

TAKRAW

Introduction

Takraw is the international ball game of south-east Asia, most remarkable for the rule that in none of its many variations may the ball touch the hands or the ground. The ball ("takraw") is of woven rattan, and must not be more than 40cm (16in) in circumference, nor more than 200g (7oz) in weight. The principle of all forms of the sport is to hit the ball with the finest possible precision in the most difficult circumstances imaginable.

Venue

Hoop takraw, the most popular form of this game in Thailand, is played on a circular field 16m (52ft) in diameter, spaced round the perimeter of which stand the members of both teams (usually seven a side).

6m (20ft) above the centre of the circle is suspended the goal, usually a cluster of three hoops, each 40cm (16in) in diameter, upright, and joined together at the rims like the faces of a triangular prism.

Rules

To score, the ball must be hit through one of the hoops, to drop into an open-ended net hanging below, like that under a basketball goal. Players of the same team hope to retain possession of the ball, if it misses the goal, preventing their opponents from being able to shoot. The more difficult or stylish the shot, the more points are awarded by the judges if it succeeds.

A simple kick scores the lowest; shots with knees, elbows, or shoulders rather more; and most of all, the classic shot in which the ball is kicked with both feet together behind the back, and through a circle made by the player holding out his arms behind him. If the ball touches his hands, or the ground, it becomes dead.

A skilled group, with exceptional concentration, may keep it up for an hour. A legendary Thai maestro, Daeng, was said to have an infinite variety of shots, the most spectacular of which was to drop face down on all fours and rebound from the ground to strike the ball with his rump. (For net takraw, a form of the game comparable to BADMINTON see SEPAK TAKRAW).

TEJO
Introduction
Tejo is a Colombian game which is similar to PETANQUE, but instead of a jack, gunpowder charges are buried in the mud. The object is to detonate one of these charges.

History
Tejo pre-dates the Spanish conquest. It originated among the Muisca Indians. Among the games they invented was one in which gold discs were thrown as close as possible to a stump in the ground. After the Spaniards wiped out the Indians Tejo disappeared and did not reappear until the mid-nineteenth century. In the 1950s explosives started to be used and by 1954, Tejo was approved by the Colombian Olympic Committee as an official sport, a national Tejo league was formed and a set of competition rules was established. Today there are over 800,000 players in the national league and, since the 1990 Copa de las Americas tournament, teams from Ecuador, Florida, Guatemala, Mexico, Panama and Venezuela have applied.

Rules
The game is played on a carefully prepared patch of muddy ground and competitors take turns at hurling stones or discs at a target.

TOBOGGANING, LUGE
Introduction
Tobagganing is the sport of sliding down ice-covered tracks on small sleds, one variety of which, the luge toboggan, is ridden in a sitting position, in contrast to the forward-prone of a Cresta run "skeleton" rider.

History

Lugeing, in its modern competitive style, is comparatively young as an organized sport. It was not included in the Olympic Games until 1964, but its ancestry goes back many centuries. The sport's origins are believed to be older than those of SKIING and it is probable that in the times when the ancient Greeks celebrated their original Olympic Games, sled-like vehicles were used by inhabitants of the Alpine countries for transport as well as for pleasure.

As a winter recreation, tobogganing is recorded in sixteenth century documents. In 1520 Hans Sachs described the enjoyment he derived from it; and in 1530 Conrad Schwarz wrote a treatise about it, using the word "rodel" (German for toboggan).

The development of lugeing as a racing sport is traceable from the middle of the nineteenth century, when British tourists started sled-racing on snowbound mountain roads in the Alps. Out of this, three sports emerged – BOBSLEIGH, Cresta Run tobogganing and luge tobagganing.

Venue

The courses are all artificial with a cement infrastructure, and length ranges from 1000m to 1250m long in the men's single lugeing event. For women's singles, men's doubles and juniors the length ranges from 800m to 1050m. The gradient must not exceed 10% and there are certain features which should appear on the course. It should have a right-hand and left-hand bend, hairpin, S bend and labyrinth as well as straight sections. A starting ramp must be provided.

Rules

The techniques of lugeing have altered appreciably. The first racers used sleds similar to those used nowadays by children. The first European championship riders in 1914 steered by touching the track with their hands, wearing gloves studded for the purpose with little iron points. The modern flexibility of the sled through the manipulation of the front runners has made this technique outdated.

When turning, the luge tobogganer makes three basic movements: (1) the pulling up of the runner on the side to which s/he intends to turn, which makes the runner's aft tip brake a little; (2) the pushing in of the fore end of the runner on the opposite side to which s/he intends to turn; and (3) the placing of the weight on the outward runner, which makes it go faster than the inward runner.

Each one of these three movements makes the sled turn a little. The rider must find the right combination of the three for every particular circumstance. Due to these improvements and the progress in run-building, speeds have increased greatly.

Although riders used traditionally to adopt an upright sitting posture, the Germans, during the mid-1960s achieved aerodynamic advantages by leaning further backwards, and this technique has since become more general.

Luge runs are similar to bobsleigh runs, but are steeper (maximum average gradient, 11%) and the corners are narrower, so a heavy competitor has hardly any advantage.

TOUCH BALL
Introduction

Touch ball is a ball-and-goal team game, in effect a no-contact form of RUGBY football. In Finland it is called "salamapallo", or "lightning ball".

History

Touch ball was devised to meet the demand for an uncomplicated game with scope for skill development which could be played with simple equipment, on rough or uneven ground – hence there is no physical contact running, i.e., sprints and rests.

It was originated by J.B. Hogg, a physical education teacher at Dalziel High School, Motherwell, Scotland and Professor Lauri Pihkala, the Finnish athlete, sports writer, and theorist.

It was first demonstrated in 1961 at Vierumaki, the National Sports Centre in Finland. The rules were finalized at Santahamina near Helsinki by an international group in 1965.

Venue

The game is played on a rectangular pitch and adults may play nine-a-side on a pitch 100m by 50m (109.5yds x 55yds) for four 15-minute periods; six-a-side on a 70m x 35m (76.5yds x 38.25yds) and three-a-side on a 50m by 25m (55 x 27.5yds) pitch, in both cases for four 10 minute periods.

Rules

To start the game, and at free throws and throw-in, all players except the one in possession of the ball are in the crouch position with one hand touching the ground. The player with the ball starts the game by passing through his legs to a team mate behind. From that point progress must be by running with the ball; it is only permitted to pass or knock in a backward direction. If the ball is passed or knocked forward the other side receives a free throw.

If a player in possession of the ball is touched with the hand on the back, between shoulders and hips, he must pass the ball within three strides, for no longer than two seconds. If he does not do so the penalty is a free throw to the other side. A player may not be impeded or obstructed when passing.

A free throw is taken with the ball grounded and no member of the defending team allowed nearer than 5m (16ft 5in) from it and on a line parallel with the own goal area.

A throw-in is taken if the ball or a player holding the ball touches or crosses the side or goal line. It is taken from the point where the ball went out; no player may approach nearer than the marked 5m line from the touch-line or in-goal line.

If a defending player is touched in his own in-goal area the attacking side takes a free throw on the 5m line. If an attacking player is touched in the opposing area the defending side takes a free throw on the 5m line.

The game is controlled by a referee and two touch judges.

Equipment

It is played with a Size 4 or 5 rugby ball.

Scoring

A player scores if he grounds the ball inside the opposing in-goal area without being touched. He scores three points if the touchdown is in the centre area, two if in one of the side sections.

TRAMPOLINING

Introduction

Trampolining is an individual acrobatic sport consisting of various manoeuvres in the air performed with the aid of an apparatus called a trampoline.

History

Trampolining began in the USA, but its precise origins are not known. When trampolining was introduced as a sport in

England, it was known as "rebound tumbling", but this name seemed too technical, and trampolining was adopted. The word "trampolin" in Spanish means diving board.

Along with running, swimming and climbing, jumping up and down has always been one of our natural activities. In the Middle Ages a plank of wood was improvised to make a take-off surface for jumping over, through and on to objects; in modern times this apparatus, when used by circus acrobats, was called a teeter board. But acrobats wanted to turn more somersaults and twists, which meant they needed more time in the air and a more powerful take-off. Again the circus provided the answer. The trapeze artist, not satisfied with their aerial manoeuvres, upon landing in their safety net rebounded to perform extra somersaults and rebound tumbling developed from this. In the wastelands of the Arctic, Eskimos have been known to stretch walrus skins between stakes and jump up and down on them for enjoyment.

In 1936, an American diving and tumbling champion, George Nissen, who was a great lover of acrobatics, especially the flying trapeze, realized that something more could be made of the safety net and he made his first trampoline in his father's garage in Cedar Rapids, Iowa (USA). Nissen put a great deal of thought into the prototype. It had to be of a reasonable size to be safe, and not so large that it would take too much space; strong enough to withstand continual jumping up and down; high enough to prevent the performer hitting the floor; and above all, if it was to be of educational value, easy for school children to store and transport. The first unofficial competition was held in the USA in 1947 during the National Athletic Union gymnastic championships.

Trampolining

Venue

Trampolining competitions usually take place indoors since high winds and sun could cause difficult and sometimes dangerous conditions. A minimum headroom of 8m is required for competition performance. For synchronized competitions, the trampolines must be parallel and 2m apart.

Rules

Trampolining, very much an individual sport, is basically a challenge to perform as many twists and turns in the air as possible before returning to the trampoline surface. The performer also has to show extreme control and fine execution to gain marks for the difficulty of his or her moves, plus the technique with which s/he performs them. S/he also has to put ten movements together, one after the other, without repetition. Male and female performers compete in their own divisions.

Each competitor must perform the compulsory routines which are marked purely on form and execution by the form judges. The four judges work out of 10 marks, deducting tenths of a point for form breaks, such as bent legs, loss of height and excess movement in any direction. They then display their marks simultaneously for all to see.

The highest and lowest are disregarded and an average of the other two marks is recorded. Each competitor follows their compulsory routine with a voluntary routine. The competitor with the lowest mark performs first and the voluntary routine is completely of their own choice, but must not have any repeated skills. The voluntary routine must be written on a prepared form and handed to the referee one hour before the competition begins. Each of the ten skills is awarded a difficulty rating depending on the number of somersaults and rotations performed.

The rules for judging synchronized trampolining, another form of the sport, are the same. Two trampolines are used side by side and two performers of the same team carry out exactly the same manoeuvres, keeping in time with each other as closely as possible. Marks are deducted for unsynchronized landings.

Equipment

The trampoline has a steel frame, braced in such a way as to ensure that a landing in the bouncing area (the "bed") may be made without fear of hitting any structural members. The bed is made of nylon straps, 1in or 0.5in (25mm or 12.7mm) wide, stitched together under tension to form a mesh which will allow air to pass freely when it is depressed. The bed is secured to the inside of the frame by means of springs or an elastic suspension. The frame is covered by padding. A pit trampoline is set in the ground so that the top of the frame is level with the ground. The frame height is approximately 1m and between 3.6m and 4.3m long and 1.8m and 2.15m wide. The jump zone must be clearly marked out in red in the middle of the bed.

Scoring

The scores of the compulsory and voluntary routines are added and the competitors with the ten highest scores go forward to the final. Again the lowest-scoring competitor performs first, putting tremendous pressure on the leader of the competition. The ten finalists then have to perform one more voluntary routine which may or may not be the same as their first. Usually it is the same, since it is extremely difficult to maintain a high difficulty rating without repeats in more than one voluntary routine. After each finalist has performed, their marks are added to their previous scores and the competitor with the highest score is the winner.

Clothing

Male trampolinists wear leotards and long trousers while women wear leotards.

TRAPBALL

Introduction

This was a ball-and-stick team game, one of the many, usually energetic, sports especially associated with Shrove Tuesday, but played by children at all times of the year. It was certainly played in the fourteenth century and possibly earlier than that. It remained popular until late into the ninteenth century in some parts of Britain, particularly in the north of England. It was basically a form of ROUNDERS or latter-day BASEBALL except that the ball was projected into play by means of a trap, not thrown into the air by a pitcher.

History

There were traces of this game, and balls of leather and wood, in the Pharaohs' tombs of 4,000 years ago. The game could be played from the centre of a large ring – if a player failed to strike the ball (or "cat"), as it was tipped into the air, beyond the ring's limits, he was out. Otherwise he counted the aggregate of the distances he had struck the cat away from the centre of the ring during his innings, and set this score against that of his opponents. If the ball was caught by members of the opposing team before it touched the ground, all the "ins" were "out" and the other side went in to bat.

Venue

The game could be played on any open space, without special regard for the surface or the existence of natural hazards. When possible, and probably most frequently, a smooth area of grass on common land was used.

Rules

The trap was a stand holding a spoon-shaped piece of wood in the bowl of which the ball was placed. The spoon moved on a pivot, and when the end furthest from the ball was struck the ball was projected into the air. The batsman then had to strike the ball with his staff. Members of the opposing side were placed around the trap with the object of either catching the ball before it touched the ground or, failing that, collecting the ball from the place where it came to rest, bowling it with the intention of hitting the trap before the batsman completed his round.

The simple nature of the game and its equipment imposed little limitation on the number of players on each of the two sides.

Equipment

The basic equipment was a ball, a staff or stick and a wooden trap.

TROTTING, OR HARNESS-RACING

Introduction

This sport is a form of horse-racing in which the rider is towed along in a small cart. Whereas in horse racing the animals taking part are called thoroughbreds, trotting horses are called standardbred and also have long pedigrees. Driven by small two-wheeled vehicles, horses compete and try to finish first.

History

Trotting owes its origin to the invention of the wheel and the building of the first cart. Archaeologists working in Asia Minor discovered evidence in 1930 that trotting races were held as early as 1350BC. In the Roman Empire, chariot racing became one of the favourite sports and it is probably from the Romans that trotting took its roots as a world-wide sport.

Although since then noblemen the world over have raced horses in every manner imaginable to pass the time and encourage sport, it was not until the eighteenth century that the foundations of harness-racing, as it is known today, were laid.

Venue

An oval racetrack of mixed materials, dirt and clay, can be set for different race lengths. Courses vary, including the distance from the start to the first turn and the length of the "home stretch" (final straight run to the finish). The "wire" is a real or imaginary line from the centre of the judges' stand to a point immediately across and at right angles to the track.

Rules

The name "standardbred" denotes that the horse has to race up to a certain standard of speed. This, akin to "par" in golf, had steadily decreased in a time sense over the years as better breeding methods have produced faster horses.

There are two kinds of standardbred horse, the trotter and the pacer. The difference between the two is in the way they move their legs, called their "gait". The trotter races free-legged and has a diagonal gait, which is the near foreleg and off hindleg working in unison and vice versa. A trotter has a high knee movement and a left-to-right nodding of the head. A pacer moves both left legs in unison and then both right legs. The pacing gait is a piston-like action and is referred to as the lateral gait. The pacer sways from side to side while racing and in most cases will wear hopples – leather or plastic straps connecting front and rear legs on the same side.

Trotting can be likened to a person in a walking race where they must go as fast as they can without crossing the dividing line that separates a walk from a run. So it is with trotters and pacers. The driver must know when s/he has pushed a horse to its limit and yet be able to keep up speed in a fighting finish without going into a gallop. When a horse gallops it is referred to as a "break" and no horse may gain any advantage from it. When a horse makes a break it must be taken to the outside of the field, allowing its opponents the advantage of a run through on the inside, and must not rejoin the race until it has been returned to a trotting or pacing gait. Should a runner gain any advantage from galloping, or continually make breaks, it will be disqualified.

Pacers are slightly faster than trotters – although very little time separates the world records for the two gaits – and usually they can get off to a better start. Races take place at 25–30mph (40–48km/h) for the mile distance and driving can be quite hazardous. This has been minimized by making drivers prove themselves competent to handle a horse and cart (or "sulky") before being granted a licence, and by constructing tracks with plenty of room for manoeuvre.

Equipment

The cart is often lightweight (around 39lb, 17.7kg) and has an open dual wheel vehicle which carries only the driver and is drawn by one horse. Two shafts connect the harness (the gear or tackle which is attached to the horse and enables it to pull the cart). Harness horses wear pads (known as boots) on their legs because they are liable to knock and rub their legs in racing. Boots are of several kinds, such as elbow boots (worn high on the front legs), knee boots, quarter-boots to protect the tender quarter (heel of the foot) in front and bell boots encircling the pastern, just above the hoof. Another aid is a headpole, which is fastened alongside some horses' heads. This stops the horse turning its head to the side opposite that on which the pole is worn.

Clothing

Drivers wear protective helmets with chin straps and whips. They usually wear distinctive coloured jackets.

TUG OF WAR

Introduction

Tug-of-war is a contest of strength and skill between two teams pulling against each other from opposite ends of a long, thick rope.

History

Few athletic events have a history reputedly so long and yet so scantily documented as tug-of-war. It is said to have originated in the harvest-gathering of ancient China; to have been used to train slaves to haul stones up the Sphinx; to have developed from the routine used by sailors in hoisting sails and by soldiers in hauling guns up the mountains of India's north-west frontier. There does not seem to be any firm evidence, however, any more than there is of the origin of the name itself.

It is also supposed, at least in England, to be a peculiarly English sport with deep roots in the rural communities of the eighteenth century; but there is no doubt that it flourished as an inter-village competition in England in the nineteenth century, when opposing teams often began the pull on opposite sides of the river that separated their territories. By 1880 it had developed well enough to be recognised by the Amateur Athletics Association (AAA), and it became an approved event at athletic meetings.

Venue

The site on which the tug-of-war takes place should be flat, measuring a minimum of 60yds by 12yds, ideally oval in shape and surrounded by a barrier to prevent encroachment by the spectators. The wider the "arena" the better, thus making it possible to change the pulling area and reduce damage to the ground.

In outdoor venues, one line is marked on the ground at right angles to show where the centre of the rope must be at the start of competitions. There are also five tapes or markings fixed to the rope: 1 A red tape or marking at the centre of the rope which will be level with the ground rope at the start of every pull; 2 Two white tapes or markings, each of 4m, either side of the red centre tape or marking; 3 Two blue tapes or markings each 5m either side of the red centre tape or marking. The first puller in each team shall grip the rope within 30cm of these outer blue tapes or markings.

Indoors there must be a mat for indoor tug-of-war with a minimum length of 27.4m and width of 90cm. There should be three lines on the ground or mat, at least 4m apart with a red centre line and two white lines.

Rules

A pull is won when one of the white tapes or markings has been pulled over the mark on the ground (4m), and is signalled by the judge who blows their whistle and points in the direction of the winning team.

During actual pulling, each side-judge is in a position alongside the competing team, on the opposite side of the rope to the judge. In the event of the judge signalling a caution, the side-judge shall inform the offenders, naming the team and adding "first caution" or "final caution".

Borrowing

A maximum of two men may be borrowed for a specified weight competition but no club shall be allowed to borrow any man for any competition at catchweight where eight pulling members from that team are or have been present. A man injured in a previous competition may be substituted in a catchweight team at the discretion of the chief judge.

Dropping a Man

If one team loses a player through injury the decision to "drop a man" from the opposing team is left entirely to the discretion of that team's coach. The "dropped man" shall rejoin his team for the next round, but the injured man may not return in that day's competitions. However, in all championships recognized by the Tug-of-War Association, and any designated by the Services, if a player is dropped through injury, the opposing team shall not drop a player.

Anchor Man's Grip

Initially, the anchor man takes up his position and places the rope around his body in the approved manner for the inspection of the judge. The approved manner: the rope must pass under one armpit diagonally across the back and over the opposite shoulder from rear to front. The remaining rope shall pass in a backward and outward direction and the slack shall run free. He shall grip the standing part of the rope with both arms extended forward.

Pullers Grip and Position

From the start the rope must be taut, every pulling member shall hold the rope with both bare hands by the ordinary grip, i.e. the palms of both hands facing up, and the rope shall pass between the body and the upper part of the arm. Any other hold which prevents the free movement of the rope is a lock and is an infringement of the rules. The feet must be extended forward of the knees and team members should be in a pulling position at all times.

Infringements

Competitors can be disqualified for: sitting; leaning (touching the ground with any part of the body other than the feet); locking the rope (no knots or loops or locked across any part of the body or member of the team); incorrect grip; incorrect propping (holding the rope in a position where it does not pass between the body and the upper part of the arm); climbing (passing the rope through the hands); rowing (repeatedly sitting on the ground whilst the feet are moved backwards); incorrect anchor man's grip; footholds (making indents in the ground in any way before the command "Take the strain" is given); foul or abusive language; talking to the coach during the pulling; and use of water (for any purpose).

Cautions

For any infringements during the pull, a judge shall, in addition to naming the team, call "First caution" clearly pointing with one finger, or "Final caution" clearly pointing with two fingers in the direction of the offenders. A team will be deemed guilty of an infringement even though only one member offends. Only two cautions can be given in any one pull. However, the judge has the authority to disqualify a team or teams without caution for any offence against the rules.

Equipment

The rope is not less than 10cm and not more than 12.5cm in circumference, without knots or other holdings for the hands, and is a minimum of 35m in length and 38mm diameter.

Rope markings

There are three tapes or markings fixed to the rope:

(i) A red tape or marking at the centre of the rope which is level with the centre red ground tape or marking at the start of every pull.

(ii) Two blue tapes or marking each 2m either side of the centre red tape or marking. The first puller in each team shall grip the rope within 30 cm of these outer blue tapes or markings.

Clothing

Appropriate shirts, shorts, stockings and approved footwear. Boots must not be "faked" in anyway, i.e. the sole, heel and the side of the heel shall be perfectly flush. No metal toe-caps or metal toe-plates are permitted. Metal heel tips that are flush on the side and bottom of the heel are permitted. Team coaches should wear track suits with the name of their team clearly marked on the back in line with the shoulders.

UNDERWATER HOCKEY

Introduction

Underwater hockey is a game introduced in South Africa in the

1960s and adopted in England, and is played by skin-divers in swimming pools. Teams are usually teams of six using miniature hockey sticks.

Venue

The swimming pool should be 6–10ft (1.8–3.0m) deep. The playing area itself is 20–25m by 10–15m.

Rules

The puck is placed in the centre of the pool – on the bottom – while the members of both teams are on the surface. To score a goal the puck must be hit against the opponent's end of the pool. In England the game is sometimes known as "Octopush".

The stick is used to push or flick the puck along the bottom of the pool. At the end of the pool is a goal area. The object of the game is to flick the puck into your team's goal. An international game is 30 minutes long with 2 minutes at half time.

The only skills you need are duck diving, swimming flat on the bottom of the pool, turning on the bottom of the pool, passing the puck and being able to stay under water.

Equipment

A puck, as in ICE HOCKEY and a hockey stick.

Clothing

Players wear swimming costumes and a mask, snorkel, flippers and protective gloves.

UNDERWATER SWIMMING

Introduction

Underwater swimming, also known as skin-diving, free diving, or sub-aqua diving, is a popular water sport.

Underwater Swimming

History

Man has been swimming and exploring underwater since earliest times, gathering shellfish for food and coral for decoration. The eminent biologist, Hardy, even suggests an aquatic phase in man's evolution. There is no doubt that man is one of the few land animals able to swim effectively under water and Hardy suggests that man's hairlessness (other than his head which would have been held out of the water) indicates an aquatic habitat during a period when lack of food on land forced him to seek shells and worms, fishing with his hands in shallow coastal waters.

Before the first diving apparatus was invented, underwater swimmers who held their breath while diving became famous. Such a man was Scyllis, the Greek, who in 460BC together with his daughter Cyana, sank Persian ships at their moorings and recovered treasure from them. Rome also had a regiment of amphibious soldiers known as "Urinatores" who dived with their mouths filled with oil which they dribbled out drop by drop. Pearl divers were operating in the Persian Gulf in 1331, using breath-holding techniques and goggles made of tortoiseshell. Women divers, or "amas", have been operating for hundreds of years in Japan and Korea.

Many devices to allow man to breathe under water by leading air down a pipe from the surface were designed and built in subsequent centuries. These cumulated in the development of the diving helmet by Deane of Whitstable and Siebe in the early years of the nineteenth century. The history of the sport of underwater swimming, however, is bound up with the development of diving apparatus that would allow man to be completely independent of lines and contacts with the surface – equipment that would enable him to swim freely like a fish, rather than plod slowly across the sea bed in heavily-weighted boots and breastplate. One of the first designs for a self-contained diving dress appeared in the notebooks of Leonardo da Vinci. Nearly two centuries later, in 1680, an Italian mathematician, Borelli, designed a self-contained apparatus. Borelli's equipment included a metal helmet with a system designed to regenerate the air and a device to alter the diver's displacement so that he could rise or sink as required.

Rules

All underwater swimmers begin by becoming snorkel divers, swimming on the surface between brief breath-holding dives.

Potential divers have to be competent swimmers. The snorkel diver will usually learn to use his/her mask, fins and tube in a pool or in shallow water. As the human eye is designed to see in air, clear vision is impossible underwater unless a face mask is worn. The face mask covers the eyes and nose, but leaves the mouth free for breathing through the snorkel tube (or aqualung mouthpiece). Masks are made out of moulded rubber with toughened glass in the single face plate which prevents the double vision caused by ordinary swimming goggles.

Indentations in the rubber on the lower edge of the mask allow the nose to be held through the mask. Blowing through the nose then allows the diver to adjust or clear his/her ears of the increasing pressure by passing air through the Eustachian tubes to the inside of the eardrum. The design of mask also allows the diver to blow air into it from his/her nose in the event of its being squeezed against his/her face by the water pressure. To prevent misting during the dive, divers usually spit into their masks and then wash them out before entering the water.

Toughened rubber fins are worn on the feet and provide the necessary propulsion, leaving the hands free to manipulate other equipment. The diver uses a slow, wide, crawl-kick, which presses the surfaces of the fins against the water thus forcing him/her forward.

The third item of basic equipment is the snorkel tube. This does not allow the diver to breathe underwater, but to breathe easily while on the surface, without lifting or turning the head. In this way, the diver can keep a continual watch on the sea-bed below. When the snorkel diver descends, his/her tube fills with water, but this is blown when s/he exhales on returning to the surface.

Snorkel divers leave the surface by means of a "duck dive". The diver lies flat, takes a deep breath, bends from the waist, and glides down until his/her fins are underwater and can be used to swim down.

Equipment

The basic equipment is a face mask, snorkel tube and a pair of foot fins or "flippers". Spear-fishermen add an underwater gun to this equipment and experts may reach depths of 100ft (30m) while holding their breath. Snorkel diving is also essential preliminary training for the main branch of the sport, diving with an aqualung.

Clothing

Most underwater swimmers need protection against cold; this is provided by a neoprene wetsuit, consisting of a jacket, hood, trousers, bootees, and, if necessary, gloves.

VOLLEYBALL
Introduction

Volleyball is a team game played with six players on each side. In play, two teams, each of six players, take up positions in their respective courts and aim to deliver the ball over the net and to "ground" it in their opponents' court, while preventing it from touching the floor of their own.

History

Volleyball, like BASKETBALL, was developed in the USA, and owes its beginning to the YMCA movement. The physical fitness instructor at the YMCA at Holyoke, Massachusetts, in the last decade of the nineteenth century, W. G. Morgan, formulated the game of volleyball in 1895 especially for middle-aged men who found basketball too vigorous. Morgan wrote later: "There was a need for a game which all age-groups could play, and above all I felt that this game should be enjoyable. To begin with we used a basketball and batted it up with the hands; then we placed a net between the teams. We found the basketball unsuitable by reason if its size and weight, and we therefore asked Spaldings to make a special ball of calf skin."

As the game progressed, certain skills developed, and soon teams wished to play against each other on a competitive basis. Thus volleyball moved beyond the original concept of its founder for, in addition to being a purely recreational game, it now took on the status of a serious team sport. From the beginning, the ball had to rebound from player to player; holding, catching, pushing and throwing were not allowed, and this is still one of the important characteristics of the game.

It was not until after the First World War that teams of six became established. Skills grew more sophisticated, and gradually the mode of play, i.e. receive, set pass, smash, evolved. The service was by now required to be direct from server to opponents, and the whole concept of tactical play with attack and defence systems began to develop. The International Volleyball Federation (FIVB), founded in 1947 to formalize and regulate international rules and competitions, now has over 100 member countries. Volleyball now features in the Olympic Games.

Venue

The court is a rectangular area 18m by 9m (59ft 0.75in by 29ft 6.5in), divided into two equal square courts by the centre line, above which spans a taut horizontal net at a height of 2.43m (7ft 11.6in).

Rules

Play begins when the server, standing behind the base line and in the service area, strikes the ball with one hand or arm to deliver it over the net and into the opposite court. Here a member of the receiving team attempts to save the ball and in the same movement to loft it for a team mate to play.

Each team is allowed to contact the ball a maximum of three times before returning it to the opposite court, but any one individual may not touch, or be touched by it, twice in succession (a "double hit"), and the ball must always be played cleanly by the hands, with no suggestion of holding ("held ball"), lifting, or carrying. Indeed, the whole character of the game stems from the finesse, precision and elegance which this handling rule engenders.

Play continues in the form of a rally until one team allows the ball to touch the ground in its own court, or fails to return it correctly. If such a rally is won by the serving team, a point is

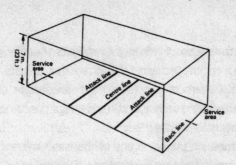

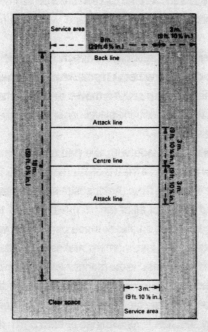

Volleyball Court

Shaded area in the plan view (below) is the recommended clear space 3m (9ft 10.13in) deep on all sides of the playing space. (For indoor volleyball the clear space may be 1m (3ft 3in) wide, and in outdoor play not less than 2m (6ft 7in) wide.) The service area must have a minimum depth of 2m at each end. In the perspective view (above) the fine lines indicate the vertical depth of the court, which must be free of any obstruction to a height of 7m (23ft).

added to its score; if won by the receivers a "side-out" occurs, whereupon the receiving side is entitled to take the next service. Players of this team must now rotate one place clockwise before service, and in this way all players take a turn in each position during a "set".

A "front-line player" is any of the three nearest the net, numbered 2, 3 and 4 in the rotation order. Similarly, a "back-line player" occupies the back row and will be numbered 1, 6 or 5.

On receiving the ball from the opponents, a defending player returns it near to the net in his/her own court, where a "set-pass" specialist (the "setter") moves to a "set" the ball with a high pass which a front-line player can smash to the floor of the opponent's court.

The "block" is made with the hands and arms near, and above, the net and is a means of attempting to stop the smash (or "spike") coming from the opposite side. The block may be performed by any or all of the front-line players. The "tactical ball" (or "dump") is an attack made by a player who feigns a smash, and at the last moment makes a soft pass over the block. The "volley pass" is the manner in which the ball is struck above shoulder level using the fingers of both hands simultaneously, while the "dig pass" is the action of striking the ball below shoulder level with one or both arms. The one-arm dig pass is less reliable and is usually used only when diving to recover the ball. The two-arm dig pass is performed with the hands clasped and the arms extended.

Two tactical moves are the "switch", in which the front-line and back-line players move laterally to positions on court where their individual abilities may be used to advantage, and the "penetration" in which a back-line player moves forward to the net, after the service, in order to act as setter, freeing all the front-line players to take part in the smash. A back-line player may only make a smash if they take off behind the attack line.

"Overlapping" is a positional fault. At the moment the ball is served, the back-line player must be behind the corresponding front-line player, the position of players being judged according to the positions of their feet.

Equipment

The ball used is 65–67cm in circumference and 250–260g in weight. It must be of one colour, without laces and made of a supple leather case, with a bladder of rubber or similar material. The volleyball net is 31ft 2in (9.5m) long, 3ft 3.5in (1m) deep, and of a mesh whose squares are 4in (10cm) wide. A double thickness of white canvas or linen, 2in (5cm) wide, should be stitched across the top.

A removable band of white material, 2in (5cm) wide and 3ft 3.5in (1m) long, should be fixed at the sides of the net above and perpendicular to the side lines. Often in matches, parallel to the tapes and just outside them, two flexible aerials are fastened to the net at a distance of 30ft 10in (9.4m) from each other. These two aerials are 6ft (1.8m) long, with an approximate diameter of 0.4in (10mm), and are of fibreglass or similar material and extend 2ft 8in (80cm) above the top of the net.

Scoring

Points are scored only by the serving team, and the first team to reach 15 points wins the set, providing that they have a lead of 2 points. If at 15 the lead is less than 2, e.g. 15–14, play continues until a 2-point lead is established. A match is decided by the best of three or five sets as agreed prior to commencement, although all international and national league matches must be played to the best of five.

Clothing

Clothing should consist of a vest or jersey, shorts, and light pliable shoes (rubber or leather) without heels. Players must not wear any object or article which may cause injury during play. Players must dress in neat clean clothes of the same colour. If the weather is cold they may play in numbered track suits. Jerseys with long sleeves are usually preferred, to protect the arms when "digging" the ball.

WATERPOLO

Introduction

As the name suggests, water polo is a ball game played in the water. In the late nineteenth century, when the game was being pioneered in Britain, it was also called football-in-the-water, and the basic aim, as in Association FOOTBALL, is for the attacking side to get the ball into the net of the defending side, usually after a series of passing movements.

History

Britain was the originator of the game. As far back as 1870, or earlier, a game in the water, with a ball, was being played. As it bore some relation to soccer, it became known as "football-in-the-water". But it was not until 1885, after much thoughtful pioneering work and pressure from Scotland and the Midlands, that the governing body for the sport (The Swimming Association of Great Britain, later to become the Amateur Swimming Association) recognized the game.

The early rules were primitive and varied from area to area.

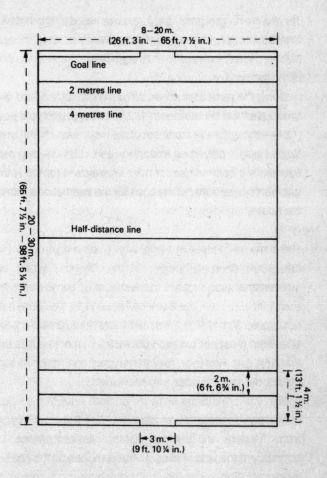

Water Polo Field of Play

The minimum distance from the goal line to the back of the goal net (not shown in the diagram) is 30cm (11.75in). The minimum depth of water is 1m (3ft 3in).

There were no goal posts and a goal was called a "touch-down" (shades of rugby football), since the swimmer could score by placing the ball with both hands anywhere along the full width of the bath end or pontoon.

Slowly the game took shape. William Wilson of Scotland, who drew up a local set of rules in 1877 and suggested goal posts (1879) – though these stood out of the water at each end of the field of play – played an important part in its development. Eventually a common set of rules was agreed for the British game and these became the basis for the international rules of the future.

Venue

The game takes place in a pool with water a minimum of 1m (3ft 3.5in) deep, although for the Olympic, world and international tournaments the water must be nowhere less than 1.8m (5ft 11in). The distance between the goal lines must not exceed 30m (98ft 5.25in) nor be less than 20m (65ft 7.5in). The width must not exceed 20m (65ft 7.5in) nor be less than 8m (26ft 3in). However, for international and major national events, the maximum playing area is used.

Distinctive marks are provided on both sides of the field of play to denote the goal line, 2m (6ft 6.75in) and 4m (13ft 1.5in) from that line, and the half distance (or centre) line. The boundary of the field of play, at both ends, behind the goal line is 0.3m (11.75 in).

The goal posts and crossbar are of wood, metal or synthetic material (plastic), with rectangular sections of 0.075m (3in) squared with the goal line and painted white. The goal posts must be fixed rigid and perpendicular and be equidistant from the sides and at least 0.30m (11.75in) in front of the ends of the field of play of any obstruction.

The inner sides of the goal posts are 3m (9ft 10.25in) apart. The underside of the crossbar is 0.9m (2ft 11.5in) above the surface of the water when the water is above 1.5m (7ft 10.5in) from the bottom of the bath and 2.4m (7ft 10.5in) above the surface when the depth of the water is less than 1.5m.

Limp nets are attached to the goal fixtures to enclose the entire goal space, securely fastened to the goal posts and crossbar and allowing not less than 0.30m (11.75m) clear space behind the goal line everywhere within the goal area. There may be no standing or resting place for the goalkeeper in the area of the goal except the floor of the bath.

Rules

Water Polo is one of the events in the programmes of most major swimming competitions, such as the World Championships, Olympic Games, European Championships and Pan-American Games. The only important event in which there is no water polo is the British Commonwealth Games.

The game lasts for four periods each with seven minutes of actual playing time. There is a two-minute interval between each period for changing ends while players in the water may only leave at an interval when injured or with the referee's permission. Referees may suspend play for up to three minutes for accidents or injuries.

If there is a tie and a result is required, there is a five-minute break, then two periods of three minutes play with a one-minute interval between. The pattern is continued until a decision is reached.

Equipment

The ball must be round and fully inflated, with an air chamber with self-closing valve. The circumference must not be less than 0.68m (2ft 2.75in) nor more than 0.71m (2ft 4in). The ball must be waterproof without external strappings and without a covering of grease or similar substance. Its weight must not be less than 400g (14oz) nor more than 450g (15oz).

Scoring

A goal is scored when the ball completely crosses the goal line between the posts and under the crossbar – providing it has not been punched and at least two players have touched it after a start or restart (not including the goalkeeper's attempts to save the ball). The team that scores the most goals wins.

Clothing

Players wear swimming costumes or swimming trunks, while one team must wear blue caps the other white. Goalkeepers wear red caps. No player may grease or oil their body.

WATER SKIING

Introduction

Water skiing is the act of planing on the surface of the water, in an upright position, by means of two flat boards, known as skis, which are attached to the feet. The skier is towed by a rope attached to the rear portion of transom of a power boat which is capable of speeds in excess of 15mph (24 km/h).

History

Water skiing derives from snow SKIING and aquaplaning. In the snowfields, villages have for many years held ski-tow races where the skiers are pulled along by sure-footed ponies. This sport is akin to present-day water skiing; the skier leans backward, resisting the forward motion of the galloping horse, just as the water skier resists the acceleration of the power boat. It had been known for at least a century that canoes would plane on incoming breakers and that, where these breakers were prolonged, quite long runs could be achieved.

With the development of the motor boat, first as a displacement hull and later as a planing hull, enthusiasts conceived the idea of a swimmer being towed on a flat board or aquaplane. One such enthusiast was the American, Fred Walter, who in the early 1900s filed the first patent for a pair of water skis which were probably no more than sophisticated aquaplanes. At the same time, in the Haute-Savoie province of France, a group of French army officers are reputed to have used their snow skis as aquaplanes in tow behind a boat on Lake Annecy. Improbable as this story is, water skiing was definitely beginning to emerge as a sport and in 1935, on Long Island, USA, the first competition was watched by a large crowd. Only four years later the first American national championships were arranged by a newly formed governing body.

Similar developments took place at French resorts on the Mediterranean coast and, in 1946, the increase in the number of countries taking part in the sport made possible the formation of an international controlling and co-ordinating body, known as the World Water Ski Union (WWSU). In the colder climate of Great Britain the sport took longer to develop. Even so, the British Water Ski Club was founded in 1949 and started skiing at Ruislip, Middlesex.

Rules

The water skier holds a handle at the end of the tow rope, assuming a slight backward lean so that their body provides the necessary resistance to the speed by which the planing position is achieved. Providing the water is comparatively calm, planing or skiing is a simple movement. Since balance is all-important, the most critical and difficult operation is the start, of which there are four main types: the beach start, the dock start, the deep water start and the scooter start.

In a beach start the skier sits in the water holding the tow bar, with the skis 6in (152mm) apart, tips turned slightly inwards and in line with the stern of the boat. From this position they lean forward in a crouch as the skis point to the surface of the water – the boat accelerates smoothly and the skis rise to the surface against the pressure of the water. The dock start is a short cut to the planing position whereby the skier sits on the dock or pontoon and, with the acceleration of the boat, is launched on to the surface of the water. The deep-water start is an elaboration of the beach start and is achieved from exactly the same basic position of the body and skis. It is invaluable when a skier wishes to restart a run after a fall. The scooter start is similar to the dock start in as much as it is a method of dry launching. It is used by mono-skiers who, equipped with one ski, step from the shore on to the water with a "scooting" action as the boat accelerates.

Turning is an essential part of skiing technique. From a line directly behind the boat a skier is able to make simple turns by crossing outside and back into the wake made by the boat. In the initial stages a turn is made simply by pointing the whole body in the required direction.

Equipment

There are various types of ski which are used for the different events but no ski must be wider than 30% of its length and skis must be safe with no dangerous splinters or chippings. The tow line is approximately 20m (65ft) long and is fixed at the centre line of the boat. The lines must have 12 strands with 60 yarns per strand; a diameter of 6.3mm at a 5.5kg load and a minimum breaking load of 590kg.

• BAREFOOT SKIING

This was introduced by Dick Pole jr at Cypress Gardens in Florida (USA), in 1947, and is still used as a stunt by those who have the nerve and tenacity. It does not hurt the feet unless continued for a long time when there is danger of the friction causing a burn. Launching is usually achieved by stepping off a single ski, while planing, on to one foot. When this is taking some of the body weight, the other foot is taken out of its binding and placed on the water. Some skiers can perform tricks while barefoot skiing and several experts are able to jump out of their skis, landing in the planing position on bare feet. Starts can also be made from stomach or back positions. Running starts from the jetty or beach are becoming popular and in barefoot competitions a miniature jump is used. Distances in excess of 8m (26ft) have been achieved. Slalom is also performed on bare feet.

• SKI KITE-FLYING

The kite is a framework of light alloy covered with over 7sq m (75sq ft) of canvas. Wearing either one or two skis and attached to the kite by a body harness for safety, the skier is towed by the boat into the wind. Depending on wind speed, the performer will glide at speeds of about 64km/h (40mph.) and heights of well over 30.5m (100ft) have been recorded. For a landing, the boat reduces speed and the skier and kite glide on to the water. In competitive flying, the skier will fly a slalom run on a similar course to regular slalom: a second discipline is a series of acrobatic feats to be executed on a points system, e.g. open swan position, somersault over bar, etc.

Figure skis ("retournement" or trick skis) are considerably shorter than general-purpose skis. They are banana-shaped at their extremities and without fins so that they will run forward, backward, or sideways.

• SLALOM

The slalom course is 259m (283yds) long and 23m (75ft) wide with gate and turning buoys moored on the outer limits. The skier "virages" from side to side in order to turn round the outer side of each buoy. Boat speeds are approximately 52km/h for women and around 55km/h for men increasing at 2km/h intervals after each successful pass through the course to a maximum of 58km/h.

In the slalom event the boat passes down the centre of the slalom course, while the skier swings across its wake to pass six buoys on their outside. The skier must then follow the boat through the central gate at the end of the course.

Scoring

Competitors have two runs, and for the run to score, the competitor must have followed the boat through the course entry gate and have left through the end gate. The tow rope is shortened on each run and points are awarded according to competitors' proximity to the correct time, the number of buoys effectively negotiated, and the number of times the competitor returns to the boat's wake on the way to the buoys.

To perform a jump, the skier is towed from the water up a

ramp measuring approximately 7.3m (24ft) long by 3.9m (13ft) wide. The height of the ramp may be varied up to 1.8m (6ft) to accommodate both men's and women's events. The boat for men travels up to 57km/h and 51 km/h for women. In order to reduce friction and the risk of accidents, the ramp is coated with prepared wax and kept continually wet. Part of the lower end is under water to allow smooth entry by the skier. As the boat, travelling down the centre of the course, approaches the ramp, the skier holds the course steady from a position outside the wake furthest from the ramp. In competition the water skier has two jumps in the first round and three jumps in the final round.

• TRICK SKIING

This forms part of the traditional group of water ski competition (slalom, jumps and tricks).

Competitors perform on specially designed skis and are allowed two 20-second passes within two sets of buoys, 175m (574ft) apart. Within this time and distance they are required to perform as many tricks as possible to the satisfaction of the judges. The judges' stand is located on shore approximately midway between the two buoys. Marks are awarded by the judges for each trick.

Scoring

Skiers perform the tricks and each trick successfully completed inside the course has a tariff value according to its difficulty. The scores are then totalled for both passes to give a score for the round.

WEIGHTLIFTING

Introduction

Weightlifting is a competitive sport (not to be confused with weight training), whose object is to find the person who can lift the biggest weight. It is a world-wide sport and on the programme of the Olympic Games and all regional games.

History

Lifting heavy stones was a pastime in early antiquity and in Greece huge boulders inscribed with the names of athletes purported to have lifted them hundreds of years BC can be found. The custom persisted in many parts of Europe through the Middle Ages into comparatively recent times. There is a huge stone weighing 400lb (181kg) in the courtyard of the Munich Apothekerhof castle. An inscription on the wall above it says that Duke Christopher of Bavaria proved his manhood in 1490 by lifting it and throwing it. Such feats became a test of manhood in many countries. Manhood stones or "clach cuid fir" can be found in some Scottish castles.

Modern weight-lifting with bar-bells and dumb-bells became popular towards the end of the nineteenth century and was fostered by strong-man acts in circuses and music halls. The first championship open to the world was held in the Café Monico, London, on 29 March 1891 and was won by Levy of England. The first Olympic Games in 1896 also featured weight-lifting.

Venue

The competition platform must be square, measuring 4m on each side. When the floor surrounding the platform has similar or the same colouring, the top edge of the platform must have a different coloured line of at least 150mm. The platform may

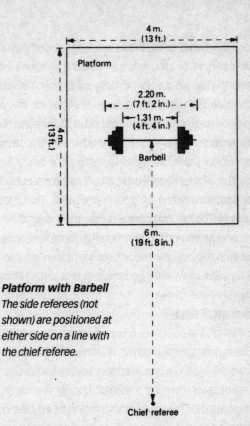

Platform with Barbell
*The side referees (not
shown) are positioned at
either side on a line with
the chief referee.*

be made of wood, plastic or any solid material and may be covered with a non-slippery material. The height of the platform must be 50–150mm.

Rules

The IWF recognises two lifts known as the "snatch" and "grab" and they must be executed in the following sequence.

The snatch: the barbell is placed horizontally in front of the lifter's legs. It is gripped, palms downwards and pulled in a single movement from the platform to the full extent of both arms above the head, while either splitting or bending the legs. During this continuous movement, the bar may slide along the thighs and the lap. No part of the body other than the feet may touch the platform during the execution of the lift. The weight that has been lifted must be maintained in the final motionless position, arms and legs extended, the feet on the same line, until the referees give the signal to replace the bar-bell on the platform. The turning of the wrists must not take place until the bar has passed the top of the lifter's head. The lifter may recover in his or her own time, either from a split or squat position, and finish with the feet on the same line, parallel to the trunk and the bar-bell. The referees give the signal to lower the bell as soon as the lifter becomes motionless in all parts of the body.

The Clean and Jerk

For "the clean", the bar-bell is placed horizontally in front of the lifter's legs. It is gripped, palms downwards and pulled in a single movement from the platform to the shoulders, while either splitting or bending the legs. During this continuous movement, the bar may slide along the thighs and the lap. The bar must not touch the chest before the final position. It then rests on the clavicles, or on the chest above the nipples, or on fully bent arms. The feet return to the same line, legs straight, before performing "the jerk". The lifter may take this recovery in his or her own time and finish with the feet on the same line, parallel to the plane of the trunk and the bar-bell.

For the jerk, the athlete bends the legs and extends them as well as the arms to bring the bar-bell to the full stretch of the arms vertically extended. He or she returns the feet to the same line, arms and legs fully extended and waits for the referees' signal to replace the bar-bell on the platform. The referees give the signal to lower the bar-bell as soon as the lifter becomes motionless in all parts of the body.

A maximum of 3 attempts is allowed on each lift.

After the clean and before the jerk, the lifter may adjust the position of the bar. This must not lead to confusion. It does not mean the granting of an additional jerk attempt but allowing the lifter to:

1) Withdraw the thumbs or "unhook" if this method is used.

2) Lower the bar in order to let it rest on the shoulders if the bar is placed too high and impedes the breathing or causes pain.

3) Change the width of the grip.

General rules for all lifts

The technique known as "hooking" is permitted. It consists of covering the last joint of the thumb with the other fingers of the same hand at the moment of gripping the bar. In all lifts, the referees must count as "No lift" any unfinished attempt in which the bar has reached the height of the knees. After the referees' signal to lower the bar-bell, the lifter must lower it in front of the body and not left it drop either deliberately or accidentally. The grip on the bar may be released when it has passed the level of the waist.

A competitor who cannot fully extend the elbow due to an anatomical deformation must report this fact to the three referees and the jury before the start of the competition. When snatching or cleaning in the squat position, the lifter may help the recovery by making swinging and rocking movements of the body. The use of grease, oil, water, talcum or any similar lubricant on the thighs is forbidden. Lifters are not permitted to have any substance on their thighs when arriving in the competition area. A lifter who uses any lubricant is ordered to remove it. During the removal, the clock goes on. The use of chalk (magnesium) on the hands, thighs, etc., is permitted.

The following are forbidden for all lifts:

Pulling from the hang.

Touching the platform with any part of the body other than the feet.

Uneven or incomplete extension of the arms at the finish of the lift.

Pausing during the extension of the arms.

Finishing with a press-out.

Bending and extending the elbows during the recovery.

Leaving the platform during the lift, i.e. touching the area outside the platform with any part of the body.

Replacing the bar-bell on the platform before the signal.

Dropping the bar-bell before the signal.

Failing to finish with the feet and the bar-bell in line and parallel to the plane of the trunk.

Failing to replace the complete barbell on the platform, i.e. the complete bar-bell must first touch the platform.

Incorrect movements for the snatch:

Pausing during the lifting of the barbell.

Touching the head of the lifter with the bar.

Incorrect movements for the clean:

Placing the bar on the chest before turning the elbows.

Touching the thighs or knees with the elbows or upper arms.

Incorrect movements for the jerk:

Any apparent effort of jerking which is not completed. This includes lowering the body or bending the knees.

Any deliberate oscillation of the bar-bell to gain advantage.

The athlete and the barbell have to become motionless before starting the jerk.

Equipment

The bar-bell consists of the bar, discs and the collars. The men's bar should weigh at least 20kg, while the women's bar should be 15kg. The discs are all coloured appropriately according to weight ranging from the heaviest red disc (25kg) down to the lightest chrome discs (0.25, 0.5 or 1.25kg). In order to secure the discs to the bar, each bar is equipped with two collars weighing 2.5kg each. Finally, the bar must be loaded with the largest and heaviest discs inside the smaller ones in descending order of weight towards the outside.

The costume may be one-piece or two-piece but must cover the trunk of the competitors. It must also be close fitting, collarless, must not cover the knees or elbows and may be of any colour. Socks may be worn but they must not cover the knees. A T-shirt may be worn under the costume. The sleeves must not cover the elbows. This shirt must be collarless. Closefitting leotard/cycling shorts may be worn under or over the costume. They must not cover the knees. But, a T-shirt and trunks must not be worn instead of the costume. Competitors must also wear shoes to protect their feet but the shoes must not give the athlete an unfair advantage or additional support. Competitors may wear special fingerless gloves but these gloves may cover only the first phalanx of the fingers. If plasters are worn on the fingers, there has to be a visible separation between the plasters and the glove.

Bandages, tapes or plasters may be worn on the wrists, the knees and the hands but may not cover more than 100mm of skin on the wrists and 300mm of skin on the knees. There is no length limit. However, no bandages are allowed on the elbows, trunk, thighs, shins and arms. In the event of an injury, plasters may be allowed on the shins. The wearing of one type of bandage may be authorized on any part of the body, but there has to be a visible separation between the costume and the bandage(s).

WINCHESTER FIVES

Introduction

Winchester Fives is a game played between four players, two on each side, in a court enclosed by four walls. The players use both hands, and gloves are worn. It is not impossible to play singles, but the shape of the court makes it unrewarding for competent players.

History

The peculiarity of the Winchester court has no obvious explanation. A few schools copied it more or less and it is quite possible that the idea for it came from the REAL TENNIS court, serving the same purpose of changing the direction of the ball if it strikes the face of it. Very few courts have been built in recent years. (See also ETON FIVES).

Venue

The courts at Winchester College are nearly the same size as a standard RUGBY FIVES court, namely 28ft (8.5m) long and 18ft (5.5m) wide. However, the back wall is 14ft (4.3m) high and the width is not identical throughout. Because the game is played in only a few schools there is no standard court and no association. The Winchester court is not quite rectangular. On the left-side wall there is a buttress, which is really a projection of the wall, 9ft 10in (2.99m) from the front wall. Here the wall changes direction at an angle of 135° for a distance of only 9.75in (25cm), making the back portion of the court very slightly narrower than the front. This projection or buttress dictates much of the positioning and tactics of the game.

Rules

Partners divide the court between front and back. The front player takes everything he can, volleying frequently, while his partner at the back does his best to return every ball that passes his partner; his main object if he cannot score the point himself, is to play his return so that the front player has a good chance of winning the point next time.

The variety introduced into the game by the buttress is considerable. Whereas the Rugby fives player can only create a difficulty for his opponent by the closeness and the differing speeds by which he hits the ball down the left-hand side wall, the Winchester player can keep his opponents in doubt by playing the ball so that it remains uncertain until the last moment whether the ball will hit the buttress and so change direction.

In Winchester fives the left-handed player, that is the player whose left hand is the stronger of the two, is at some advantage in rallies. This is because, in theory, he finds it easier to play the ball down the left-hand side wall and with greater variety and control than a right handed player. At the same time he is not at a disadvantage when serving. There is nothing to prevent him from electing to serve into the left-hand corner but if he does so he is gaining no advantage from the existence of the buttress on the left-hand side wall. For the right handed server the buttress adds to the opportunity for scoring an outright point or ace, although the opportunity is reduced since either opponent may return the serve. The game puts a proper premium on good partnership. There is less enjoyment for partners of uneven abilities and more for those who can rely successfully on one another.

Scoring

The scoring follows the same pattern as the Rugby game.

WIND SURFING

Introduction

Windsurfing is a sport which is a mixture of SURFING and SAILING.

History

Windsurfing is a young sport, its roots can be traced by to southern California where two men, Jim Drake, a sailor, and Hoyle Schweitzer, a surfer, got together and combined two sports into Wind Surfing in 1968. The heart of the invention (and patent) was mounting a sail on a universal joint, requiring the sail to support the rig and allowing the rig to be tilted in any direction. This tilting of the rig fore and aft allows the board to be steered without the use of a rudder – the only sail craft able to do so. In the early 1970s, only one board, Schweitzer's Windsurfer, was mass produced. The early 1980s was a period of tremendous growth for windsurfing, racing participation was incredibly popular, the professional World Cup tour began and the sport was awarded with Olympic status in the 1984 Los Angeles Games.

Venue

Two types of course are normal for the slalom event, depending on the conditions. In very large surf it is usual to set only two buoys, one close to the shore, the other outside, beyond the waves. Racers then have to round each mark in a "figure of eight" at least twice before finishing. Sometimes venue organizers can set up to six buoys in a "downwind" pattern, and each competitor rounds each mark once only.

Rules

There are many different types of wind surfing, but cruising is the most popular form, and involves simply "cruising" across the water.

Freestyle sailing involves putting your board and sail through a series of tricks and manoeuvres that could include turns, rail rides and sail spins. The routines are judged by a panel of experts and the most consistent performer with the most varied tricks wins.

Slalom Sailing Racing is the most popular form of high-wind sailing. This is a knockout contest, run in heats of eight to ten races at one time, with the first four or five competitors to finish advancing through to the next round, and so on up to the final. The heats can be started in two different ways: with a "Le Mans" type running start with racers lined up on the beach, who then run into the water and launch together; or with a water borne start across an imaginary line between marks on the water.

Wave performance demands some finely-tuned skills and is regarded as the most spectacular of all. The contest is "man-on-man," a surfing term for one racer against another, the best advancing into the next round.

Scoring

The judges score each move in the contest area in three categories: jumps, transitions and surfing. The more difficult, innovative and varied the moves, the higher the scores. In competitions the first place finisher scores 0.7 of a point, the

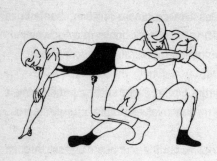

Freestyle

Graeco-Roman

Cumberland and Westmorland

Freestyle

Sumo

Styles of Wrestling

second 2 points, the third 3 points and so on. In a series of races the winner is determined by the lowest totalled points.

Equipment

Any type of board and sail maybe used. The Lechner 390 is the racing board chosen for use by competitors in the Olympic Games.

Clothing

Windsurfers often wear a functional windsurfing wetsuit and even booties to protect feet from rocky and reefy bottoms.

WRESTLING

Introduction

Wrestling, now more precisely called amateur wrestling, is an individual combat activity in which strength, skill and stamina combine to make it one of the most basic sports. There are two major types of wrestling: amateur and Graeco-Roman.

History

Wrestling is one of the oldest and most basic of all sports. Although the FILA was not founded until 1921, events had been staged for thousands of years before. Many of the holds and throws used now in the Olympic Games and world championships are the same as those used in the championships of the ancient civilizations of Egypt, Crete, China and particularly Greece. However, the origin of wrestling probably precedes even the earliest of these, since the cavemen almost certainly practiced headlocks, throws and strangleholds to defend themselves. Thus, from a necessity for survival, wrestling became a sport.

Certainly the Egyptian civilization, which was established about 3400BC, practiced wrestling, as shown in wall paintings at Beni-Hasan. On one wall there are over 200 wrestling groups and the bout ends as in modern times, when a competitor's shoulders are pinned to the ground. There are even records of some typical conversations between the wrestlers during matches. Wrestling events also took place in the Babylonian and Assyrian civilizations and in China, where the upper classes practiced a method which also included boxing and kicking – perhaps one of the origins of KENDO and KARATE.

But it was in Greece that the sport really developed. There are references to wrestling in both the *Iliad* and the *Odyssey* and it was introduced to the Olympic Games in 704BC. Theseus is credited with having laid down the first rules of wrestling in about 900BC. The rules were simple for the Olympic event – a fall was gained when any part of the body except the feet of either competitor touched the ground. The first competitor to get two falls was the winner. By the end of the nineteenth century, two styles were used in competition. Graeco-Roman (holds only above the waist) were in the Olympics of 1896 and freestyle was added in 1904.

Venue

Both these styles are fought on a raised platform with sloping sides. No ropes are used. The mat is 6–8m (19ft 8in–26ft 3in) square (8m for Olympic Games and World Championships and 6m for international matches) with a surrounding safety area of matting 2m (6ft 7in) wide.

Rules

Each bout is scheduled to last nine minutes, consisting of three minute "rounds", with a minute's rest between each. A "fall" or disqualification, however, may halt the contest before the scheduled end.

The referee calls the contestants to the centre of the mat and examines them to ensure that they are wearing regulation costumes.

A fall is given when both an opponent's shoulders are held in contact with the mat for one second. The referee strikes the mat with his hand and sounds his whistle. If no fall has been obtained by the end of the bout, both wrestlers are brought to the centre of the mat on either side of the referee. The judge's score-sheet is brought to the mat chairman who examines it and declares the winner by raising the plaque of the same colour as the winner's costume.

The referee administers warnings and cautions to wrestlers for passivity, foul holds and other infringements of the rules. A wrestler at fault is given a warning and if he offends again he is given a public caution. The referee promptly stops the bout, holds the wrist of the wrestler at fault and raises his other arm overhead, and the judge gives 1 point to the offender's opponent. Should the same wrestler offend again he is given a second public warning and a further point is awarded to his opponent. When this occurs, an additional official is brought in to assist the mat chairman. Should the wrestler offend yet again, he is disqualified and declared the loser.

Freestyle is the most popular and probably the most entertaining of the major styles. It developed from Lancashire and catch-as-catch-can styles. Any fair hold, throw or trip is allowed and all bouts are governed by international rules.

Wrestlers can only attack using their legs in freestyle and the duration of the bout is usually about five minutes without a break.

The following are fouls and not allowed:

Pulling of hair, flesh, ears, and private parts, or holding an opponent's costume.

Brawling, kicking, punching, or twisting of fingers or toes.

Applying holds liable to endanger life or limb.

A throw following a hold applied in the standing position from behind, when the opponent is turned with his head pointing downward, must be made from the side and not directly downwards. In any throw made from the standing position, the wrestler making the throw must touch the mat with his knees before his opponent's body reaches the mat, to lessen the impact and save injury.

Forbidden Moves:

When a competitor assumes a wrestler's bridge (resting his head and feet in an arched position with his back towards the mat), pressure to break this bridge must be applied directly downward and forward towards the head.

A full nelson – when a wrestler passes arms under his opponent's armpits from behind and clasps his hands behind the back of the other's neck – must be applied only sideways and not directly downward.

The the bending of an opponent's arm behind his back more than 45°. Scissor-grips to the head or body (but these may be applied to the leg), and head-holds using both arms.

The chief standing throws are:

The cross-buttock, in which a competitor heaves his opponent over his hips.

The flying mare, where he hurls him over his back, using his opponent's arm as a lever.

The double-thigh pick-up, where the wrestler scoops his opponent on to the mat by catching him behind his legs.

The ankle-and-leg dive, where he takes him off balance by grabbing one leg.

The standing arm-roll, where he clasps his opponent's arm and then, wrapping it round his own body, rolls him to the ground.

The chief ground holds are:

The nelson holds, where the competitor traps an arm and levers his opponent into a defensive position.

The cradle hold, where the wrestler pins his opponent with one hand over his head and the other through his crotch.

Scoring

The scoring system is very complicated but can be followed on the public scoreboard which shows how many points each competitor has at any stage of the bout. The referee indicates scoring points by raising his hand and signalling with the thumb and first two fingers the points scored – one, two or three as the case may be. The judge records the score on a score sheet and raises a plaque, coloured red or blue, indicating the number of points. If he disagrees with the decision of the referee he raises a white plaque. The mat chairman then decides the points to be given, which the judge must record on the score sheet.

1 point is given for executing a takedown, executing a reversal, forcing an opponent down on to one or both arms, a hold illegally blocked, an opponent leaving the mat, and others. A 15-point lead stops the contest. A bout can also be won by

technical superiority. 2 points are given for putting an opponent in danger from various ground moves (for example, rolling an opponent across the shoulders). 3 points are given for lifting an opponent from the mat, or a standing move that puts the opponent in danger with his back to the mat. 5 points are given for executing a grand technique, a move from the mat that takes an opponent off the ground and then to a position where his shoulders are in immediate danger. If the move does not cause immediate danger, it only scores 2 points.

Clothing

Wrestlers often wear regulation costumes, one of them red, the other blue. In minor events different coloured anklets are worn. The costumes are leotards, leaving the upper chest and shoulders bare. Light boots and socks are usually worn on the feet.

• GLIMA

This is practiced almost entirely in Iceland and has been popular for over 900 years. Glima is derived from the words "glitra" and "glampa", which meant "something that flashes or sparkles". The winner is called "The King of Glima" and the most outstanding "kings" have weight over 90kg (14st 2.5lb).

Before the twentieth century competitors gripped each other's trousers but in 1908 a harness was introduced. This consists of straps round both thighs, which are linked by vertical straps on the outside of each thigh. Each competitor puts his right arm over the top of his opponent's hip at the back, and the left hand holds on to a strap outside the thigh just below each upper end of the thigh bone.

Each round is of two minutes and a winning fall is scored if a competitor is thrown to the ground. Hip and ankle throws are particularly common. A fighter must keep hold of his opponent's harness and if a competitor loses his grip the bout is stopped. There is no ground wrestling.

• GRAECO-ROMAN

The rules, training and preparation are largely the same as for freestyle. The major difference is that a wrestler is not allowed to seize his opponent below the hips, nor to grip with the legs. Pushing, pressure, or lifting with the legs when in contact with a part of the opponent's body are forbidden.

Most wrestlers concentrate on either the more fluid freestyle or on the classical Graeco-Roman. But whichever they are more proficient in, they can still put up competent performances in the other style. Some wrestlers, particularly below the top international class, compete in both.

In addition to freestyle and Graeco-Roman, inter-collegiate wrestling is practiced in America. It is similar to freestyle but a few of the rules differ. A bout of nine minutes' duration is controlled by a referee, who awards the points, and a timekeeper. A fall is given when both a contestant's shoulders are in contact with the mat for two seconds. If no fall takes place the referee declares the winner, taking into account aggression and whether either of the wrestlers has scored near falls. If a draw results, a further two minutes' wrestling takes place, after which a decision must be made.

• KUSHTI

This is the national style of wrestling practiced in Iran. Contest take place on grass-land and the competitors wear tight-fitting leather trousers. The winner of the bout is the wrestler who throws his opponent on to his back on the ground. In competitions, the winner is the wrestler with the most throws to his credit.

• SCHWINGEN

This form of wrestling has been practiced in Switzerland for hundreds of years. The competitors are clothed in a vest and short leather trousers and commence a bout by taking hold of each other's trousers at the back and one of the trouser legs. On the referee's command they start wrestling, the object being to throw the opponent to the ground. For the throw to be correct the thrower must have hold of his opponent's trousers when he touches the ground. In a competition or championship a wrestler is eliminated when he has been thrown twice. Each competitor wrestlers every other, the winner being the wrestler who has the most throws to his credit.

• SUMO

This is Japan's spectacular national sport which attracts thousands of spectators to the 15-day championship events which are staged six times a year in Japan's major cities. In sumo the competitors' centre of gravity must be as low as possible and few outstanding wrestlers weigh less than 130kg (20st).

The highest position possible in sumo is "yokozuna" – grand champion – but there have been only a few who have achieved it, rarely more than two or three at any one time. The award is made by the Japan Sumo Association, which controls the sport.

Wrestlers are trained from youth under a rigorous selection and preparation policy. But all aim eventually to compete in six major annual events. Competitors wear loin-cloths, and the reigning champion enters the ring with a sword-bearer and attendant. The object of the sport is to force an opponent out of the 12ft (3.66m) circular ring. At the start of a bout, the wrestlers face each other, with both feet on the ground, in a crouching position, with both hands firmly clenched in front. Any hold is allowed, the winner being the wrestler who forces his opponent out of the ring. The sport is surrounded by great ceremony – purifying salt is hurled into the ring and the two competitors glare at each other, pounding their fists on the ground before each contest.

• YAGLI

Yagli wrestling is a national sport in Turkey and attracts large crowds to its tournaments. Contestants wear long leather breeches and the body is smeared with grease. A contest ends when one of the competitors is thrown with one shoulder and one thigh touching the ground. The annual Kirkpinar contests attract an entry of over 300 wrestlers from all parts of Turkey, and the event lasts for three days.

YACHTING
Introduction

Yachting is the use of a small sailing and power craft for pleasure, either competitively in racing or individually in cruising. Yachting is essentially a participation sport.

History

Taking to the water in small boats for pleasure dates back at least to the time of Cleopatra's barge, and, in the ancient civilizations of the Mediterranean, probably earlier. Small, privately owned craft were used where water transport was a regular part of daily life. Yachts existed in ancient Egypt and the Romans sought relaxation afloat on the Italian lakes.

Modern yachting was pioneered in Holland in the seventeenth century when travel along the miles of sheltered Dutch waterways was difficult without boats. The word "yacht" is of Dutch origin (from "jaght", the name given to pleasure craft developed from the small cargo or passenger carriers). An early convert to yachting was Charles II of England, who spent nearly ten years in exile in the Low Countries until the Restoration in 1660. The first clubs were started in the eighteenth century, but modern racing took form in the early 1800s under royal sponsorship.

Venue

Courses vary according the type of race taking place.

Rules

The yachts usually start between two marks (usually buoys) and race around until they reach the finish which is marked in the same way as the starting line. There may be a time limit for finishing the race.

Because it is impossible for yachts to wait stationary behind the starting line until the signal, skill is required of helmsmen and crews in the preceding ten minutes to position their vessels in the most advantageous way, taking into account the tide, the direction of the wind and any nearby obstructions, including competing yachts. Ideally a yacht should be on an unobstructed heading for the first mark or, if this is to windward, at the most advantageous end of the line for her

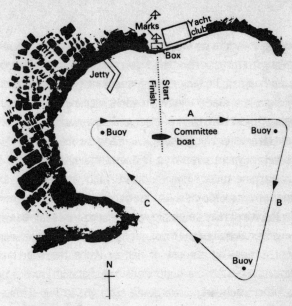

Yacht Racing Course

If the wind is easterly the first leg of the course A) will be a "windward leg". If the wind is anywhere south of east the southern (seaward) end of the starting line will be the most advantageous position. For other winds courses could be laid out differently. A special box on shore, in line with the marks, may have a balcony for officials judging the start and finish of the race.

first windward leg, and travelling at her best speed, immediately behind the line as the starting signal is made. Until s/he is in the starting area, testing the weather and scrutinizing the competition, a skipper cannot finally decide on his/her tactics, although a good start can be the most important factor in the race.

Once the race is under way, yachts are governed by rules designed to prevent collisions and obstruction to other competitors. These two aims are complementary. When tacking, the yacht on the port tack (steering through the wind blowing from her port, or left, side) must keep clear of a yacht on starboard (right) tack. Other fundamental rules for avoiding collisions are that a windward yacht (occupying an upwind position) must keep clear of a leeward (downwind) yacht, and a yacht clear astern must keep clear of a yacht ahead of her.

When a yacht overtakes and establishes an overlap to leeward, she must allow windward yacht ample room and opportunity to keep clear. The tactic of "luffing" (turning round into the wind) may be employed by a yacht threatened with being overtaken, but she must not do this when the overtaking yacht is drawing abreast of her, or when the overtaking helmsman has his/her opponent's "mast abeam" to prevent the other yacht from exercising her right to luff. If this is ignored, then a protest may be lodged. There are other rules to decide right of way when a yacht is tacking or gybing (filling the sails on the other side when running before the wind). A yacht which is tacking or gybing must keep clear of another settled on a tack, and if she wants to alter course to gain a right-of-way position over an opponent, she must do this far enough away to avoid causing the other yacht to alter course until the manoeuvre is completed. When two yachts are tacking or gybing, the port-side vessel must keep clear.

One of the most important sections of the right-of-way rules governs the rounding of course marks (buoys, moored boats, or posts). It is here that racing is at its closest, with yachts converging to round the mark with as little wasted distance as possible. The rules specify that a yacht shall not "squeeze" another between herself and the mark. Conversely, an overtaking yacht must not claim room between a yacht ahead and the mark, if the yacht ahead cannot give her room.

That the rules combine the requirements of safety and fair play is demonstrated when two yachts are approaching an obstruction or shallow water. If the yacht nearer the danger cannot alter course to clear it without risk of a collision, she must hail for room to tack (usually by calling "water"). The yacht which needs room must give the other time to keep clear – and to satisfy the race committee that she did so, in the event of a protest. When the obstruction is a course mark, a yacht which is forced to tack to avoid it does not have right of way over a following yacht which is laying out the mark correctly.

Equipment

Modern racing craft make use of the latest man-made plastics available. Their spars are either aluminium or carbon-fibre while the sails are either of "dacron", "mylar" or nylon. For the Olympic Games there are four different types of craft used: the Mistral sailboard; the dinghy; keelboats; and catamarans.

Scoring

There are separate point systems for the Olympics and regular events and a series of races may be run from each class. The lowest total point score over all races wins.

Olympic	Low Point	(most common)
First place:	0	0.75
Second:	3	2
Third:	5.7	3
Fourth:	8	4
Fifth:	10	5
Six:	11.	76
Seven and over:	Finish place plus six	

- # CRUISING
  The non-competitive side of yachting, usually involves making a passage either under sail or power from one port to another and spending at least one night away from the yacht's base. A cruise might be anything from a circumnavigation of the globe to a weekend camping expedition in a sailing dinghy in esturial waters.

- # OCEAN RACING
  For yachts, involving long passages over open water, with vessels sometimes out of sight of each other and of land for days, has influenced yacht design with regard to sea-keeping qualities, rig and habitability. Crewing in an ocean race demands experience and stamina of a high order.

  Such races vary in distance from less than 200 miles (322km) in the waters of the English Channel and the North Sea (where they are more accurately called offshore races) to events such as Transpacific, held every two years since 1926, the distance of which is 2,600 miles (4,184km).

YACHTING, ICE
Introduction
This follows similar principles to water-borne YACHTING, using runners instead of wheels and sometimes a far greater area of sail. Four times the wind speed is often achieved.

The Dutch went sand yachting on wooden wheels four hundred years ago. This was probably the first use of such a vessel for sport, though land yachts were probably used for carrying goods in the ancient civilizations of Egypt and China. It was in Holland, too, that ice yachting first developed in the second half of the eighteenth century. Though sand yachting has been organized at club and national level in Europe throughout the twentieth century, it remained a rare pastime until after the Second World War. Since then there has been something of a boom in the sport, particularly in the USA, where the deserts are ideal for racing.

YACHTING, SAND
Introduction

Sand and land yachting, in their most primitive state, require a small sailing dinghy to be mounted on a simple chassis with three or four car wheels. In suitable conditions, the boats can be propelled by the wind over firm sand, tarmac, concrete or any other level surface. The sail is operated as it would be in yachting on water and the direction controlled by a steering wheel or pedals.

As the sport developed, boats of a more sophisticated design, capable of high speeds and delicate manoeuvres, came into use. In Europe, the vessels usually have a canoe-like body, or fuselage, often of fibreglass, which may be as long as 24ft (7.3m) with an 18ft (5.5m) wheelbase and 24in (61cm) diameter tyres. Only one sail is used, but on the largest yachts its area may be as much as 400sq ft (37 sq m). Some vessels have a crew of three.

American yachts are smaller, lighter and faster. The body often consists only of an open chassis 10ft (3m) long, with room for the pilot alone. The sail area is about 45sq ft (4sq m), but on a hard surface these craft are capable of at least double the speed of the following wind.

Index

Aikido **8**
Aquabobbing **9**
Archery: **11**
   Archery Darts/Golf **12**
   Clout Shooting **12**
   Flight Shooting **13**
   Popinjay Shooting **13**
Archery, Crossbow **14**
Archery, Target **16**
Athletics: **18**
   Discus **20**
   Hammer **21**
   High Jump **23**
   Hurdling **24**
   Javelin **24**
   Long Jump **25**
   Pole Vault **26**
   Relay **27**
   Shot Put **28**
   Steeplechase **29**
   Triple Jump **30**
Austball **31**
Autocross **31**
Badminton **32**
Ballooning **38**
Ballroom Dancing **39**
Bandy **40**
Baseball **42**
Baseball, Welsh **46**
Basketball **48**
Batinton **59**
Beach Volleyball **61**
Biathlon **63**
Biathlon, Skiing **64**
Bicycle Polo **66**
Biddy Basketball **70**
Billiards, Carom **71**
Billiards, English **73**
Bobsleigh **75**
Bowl-Playing **78**
Bowls:
   Canadian Five Pin **79**
   Crown Green **80**
   Indoor **82**
   Lawn **83**
   Tenpin **86**
Boxing **88**
Boxing, Chinese **92**
Boxing, Thai **94**
Broomball **95**
Bull **97**

Caber, Tossing the **99**
Camel Wrestling **100**
Camogie **100**
Canoe Polo **102**
Canoe Sailing **103**
Canoe Slalom **104**
Canoeing: **107**
   Long Distance **109**
   Sprint Racing **110**
   Wild Water **111**
Club Ball **112**
Cricket **113**
Croquet **123**
Curling **129**
Cycle Ball **132**
Cycling **133**
Cyclo-Cross **138**
Dakyu **141**
Darts **141**
Deck Cricket **143**
Deck Games **144**
Deck Quoits **146**
Deck Tennis **147**
Diving **150**
Equestrian Events: **155**
   Dressage **156**
   Showjumping **158**
   Three Day Event **160**
Eton Field Game **165**
Eton Fives **170**
Eton Wall Game **174**
Fell Running **178**
Fencing **179**
Fishing: **186**
   Course Fishing **186**
   Sea Fishing **187**
   Still Fishing **188**
Fly Ball **189**
Flying, Sporting: **189**
   Air Racing **190**
   Air Touring **191**
   Record Breaking **192**
Football:
   American (College) **193**
   American (Professional) **200**
   Association **202**
   Australian Rules **209**
   Gaelic **215**
   Harrow **218**
   Winchester College **223**
Futevolei **226**

Gliding **227**
Golf **232**
Grass Skiing **241**
Gymnastics: **243**
    Alloy Rings **244**
    Asymmetric Bars **245**
    Balance Beam **246**
    Floor Exercises **246**
    Horizontal or High Bar **247**
    Parallel Bars **248**
    Pommel Horse **249**
    Vaulting Horse **250**
Handball **250**
Handball, Court **255**
Handball, Irish **259**
Hare and Hounds **260**
Hockey, Field **261**
Hockey, Indoor **267**
Holani **269**
Horse Racing **269**
Horseshoe Pitching **272**
Hurling **273**
Ice Hockey **277**
Ice Skating: **284**
    Figure Skating **285**
    Ice Dancing **287**
    Pairs **288**
    Singles **288**
    Speed Skating **290**
Ice Yachting **292**
In-Line Roller Hockey **295**
Jeu Provencal **297**
Jousting **300**
Joutes Lyonnaises **302**
Judo **303**
Ju-jitsu **309**
Kabaddi **310**
Karate **313**
Karting **322**
Kendo **326**
Kick Boxing **332**
Kite Fighting **334**
Knur and Spell **335**
Korfball **338**
Kuningaspallo **342**
Lacrosse, Men's **343**
Lacrosse, Women's **348**
Lawn Tennis **352**
Logrolling **357**
Marathon **358**
Moto-Cross **359**

Motor Racing: **361**
    Autocross **364**
    Drag Racing **364**
    Formula One **365**
    Hill Trials **365**
    Indy Car Racing **365**
    Road Rally **366**
    Sedan and Sports Car **366**
    Single Seater Racing **366**
    Slalom Racing **367**
Motorcycle Racing: **367**
    Drag Racing **370**
    Grass Racing **370**
    Ice Racing **371**
    Long Track Racing **372**
    Sand Track Racing **372**
    Speedway **373**
    Sprinting **374**
Mountain Running **375**
Netball **375**
Nine Men's Morris **382**
Orienteering: **383**
    Cross Country Orienteering **385**
    Line Orienteering **386**
    Route Orienteering **386**
    Score Orienteering **386**
Padder Tennis **387**
Paddleball **389**
Parachuting: **391**
    Competition Parachuting **392**
    Freefall Relative Work **392**
    Para-Ascending **393**
    Para-Gliding **394**
Pato **394**
Pelota: **396**
    Jeux Directs **399**
Pesäpallo **401**
Pétanque **404**
Pigeon Racing **407**
Ping Ball **410**
Polo **410**
Polocrosse **416**
Pool **418**
Powerboat Racing: **419**
    Drag Boat Racing **420**
Punting **421**
Quoits **423**
Race Walking **425**
Rackets **427**
Real Tennis **431**
Rhythmic Gymnastics **438**

Index

Ring Tennis: **440**
   Beach Tennis **442**
Rock Climbing **442**
Rodeo: **443**
   Bareback Bronc Riding **445**
   Bull Riding **445**
   Calf Roping **446**
   Saddle Bronc Riding **447**
   Steer Wrestling **447**
   Team Roping **448**
Roller Hockey **448**
Roller Skating: **452**
   Dancing **453**
   Figure Skating **453**
   Speed Skating **453**
Roque **454**
Rounders **455**
Rounders, Irish **459**
Rowing: **459**
   Sculling **464**
   Skiff Racing **465**
Rugby Fives **465**
Rugby League Football **469**
Rugby Union Football **473**
Sailing **479**
Sepak Takraw **479**
Shinty **481**
Shooting, Air Weapons **484**
Shooting, Clay Pigeon **486**
Shooting, Pistol **490**
Shooting, Rifle **495**
Shuffleboard **498**
Skibobbing **500**
Skiing: **502**
   Alpine Skiing **506**
   Nordic Skiing **507**
   Ski Jumping **508**
Skittles: **509**
   Devil Among theTailors **512**
   Hood Skittles **513**
   Long Alley **514**
   Ninepins **514**
   Old English Skittles **515**
Sled Dog Racing **516**
Snooker **517**
Snowboarding **518**
Softball **520**
Spaceball **524**
Squash Rackets: **527**

   Doubles **530**
Stoolball **531**
Surfing: **535**
   Bellyboard Surfing **535**
   Body Surfing **535**
   Surf Canoeing **536**
Swimming: **542**
   Backstroke **545**
   Breaststroke **546**
   Butterfly **547**
   Freestyle **548**
   Medley Swimming **548**
Swimming, Open Water **549**
Swimming, Synchronized **550**
Table Tennis **553**
Takraw **558**
Tejo **560**
Tobogganing, Luge **560**
Touch Ball **562**
Trampolining **564**
Trapball **568**
Trotting **569**
Tug of War **572**
Underwater Hockey **576**
Underwater Swimming **577**
Volleyball **581**
Waterpolo **586**
Waterskiing: **589**
   Barefoot Skiing **592**
   Ski Kite-Flying **592**
   Slalom **593**
   Trick Skiing **594**
Weightlifting **596**
Winchester Fives **601**
Windsurfing **604**
Wrestling: **607**
   Glima **612**
   Graeco Roman **613**
   Kushti **613**
   Schwingen **614**
   Sumo **614**
   Yagli **615**
Yachting: **615**
   Cruising **620**
   Ocean Racing **620**
Yachting, Ice **620**
Yachting, Sand **621**